Sponsored by Armstrong Wolfe

ARMSTRONG WOLFE
Collaborative Ventures

Donkey Mail and Bully Beef; The Art of Survival

In aid of GCF Bosnia, registered charity number 1155036

First published in Great Britain in 2018 by Armstrong Wolfe on behalf of GCF Bosnia

Eagle Tower, Montpellier Drive, Cheltenham, Gloucestershire GL50 1TA United Kingdom

www.gcfbosnia.org

Copyright © 2018 Armstrong Wolfe

Design and production: Rob Walster, Big Blu

Edited by Kate Owen-Dixon

For general information, please contact +44 203 664 8863 (UK) or email dmbb@armstrongwolfe.com

ISBN 978-1-9996177-0-7

CONTENTS

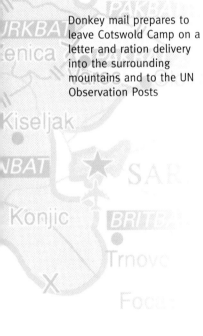

Donkey mail prepares to leave Cotswold Camp on a letter and ration delivery into the surrounding mountains and to the UN Observation Posts

DEDICATION

To all the stars in the universe, as one of them is
my father looking down on me.

To the three hundred and thirty men and women of 1RGBW (Goražde Force),
United Nations Protection Force (August 1994–March 1995).

IN REMEMBRANCE

BEN HINTON

CHRIS TURNER

MARTIN DOWDELL

PHILLIP ARMSTRONG

They shall grow not old, as we that are left grow old:
Age shall not weary them, nor the years condemn.
At the going down of the sun and in the morning
We will remember them.

THE 1ST BATTALION, THE ROYAL GLOUCESTERSHIRE, BERKSHIRE AND WILTSHIRE REGIMENT

IN MEMORIAM

Pte Ben Hinton

Ben Hinton died tragically on 9 September 1994 whilst on a UN peacekeeping mission in the Goražde enclave in eastern Bosnia. His Saxon left the road in the mountain region.

Ben Hinton was twenty-two years old. He joined the Gloucestershire Regiment in March 1990 and served in Catterick, Canada and Northern Ireland.

Ben Hinton lived life to the full and had a tremendous character. He was always cheerful and had the respect of both his platoon and company. He had proved himself a professional, committed and proficient solider and sportsman.

He had also served as a Junior NCO in 1992/3, having successfully passed a potential NCO's cadre. His humour was infectious, and his antics long remembered. He, along with his section, had quickly built a close and professional relationship with both Serb and Muslim locals.

Pte Phillip Armstrong

Phillip Armstrong died with two of his comrades whilst on a UN peacekeeping mission in Goražde, eastern Bosnia, on 12 September 1994. He was twenty-one years old.

Phillip Armstrong joined the 1st Battalion, The Gloucestershire Regiment in 1999, having previously trained as a junior soldier for a year at Shorncliffe, Kent. He served in the USA, UK, Northern Ireland, Germany and France.

He was a well-respected, professional and friendly soldier who was utterly trustworthy and reliable. He had a sense of humour that was an inspiration to us all and especially his close friends. He loved the outdoor life that soldiering offered and often spent his leave hill-walking and climbing. He possessed a tremendous enthusiasm for all that he participated in. He had completed several specialist courses, which he passed with flying colours.

Pte Martin Dowdell

Martin Dowdell followed in his father's footsteps and joined The Duke of Edinburgh's Royal Regiment (Berkshire and Wiltshire) in 1991. He served in the UK and had already completed one operational tour in South Armagh.

In 1994, after the formation of 1 RGBW, Dowdell served with A Coy and continued to prove himself as a professional and popular soldier. He always had an answer to everything and enjoyed having the last word in a discussion. He will be remembered for his politeness and his hardworking nature, as well as his talent as a sportsman, playing hockey and football to a high standard. His sense of humour, together with his cheerfulness, were widely appreciated, especially by his platoon.

Martin Dowdell died with two of his comrades on 12 September 1994. He was part of a patrol conducting UN peacekeeping operations in the Goražde enclave in eastern Bosnia when his Saxon APC left the road.

Pte Christopher Turner

Chris Turner joined The 1st Battalion in May 1994. He was recruited in Salisbury by the same sergeant who was later his platoon commander in Bosnia. Chris Turner died suddenly and tragically in the second accident involving Saxon vehicles in four days. He was eighteen years old. He was proud to have been able to follow in the footsteps of his uncle, Sgt Hopgood, who served in the 1st Battalion.

Chris Turner was a quiet, hard-working soldier. He was very keen to learn and rapidly gained the respect of his comrades. He was always cheerful and had a great sense of humour, always seeing the funny side. He was also a keen sportsman, representing the Company at running and steeple chase.

CHARITABLE CAUSE: GORAŽDE CHILDREN'S FOUNDATION

All proceeds from the sale of this book and its launch event will be donated to Goražde Children's Foundation (GCF Bosnia).

GCF Bosnia is a UK-based charity that is committed to helping rejuvenate the previously war-torn town of Goražde in Bosnia. The charity specifically supports Goražde Primary School and seeks to provide a brighter future for its students.

It was founded in 2012 by Maurice Evlyn-Bufton in memory of four of his comrades who were killed on United Nations' duty whilst deployed on Operation Grapple in the eastern enclave of Goražde.

Through various fundraising events, including a marathon as well as the proceeds from all three of Maurice's published books, the charity has raised over £65,000 at the point of publication.

These funds have been used to build an English language centre for the school, provide books and educational materials, and refurbish their previously war-scarred playground into an all-purpose Astro Turf that the children can now play sport on again.

If you have purchased this book, thank you.
Your money has been donated to GCF Bosnia.
To make a donation to the charity, please visit gcfbosnia.org
and donate via our JustGiving page.

For more information on GCF Bosnia, see page 379, or visit GCFBosnia.org

WITH THANKS

I would like to thank the following individuals for their generosity towards my charity and support in bringing this book together:

Kyle Dickens
Nick Doddy
Rajeev Mehta
Zeynep Kudatgobilik
Andrew Batchelor
Stuart Crotaz
Vanessa La Santa
Esteban J. Benavides
Darren Jarvis
C J Richardson
Thomas Lack
Charles L. Rose
Paul Beedle
Jason Pugh
David Flowerday
Stephen Ellis
David Tarling
Rania and Hannah Hart
Chloe and Bobby Hart
Brian Halligan
Andrew Stevens
Marc Leaver

Diana Evlyn-Bufton
Nick Lovett
Mike Wolff (late 1 DWR - Gorzade
    May - Sept 1994)
Overthrow Decorators and Carpenters
Lena and Daryl McDonald
Mark Compton
Simon Fawcett
Adam Tyrell
Fiona Grandison
Nicholas Jenkins
Amelia Rose Reddan
Oscar William Reddan
Alan Leigh
Wen Si
Larry List
Simon Longden
George Nunn
Graham Warby
Trina Jackson
David Grosse
Stephen Miller

Peter McCarthy
Rob Scott
Angus Jones, Trinity Restaurant
Adam Byatt, Trinity Restaurant
Tom Groom
Maggie and Jerry Collier
Roger Marc-Noirot
Jason Hope
Aviral Rai
JC, Lexi and Willem Hambro
In memory of June Mascal
Cara Schulze
Toby Billington
Jamie Hamilton
Rick Sears
Simon Powell
Mark H. Roth
Clement Coudron
John M Coleman
Paul Maley
Doris Honold
Julie Paas
Oliver Bader
Stuart David James McClymont
Emily J Shepperd
Joe Abboud
Jean-Renaud Grasset
Shawn Feeney
Ralph Orciuoli
Miriam Flood
Farhan Amin
The Norena Family
Oliver Bettin
Peter A Bowden
Richard Turner
Ian McCartney
Simon Anderson
Tim Rooke
Neil Smith

Ed Steel
Mark Price
Marc Walby
Nick Borzellino
Cameron Dick
Warren Young
George Koutzen
Fang Bourne
David Griffith
Mark Selvarajan
Dan Cole
Simon Redpath
Donna Holt
Craig Beevers
Dr. Sven S. Kasper
Simon Rees-Goddard
Graeme Harker
Andy Powell
Jayne Howatson
Jitinder Bhandal
Simon Bennett
Peter McCarthy
Remi Ferrer
Bhargav Aghase
Phil Redden
Andrew De Groot
Neil Smith
Remi Ferrer
Andrew Batchelor
Suresh Pathmanathan
Steve Krueger
Kashyap Bhatia
Elliot Evlyn-Bufton
David McLagan
Ian Anderson
Chris Severson
Roger Evlyn-Bufton
Huw Fullerton

ABOUT THE AUTHOR

Maurice Evlyn-Bufton was born in Ludlow, Shropshire. He spent his early years in the Welsh Marches, went to boarding school in the county, and spent his childhood summers in the green and wonderful countryside of Herefordshire.

Maurice is a graduate of Cardiff University, which he completed through an Army scholarship. He attended the Royal Military Academy Sandhurst, and was commissioned into The Gloucestershire Regiment. He saw service in the Balkans War, where he was 2IC of the British UN forces protecting the south bank of the River Drina, dissecting the safe haven of Goražde.

He has returned to Goražde on several occasions and has raised funds through his charity, GCF Bosnia, for the primary school in the town, in honour of his comrades who died in service in 1994–95. His efforts have funded the school's first English classroom with an extensive library, and the refurbishment of the playground, turning it into an AstroTurf football pitch and tennis court.

In 2011 Maurice set up his own advisory business, Armstrong Wolfe (named after two young officers from his regiment who fought with bravery at the battle of Salamanca in 1812), which is focused on conduct and ethics training for banking and the provision of executive search.

He has published two books about the banking sector, one on the Chief Operating Officer and one on the Chief Control Officer, with both publications' profits being donated to his charity. Donkey Mail and Bully Beef was printed in 2018, with all proceeds being donated to GCF Bosnia.

Maurice is married to Joanna and has three sons, Simon, Monty and Alfie. They are expecting a fourth child in November 2018. He lives in Gloucestershire, England, and spends his spare time with his family, marathon running, mountaineering, walking his dogs, writing and carrying out his charity work.

CONTRIBUTORS

The following individuals have been an enormous help in shaping this book and bringing it to life. They gave up their time to meet with me, answer my questions, and share their stories and personal photographs.

Andy Grant

During his Bosnian tour from 1994-5, Reverend Andy Grant served in A Company as an acting section Second in Command. The tour was cut short for him due to an injury in the September, but he returned in January 1995 to finish the tour. He is now a vicar in the Church of England in Middlesbrough. He is married, has three children and three grandchildren.

Andy Paddon

Andy was a Corporal and section commander in B Company whilst in Goražde. He currently works as an Operations Manager for a Risk Mitigation Security Company in Iraq. When back in the UK, he lives with his long-term partner Kathryn and his two stepchildren, Sarah and Mark.

Danny Ashton

Danny was a Private in 3rd Platoon A Company 1RGBW, operating from OP 9, OP 7 with stints at OP5 and OP6a as well as undertaking patrols and guard force in Cotswold Camp. Today, he is still serving in the army with The Rifles as a Colour Sergeant Sniper instructor at the School of Infantry in Warminster. He now lives in Tewkesbury.

Darren 'Taff' Davies

Darren held the position of section commander, Corporal, 1RGBW whilst serving in Goražde. He is now a Warrant Officer, and works with the 160th Infantry Brigade and at HQ Wales as a Training Safety Advisor. He lives in Cwmbran, South Wales, and has three children.

Dave Hill

Dave Hill was a Private with 1st platoon A Company, part of the Machine Gun attachment from support company. He operated in Goražde on the west bank OP's 6,8 and 9. Today, he is a builder by profession and is happily married with two adult children.

Ed Brown

Major Ed Brown MDE was the Officer commanding for A Company in the 1RGBW Regiment. He retired as a Brigadier in 2015 having commanded 1 RGBW in Northern Ireland 2000-2003. Since then he has become Head of Operations for Mercedes Benz in Kuwait. He has been married since 1993 and has three daughters who are currently at university.

Gary Cox

Gary Cox was in SF Platoon, 1st RGBW attached to B Company whilst in Goražde. He served in the army for ten years, with postings in Northern Ireland, Hong Kong, Hawaii, USA, Germany and Catterick Garrison. Gary is now married with three children and is the managing director of an electrical calibration company. He left the army in 1996 but is still an adult instructor for Army Cadet Force.

Gary McDade

Gary was educated at Wycliffe College in Gloucestershire and King's College, London. He was commissioned into The Gloucestershire Regiment at Sandhurst in 1993, returning as Chief Instructor in 2011. He served as a Platoon Commander in B Company in Goražde. Gary served in the army until 2014, and is presently Executive Officer, European Union Training Mission in Mali.

Gary Morley

Gary was attached to B Company whilst serving in 1RGBW in Goražde, working with the Company and Battalion Intelligence cells gathering information, as well as providing refugee support. Since leaving the army in 2002, he has continued to support young families and is now a Family Support and Attendance Officer at Risedale School in Catterick Garrison. He is married with two daughters.

Ian Harris

Ian Harris was commissioned into The Gloucestershire Regiment in 1980. This regiment amalgamated with The Duke of Edinburgh's Royal Regiment into RGBW in April 1994. During this 1994 UN tour Ian was the officer commanding A Company 1RGBW. He retired from the army in 2015 after thirty-five years of service. He now works for a large defence company.

Ivor Wood

Whilst in Goražde, Ivor was (WO1) Regimental Sergeant Major. After over thirty years of military service and being commissioned to end his career as a Quartermaster, he retired from the army to move into counter terrorism and security. He is a committed family man with three children.

Jason 'Jay' Hicks

Whilst in service and in Goražde, Jay was a Reconnaissance Platoon Signaller and additionally a medic for C Company. He served in the army between 1990-2006, with postings in Northern Ireland, Bosnia, Kosovo, Sierra Leone, Afghanistan, Iraq, Germany, Cyprus, and the UK. He now lives in Newcastle with his wife, two sons and cat called Rambo. He is the co-founder of a security risk management company 'Athena Risk', which enables UK organisations to mitigate overseas risks.

Jonathan Smith

Jonathan Smith was a Private in the 1st Battalion of The Gloucestershire Regiment and then the 1RGBW. He was transferred from drums /mg platoon to C Company for the duration of the tour at Bugojno, Goražde and the surrounding areas.

Julian 'Clarence' Heal

Clarence was a Private in the Mortar Platoon 1RGBW. He left the army in 2014 after completing twenty-four years of service, ending his service in 1Rifles in Headquarters' Company. He now lives in Chester working as a Security Officer at Airbus. Clarence is married happily to Lea and is the proud uncle to three nephews.

Mark Spandler

After being commissioned into The Gloucestershire Regiment at Sandhurst, Mark enjoyed sixteen years military service, including being a Platoon Commander in A Company in Goražde. He joined G4S Secure Solutions Group in 2007 in Afghanistan and worked with the Company through to 2017. He is now director of Security Risk Management ISS Facility Services.

Neil 'Slug' Southern

Neil was a Corporal and acting Platoon Sergeant of 6 Platoon, B Company when in Goražde. He now teaches English as a second language to pupils of Gypsy, Roma and Traveller heritage. He is married to Lindsay, a vicar in the Anglican church, and has two children.

Nihad Gluscic

Nihad was fourteen years old during the conflict in Goražde. He is now an Assistant Attaché for the Defence Section of the British Embassy in Sarajevo. Nihad enjoys skiing, sailing and music. He also plays guitar in a band called 'Exclusion Zone' that was formed in Goražde at the time. He is married with two children.

Pat 'Joey D' Deacon

Joey served from 1984 to 1998 with 1GLOSTERS and 1 RGBW. His tours of duty included Berlin, two tours of Northern Ireland, Africa, USA, Belize and Bosnia. He spent six years as a Physical Training Instructor and the remainder of his time as a section commander, as a Lance Corporal and Corporal. He lives in Bream in the Forest of Dean with his wife and his two boys. He works as a senior shop steward for Unite at a paper mill in Lydney.

Patrick Davidson-Houston CBE

Patrick was the Commanding Officer, 1st Battalion , The RGBW Regiment in Goražde. He is now a Senior Advisor for the Stabilisation Unit, Foreign and Commonwealth Office in London. He is married with three children.

Patrick Irwin

Reverend Patrick was the RGBW Chaplain. Whilst in Goražde he was the Goražde Force Chaplain, helping different nationalities serving alongside the RGBW. As an Anglican priest, he joined the Royal Army Chaplains' Department in 1992 and retired in 2010. Reverend Patrick now works as a temporary Chaplain in the Anglican Diocese across Europe and is also The Royal British Legion Chaplain to Normandy.

Patrick Hyde

Patrick was a Private in 4 Platoon, B Company, during Op Grapple in 1994 – 1995 in Goražde. Today, he is still serving and is a Captain in 1 RIFLES, as its Quartermaster. He has a son named Henry and a daughter named Evie.

Patrick Tomlinson

Patrick was Company Commander, B Company whilst serving in Goražde. He was responsible for monitoring the territory east of the River Drina. After over thirty years of military service, Patrick left the army and moved successfully into Business Continuity and Crisis Management.

Simon Gray

Simon held the rank of Major and was the Commanding Officer for B Company whilst in Goražde. He is still serving in the Rifles Regiment after a final appointment based at the UK Defence Academy following three years Loan Service instructing at the Joint Services Command and Staff College, Doha, Qatar. He is now married to Louise, lives in West Oxfordshire and has three children.

Stephen Oxlade

Stephen was the 1st Battalion RGBW Second in Command in Goražde 1994, working closely and directly with the Commanding Officer. He is now retired from the army and runs his own company.

Tom Bailey

Tom Bailey was studying at the University of Bristol for his undergraduate History degree when Maurice approached the university for help researching this book and Tom's interest in combat motivation in soldiers drew him to the project. He met with the author and helped to conduct around twenty interviews with Maurice's former comrades before joining him on a trip to Bosnia in 2012. He now works at Imperial College London.

Tony Bird

Tony was a driver in the Royal Logistic Corps, Op Grapple 5 British Logistics Battalion. He was originally based in Split and was attached to the Goražde Force between Kiseljack and Goražde. He has left the army and is happily married; a family man with a daughter, whom he hopes 'will never have to hear about the horrors of the Bosnian War'. He now works as a driver and training manager, instructing people on how to transport dangerous goods and explosives.

ACKNOWLEDGEMENTS

I would like to thank Ian Harris for taking me back to Goražde in 2012, for without his initiative and the well-organised trip he took the time to bring together, this book and the charity GCF Bosnia would not exist.

To the old comrades who came with me on this adventure, reuniting me with my love and affection for my Army days, and the privilege that I had been gifted to serve with them and so many others: Danny Ashton, Blaine Bradbury, Leigh Deacon, Joey Deacon, Andy Grant, Ian Harris, Clarence Heal, Andy Paddon, Willo Williams, Slug Southern, Mick Stacey and Patrick Irwin. To Tom Bailey, a youthful and intelligent young man and at the time an undergraduate at the University of Bristol, who came along on the trip and supported me in my writing and meanderings.

My heartfelt thanks to the teachers and children of Goražde Primary School for being my inspiration, and for their consistently welcoming and splendid hospitality. More so, for the purpose they gave me: to do something and to give back to those in greater need than most of us.

Special thanks to Patrick Davidson-Houston (my former CO in Bosnia) and Patrick Tomlinson (my OC), for their support and contributions to this book. To Ed Brown, Simon Gray, Stephen Oxlade and Ivor Wood similarly for their contributions and the many voices heard within its pages. Patrick Tomlinson needs a special note for being my leader whilst on tour in Bosnia, and for suffering and tolerating my inconsistencies. Ironically, in my annual report – my last in the Army, written by Patrick in 1995 – of the eleven categories, he graded me 'excellent' in ten. The only one graded 'very good' was the 'written word'; I hope I may be graded 'excellent' twenty-three years later with the publication of this book!

For the knowledge the worldwide web gave me, a window into a library of eternal and bottomless facts and detail. The texts, periodicals, articles and papers that assisted me can be found on page 388.

To my darling wife Joanna: for her constancy, her loving support and tolerance in letting me burn the midnight oil and awake with the sparrows to undertake this task.

To my boys, Simon, Monty and Alfie and at the time of writing, my unborn son who, God willing, will be born healthy and happy in November 2018 and be christened Oliver. He will be blessed and christened by the Reverend Andrew Grant, whose story you will find in this book and to whom my wife and I owe our gratitude in many ways.

I dedicated this book in part to my father David, who passed away in 2008, but I leave the final acknowledgement to my mother, Diana. My rock, my star and my distant support when I was away in Bosnia, she has remained so throughout my life. She kept and protected my letters sent home when I was away on duty and allowed me to bring them to life again in this memoir.

FOREWORD

BY GENERAL SIR MICHAEL ROSE, KCB, CBE, DSO, QGM

By 1994, the United Nations had deployed over 23,000 young peacekeepers to Bosnia in order to deliver aid to 2.7 million people caught up in the region's three-sided civil war.

The majority of these peacekeepers were volunteers who believed that it was their duty to help others, no matter how risky the mission. Sadly, many of them were killed or injured during the three-year period for which the war lasted, of whom seventy-two were British.

However, their deaths were not in vain as the UN presence in Bosnia undoubtedly prevented the country from being overrun by the Serbs and, of course, without the humanitarian aid that was delivered, many more thousands of Bosnians from all sides of the conflict would have perished through hunger or disease.

Following UN-brokered deals, the war did not end sooner because the USA -tacitly supported by NATO- armed the Bosnian Muslims in direct contravention of the UN Security Council resolutions that the international community had been signed up to in 1992 at the start of the war.

This illegal arming of the Bosnian Muslims undoubtedly derailed the efforts of the UN to bring about peace. It caused a prolongation of the war and thereby the suffering of the people of Bosnia, and without any significant territorial gain for the state of Bosnia. It was a clear betrayal, of not only the UN peacekeepers and the people of Bosnia, but also of international convention. It is also clear that if the USA had allowed President Izetbegovic to sign up to the Stoltenberg Owen peace plan in July 1994, the massacre at Srebenica would never have happened.

This book serves as a useful reminder of the confusion, difficulties and dangers faced by those brave soldiers serving in the UN mission in Bosnia, at a time when the international community lacked strategic coherence. It also serves as a moving testimony to the four British soldiers who died whilst serving with the RGBW in 1994.

GENERAL SIR MICHAEL ROSE

General Rose was enlisted in the Territorial and Army Volunteer Reserve as a private soldier and was commissioned into the 5th Bn The Gloucestershire Regiment in 1959, transferring to the City of London Yeomanry as a second lieutenant later that same year.

After graduating from Oxford University, General Rose joined the regular Army and the Coldstream Guards. His distinguished career led him to be the commanding officer of the Special Air Service Regiment, notedly being in charge of the Special Forces during the Iranian Embassy Siege and later during the Falklands War.

In 1994 he was appointed Commander UNPROFOR Bosnia during the Yugoslav Wars. He retired from the army in 1997.

"A trip up into the nearby rugged mountains offers spectacular scenery, but also more scenes of destruction."

CHAPTER 1

A TOWN CALLED GORAŽDE

During the spring of 1994, the war in Bosnia was well under way and the Bosnian Serbs – with political and military support from Serbia itself – controlled most of eastern Bosnia. Three cities with Muslim majorities, however, had managed to resist the onslaught: Srebrenica, Žepa and Goražde (gor-AHZH-duh). All three remained islands – enclaves – within territory dominated by the Bosnian Serbs. These cities also held many Muslim refugees who had been "cleansed" by the Bosnian Serb army from the surrounding countryside.

Srebrenica and Žepa would eventually fall (and Srebrenica would become the scene of a horrific massacre, brought back into the consciousness with the arrest and subsequent trial of General Ratko Mladić many years later). Goražde, however, managed to hold out despite a concerted effort by the Bosnian Serbs to take the city and empty it of its Muslim citizens. Goražde lay in eastern Bosnia, along the Drina River and not far from Serbia proper. More importantly to the Bosnian Serbs, it lay along a vital road linking Foča and Višegrad, two cities already under Bosnian Serb control. It was a small island in the vast territory controlled by the Bosnian Serbs – the part of Bosnia that would be called Republika Srpska (in Serbian, Република Српска) – or "Serb Republic", though not to be confused with the neighbouring country, the Republic of Serbia.

Beginning in April 1994, Bosnian Serb forces, under the command of General Mladić (later indicted as a war criminal), began a siege of the city. Bosnian Serb artillery rained death and destruction from the surrounding hills. Finally, the international community had seen enough. For years it had dithered and negotiated whilst the worst atrocities on European soil since the Nazi era mounted and the Bosnian Muslims (the "Bosniaks") were brutally removed from ever-expanding regions of their homeland.

Right: The three Muslim enclaves surrounded by Serb forces: Srebrenica, Zepa and Goražde

January 1995

On April 10, 1994, decisive action came at last in the form of US Air Force F-16s operating under UN and NATO command and NATO troops attacking Bosnian Serb artillery positions outside Goražde. It was the first NATO ground assault in the forty-seven-year history of the alliance, but it did nothing to stop the attack on Goražde. It was the Bosniaks themselves who managed to prevent their town from being absorbed into the Republika Srpska.

In 1995, Goražde remained a Muslim island surrounded by the Republika Srpska. It was connected to rest of the Muslim–Croat Federation (non-Serbian Bosnia–Herzegovina) by a narrow isthmus. This convoluted gerrymander – a textbook example of "Balkanisation" – was enshrined by the 1995 Dayton Agreement that finally ended the war in Bosnia.

Above: General Mladić looking into the city of Goražde from its surrounding hills

The remnants of war remain readily apparent more than twenty years after armed hostilities ceased. Houses and other buildings throughout Goražde that were bombed out or riddled with the pockmarks of Serbian bullets and shrapnel, remain as monuments to the war. A trip up into the nearby rugged mountains offers spectacular scenery, but also more scenes of destruction. There is also a monument on one of the sites from which Bosnian Serb tanks and artillery lobbed deadly rounds into a city of civilians below them, close enough to murder innocent women and children but far enough away that the killing remained impersonal.

Heading north toward Višegrad, one soon leaves the enclave and enters the Republika Srpska. There is no border crossing, just a battered sign by the side of the road, where the flag changes from the blue and gold of Bosnia–Herzegovina to the red over blue over white of Serbia (the inverse of the Russian flag). The alphabet changes from Latin to Cyrillic. The places of worship change from mosques to Orthodox churches. Even the cemeteries change.

If you look closer still, hidden in the undergrowth on the hilltops surrounding Goražde, you will find remnants, now dusted and decaying, of observation posts, once where the sandbags were painted white, where the British soldier clapped his hands to keep them warm in the cold Yugoslavian winter. Here is the unregistered and largely unrecognised contribution of the British infantry battalions that came to the town of Goražde and patrolled a corridor around its embittered core to shield its people.

For most of the British soldiers entering Goražde this was the culmination of a long journey from walking into the Army recruitment office, taking the Queen's shilling, through training to real-time operations. This was what they were qualified to do and wanted to do. They had not sought war or conflict but had trained for it and finally they would be able to carry their weapon, loaded, at the ready, with a real-time threat and for what they believed to be a just cause.

In Goražde, a faraway place unknown to them, they would be at one with their comrades, platoon, rifle company and, in the case of 1RGBW (The Royal Gloucestershire, Berkshire and Wiltshire Regiment), part of a newly amalgamated regiment. At last they were doing what they joined the Army to do. In the Yugoslavian hills they would patrol the untested, muddied and wood-lined paths that crossed the mountains and valleys above Goražde and down to the River Drina below.

The British observation posts, nestled high on the hillsides, looked out across the striking Yugoslavian mountains. Often for the soldiers in these makeshift shelters, the clouds would carpet the view below them, the snow-clad peaks pushing up through this softness. Outside Northern Ireland, this was the first taste of soldiering for most. What this book seeks to explore and record are the thoughts, emotions and recollections of those soldiers and officers of 1RGBW and attached personnel who spent six months wearing the blue beret of the United Nations as part of Operation Grapple.

In my investigations I discovered this taste of action was both beautiful and tragic. It was for many their solitary moment of operational duty, for others the

Goražde September 1994

start of a distinguished military career that saw them undertake multiple operational tours in the Middle East, mostly Afghanistan and Iraq. What was surprising and consistent was that, despite such differences in post-Goražde experiences, Operation Grapple was a time that all of those I reconnected with and interviewed will never, can ever, forget.

The central and core chapters of this book capture these memories, and to this end I thank all who took time to contribute. I have added to their thoughts by including my letters home and half-hearted attempts at poetry, which capture my own thoughts and emotions from this time.

A MUSLIM TOWN CALLED GORAŽDE

Goražde's children, at street corners, cluster from the cold
Brightly clad, trousers frayed, shoes now worn and old
Fresh faced, young and beautiful, hardened by this war
A richness in their happiness, clothes that show they're poor
In these wind-chilled hands, where games are held so tight
Are handmade wooden weapons, carved to play not fight

Their Fathers and their brothers are dressed in combats new
With rifles shouldered high, they present an earthly view
A weathered face, no arrogance, no intention to offend
Detached from their children whom now they must defend
While on the hills surrounding, huddled close on benches
Females lean on shovels behind their well dug trenches

At night the town is quiet, the Drina Valley sleeps
While sheathed in woollen blankets mothers turn to weep
Where once her man did rest an emptiness is found
His body wrapped in satin now lies in holy ground
As war shows signs of ending her legacy is born
A lonely child, embittered wife, a family left forlorn

Note: Written week one September 1994, upon returning from an early morning patrol and coming across a group of elderly women digging and enhancing the front line trenches.

DOBRO DOŠLI
WELCOME

GORAŽDE

"4 soldiers of my battalion gave their lives whilst deployed to Goražde; 72 British servicemen gave their lives whilst on operations in Bosnia and Kosovo throughout the entire UN Balkan deployment."

CHAPTER 2

4 AND 72 – FORGOTTEN LIVES

There are 4 and 72 reasons I decided to write this book.

Four soldiers of my battalion gave their lives while deployed to Goražde, and seventy-two British servicemen gave their lives whilst on operations in Bosnia and Kosovo throughout the entire UN Balkan deployment.

For my battalion, a newly formed battalion, the loss of four young men, comrades and friends, was a sobering and for some heart-rending experience. I revisit this subject later in this book, which is dedicated to their remembrance. The four young men who will not be forgotten are Privates Phillip Armstrong, Martin Dowdell, Chris Turner and Ben Hinton, from Almondsbury in south Gloucestershire, Royal Wootton Bassett and Amesbury in Wiltshire, and Christchurch in Dorset respectively. Their names rest on commemorative plaques in the valleys of Goražde.

They were among some 350 soldiers from 1RGBW, which was on its first operational tour in 1994–95. So, 350 soldiers for six months, leaving a collective legacy of 175 years of service to the town.

IN MEMORY OF
A MUCH LOVED SOLDIER AND FRIEND
PTE BEN HINTON
A COMPANY - 1ST BATTALION
THE ROYAL GLOUCESTERSHIRE BERKSHIRE
AND WILTSHIRE REGIMENT
KILLED IN A VEHICLE ACCIDENT
ON 9 SEP 94
WHILST OPERATING FROM THIS
UNPROFOR BASE

IN MEMORY OF
THREE MUCH LOVED SOLDIERS AND FRIENDS
**PTE PHILLIP ARMSTRONG
PTE MARTIN DOWDELL
PTE CHRIS TURNER**
A COMPANY - 1ST BATTALION
THE ROYAL GLOUCESTERSHIRE BERKSHIRE
AND WILTSHIRE REGIMENT
KILLED AT THIS SPOT
ON 12 SEP 94
IN A VEHICLE ACCIDENT
WHILST ON AN UNPROFOR PATROL

The commemorative plaques to the fallen comrades that were taken from Gloucester, to Goražde, in 2012

I questioned whether or not I should write this book. Was is it deserved or warranted, when you consider the ferocity of the conflicts the British Army has been engaged in during the interim period in Iraq, Afghanistan and other locations? My journey to Goražde in 2012 and the subsequent conversations with many ex-1RGBW soldiers gave me the purpose to do so. Regardless, what more reason do you need than to honour the names of four young men who died in service, irrespective of their era of this service, the role they played, the conflict in which they gave their lives, or the manner of their death? They enlisted with equal intent to serve, acted with equal enthusiasm and will be, and have no doubt been, missed equally by friends and family as all those who served before or afterwards.

Since the end of the second world war, 2016 was only the second year so far in which British military engagements have not resulted in the death of at least one member of the armed forces; 1968 was the other.
In all, Britain has been involved in 29 deployments since 1945 and has suffered a total loss of 7,186 lives (The Economist, online 2016)

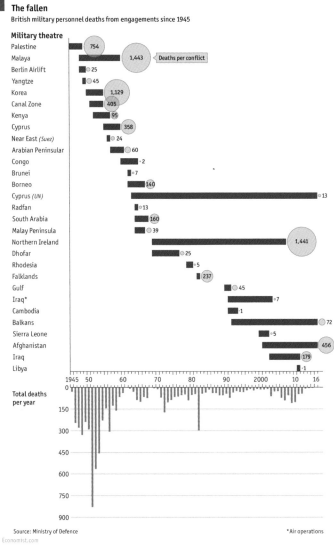

The fallen
British military personnel deaths from engagements since 1945

Source: Ministry of Defence
Economist.com

*Air operations

10

The enduring and never fully answered question, asked by many who have followed the numerous conflicts the British Army has been involved in post-Second World War and the generations that have been witness to the loss of British life during this period, has been whether each investment in human life has been worth it. More so for those who have lost loved ones for they have to dig deeper on this quest, inevitably most having to balance their own sense of loss or perhaps injustice and anger with a sentiment linked to "whatever we feel, this person died doing what they chose to do and loved" or more certainly in the post-National Service and professional, volunteer era, 1963 to date.

Later I tell of a moment in the primary school in Goražde in 2012 that gives colour to my own quest for an answer to this question. As for our overall contribution to the UN effort, an article by Thomas Harding in Banja Luka in the Daily Telegraph (24 March 2007) offers a view:

> *Fifteen years of hazardous operations that cost the British Army 55 (72 when including Kosovo) dead but kept thousands of Bosnians alive comes to an end today as the last troops fly home.*
>
> *With democracy established and the warring factions able to live without killing their neighbours, the European Council decided that the path was clear to reduce the European Force to 2,500 from a mission that once numbered 60,000 NATO troops. As an indication of how long the deployments in Iraq and Afghanistan might last, some officers believe that the decade-and-a-half of enforcing peace in Bosnia provides a realistic timeline.*
>
> *But as the last 130 troops from the Welsh Guards boarded an RAF VC10 to leave Banja Luka, Brigadier Chris Murray, the commander of British Forces in Bosnia, said it was a historic and key moment for the British Army.*
>
> *"This country was devastated and in bits when we arrived," he said. "We can go home now because we have created the conditions for a safe and secure environment."*
>
> *From day one the Army had played a "pivotal role" in preventing thousands of lives being lost and had stopped the country from sliding into the "carnage and chaos" of the early 1990s.*

There are many arguments in support and against this view, but generally British military intervention and its contribution to the UN effort in Bosnia has been seen in a positive light, one that most likely saved the suffering of many and alongside the other UN forces within UNPROFOR (United Nations Protection Force), helped the geopolitical situation to run its course and take Bosnia eventually to peace.

It is interesting that any sense of failure at the time was expressed more by the soldiers than national or international politicians, their masters. There was a genuine frustration that we could not do more, that we could not have been, or rather should have been, more robust in our interpretation of the terms of the mandate and its operational application on the ground. There was a sense, a belief, that if the British Army had been in Srebrenica the catastrophe would not have happened and this frustration, I believe, ran through the three battalions that were deployed to Goražde.

The failure of political leadership during this period, discussed also in the chapter investigating leadership and camaraderie, has been dissected many times by many in and out of Bosnia. This is as opposed to any failure at operational level by the soldiers themselves to execute on the orders given. An international and political institutional guilt has remained over the Srebrenica situation, as outlined in an article in The Economist, written more than fifteen years after the event and brought into retrospective consideration as the international community struggled to reach a consensus over what action should be undertaken in Libya, as follows:

> As the debate continues over how far Britain should (and realistically can) push calls for a no-fly zone over Libya, it is no surprise to hear politicians urging caution citing Britain's entanglements in Iraq and Afghanistan as unhappy models to avoid.
>
> What I had not expected, but should have expected, was how many voices for action cite the example of Bosnia, and the Balkan wars of the 1990s. It is not just that Europe's shameful failure to prevent genocide in the Balkans was a formative experience for a whole generation of British ministers. Some close observers of Balkan suffering now hold key posts in the present-day coalition government.
>
> Elder statesmen still shivering under Bosnia's long shadow include Sir Malcolm Rifkind, whose plea for a no-fly zone in yesterday's Times had a distinctly confessional edge. Sir Malcolm called for: "An open and urgent supply of the necessary weapons to the insurgents so that they can fight Gaddafi on equal terms."
>
> Otherwise, he said: "We will repeat the mistake of the Bosnian war – when the UN embargo had much less impact on the Bosnian Serbs who were, already, heavily armed. Having been Defence Secretary at that time I have, in retrospect, felt that that was the most serious mistake made by the UN."
>
> Lord Ashdown, the former Liberal Democrat leader and the international community's high representative for Bosnia and Herzegovina between 2002 and 2006, also seemed to be wrestling with old ghosts in his essay for the Financial Times. Tearing up coalition niceties, Lord Ashdown begins with a direct swipe at the Conservative government of John Major: "Commenting on Libya the other day, former British prime minister John Major said, 'Events alter opinions.' He was right, and he should know. At the start of the Bosnian war, very few were calling

for military intervention (and the Major government was strenuously resisting it). By the end of the war, almost no one wasn't. What changed the situation was events – and specifically Srebrenica and the infamous mortar bomb massacre in Sarajevo's Markale market. The problem is that between the two, about a quarter of a million people were killed, 2 million driven from their homes, the United Nations was humiliated, and international rhetoric was shown to be sham.

Lord Ashdown goes on: "As with Bosnia, we must calculate not just the risks of action, but also the risks of inaction. Here too, the risks of standing by and doing nothing are greater than those that would be incurred by a careful, graduated and proportionate response designed to assert the primacy of international law and enable the people of Libya to make their own choice about their government."

Such memories live on in the current corridors of power. Lord Ashdown's former political adviser from his days in Bosnia, Edward Llewellyn, is now chief of staff to David Cameron in Downing Street. Over at the Foreign Office, the top political aide to the Foreign Secretary William Hague is Arminka Helic, a Bosnian Muslim by background, whose family fled the violence of the Balkans wars.

None of this is to suggest some murky axis of ex-Bosnia hands is running Libyan policy. It is more a reminder to think beyond the most recent template of Iraq and Afghanistan, and to remember the powerful impact that failure in the Balkans had on modern British politics.

Mr. Blair's recent memoirs trace his own conversion to a doctrine of liberal interventionism back to the ethnic cleansing that broke out in Kosovo in 1999. One passage leaps out, in which the former prime minister recalls his efforts to persuade other European leaders to act: "Very early on, they were prepared to commit to the necessary expressions of disgust at what was happening and demand that it stop but were insistent that any military threat should explicitly rule out the use of ground forces."

This was a hopeless tactic, Mr. Blair suggests, since it told Slobodan Milosevic, the Serbian leader, that if he could withstand an air campaign he could survive. He goes on: "It is amazing that people constantly miss the importance of the fact that any threat made in international affairs must be credible. The absence of credibility increases the likelihood of confrontation. The recipient of the threat doesn't believe it, so he carries on; then the very choice you are trying to avoid – go to war or not – is the one you are forced to make."

Is that just special pleading by a prime minister who undertook wars of choice under the guise of necessity? Today's European leaders seem to have made their choice for now – no war.

Is that a sustainable decision? That may depend on whether Europe can live with a failed state (or tribally-tinged civil war) where Libya currently sits on the map, a short boat ride from the shores of the EU. Small wonder that policymakers are wrestling over memories of the Balkans.

THE CRISIS IN LIBYA, BOSNIA'S LONG SHADOW OVER BRITISH FOREIGN POLICY (THE ECONOMIST, 15 MARCH 2011)

More worrying still is the unfolding evidence that Srebrenica not only could have been prevented, it was known that it was to happen and the three major powers, the US, Britain and France were complicit in this failure, as The Guardian newspaper outlined in July 2015 in its article *How Britain and the US decided to abandon Srebrenica to its fate*:

> *New research reveals that Britain and the US knew six weeks before the massacre that the enclave would fall – but they decided to sacrifice it in their efforts for peace.*
>
> *They will fill the VIP stands at Srebrenica next weekend to mark the 20th anniversary of the worst massacre on European soil since the Third Reich; heads of state, politicians, the great and good.*
>
> *There will be speeches and tributes at the town's memorial site, Potocari, but the least likely homily would be one that answered the question: how did Srebrenica happen? Why were Bosnian Serb death squads able, unfettered, to murder more than 8,000 men and boys in a few days, under the noses of United Nations troops legally bound to protect the victims? Who delivered the UN-declared "safe area" of Srebrenica to the death squads, and why?*
>
> *Over two decades, fourteen of the murderers have been convicted at the war crimes tribunal in The Hague. The Bosnian Serb political leader Radovan Karadžic and his military counterpart, General Ratko Mladic, await verdicts in trials for genocide. Blame among the "international community "charged with protecting Srebrenica has piled, not without reason, on the head of UN forces in the area, General Bernard Janvier, for opposing intervention – notably air strikes – that might have repelled the Serb advance, and Dutch soldiers who not only failed in their duty to protect Srebrenica but evicted terrified civilians seeking shelter in their headquarters, and watched the Serbs separate women and young children from their male quarry.*
>
> *Now a survey of the mass of evidence reveals that the fall of Srebrenica formed part of a policy by the three "great powers" – Britain, France and the US – and by the UN leadership, in pursuit of peace at any price; peace at the terrible expense of Srebrenica, which gathered critical mass from 1994 onwards, and reached its bloody denouement in July 1995.*
>
> *Until now, it has always been asserted that the so-called "endgame strategy" that forged a peace settlement for – and post-war map of – Bosnia followed the "reality*

The disaster and massacre at Srebrenica will haunt the people of central Bosnia for generations

on the ground" after the fall, and ceding, of Srebrenica. What can now be revealed is that the "endgame" preceded that fall and was – as it turned out – conditional upon it.

The western powers whose negotiations led to Srebrenica's downfall cannot be said to have known the extent of the massacre that would follow, but the evidence demonstrates they were aware – or should have been – of Mladic's declared intention to have the Bosniak Muslim population of the entire region "vanish completely". In the history of eastern Bosnia over the three years that preceded the massacre, that can only have meant one thing.

Srebrenica nestles in a verdant valley, among mountains that rise from the banks of the river Drina. It is the location of a famous silver mine – srebro means silver. But by July 1995, Srebrenica had been a living hell for three years.

In the spring of 1992, Bosnian Serb troops had launched a hurricane of violence in pursuit of a racially pure "statelet", after multi-ethnic Bosnia voted for independence from disintegrating Yugoslavia. And nowhere more savagely than in eastern Bosnia, where entire villages were eradicated, towns torched, their populations killed or put to flight by what Karadžic called "ethnic cleansing".

Survivors fled into three eastern enclaves where the Bosnian republican army had resisted: Goražde, Žepa and Srebrenica, their populations swelled by displaced deportees, cowering, bombarded relentlessly and largely cut off from supplies of food and medicine. The population of Srebrenica swelled from 9,000 to 42,000, and by

15

March 1993 the situation was sufficiently horrific for a French general, Philippe Morillon, to lead a convoy into the battered pocket and, appalled, promised: "You are now under the protection of the UN. I will never abandon you." The UN duly proclaimed Srebrenica as one of six "safe areas" to be defended by the United Nations Protection Force (our emphasis), or Unprofor.

The following month, April 1993, the UN security council passed a resolution whereby any peace in Bosnia must "be based on withdrawal from territories seized by the use of force and 'ethnic cleansing'." And in the same month, a report from that same security council warned specifically of a "potential massacre in which there could be 25,000 victims if Serb forces were to enter Srebrenica".

Its fears were justified: Karadžic promised the Bosnian Serb assembly the following July that if his army entered Srebrenica there would be "blood up to the knees".

Two years later, Srebrenica remained under relentless siege, while the UN, European Union and Contact Group of five nations dealt for peace. Bosnia's carnage had confounded the world's most experienced diplomats; ineffective talks and plans had played out and failed for three bloody years. All the while, Karadžic's hand was eagerly clasped beneath the chandeliers of London and Geneva; diplomats also courted the Serbian president, Slobodan Miloševic, while Mladic dined and exchanged gifts with the UN's military commanders, soldier to soldier, as they ineffectively sought his co-operation.

By spring 1995, the Contact Group – the US, UK, France, Germany and Russia – appeared to abandon the 1993 resolution against rewarding ethnic cleansing, as it sought to partition Bosnia between a Serb statelet and a Muslim–Croat federation. Then the French foreign minister, Alain Juppé, had privately confided the working map in mid-1994: it showed the three eastern "safe areas" to be contiguous with one another and part of the federation.

But Miloševic complained to the Contact Group's negotiator, an American, Robert Frasure, that the safe areas constituted "a monstrous excrescence" within Serbian territory. Frasure reported to the national security council in Washington that Miloševic would not agree to peace unless he had a "modified" map that ceded the safe areas.

America's national security adviser, Anthony Lake, told Frasure in a memo that he favoured revising the map. The former Dutch defence minister Joris Voorhoeve recalls a meeting with Lake at which the American appeared to be "one of a number of persons – who might not like to be reminded of the fact – who then thought the enclaves were indefensible anyway ... They considered the enclaves to be very complicated situations which did not fit into a future map."

Lake, who is now head of the UN Children's Fund, Unicef, said last week:

16

"While holding the position of executive director of Unicef, whose humanitarian mission depends on its non-political character, I have had to decline, often regretfully, to speak publicly about events in my previous career as a government official. I apologise and wish it were otherwise, for there is no doubt about the importance of the war in Bosnia. There was no issue about which I cared more deeply."

A CIA memo, since declassified, described the eastern safe areas as "fish bones in the throat of the Serbs". Frasure later told a meeting that he saw "one last card. To make a deal with a Chicago mafia boss, one must be ready to give enough ground to ensure he will fulfil his part of the contract. It's the same with Milošević."

A counsellor to President Clinton, Alexander Vershbow, would recall in 1998 that by June 1995, "Srebrenica's future seemed pretty gloomy. We were already then considering that some kind of swap for at least the smallest of the eastern enclaves for more territory would be wise."

France and Britain agreed: General Bertrand de La Presle, adviser to the president, Jacques Chirac, would later visit Mladic on 29 May, with a message "from the French president and the French government". According to Mladic's notebooks, found in his flat while he was on the run, it said: "France clearly understands your concern, that you do not want the Contact Group map. Since last fall [1994] three amendments to the Contact Group proposal have been adopted on the initiative of France and Great Britain … The map can change through negotiations."

On 3 June, at a meeting in Paris, Britain's defence secretary, Malcolm Rifkind, would urge that the enclaves were "untenable". Rifkind said last week: "The UN declared safe areas with, in their judgment, a minimum troop requirement to make them so. Britain increased its numbers in Bosnia and so did France, but not others. They can call them safe areas, but you have to put enough troops there to make them safe, otherwise they are untenable."

Pressure was put on the Bosnian president, Alija Izetbegovic, to concede Srebrenica and the other safe areas. "The message was clear: the enclaves have no future," recalls the Bosnian government's chef de cabinet, Mirza Hajric. Izetbegovic had told civilian authorities in Srebrenica back in September 1993 that surrender of their town might be the price of peace; they refused to discuss it. In April 1995, the presidency summoned fifteen military commanders from Srebrenica to the government-controlled town of Tuzla, forbidding them to return. The protection of the safe area was, the government argued, the duty of the international community.

Meanwhile, on 8 March, the Bosnian Serb military command had issued "Directive 7", which escalated what had, until then, been called the "slow suffocation of the enclaves" and now ordered "combat operations to create an unbearable situation of total insecurity of life with no hope of survival or life for inhabitants of Srebrenica and Žepa". The directive demanded the "permanent removal" of Bosnian Muslims to "liberate definitively the entire Drina valley region".

Mladic told the Bosnian Serb assembly of his plans for the Bosniak population of the enclaves: "My concern is to have them vanish completely." Both the directive and Mladic's speech were known to western governments.

On the same day, 8 March, Mladic met the British general Rupert Smith, the head of UN peacekeeping in Bosnia, at the Hotel Panorama in "cleansed" Vlasenica. According to Smith's military adviser, Lt Colonel James Baxter, "Mladic took out the map and drew a scratch over each of the enclaves".

During March, says the then head of military planning at the UN peacekeeping department, General Manfred Eisele, the department and the Netherlands pushed for reinforcements for Dutch troops in Srebrenica. The proposal was overruled by the US, he says, on grounds that the enclaves were "untenable" and US helicopters would be used to transport the reinforcements.

The US policy-making Principals Committee, meeting on 19 May, expressed its view that: "The only realistic option is to seek Allied support for an Unprofor pull-back from vulnerable positions" – ergo, the safe areas – "coupled with more robust enforcement of the remaining mandate, including Nato air strikes."

The French general Bernard Janvier, overall commander of UN troops on the

General Mladić has come to represent the evil that ran riot throughout Bosnia in the early 1990s

ground, told the security council member states on 24 May that: "The enclaves are indefensible, and the status quo untenable." He said UN troops were too vulnerable in the safe areas, and should either be reinforced, or withdrawn to make way for air strikes.

The following day, 25 May, any prospect of further air attacks collapsed anyway as 400 UN troops were taken hostage by Serbs, in retaliation for an air strike.

Two days later, presidents Clinton and Chirac and the British prime minister, John Major, spoke by telephone to discuss a response, including halting air strikes. Next day, 28 May, according to the declassified US national security archive, the Principals Committee formalised a decision, apparently made during the phone call, "to suspend the use of Nato air strikes against the Serbs for the foreseeable future".

Lake, in a memo to the president, outlined the need of secrecy: "Privately we will accept a pause on further air strikes but make no public statement to that effect."

During early June, the UN military monitor in Srebrenica, the Kenyan colonel Joseph Kingori, reported to peacekeeping headquarters that the Bosnian Serb "Colonel [Vlatko] Vukovic insisted on trying to find out what would be the reaction of the United Nations if the Bosnian Serb army would capture the enclave and expel the population – literally, all the people living inside that enclave".

In later testimony at the International Criminal Tribunal for the former Yugoslavia, Kingori testified that he had reported that any "safe passage" granted to those leaving the area "did not apply to those considered as war criminals", ergo, men of fighting age. Kingori's reports went apparently unheeded.

On 2 June, Mladic ordered a "destruction of the Muslim forces in these enclaves". Voorhoeve insists that western leaders knew of this order, but that he and his troops were kept in the dark. "The intelligence services of at least two of the five permanent members of the UN security council knew already at the beginning of June 1995 – a month and a half before the attack – that the Serbs intended to capture, in the coming weeks, the three Eastern enclaves – meaning Srebrenica, Žepa and Goražde, "Voorhoeve says. "These two big countries had advance knowledge of the Serbian battle plans and did not share it with the Netherlands."

The Observer has independently verified this, and the two countries were the US and the UK.

Smith, Janvier and the UN's special envoy to the Balkans, the Japanese diplomat Yasushi Akashi, met on 9 June in Split, where Janvier pushed for ceding the enclaves, saying: "Most acceptable to the Serbs would be to leave them the enclaves. It is the more realistic approach and it makes sense from the military point of view." He added: "But this is unacceptable to the international community."

Smith was forthright, warning Akashi of a forthcoming "crisis that, short of air attacks, we will have great difficulty responding to".

A whole month passed while Mladic prepared his assault and, it transpired, the massacre. On 6 July, he ordered his tanks to advance. Two days later, a UN military observer reported: "The Bosnian Serb army is now in a position to overrun the enclave. Since the UN response has been almost non-existent, they will continue until they achieve their aims."

On the same day, despite American reconnaissance planes portraying the alarming situation around Srebrenica, a cable from US intelligence in Zagreb informed Janvier's HQ, also in the Croatian capital, that the Bosnian Serbs had "no interest in occupying Srebrenica given that they have no idea what they would do with all the local Bosnian Muslims".

Also, on 8 July, Akashi and generals Smith and Janvier met at UN headquarters in Geneva. Smith was told to return to his holiday on the Croatian island of Korcula while Akashi, the only man in the Balkans with authority to order air strikes, went to Dubrovnik for a two-day break.

The Bosnian leadership in Sarajevo warned the UN on 8 July that "genocide against the civilian population of Srebrenica may occur" but did not call for evacuation. The populace chose to remain, wrongly believing the world would comply with legally binding obligations to protect them.

The stories of the fall and ensuing massacre are well known. Srebrenica's inhabitants sought protection at the Dutch HQ but were expelled. The UN's envoy, Akashi, sent a cable: "The Bosnian Serb army is likely to separate the military-age men from the rest of the population, an eventuality about which Unprofor will be able to do very little." Indeed, Dutch soldiers watched Mladic's troops separate women and young children (for expulsion) from men and boys (for killing). Many of them had been expelled from the compound.

Early on 12 July, the Dutch commander in Srebrenica, Colonel Ton Karremans, met Mladic, with orders to "let the Serbs organise the transport" of civilians out of Srebrenica. But, says General Onno van der Wind of the Dutch defence ministry, the UN then provided 30,000 litres of petrol, which proved necessary for the genocide. "After Unprofor approval," says Van der Wind, "the fuel was delivered in Bratunac [the Bosnian Serb HQ outside Srebrenica] after the arrival of a logistical convoy." The UN petrol was used, he says, to fuel transport of men and boys to the killing fields, and bulldozers to plough the 8,000 corpses into mass graves.

The mass murder was later described at The Hague by Judge Fouad Riad as "written on the darkest pages of history". A sole "executioner" to turn prosecutor's evidence at the trials, Dražen Erdemovic described how death squads asked to sit down — they were so tired, killing wave upon wave, busload after busload, of men and boys.

One of the very few men to survive the killing fields, Mevludin Oric, recalled: "I just threw myself on the ground; my nephew shook, and died on top of me."

20

Mevljudin remained lying, face down, all day. "When they finished shooting, they went to get other groups. They kept bringing new rounds of men. I could hear crying and pleading, but they kept on shooting. It went on all day."

For a while, Mevludin lost consciousness. "When I came round, it was dark, and there was a little rain. My nephew's body was still over me; I removed the blindfold. There was light coming from bulldozers that were already digging the graves. By now, [the Serbs] were tired and drunk, still shooting by the light of the bulldozers. They went to those who were wounded and played around with them. 'Are you alive?' And if the man said 'Yes', they would shoot again. Finally, they turned off the lights.

"I started to move a little. I got my nephew off me. I arose and saw a field full of bodies, everywhere, as far as I could see. And I cried; I could not stop myself." Amazingly, "there was another man on his feet. I thought I was dreaming, seeing things. I walked towards him; I had to step on bodies to get to him – there was no patch of land without bodies. I hugged and kissed him – his name was Hurem Suljic." Mevludin and Suljic walked through the forests to Tuzla, narrowly escaping discovery and death many times. Their journey to safety took eleven days.

According to declassified US cables, details of the killings reached western intelligence and decision makers soon after they began on 13 July; CIA operatives watched almost "live" at a satellite post in Vienna. From that day, spy planes caught what was happening. "Standing men held by armed guard. Later pictures show them lying in the fields, dead," according to one cable.

Row upon row of tombstones lie silently and capture the magnitude of Srebrenica's disaster and tragedy

21

A senior state department official insists: "All US partners were immediately informed." Yet the slaughter was allowed to run its course, no attempt made to deter the killers, or to locate the men and boys, let alone rescue them.

The next day, 14 July, the UN security council said it feared "grave mistreatment and killing of innocent civilians"; it said it had received "reports that 4,000 men and boys have gone missing". But the diplomats continued business as usual.

That day, the European Union's special envoy, Carl Bildt, met Mladic and Milošević while the killing machine was at full throttle, though he seems not to have mentioned the massacre. Bildt says that he urged Mladic that "boys and young adults from Srebrenica who have been taken to Bratunac need to be released". He said the Red Cross should be allowed to register prisoners. Bildt had foremost in mind, it seems from his memoirs, the release of thirty Dutch hostages, and wrote a report after the encounter saying: "Mladic readily agreed to most of the demands on Srebrenica."

On 15 July, Bildt met Mladic again – and Milošević – for lunch with Akashi and Smith. Only Smith raised the issue of "information on mass killing and rape" and threatened force "if UN forces are attacked". But all the group got in return was an assurance that Dutch soldiers would be free to leave on 21 July, with their equipment and the 30 hostages, and with that the delegation left.

Bildt told The Observer last week: "It was clear that knowledge of what really happened" at Srebrenica, "wasn't there until considerably later. On the meetings of [July] 14–15, there are also good UN cables," he said, which "will be released", after a conference this week. He continued: "There were certainly extensive discussions of, and clear reactions to, Srebrenica also on the 15th. Free and immediate access for ICRC and UNHCR to Srebenica to register and help POWs was among the key points. I see that you have seen the brief Mladic account of what was agreed. Worded differently and briefer than UN account but no difference in substance."

The war ended after the Dayton peace agreement of December 1995, after the US envoy, Richard Holbrooke, negotiated a map that ceded Srebrenica and Žepa, but kept Goražde in the federation. Holbrooke told Bosnian Hayat TV in 2005, on the 10th anniversary of Dayton: "I was under initial instructions to sacrifice Srebrenica, Goražde and Žepa".

Seasoned diplomats insist the massacre came as a surprise. The US assistant secretary for human rights, John Shattuck, said: "We had the Omarska model in mind" – ergo, that Mladic would imprison men in camps, for use as "an extremely valuable bargaining counter to gain territorial exchange or even political concessions" as Richard Butler – the US intelligence officer who worked as the Srebrenica military expert at the International Criminal Tribunal for the former Yugoslavia – put it.

A US briefing paper on Srebrenica reads: "We did not have any information

BROJ ŽRTAVA
GENOCIDA PREMA
POJEDINIM OPĆINAMA
KOJI NIJE KONAČAN

BRATUNAC
BIJELJINA
FOČA
HAN PIJESAK
ROGATICA
SARAJEVO
SOKOLAC
SREBRENICA
SREBRENIK
UGLJEVIK
VIŠEGRAD
VLASENICA
ZVORNIK

8372...
UKUPAN BROJ ŽRTAVA
KOJI NIJE KONAČAN

Srebrenica today carries the memories of its recent past, cast in stone as a permanent memorial to the 8372 that were massacred by the advancing Serb Army.

on any Bosnian Serb intent to commit atrocities against the Muslim defenders or population of Srebrenica."

Pauline Neville-Jones, then political director at the British Foreign Office, argued as late as 2009: "It still remains to be established whether the Serbs had a long-range intention to do just that [massacre men and boys]. Serb forces engaged in an ethnic cleansing campaign to rid Srebrenica of its Muslims [which] eventually became genocide when the decision was made to separate men targeted for extinction."

Jean-Claude Mallet, the director of strategy at the French defence ministry, says in an interview: "I had no illusion that atrocities would be committed. We had reported that. But never such as the ones that occurred."

The International Criminal Tribunal for the former Yugoslavia rejects these views, ruling that the killings were premeditated well in advance. In the conviction of the Bosnian Serb general Radislav Krstic for aiding and abetting genocide at Srebrenica, the court ruled: "Without detailed planning, it would have been impossible to kill so many people in such a systematic manner in such a short time, between 13 July and 17 July."

The International Court of Justice would rule in 2007: "It must have been clear that there was a serious risk of genocide in Srebrenica."

France's foreign minister at the time, Alain Juppé, says in an interview: "We all

23

knew the men would be annihilated, or at least that the Serbs were not sparing the lives of prisoners."

Not a single politician, diplomat or senior soldier saw fit to resign over the betrayal of Srebrenica. It will be interesting to see if anything approaching an apology – let alone a reckoning – by Britain, America or France is spoken next weekend. Most of those involved were promoted or moved on to lucrative positions. After he had left the government, the former British foreign secretary, Douglas Hurd, who had chastised attempts at intervention to help Bosnia, along with Neville-Jones, famously beat a path to Belgrade to engage Milošević – just before he was indicted for genocide – on behalf of the NatWest Markets bank.

The reaction of Akashi to the killing, as it began on 13 July, was to assure that the UN "should not fear an international outcry as at no time have Unprofor drivers or vehicles assisted in the evacuation".

Toby Gati, the US assistant secretary of state for intelligence, told the current US ambassador, Samantha Power, for a book: "Ethnic cleansing was not a priority of our policy. When you make an original decision you are not going to respond, then I'm sorry, these things are going to happen."

The then UN secretary general, Boutros Boutros-Ghali, told the BBC on 11 July 1995, when Mladic entered Srebrenica: "We have been humiliated and duped. We will have to live with it. But in several days, it will belong to the past."

Bildt, in his memoirs, insists that: "They [the Bosnian leadership] knew that the peace settlement would mean the loss of the enclave. So from this point of view what happened made things easier."

*The above was originally published as *L'affaire Srebrenica: Le Sang De La Realpolitik (The Srebrenica Affair: The Blood of Realpolitik)*, by Florence Hartmann, published by Don Quichotte Éditions, *Paris*. A translation was then published in The Observer, which is the version that has been used in this article.

This account is not conclusive on this issue, although it is important to refer to it, to put the Goražde British military deployments in the context of the overall UN plan for Bosnia. What is unnerving post the event, armed with a greater level of understanding, is the heightened sense of vulnerability you get when you understand how tenuous and disconnected the political, the UN and military agendas were at the time. Certainly, the politicians appeared to be dealing with an adversary they did not understand or certainly underestimated as to the depths and possible actions the Serbian leadership were willing to undertake. Human catastrophe beyond the desperate plight of the people of Bosnia and the possibilities of extending this to those sent to protect them was a real possibility.

From top to bottom; UN, RGBW front and rear cap badges. 1RGBW wore the UN badge whilst on tour, but were uniquely allowed to wear the Regiment's Back Badge on the reverse of the UN's blue beret

24

Such a secondary catastrophe was prevented, some by design and some by luck. The seventy-two that died could have been much more, but it is still a significant and largely unrecognised figure. When asking the question, "How many British servicemen and women gave their lives in Bosnia and the Balkans?" not one person I asked got near to the figure of seventy-two. This loss was dispersed over a period and across the Balkans, the peacekeeping tag perhaps diluted the scrutiny of the public and led to them underestimating the level of exposure our forces had to a real-time threat.

This book and my account is aimed at capturing the thoughts and reflections of those exposed to this threat to the reality of being on the ground at the pinprick of the political strategy. This is represented through the recollections of those who served whilst wearing the blue beret and back badge (uniquely 1RGBW was afforded the right to retain its regimental badge, a sphinx, worn at the back of the beret, in honour of the 28th Foot's [North Gloucestershire] action at the battle of Alexandria in 1801) through the winter of 1994 and into the spring of 1995. These memories are woven together through the interviewing of more than sixty soldiers and officers of 1RGBW who entered the beleaguered town in the late summer, taking over the operation from the Duke of Wellington's Regiment, whose soldiers have their own stories.

As a serving captain in 1994, my first and last operational tour to Bosnia had an arresting impact on my life. Since leaving the Army in 1995, I had carried and perhaps fostered increasingly romantic memories of my time with the boys on the hills and in the trenches above the distant Yugoslavian and Bosnian town of Goražde. These memories had been seen through unquestionably rose-tinted spectacles, or so I thought until my visit to the town in 2012. This turned out to be a rebirth, or rather a clarification, of these memories. I am glad I returned, as I would have regretted it later in life. My father had served with The King's African Rifles, fighting in the Mau Mau uprising in the 1950s, and one of the regrets I have was not taking him back to the slopes and jungles of the Aberdare mountains and Lake Nakuru before he passed away. He had wanted to do so.

My first thoughts about gathering memories of 1RGBW's operational tour to Bosnia were full of the hope of uncovering a singing jamboree of tales and yarns, as the soldiers would surely be an unlimited library of such stories. As outlined above, I then pondered on the question of why and with what justification. The modern, post-2000 era of military engagement is framed by ever-present TV and newspaper images. In the case of operations in the Middle East, it is the images of the deserts of Iraq and the barren, sand-dusted mountains and roads of Afghanistan. All have become sadly commonplace in the psyche of British society.

Afghanistan's death toll, more than 450 British military personnel killed and a multiple of servicemen and women injured or mutilated, has left a younger generation with images of Union Jack-covered coffins being trooped through British streets in a frequency not seen since the Second World War. It was a level of death and injury that galvanised British society in support of its armed services and led to the unrivalled success of such charitable causes as Help for Heroes.

Thankfully, mercifully, there was no such frequency of British military fatalities in the Bosnian conflict, but neither was there the insight and awareness of the soldier's daily trials and endeavours, living in true adversity with post-Cold War equipment and even poorer provisions. There was no intensive, intrusive media coverage in Goražde, no coverage at all, as this was banned by the Serbs, but neither were there the technologies of today to allow it. To most in the UK, British military intervention in Bosnia was covered by the media at a distance, with limited, and in the case of those in the enclaves, no, reporting allowed.

This led to an unawareness of the reality of the situation on the ground and a

The children of Goražde were an enduring memory for many British soldiers that served there throughout Operation Grapple. Private Danny Ashton, Gorazde 1994 on board a Saxon.

26

misunderstanding as to the dangers or hardships faced. My parents were witness to this witlessness, as their own cravings for information were fed by occasional mentions on the TV or radio or the infrequent and dated letters I sent from the enclave. We had one weekly call, a ten-minute event. Mine was at 6.10 p.m. on Sunday. I never missed one and was never late. Regardless of this set time, my mother still banned incoming calls to her and my father's home from midday every Sunday I was in Goražde.

My investigations unpicked a different perspective and changed my view. It wasn't about comparing or ranking deployments, it was about appreciating each separately and putting them in the context of their own time and unique challenges.

Danny Ashton, in 2014 a serving soldier, a sergeant in 1 Rifles, a sniper battle-hardened from tours in Iraq and Afghanistan and when in Goražde, an eighteen-year-old private soldier, put forward his own thoughts:

> *In 1994 we were the battalion of the inexperienced; from the most junior soldier to the commanding officer, we had little metal on our chests, no medals beyond Northern Ireland. We had buckets of enthusiasm, mixed equally with naivety, but we must not forget what we faced in 1994, what we dealt with and the hardships we faced and largely thrived upon. In Iraq and Afghanistan, we faced death, injury, mutilation and intensity far above that faced in Bosnia, but today when a private soldier joins an infantry battalion he or she joins a battle-hardened unit, with combat experience from the most junior soldier to the commanding officer.*
>
> *Today we have good food, accommodation and equipment, immeasurably better than we had in 1994. We would have prayed for such equipment in Bosnia. In Afghanistan we did have the ever-present danger, the unknown, but similarly we were capable and appropriately trained to deal with it. In Bosnia we dealt with humanitarian disaster, we dealt with no food, dry rations, the Saxon, the unreliability of our equipment, no contact with friends and family, the Yugoslavian winter in summer gear and life in a trench for weeks on end. Yes, it was not Iraq, not Afghanistan, but it had its own austerity, its own challenges and as an eighteen-year-old man, or rather a boy in soldier's clothing, it shaped the soldier and man I am today.*

This summary is insightful, objective and candid. It represents the précis of the career and experiences of the British Army through a period of significant change. It gives us the opportunity to remember the "4 and the 72". This transformation was driven by a change in the global order of things, from the Cold War to the War on Terror, and how the armed forces were modernised and altered to respond to these changes.

British Army fatalities in recent times are as follows:

Persian Gulf War, Operation Granby (1990–91)

The ending of the Cold War saw a significant cut in manpower. Despite this, the Army has been deployed in an increasingly global role and contributed 50,000 troops to the coalition force that fought Iraq in the Persian Gulf War. British forces were put in control of Kuwait after it was liberated. Forty-Seven British military personnel died during the Persian Gulf War.

The Balkans Conflicts and UN Intervention (1993–2010)

The British Army was deployed to Yugoslavia in 1992; initially this force formed part of the United Nations Protection Force (UNPROFOR). In 1995 command was transferred to IFOR and then to SFOR, under the command of EUFOR. More than 10,000 troops were sent. In 1999 British forces under the command of SFOR were sent to Kosovo during the conflict there. Command was subsequently transferred to KFOR. Between early 1993 and June 2010, seventy-two British military personnel died on operations in the former Yugoslavian countries of Bosnia, Kosovo and Macedonia.

War in Afghanistan, Operation Enduring Freedom (2001–15)

In November 2001 the United Kingdom, as a part of Operation Enduring Freedom with the United States, invaded Afghanistan to topple the Taliban. The 3rd Division was deployed in Kabul, to assist in the liberation of the troubled capital. The Royal Marines' 3 Commando Brigade (part of the Royal Navy but including a number of Army units), also swept the mountains. The British Army concentrated on fighting Taliban forces and bringing security to Helmand province. Approximately 7,900 British troops (including marines, airmen and sailors) were deployed into Afghanistan, making it the second largest force after the US. Around 500 extra British troops were deployed in 2009, bringing the British Army deployment total up to 9,500 (excluding Special Forces). In December 2012 prime minister David Cameron announced that 3,800 troops – almost half of the force serving in Helmand Province – would be withdrawn during 2013 with numbers to fall to approximately 5,200. Combat operations ended in 2014. Between 2001 and January 2014 a total of 454 British military personnel died on operations in Afghanistan.

Iraq War, Operation Telic (2003–2009)

In 2003, the United Kingdom was a major contributor to the invasion of Iraq, sending a force that would reach 46,000 military personnel. The British Army

4 AND 72 – FORGOTTEN LIVES

controlled the southern regions of Iraq and maintained a peacekeeping presence in the city of Basra until their withdrawal on 30 April 2009. A total of 179 British Military personnel died whilst on operations in Iraq. All the remaining British troops were fully withdrawn from Iraq after the Iraqi government refused to extend their mandate.

Northern Ireland, The Troubles (1971–2005)
Although having permanent garrisons there, the British Army was initially deployed in a peacekeeping role – codenamed Operation Banner – in Northern Ireland in the wake of Unionist attacks on Nationalist communities in Derry and Belfast and to prevent further Loyalist attacks on Catholic communities. It was deployed between 1969 and 2007 in support of the Royal Ulster Constabulary (RUC) and its successor, the Police Service of Northern Ireland (PSNI). There has been a steady reduction in the number of troops deployed in Northern Ireland since the Good Friday Agreement was signed in 1998. In 2005, after the Provisional Irish Republican Army announced an end to its armed conflict in Northern Ireland, the British Army dismantled posts and withdrew many troops, and restored troop levels to that of a peacetime garrison.

Operation Banner ended at midnight on 31 July 2007, ending some thirty-eight years of continuous deployment, making it the longest in the British Army's history. An internal Army document released in 2007 stated that the service had failed to defeat the IRA but had made it impossible for it to win using violence. Operation Helvetic replaced Operation Banner in 2007, maintaining fewer servicemen in a much more benign environment. From 1971 to 1997 a total of 763 British military personnel was killed during the Troubles. Some 300 deaths during the conflict were attributed to the British Army, including paramilitary and civilians. A total of 303 RUC officers were killed in the same period.

In the period 1991–2014 more than 1,500 British soldiers, sailors and airmen and women have lost their lives in serving Queen and country. Seventy-two of these were in the Balkans, four of this number from 1RGBW and every one of the 1,500 as equal in life as they are remembered in death. In this period, we understand the world and order within it changed, but as a retired soldier, closer to home, so has society's view of its armed forces.

If any positive can be found from the travesty of the military deployments into Iraq and Afghanistan, then it is this: Having served at the back end of the Cold War and having grown up in the 1970s and 1980s, the armed forces enjoy today, and justifiably so, a heightened and very public level of support in society. This support is much stronger than it has been for one, perhaps two, generations. This appreciation is deep-rooted, expressed by the young and the old, and cheered, not in a triumphant way, but in a deeply sentimental and respectful way, and is found as a common chorus within the shores of the United Kingdom.

This refrain is also shown by the number of people, militarily linked and not, that undertake a pilgrimage to the National Memorial Arboretum in Staffordshire. Perhaps, and more publicly, what came to represent this change was the respectful undertakings of the townsfolk of the Wiltshire settlement of Royal Wootton Bassett, as they lined their streets, head bowed in silence, as the hearse of a fallen soldier, sailor or airman or women passed by.

The National Arboretum, opened in 2001, is the site of remembrance at Alrewas, near Lichfield, Staffordshire. It gives its purpose as to honour the fallen, recognise service and sacrifice and to foster pride in our country.

It is a spiritually uplifting place and is emerging as a worldwide destination of remembrance. The idea for the Arboretum was conceived by David Childs in 1988. He believed that it would form a living tribute to servicemen and women

The National Arboretum in Staffordshire was opened in 2001. As the Armed Forces Memorial it was further dedicated in October 2007 by the Archbishop of Canterbury in the presence of the Queen.

for future generations to reflect upon and enjoy. The Arboretum was officially opened on 16 May 2001. On its hallowed walls are the names of the "4 and 72".

The genius of the Arboretum is matched by the wonderful spontaneity of the town of Wootton Bassett and its people. In the early 21st century, the town became known for the informal tributes it paid during military repatriation funeral processions that passed through the town. On 16 March 2011, Prime Minister David Cameron announced, at the start of Prime Minister's questions, that while "from September, military repatriations will no longer pass through the town of Wootton Bassett, Her Majesty has agreed to confer the title 'Royal' upon the town, as an enduring symbol of the nation's admiration and gratitude". The addition to the town's name was enacted through Letters Patent and became effective on 16 October 2011, when The Princess Royal visited the town to present formally the Letters Patent to the town council. Royal Wootton Bassett has become the third

Wooten Bassett's spontaneous and collective support and respect for the fallen became known throughout the free world and was recognised by HM the Queen bestowing Royal status in 2011

31

Royal town in the country after Royal Leamington Spa and Royal Tunbridge Wells, and the first to receive the status in more than 100 years, but it is the reason for its royal patronage and promotion that makes it the more remarkable.

What the National Arboretum and Royal Wootten Bassett both show is that deep in our society's psyche rests a profound affinity with its armed forces; deeper still a meaningful appreciation and acknowledgement of the link our nation has between its history and her men and women who have been willing to take up arms. Just as it had become unfashionable or unseemly to be proud of your nation, the very notion you could be proud of your armed forces had also been suppressed. The people of Royal Wootton Bassett were honouring their dead, our dead, a nation's fallen heroes and paying respect to their service and openly showing support to them. This, of course, is not to be confused with the decision or politics that took them into conflict or as sympathy that the armed service does not seek, but respect for those who take the Queen's shilling and knowingly accept the associated risks in doing so.

In 2014 we commemorated the start of the First World War and acknowledged and remembered inconceivable carnage. This remembrance helps reaffirm that you cannot compare what young soldiers have been exposed to from generation to generation. By numbers alone the First World War is beyond imagination, with 703,000 servicemen and women killed and 1,663,000 wounded. If you include British and Commonwealth troops, those figures rise to 908,000 killed and 2,123,000 wounded. In the Second World War 382,600 were killed and 369,267 wounded. Again, if you include British and Commonwealth troops, the figure rises to 580,000 killed and 475,000 wounded. In the Second World War a further 67,800 British civilians were also killed in bombing raids.

The words of two of England's finest First World War poets in different ways ring true today, as they did a century ago. The following poems represent extreme and counter views, from the patriotic and romantic vision of service portrayed by Rupert Brooke to the horrors of war and the satirised view of patriotism we find in Siegfried Sassoon's writings.

THE SOLDIER
By Rupert Brooke

If I should die, think only this of me:
That there's some corner of a foreign field
That is for ever England. There shall be
In that rich earth a richer dust concealed;
A dust whom England bore, shaped, made aware,
Gave, once, her flowers to love, her ways to roam,
A body of England's, breathing English air,
Washed by the rivers, blest by suns of home.
And think, this heart, all evil shed away,
A pulse in the eternal mind, no less
Gives somewhere back the thoughts by England given;
Her sights and sounds; dreams happy as her day;
And laughter, learnt of friends; and gentleness,
In hearts at peace, under an English heaven.

The soldier and the man. Rupert Brooke known for his idealistic war sonnets written during the First World War. He died on a French hospital ship moored in a bay off the Greek island of Skyros in the Aegean and was buried on the island (3 August 1887–23 April 1915)

DREAMERS
By Siegfried Sassoon

Soldiers are citizens of death's gray land,
Drawing no dividend from time's tomorrows.
In the great hour of destiny they stand,
Each with his feuds, and jealousies, and sorrows
Soldiers are sworn to action; they must win
Some flaming, fatal climax with their lives.
Soldiers are dreamers; when the guns begin
They think of fire lit homes, clean beds, and wives.
I see them in foul dugouts, gnawed by rats,
And in the ruined trenches, lashed with rain,
Dreaming of things, they did with balls and bats,
And mocked by hopeless longing to regain
Bank holidays, and picture shows, and spats,
And going to the office in the train.

The soldier and the man. Decorated for bravery on the Western Front, Siegfried Sassoon became one of the leading poets of the First World War. His poetry both described the horrors of the trenches, and satirised the patriotic pretensions of those who, in his view, were responsible for a jingoism-fuelled war (1 September 1886–1 September 1967).

Influenced by the readings of the war poets, I made my own efforts to represent my views and emotions whilst on tour. Reading them today, they appear to question the futility of the situation and render an understanding and admiration for the average (British, Serb or Bosnian) soldier found within it.

I am not on my own in the veneration of our brave servicemen and women of today, but equally I retain praise for the soldier, sailor, airman or women of all generations. They are bound together by their sense of service and duty, regardless as to what that duty demanded of them at their time in service. There is something very British about this view of service, something that stretches back through our tumultuous and eventful history and finds popular refrain today, despite such emotions being viewed as somewhat unfashionable or politically incorrect by the broader media and by some within our society.

This pride was married to a humility by those I reconnected with when researching for this book, their attitude being a testament to the nature of the British soldier. They were happy to contribute their thoughts and memories, pleased their efforts and the labours of their comrades were to be recorded.

Similarly, I will not apologise for playing out my role and thoughts in this book, for it is in a large part my story, but I wish to be clear that I am in eternal gratitude to those with whom I had the honour to serve. They have given me the richest of memories, for which I cannot express sufficient appreciation. Neither have I watered down the opinions expressed in letters at the time, to be sensitive to the reader today. There will be some that disagree with my views or question their validity; if so, let them put pen to paper, for they are free to do so, rather than scoff from the sidelines.

Laurence Binyon's most famous poem, 'For the Fallen', is the mainstay recital at Remembrance Sunday services in the UK and is an integral part of Anzac Day services in Australia and New Zealand and of 11 November Remembrance Day services in Canada. The 'Ode of Remembrance' has thus been claimed as a tribute to all casualties of war, regardless of nation

My purpose is to capture the views of the soldiers on the ground, specifically those of A and B Company. I was in B Company and therefore this book will have an emphasis on the experiences and views of the riflemen within this fighting unit. I also take views from battalion headquarters and refer to the role of politics and the United Nations, but it is to the Tommy on the ground, the riflemen at arms' opinions, I sought to hunt out, listen to and digest.

As an aging and long-retired soldier, there is only one passage I can refer to when considering remembrance: the words of Laurence Binyon and his poem, For the Fallen. It is probably the most famous and widely read war poem in English and known, in extract form, as the Ode of Remembrance. For the Fallen was first published in The Times on 21 September 1914, just a few weeks after the First World War began on 28 July that year.

Binyon was too old to enlist as a soldier in the war, but volunteered in hospitals helping wounded French soldiers, and wrote For the Fallen in Cornwall shortly after the Battle of the Marne.

> *They shall grow not old, as we that are left grow old:*
> *Age shall not weary them, nor the years condemn.*
> *At the going down of the sun and in the morning,*
> *We will remember them.*

It is with these words echoing in my head, remembering all those who have served, those who have carried injuries and for those who gave the ultimate sacrifice, that remembrance will be at the heart of this book. And so, we that served with them, their family and friends and the people of Goražde, shall remember them, our four, Privates Benjamin Hinton, Phillip Armstrong, Martin Dowdell and Christopher Turner.

More affectionately known as Ben, Bones, Dowds and Hooch.

"You wear your cap badge and fight for your regiment with pride, you serve the Queen and her country and all you expect is respect and the tools to do your job as best you can."

CHAPTER 3

TO TAKE THE QUEEN'S SHILLING

What makes a young man or woman walk into the recruiting office of the Army and commit him or herself to a military career? To serve your Queen and your country. Not the compulsory and military National Service of years gone by or the falsehood and pretence of some in public service who portray their employment as a national service, but a sacrament undertaken that will knowingly change your life and could actually take it.

Joining the Army will take you away from your friends and family and into a world of adventure and potential danger. You accept these changes and these risks readily; it is an honourable course to take and one not understood by those who don't. For many who haven't, they would, if asked, speak of childhood dreams and playing at being a soldier. For some these dreams became a reality.

Samuel Johnson wrote memorably, "Every man thinks meanly of himself for not having been a soldier, or not having been at sea." He went on to say about public servitude: "The character of a soldier is high. They who stand forth the foremost in danger, for the community, have the respect of mankind. An officer is much more respected than any other man who has as little money. In a commercial country, money will always purchase respect. But you find, an officer, who has, properly speaking, no money, is everywhere well received and treated with attention. The character of a soldier always stands him in good stead."

Can we realistically extend the thread of words some 300 years old to modern days? It would appear we can, for those former and some still serving soldiers interviewed for this book spoke of childhood influences and dreams of soldierhood. Each spoke of friends who did not take the shilling who were for ever fascinated by their stories, envious perhaps but certainly deeply interested.

The danger and associated risk in joining the military and the armed services is real, more certain today than for two generations. Surprisingly for some, the Army recruiting office was far busier in recent times of intense conflict than it is today. Ending hostilities in Iraq and Afghanistan and a pervading view among the public that Britain's military is being ravaged by defence cuts has resulted in a shortage of new recruits, one former senior officer has claimed.

Brigadier (retired) Ben Barry's comments came as military cuts left the Army of 2017 struggling to attract new recruits, leaving the force below its intended post-austerity strength. "There's no doubt that the wars in Afghanistan and Iraq acted as a recruiting sergeant — people joined knowing that they would be going out at least every two years."

Barry, a former officer and senior fellow at the International Institute for Strategic Studies (IISS) think tank, told the Financial Times. "In an army that is much less busy, that adrenaline buzz and sense of adventure is going to go down. Recruiting has struggled as a result and with the public image being one of a shrinking army, potential recruits are even less interested."

HM Queen Elizabeth II has been the head of the British Armed Forces since 1953

This would suggest it is not so much the sense of service as the adventure and the associated adrenaline rush that comes with it that moves someone to take the shilling. This in turn would be to oversimplify the situation and hence be an insult to those who do enlist. They may not have this overriding sense of service driving them at the point of signing up, but as they go through their training they become increasingly aware of the burden of responsibility bestowed upon them in honouring and upholding the reputation of those who have gone before them, and of a very open and deep-rooted allegiance to the sovereign, the Queen, as their commander-in-chief.

The commander-in-chief of the British armed forces is a position vested in the British monarch, who as sovereign and head of state is head of the armed forces. Long-standing constitutional convention, however, has vested de facto executive authority, by the exercise of royal prerogative powers, in the prime minister and the secretary of state for defence; and the prime minister (acting with the support of the Cabinet) makes the key decisions on the use of the armed forces. The Queen, however, remains the "ultimate authority" of the military, with officers and personnel swearing allegiance only to the monarch, as the head of the armed services.

The Queen therefore embodies the British military's history and her country. She is the focus point for the military and those who serve within it. This line of allegiance ensures that the armed forces are for the purpose of protecting the country and its people, not of government. There are, no doubt, some republicans hidden in the armed services, but I would have a guess that they are few and far between.

I am a Royalist and unashamedly so. Taking this route and swearing such an allegiance was a positive contributing factor in my decision-making when joining the Army. You could argue that, in US terminology and parlance, I am a patriot. Herein is an interesting point, as a patriot is a person who vigorously supports his or her country and is prepared to defend it against enemies or detractors. In my formative and youthful years, my and my country's enemy or perceived philosophical adversary was not the War on Terror* that frames western military, legal and international response today.

*The War on Terror is a metaphor of war referring to the international military campaign that started after the September 11 attacks on the United States. US President George W. Bush first used the term "War on Terror" on 20 September 2001. The Bush administration and the western media have since used the term to argue a global military, political, legal, and conceptual struggle against both organisations designated terrorist and regimes accused of supporting them. It was originally used with a focus on countries associated with Islamic terrorism organisations, including Al-Qaeda and like-minded organisations.

In the late 1980s the threat was the Soviet Union and the great ideological battle of the 20th century: East verses West, communism verses capitalism, democracy verses dictatorship. The armed forces were entrenched in Germany, their very military presence being the counterbalance to the possibility of war, and only the fleeting months of the Falklands War had interrupted this military stalemate, which had set the parameters of military service for a generation.

Did this impasse influence those joining the armed forces or are the decision-making criteria fundamentally the same from generation to generation? It was against this backdrop, with the end of the Cold War and the advent of the evolution of a more proactive and widespread United Nations interventionist policy, that the Yugoslavian conflict unfolded. New possibilities of adventure, an opportunity to soldier properly, were provided by this change. It gave an opening for the British soldier to look beyond the streets of Northern Ireland to test his chosen course, career, vocation and the extensive training he had undertaken.

If the opinions of sixty soldiers and officers now in their forties and fifties, and many of them beyond military service, are to be considered, it does suggest a consistent reasoning as to why any young man or woman would take this step. A simple yearning for adventure and, unfashionable as it may be, a sense of service and a desire to do the right thing remain present, albeit they will have a different weighting for everyone. Undoubtedly the role of the media in the modern era has influenced today's generation, not least bringing the reality of operational service into our living rooms. However, the interviews of those of the Northern Ireland and Bosnian UN generation demonstrates a commonality in purpose:

Lieutenant Gary McDade
OP2 Goražde, 1995

"*It was youthful exuberance, the choice between acting, teaching or soldiering. I couldn't act, felt I could teach in later years and soldiering offered a route to adventure.*" Major Patrick Tomlinson

"*It was a sense of duty, I wanted to play my part against Communism.*" Private Danny Aston

"*My Company Sergeant Major at boy time cadets was an ex Gloster. He painted a life that seemed so full of laughter, adventure and manly trials. My career was set at a youthful age through this contact.*" Corporal Taff Davies

Taff added, "*The patriotism of The Falklands War, the images of the returning soldiers left an undeletable image,*" which was echoed by Corporal Des Moore, "*I had family history in the Army, but The Falklands sealed my fate.*"

Many had immediate family connections, "*My father was in the US Air Force, from a young age I was a cadet, as long as I can remember I always wanted to be a soldier.*" Lieutenant Gary McDade

As for me, my father had served with The King's African Rifles and in the sitting room at my parents' home above the fireplace hung a portrait of his

40

father, my grandfather, in military uniform (he was in The Worcester Yeomanry), painted by his best friend in the First World War, a South African artist called Bertrum Dumbleton.

My bedroom had Airfix Spitfires and Hurricanes hanging from the ceiling battling with German Messerschmitts and my bookshelves had Victor annuals and comics stacked high. Each Saturday my father and I used to go down to the local market to buy second-hand copies of 'Battle' or 'Commando', the iconic 7in by 5½in, 68-page war story comics with coloured cover and black and white interior.

I have all thirty Victor annuals, from its first in 1964 to its last in 1994, although the comic ended in 1992. Remarkably, as I researched for this book, I discovered Commando is still going strong and upon finding this out I subscribed to a twice-monthly delivery to set my weekend in motion, as I did as a child every Saturday morning. For those similarly inclined you can join me in this retrospective endeavour at www.commandocomics.com

My path to the Army was framed in my childhood influences and experiences, although it was not a path followed automatically, as it was not until university that I had my full military epiphany and took the Queen's shilling.

This may appear a romantic vision of servitude, but interestingly none talked of the danger, the possibility of loss of life or the consequences of injury. It would be surprising if such thoughts do not enter the mind of the young men and women signing up today in the shadow of the recent conflicts in the Middle East. It is as if this is a given, part and parcel of the deal to which you have signed and committed yourself, regardless of time of service, the possibility of such danger and risk. When taking the Queen's shilling, you accept the prospect of danger, injury and even death as being within your own covenant to the Queen and your country, unwritten in your contract and yet often written about in the open media. Death in the name of your Queen and your country; it sounds poetic and absurd, so what is it that engenders such a sense of purpose and possible sacrifice?

My research suggests this decision is not made in youthful ignorance or innocence, but that it is much more complicated than this. The decision is both individual and collective, it is influenced certainly by the events of our time, where globalisation throws duties upon our forces and where the personalities of the government of the day can influence the willingness and enthusiasm of our military to be deployed. The experiences therefore of the soldier, sailor or airman or women in service are influenced by politics, time, opportunity, personality and luck (or bad luck depending on how you look at it).

The web of personal influences that shape a decision to consider the armed services as a career are very different, unique to that person, but at its heart service, adventure and seeking a purpose played a role in the decision of all I

41

Above: Prime Minister Margaret Thatcher, known as the Iron Lady, established an impenetrable partnership and understanding with the U.S. President Ronald Reagan, delivering a unified voice against Soviet Union aggression, expansion and communist ideology.

"For those happy to talk, most had joined in the same era as me, the Cold War generation. Then, the threat to our nation's security was very different. The possibility of war with the Soviet Union was real; if it happened it would not be localised and would perhaps have catastrophic, even cataclysmic, consequences for the world."

Left: As a child in the 1970s it was not unusual to dig makeshift shelters, designed to combat the strong possibility of attack and even nuclear attack by the Soviet Union

The tangible threat of the Soviet Union influenced some to join the Army out of a sense of duty

The return of HMS Invincible to the U.K. rejuvenated a sense of patriotism and gave rise to many joining the Armed Services.

The Royal Marines 'Yomp' across the Falkland Islands, with no helicopters in support, came to represent the war and the arduous conditions overcome by the British forces in their recapture.

asked. For those happy to talk, most had joined in the same era as me, the Cold War generation. Then, the threat to our nation's security was very different. The possibility of war with the Soviet Union was real; if it happened it would not be localised and would perhaps have catastrophic, even cataclysmic, consequences for the world. This statement may seem theatrical to today's younger generation, the millennials, but I can recall the tangible sense of unease and of an awareness of an anxiety. These worries as a child and teenager came to us through the continual wrangling and posturing of the White House and the Kremlin. This chess-like politics ran as if a lengthy board game throughout the Sixties, Seventies and into the Eighties, giving the impression that war was a real possibility because it was.

All-out war was an option, an option that occasionally felt a probability rather than a possibility. While this gave a definable purpose, it was felt more keenly at political levels than by those soldiers in wet, cold trenches on Salisbury Plain. Here, the repetitive nature of the training and the long periods in barracks in Germany led to poor retention and recruitment, not the fear of war, but the possibility of lack of it and adventure that led our armed services into a manning crisis.

Putting it simply, you joined the Army to be a soldier and had an expectation of what this would deliver. Living out your days on repetitive military exercises with no apparent opportunity for real adventure went against the grain of those the armed services sought to recruit and was successful in doing so. I had resigned from the Army in part due to this reason, but then extended my service to ensure I would not miss out on 1RGBW's deployment to Bosnia. I did so as I wanted to do what I had volunteered and been trained to do; to be a soldier.

Qualifying my own thoughts on this subject, drawing my conclusions, I had asked many in 1RGBW the same question: why did you join? This a question put forward in an era when the British armed forces had been engaged in war in the Middle East for more than ten years. Through modern media channels and technology, what the armed services do and how they do it is far better known, understood, documented and discussed by society and its armchair warriors. In the studios of our television and radio networks, within the open domain of the internet, the library of material available allows analysis of a depth not known before, where men and women chit-chat on the subject in now smokeless bars and public houses, where opinions are further expressed in the sitting rooms and gardens of our country.

Almost daily our TV screens are occupied by images and accounts of the exploits of our armed forces, home and abroad. Their actions, their station, their challenges, are better known and arguably better understood than at any time in history. A pride in our armed services has been rediscovered, re-established and cemented, as there now exists a social and even corporate level of responsibility towards our armed services, and to what the Americans term veterans, although we have some way to go to meet the American levels of appreciation of its former soldiers. This rediscovery has evolved steadily in the years since Iraq was invaded and as we enter a new era, the British soldier and the armed services generally occupy a place in the nation's psyche, one of respect and belonging to the very fabric of our society.

This is, of course, good and justified news and in no small part a by-product of the modern media. However, as the National Memorial Arboretum in Staffordshire attests, over 16,000 men and women of the armed services have died since the end of the Second World War whilst on duty. We must not therefore focus on today and forget those of yesteryear by doing so.

Within the ongoing service and sacrifice of the armed services, the role of the British soldier when wearing the blue beret of the United Nations is little known. It is appropriate that my sole service was when wearing blue, because my parent regiment, The Gloucestershire Regiment, found honour and glory when taking part in possibly the most significant UN deployment and co-ordinated action since the Second World War, in Korea in 1951. Those of Gloster heritage within 1RGBW felt this link when we were presented with our blue berets, as we had the infamous events that the Glosters had participated in when they made history in Korea taught us as if a religious passage.

I will allow myself to digress here, for this story deserves a mention and, I hope, further investigation, so is here to whet your appetite.

On 20 April 2001 the Daily Telegraph ran an article acknowledging and celebrating the 50th anniversary of the coveted actions of the 1st Battalion, The Gloucestershire Regiment, which was titled 'The day 650 Glosters faced 10,000 Chinese':

> *One of the great tragedies of British military history will be remembered this week as 120 veterans join the Duke of York in Gloster Valley, South Korea. Fifty years ago, the valley saw a battalion of the Gloucestershire Regiment all but annihilated when its position on the Imjin River came under attack by a huge Chinese force. David Rennie in Beijing reports:*
>
> *Half a century ago, 650 British fighting men – soldiers and officers from the 1st Battalion, The Gloucestershire Regiment – were deployed on the most important crossing on the Imjin River to block the traditional invasion route to Seoul.*
>
> *They knew they faced a major Chinese attack. They did not know quite how big, or how soon. The enemy came at around midnight on April 22, 1951, a day*

earlier than the Glosters had expected. The Chinese had marched seventeen miles to the river's edge and, rather than stop, simply continued across the river. As appalled British patrols reported "huge forces" advancing on them, it became clear that China had sent an entire division – 10,000 men–- to smash the isolated Glosters aside in a major offensive to take the whole Korean peninsula.

The Rev Sam Davies conducting Sunday Service for 1st Battalion, The Gloucestershire Regiment in Korea 1951. This was before the Battle of Imjin River. Photo courtesy of George Streatfeild

In all, the United Nations forces seeking to repulse the communist onslaught had some 3,000 men guarding the twelve-mile line on the river. They consisted of Glosters, The Royal Ulster Rifles, The Royal Northumberland Fusiliers, Belgian forces and other supporting units.

All the units fought bravely, but it was the tragedy of the Glosters, who lost 622 men and officers to death, injury or captivity, which shook the world. Captain Anthony Farrar-Hockley, a young Glosters' adjutant, was one of those waiting.

Now Gen Sir Anthony, he recalled the last hours before the attack. "The Glosters were holding an ancient invasion route to Seoul – the key ford across the Imjin River where vehicles could cross. On the day of the 21st, we saw lots of little groups of the enemy getting into position."

Aircraft reported that the Chinese were filling in anti-tank ditches on approach roads and releasing smoke clouds to hide troop movements. What the Glosters did not know was that Chinese "deep reconnaissance units" were already above them gazing down from Kamak-san, the 2,000ft peak that separated the Glosters from the rest of the line of defence.

On Sunday the 22nd, as men prepared for a major battle, Protestant and Catholic padres of the whole British brigade preached to packed congregations. At midnight, the main body of the Chinese division, part of the Sixty Third Army, arrived at the ford and poured in their thousands across the river.

The Chinese fell on the defenders like "a swollen wave … breaking on the shore", Sir Anthony records in his official history of the war. Some of the Glosters waited in the dark in prepared ambushes. As battle raged nearby, one unit waited for four hours until the rattling of tin cans on barbed wire revealed that the enemy was almost upon them. The defenders unleashed a hail of small arms fire, grenades and mortars to murderous effect. But still the attackers came and in ever greater numbers. By daylight on Monday, the scene was "grim". Chinese forces had reached the heart of the lines that had been dug and wired with such care and swarmed across the endless hills and clifftops overlooking the river valley.

Now the Glosters were being fired on from their own prepared hilltop positions. One Chinese machinegun post was set up on the key summit of Castle Hill. Lieutenant Philip Curtis "ran forward alone, a pistol in one hand, a grenade in the other". Missed by the first wave of fire, he was killed by the second as his grenade fell into the Chinese position, destroying it. Lieutenant Curtis was awarded a posthumous VC.

By Tuesday, ammunition was running out and the Chinese poured fire from all sides on desperate bands of men as they scrambled down sheer, rocky slopes for the cover of gorges or trees. The British tried to resort to ingenuity as their supplies ran out. The Chinese, who lacked radios, were using trumpets to direct their battalions. Sir Anthony's history records: "Drum-Major P.E. Buss was instructed to sound a range of British calls to confuse the enemy – to excellent effect".

Slowly, it dawned on the US-led High Commanders, well to the Glosters' rear, that nothing short of a division would now be able to rescue the trapped men. But such an effort would endanger the entire line and relief never came. A debate rages to this day over whether the Glosters could have been pulled out or relieved sooner. Cultural differences were a factor in the confusion.

On Tuesday afternoon, an American, Major-General Robert H. Soule, asked the British Brigadier, Thomas Brodie, "How are the Glosters doing?" The brigadier, schooled in British understatement, replied: "A bit sticky, things are pretty sticky down there." To American ears, this did not sound too desperate. General Soule ordered the Glosters to hold fast and await relief the following morning. With that their fate was sealed. On Wednesday morning, the 25th, the young Captain Farrar-Hockley heard the news. "You know that relief force?" his colonel told him. "Well, they're not coming."

Glosters at Imjin Hill

By then, some 100 of the original 650 men were either dead or too seriously wounded to fight. All that was left was to try to break out en masse, every man for himself, to reach the American positions a few miles to the rear.

Sir Anthony explained: "The hope was that with a large number of men streaming across the countryside some would get through." The wounded were placed on top of a hill with a Red Cross flag. Their medical officer and orderly volunteered to stay with them, as did the Glosters' padre, to await capture.

Sir Anthony clapped the medical officer on the back, then prepared to lead his men for the run to safety under cover of a supporting artillery barrage. Men joined close comrades in arms or officers they had come to trust. Sir Anthony said: "At a given moment there was to be a tremendous whack of artillery, then every man should make his own way. We expected to have to cross about two or three miles through a lot of Chinese."

Only forty men escaped. Six more Glosters would have made it but were gunned down by American tanks who took their muddy, ragged figures for Chinese. A Mosquito pilot overhead averted further disaster by dropping a scribbled note, and the American forces gathered in the remaining survivors.

Sir Anthony and a dozen men ran three quarters of a mile, before a large force of Chinese opened up a withering fire across their line of escape. "They were firing shots across our bows. I could have ordered the men to fight on, but to what effect? I ordered the men to smash up their weapons and surrender."

Across the cold landscape, some 500 Glosters, radio operators and gunners were suffering the same process. Three days after the Battle of Imjin River began, they were prisoners of war.

The regiment was christened the Glorious Glosters after this battle, fighting back to back against the odds, wearing the back badge throughout with pride. In doing so the regiment evoked the famous action of fighting back to back at The Battle of Alexandria in 1801. This very same badge was uniquely worn with pride on the back of the soldiers' UN blue berets when we were deployed to Goražde.

The Glosters at Imjin experienced a level of intensity of battle none of the national conscript soldiers largely making up the battalion could have expected. It is impossible to compare their contribution to those of latter years, whether the soldiers patrolling the streets of Northern Ireland or Bosnia, fighting in the darkness up slopes in the Falklands or across the fields and sands of Iraq and

Lieutenant Colonel Fred Carne, commanding officer at Imjin River, was awarded the Victoria Cross for demonstrating outstanding bravery.

Afghanistan. Good luck or bad luck had our men and women facing the challenge of the day, where they could not influence what challenge they were to face or what contribution they could make, but in common, since the end of National Service in 1963, they volunteered knowing risk and danger was a possibility.

Some of those I passed out with at The Royal Military Academy, Sandhurst, speak with regret and even embarrassment about their service, more specifically those not given the opportunity to be deployed on operational duty. As one said to me, "I tend to hide the fact I was in the Army to be honest. Telling of the moment one of my sergeants arrested a drunkard in Hong Kong, as I sat in the Land Rover, as being my most dangerous in-service moment, is a disappointment to me. I was never to experience the adventure of true operations, which has cast a shadow on my military service."

This is not an unusual response to those who served their days pre-War on Terror, but it is a shame that many feel this way, as they should retain a pride that they took the Queen's shilling. It was time and lack of opportunity that prevented them from operational soldiering, not the lack of willingness to face danger or risk as they had volunteered to do.

Be it through National Service or its post-professional and volunteer era, a thread of service and duty reaches out over the years. In understanding what our young men and women have done in service beforehand, what they experienced, the chance component of these experiences, you can start to understand the DNA of this timeless thread of service and duty that links the soldier who walked into the recruitment office in the 1950s to the 1980s to those who do so today. Their decision-making criteria when joining the armed services has not been that different, although what they experienced in service can be very different and therefore how their military experiences shape them and what they carry through life is unique to each, bound by the common thread of service alone.

As one former company sergeant major (CSM) of 1RGBW put it, "My son joined the army because of me and in his first four years' service experienced more danger and risk and has more medals to prove it than I gathered in thirty years. I am strangely and silently jealous of him, whilst being fiercely proud. My tales of military service are mundane and lack colour compared to his. He has had both the good and the bad luck in joining at a time that the army has been fully engaged, I had both the good and the bad luck that it was not."

The challenge as we disengage from operations in the Middle East will be the creation of a two-tiered Army, those who have wartime experience and those joining today, who are unlikely to have the operational opportunities presented to them. It will be interesting to see how this new generation handle missing the recent past and being blessed with the luck of doing so.

Since Iraq and Afghanistan, the British public has rightly recognised the service of the British Army and is largely steadfast in its defence, although a broader awareness of the armed forces' present commitments is still required to ensure their interpretation is not limited to Afghanistan. In 2017 the Army remained deployed in one capacity or other in Afghanistan and retained a presence in a low intensity capacity in Cyprus, the Falkland Islands, Gibraltar, Northern Ireland, Sierra Leone, Pakistan and Libya. It additionally retained permanent overseas postings in Belize, the Falkland Islands, Brunei, Canada, Germany and Kenya. International opportunities of adventure still exist, albeit they are not in high-intensity operations.

Therefore, adventure and modern-day purpose given by our politicians and the generally supportive members from within society remain influences on the young to join the Army; just as the impact of images of our servicemen and women at war prompt a desire to join this fight, a romantic view of military service perhaps and its ageless sense of service to your country. There are, however, far simpler reasons that take some to the door of the recruitment office. These include following family tradition, it never being questioned that the armed services would be your career; the influence of pals, on hearing of exploits of friends in service; or opportunism when a child, when someone in a position of influence or authority, be it teacher, rugby coach or other, sows a seed of thought about joining the Army, which can be especially influential if this person is ex-military and is liked and respected. Some seek the support framework for which the armed services are renowned, the military family and associated camaraderie; some are perhaps running away from a broken heart; and finally, some see this youthful opportunity as a gateway to physical adventure, worldwide travel, mountains, rivers and the wilderness and a life you can but dream about.

Most struggle to articulate what exactly took them to take the Queen's shilling, having one or more of the reasons listed above, and it is post-service that the value of this shilling becomes apparent, as in its taking it created unforeseen opportunity, memories and mostly little regret. Most veterans would encourage the young to enlist, painting a realistic picture of the time in service. Perhaps in a world where vocational and emotional reward are not so readily found in the workplace, the Army offers a route to some sense of personal fulfilment. Your freedom and your liberty may be diluted, restricted, but these restrictions are weighed positively against the experiences with which you will be rewarded and carry with you for life.

Such an unforeseen experience was the advent of the Bosnia War, aligned to the end of the Cold War. The UK government at this time became markedly more involved in the provision of humanitarian aid, not only through the funding of UN agencies and non-governmental organisations (NGOs), but also with the tasking of the armed forces with a greater responsibility for undertaking missions outside what was the traditional area for possible NATO operations. This was formally adopted under the Strategic Defence Review (MoD, 1998), where the military tasks assigned to UK armed forces were altered to reflect the changing defence environment, the armed forces' roles within that and the new foreign policy focus. With respect to such operations, it was stated that "in a less stable world, we have seen more operations of this type … Britain will play its full part in such international efforts."

This doctrine was defined after participation in Yugoslavia and lessons learnt there undoubtedly influenced its strategy. The Yugoslavian and Bosnia deployments were evolutionary, where embedded practices of Cold War tactics and those of Northern Ireland were knitted loosely together to fit operational purpose, where a "suck it and see" approach was cobbled together within poorly written UN mandates. More so, the interpretation of these policies on the ground left the British Army exposed in disparate and vulnerable pockets across the former Yugoslavian Federation.

Retrospectively, the 1998 review recognised involvement of the military in such operations is not without challenges. It concluded a balance must be sought in allowing the civilian aid agencies a free hand in using the available military resources, while being aware that military manpower is trained to fight and engage in combat operations. What was not fully understood and accounted for was that there is quite "a wide cultural difference between the civilian aid worker and the soldier". (Hoff, 1999; Whitman, 2001).

This was certainly apparent in the deployment to Bosnia in the mid-Nineties, which was bespoke, many feeling the Army's thirty years in Northern Ireland positioned it well to cope with the complexities of peacekeeping. The addition of a humanitarian requirement was a not too complex issue to accompany within a structured military framework to peacekeeping. If the framework of peace could be enforced by the military, the humanitarian agencies would operate in co-operation, freedom and safety within it.

This change in policy, with successive British governments being willing to deploy its armed forces, make it more likely servicemen or women will see active service than in the sustained period of stand-off peace experienced throughout the Cold War, although the expectancy of what could have happened in the Cold War was, of course, far reaching and of greater significance.

You train in the expectation and understanding that this is fundamental to your safety and the safety of others, but you cannot appreciate what it feels like to hold your weapon in a live situation, finger on the trigger, live ammunition in the magazine and barrel until it happens. The reality of the situation and your position becomes starkly apparent at the point you are doing it and not before. Nor can you influence what events may unfold in your time in service, the level of intensity or, conversely, as many soldiers will attest, the protracted periods of boredom.

Unquestionably many soldiers have done braver things before and after the Army's involvement in Bosnia. Many deployed to Bosnia came and went with different experiences, differing levels of danger, where single events and timings of a succession of events were out of their control. Some experienced tragedy, some used their weapons in anger, and others' time passed comparatively untested.

However, the common bond of the British soldier is that they all share the same level of commitment; when asked to do their duty, they would respond in kind and as expected. Wherever you are, you patrol with the protection of your comrades and "mates" foremost, you wear your cap badge and fight for your

regiment with pride, you serve the Queen and her country and all you expect is respect and the tools to do your job as best you can. The ethos of service as a professional volunteer soldier is simple; it is based upon commitment, service and a natural inclination and willingness to do the right thing.

Written in January 2008, the then chief of the general staff, General Sir Richard Dannatt, summarised the values and standards of the British Army as follows:

> *The British Army has a worldwide reputation for excellence, a strong reflection of its soldiers and officers. This reputation derives from, and depends upon, unequivocal commitment, self-sacrifice and mutual trust. Our Values and Standards are vital to operational effectiveness – they are the lifeblood that sustains the Army.*
>
> *They have to be more than just words, we must believe in them and live by them. Therefore, it is the effective and coherent translation of these Value and Standards into actions that must penetrate every command and organisation until they are instinctive. Commanders create their command ethos and must ensure that Values and Standards are at the centre of it, through personal example and by educating and training their subordinates.*
>
> *The responsibility of commanders to be at the heart of this process cannot be delegated, and I hold you all accountable for it.*
>
> *The Values are about character and spirit: The Standards define our actions and behaviour: expect everyone in the Army to abide by these Values and Standards.*

There are, of course, soldiers who have fallen short of this expectation of good conduct or have not carried such standards and values, but the clear, overriding majority have done so and will continue to do so. As one retired soldier commented, "If any good has come out of the tragedy of our Middle East military deployment, it is that by the demonstration of the people of Royal Wootton Bassett lining their main thoroughfare as each fallen soldier returns to the UK or through the contributions to Help for Heroes and many other military charities, the British soldier and the Army would appear to be held with a level of respect not seen for many generations by the public they serve." He was not being vainglorious, but merely acknowledging a renewed pride in his service and for those that he fought with in Afghanistan.

The respect of the British public today appears to foster a retrospective acknowledgement for the soldiers that have gone before them. This in relation to their largely forgotten service, which can be found in a rehabilitated pride for their contribution, tucked as it is in the shadows of yesteryear and openly represented at the arboretum in Staffordshire.

Yesteryear was 1994 to 1995 for three battalions of British infantry deployed to Goražde on UN duty, a Muslim enclave south-east of Sarajevo. For them it will be a place and name that they will carry for a lifetime. The stories and memories of the soldiers of The Duke of Wellington's Regiment that went before 1 RGBW into Goražde, or of The Welch Fusiliers, who came after them, each have their place and a rightful need of recognition. This book is singularly an account and a study of the experiences, human and emotional impact on the soldiers of 1RGBW when wearing the blue beret on Operation Grapple in the summer of 1994 to the spring of 1995. It is in part to ensure an accurate representation is recorded for the soldiers of 1RGBW, who gave their all for their six months of duty and left four of their comrades whose souls will rest eternally in the valleys that feed into Goražde, as tragic evidence of this duty.

I personally hope that amidst now historic and post-Bosnian UN engagement opinions the accusations of indecisiveness and possible negligence by the UN are not unjustifiably married to and do not reflect poorly on British military operational competence. Those who made policy and defined the UN strategy for peacekeeping in central Bosnia may well have a case to defend, but the actions and duty of the soldiers on the ground sent by the UK and other governments should not be found guilty by association of incompetence or have to defend what they achieved, restricted as they were by a confused and poorly framed mandate and its supporting resolutions.

For many British soldiers, wearing the blue beret of the UN in Bosnia was a poisoned chalice. They had joined the Army with a purpose and servitude on their mind, with an expectation of what soldiering was to be and similarly what would be expected of them. Through this decision and heightened by subsequent training and regimental duty, they prided themselves in their professionalism, fortitude, behaviour and sense of duty.

This was largely neutralised, however, by the loosely scribed and not surprisingly misunderstood mandate of peacekeeping and its application on the ground. Many soldiers felt this mandate would have better served the end purpose as being one of peace enforcement, not keeping, as there was no peace to keep, but there was a job to be done in the protection of the civilians in the region, caught amidst this terrible and barbaric war. It was not the duty they

The author (right) as the Regimental Signals Officer 1Glosters with Matt Shaw, the battalion's intelligence officer, during training 1993

expected when taking the Queen's shilling, but they did not quibble or question this duty, they applied themselves to it without recourse. They did it with the expected banter, humour and downright moaning you learn to embrace and love as an officer honoured to lead such men, but under this staged performance was a simple application to their profession and trade, which was bound by their sense of duty to their pals beside them, their regiment and its history, their country and to their Queen.

1RGBW's interpretation of the mandate was one of compliant robustness, a natural evolution of the good work undertaken by The Duke of Wellington's Regiment before us. We were conscious in such an environment that no party could be trusted, and that familiarity could breed contempt. We kept both Bosnian Muslims and more so the Serbs at arm's reach, never allowing them access to our positions, although we entered theirs, enforcing the small arm embargo within the total exclusion area on both sides, ensuring our mandate was neutral and consistently enforced.

1RGBW came with a loosely defined mandate, built upon what the Dukes left them, both in policy and physically. This came with the further enhancement and building of meaningful, deep-rooted observation posts, offering protection against the Yugoslavian winter and against the possibility of Serb encroachment for our distant and sporadically dispersed troops. Through this collective endeavour at section, platoon, company and its by product, at battalion level, an identity was born for 1RGBW.

We came as a new regiment seeking an identity and left a uniformed group, proud in what we had achieved and handing over our duty in good order. There were approximately 300 men and women in our battalion group; 300 stories to tell on why they had taken the Queen's shilling; 300 stories to be told of their endeavours in Bosnia and, appropriately, done so in the 300th and tercentenary year of our regiment, founded by Sir John Gibson on 5 March 1694.

Three hundred journeys that led to one Bosnian town, unknown to all before and to be known to all in eternity, Goražde.

"Historical and national identities ran deep in Bosnia and was a sleeping giant awaiting its awakening."

CHAPTER 4

UNDERSTANDING THE YUGOSLAVIA PROBLEM

It was in the spring of 1994 when the confirmation of our deployment was communicated on battalion orders. At last the speculation around whether we were to be going to Bosnia came to an end. The next few months offered intensive training, but training with purpose and an end game. Excitement ran through the barracks and a collective spirit of intent wrapped the newly created battalion of 1RGBW.

Whether it was for my love of history or a need to generally understand and know where and why we were going, I set about reading the history of Yugoslavia and felt it my duty to be able to respond to soldiers' questions. I also felt if I knew its history it would help balance my sense of purpose. I needed to understand how Bosnia had got to the point of social–economic decay and civil war of the time, where the previously content neighbours of the Serbs and Bosnians had fallen into a state of mutually imposed brutality and criminality that had led us to being deployed into Goražde under a UN mandate.

Yugoslavia, the name given for the monarchist and later federated country of the western Balkans, evokes emotions and images of the past and the present for Europe's living generations. Resting between the two great religions of Christianity and Islam, the region has stuttered through the 20th century, migrating from empirical Austro–Hungarian asset to monarchy through invasion and occupation to integration within a federation and dictatorship to latterly disunity, separation, independent national status and restless stability.

Every passing generation will link Yugoslavia in history with Archduke Ferdinand and his untimely assassination, and the consequent, but simplified view that his death was the catalyst that led Europe and much of the world to war in 1914. Beyond this timeless association, there is a generation that marvelled at the heroism of the partisans who fought the Nazis some twenty years later, unified in their fight for national freedom. There is a generation that wondered at Tito's ability to retain autonomy, bridging soft support from the west and the material support from the Soviet Union. This he maintained to his and a lesser extent his country's benefit.

There is a generation, of which I am part, that remembers the holiday destination images of the Yugoslavian mountains, the Winter Olympics of 1984 and the alluring images of the cobalt Adriatic, portraying a sense of peace, beauty and tranquillity.

These are the generations that watched with disbelief as war and ethnic cleansing ran like a cancer throughout the Yugoslavian Federation in the early 1990s, disbelief more so that this was happening at Europe's door. This type of wanton destruction had, we believed, been left in the annals of history in 1945, strengthened in purpose by the creation of the European Union.

Today there is a generation for whom Yugoslavia is resigned to a place in history, where Croatia, Bosnia–Herzegovina, Serbia, Macedonia, Montenegro and Slovenia are independent states born from this war and where their people have discovered or rediscovered a sense of independent identity.

There will be future generations that will make judgement as to the actions in response to the atrocities that accompanied this journey to independent statehood. My generation no doubt will be found guilty of neglect, of hesitation and of retrospective abandonment.

However, events could have been much worse, and history could have painted a darker picture. Atrocities accompanying Srebrenica could have made this passage of European history unimaginable. Future records could rightly be appalled that the international community stood by, if not for the intervention, albeit the late and convoluted intervention, of the United Nations.

In hindsight, this intervention was late, but at the time the arrival of the blue beret gave a respite, and some believe, certainly to the people of Goražde, an ingredient that led in no small part to sanctuary and safety. While politicians procrastinated, and distant people suffered, the maxim of "it is better now than never" was a frustration for western observers, but a craved-for intervention by the people of Bosnia.

Hindsight is the art of the privileged blessed with the passage of time and not the gift of those in positions of leadership in the present. As they procrastinated, and people suffered, the British soldier readied him or herself for action. They were not part of the decision-making process, but their future depended upon it. They were to play a part in the long and complex history of the region and leave a legacy in doing so.

In writing this book I felt it important for the reader to understand the history of the region, a colourful and eventful one, to help put in context our purpose, the purpose underpinning Serb and Bosnian actions and the ongoing threat imposed by this complexity.

I have attempted to make this history concise and interesting, focusing on what I felt to be the key and turning points in the region's history. Some may question why I have gone so far back in history. This is linked singularly to a comment by a Serb soldier sipping intensely on his strongly-brewed, bitter-tasting coffee on the Serb sentry post found at Brdo, which was high above Goražde and one I visited frequently when patrolling: "It is our right as the true people of these lands to claim them back from Ottomans, the Muslims that still occupy our towns and cities." It seemed strange to me that a reference point for such deep-rooted discontent today, was as distant and historical as the Ottoman Empire, of which I had limited understanding from my lessons at school. It was, however, at the core of his displeasure and framed the justification for his cause.

Through my readings, it was clear that the DNA of distant, historical and national identities ran deep in Bosnia and was a sleeping giant awaiting its awakening. Such historical allegiances are found worldwide and materialise in different ways as people seek to secure independence and rediscover nationhood, be it through military action as we see with the Kurds in the Middle East or by following diplomatic and democratic routes, seen within Europe and the Basque region of Spain, or Scotland seeking separation from the United Kingdom. Nationhood runs deep and understanding this helps us understand the Balkans.

In Yugoslavia hundreds of years of entrenched and hibernating hatred had found a voice in shameful and terrible actions since the spring of 1991. What I wanted to understand was what took the Yugoslavian people, who had lived in such proximity, intertwined in all matters, to a point of heartless, unforgiving, unimaginable civil war of a scale that shocked the world.

Then, as now, I was seeking what lessons could be learned from the apparent ease to which civilisation on Europe's doorstep could and was tipped into anarchy and moral ruin.

To represent this course of history I have split it into an outline of the history of the Balkans and Yugoslavia and then an analysis and history of Bosnia–Herzegovina. The latter is obviously intertwined and born out of the former, but a narrow and informative review on Bosnia will help concentrate the mind on the events that led to the situation in Goražde. The reader will find some degree of repetition, but only when relevant to key points that demonstrate Bosnia's role in the Yugoslavian war and the Balkans more broadly.

I have intentionally taken the reader on a whistle-stop tour of this history, by simply listing events linked to important dates throughout time, which races us from the Bronze Age to the 1992–95 conflict and our arrival in September 1994. I have added notes and some colour to the events since 1995, chronologically positioned within the book, as this helps put in perspective our deployment and the old comrade visits since leaving the town in March 1995.

It may even reflect positively on the small role we played in trying to keep an interim armistice to allow long-lasting peace talks to take place, and equally highlight the impression left on many British soldiers that served in the war-torn years with the United Nations.

I hope it is sufficient to allow the reader to draw their own answers to the question I was asked on numerous occasions, "What had caused the war that we were being sent to stifle, why were we going?"

I recall my own summary and understanding as to the cause of the Balkan War being the direct result of a power vacuum created upon Tito's death in 1980:

Briefly, I would say, the former Yugoslavia was unique, being a Socialist state created after German occupation in the Second World War and a federation of six republics, which brought together Serbs, Croats, Bosnian Muslims, Albanians, Slovenes and others under a comparatively lenient communist regime.

Josip Broz Tito had been the country's inspirational leader, the iron-fist that had run the country in his own image and an astute statesman. Whilst supporting the communist cause (he had been active as a revolutionary in his early years), in 1951 he implemented a self-management system that differentiated Yugoslavia from other socialist countries. He fine-tuned his economic model and introduced market socialism, which brought economic expansion in the 1950s and 1960s, but a decline during the 1970s. His internal policies included the suppression of nationalist sentiment and the promotion of the "brotherhood and unity" of the six Yugoslav nations. He was both brilliant and brutal.

Importantly, such tensions between these groups were successfully suppressed under his leadership, although being born to a Croat father and Slovene mother in Croatia and a Catholic, in part this heritage enabled him to unite the peoples of Yugoslavia after the Second World War. Having led the Partisans, the most successful anti-Nazi resistance movement of the war, against the Nazis and the Croats, this leadership of the Serbs, Bosnians and other peoples of Yugoslavia married well to his Croatian heritage, allowing him to represent all within the federation.

However, after his death in 1980, tensions between the Yugoslav republics emerged in the void left by his passing and in 1991 the country disintegrated into inter-ethnic turmoil, which had been long term suppressed by Tito. We have borne witness to the Balkans' history and its present and now we are to be sent to help create the conditions where negotiations will hopefully lead to peace.

A simple summary, undoubtedly possessing holes in its validity, but for me and I believe my soldiers, it was close enough.

However, it is not until you read the history of the Balkans over the last 1,000 years or more that you truly understand the journey that led to the Bosnian War in 1992.

I am no historian and have turned to the worldwide web to gather impressions, thoughts and content, from Wikipedia to the BBC, from learned papers and books to anecdotal observations. To all these texts and sources and to the journalists who have written in haste and in passion about the subject of the Balkans, I thank you.

Early Civilisation through to the 19th Century

Bronze Age
Bosnia has been inhabited since at least Neolithic times. In the late Bronze Age, the Neolithic population was replaced by more warlike Indo-European tribes known as the Illyrians.

4th and 3rd Century BC
Celtic migrations displaced many Illyrian tribes from their former lands, but some Celtic and Illyrian tribes remained and mixed.

229 BC
Conflict between the Illyrians and Romans started, but Rome wouldn't complete its annexation of the region until 9 CE.

337–395
The Roman Empire split, Dalmatia and Pannonia were included in the Western Roman Empire.

455
The region was conquered by the Ostrogoths, and further exchanged hands between the Alans and Huns in the years to follow.

6th Century
Emperor Justinian had reconquered the area for the Byzantine Empire. The Slavs, a migratory people from south-eastern Europe, were angered by the Eurasian Avars in the 6th century, and together they invaded the Eastern Roman Empire in the 6th and 7th centuries, settling in what is now Bosnia and Herzegovina and the surrounding lands.

Note, modern knowledge of Bosnia in the western Balkans during the Dark Ages is very limited.

6th–9th Century

Looter invasions by the Avar and Slav horsemen bought the Slavic languages, giving way to feudalism with the might of the Frankish penetrating into the region in the late 9th century. It was also around this time that the Bosnians were Christianised, probably one of the last areas of Europe to go through this process, due to its mountainous terrain.

Middle Ages

By the Middle Ages Croatia had been acquired by the Hungarian Kingdom, and the Serbian state to the south-east was in a period of stagnation. Control over Bosnia was later contested between the Kingdom of Hungary and the Byzantine Empire.

The second Bosnian ruler, Ban Kulin, presided over three decades of peace and stability during which he strengthened the country's economy through treaties with Dubrovnik and Venice.

14th Century

Bosnian history from the Middle Ages until the early 14th century was marked by the power struggle between the Šubić and Kotromanić families. This conflict came to an end in 1322, when Stjepan II Kotromanić became Ban (Ban was a noble title used in several states in central and south eastern Europe between the 7th century and the 20th century). He was succeeded by his nephew Tvrtko, who gained full control of the country in 1367. Under him, Bosnia grew in both size and power, finally becoming an independent kingdom in 1377. Following his death in 1391 however, Bosnia fell into a long period of decline.

The Ottoman Empire 1463–1699

The Ottoman Empire had started its conquest of Europe in the first half of the 15th century. After decades of political and social instability, Bosnia fell in 1463, whilst resistance remained active for a few more centuries. Southern regions of Bosnia, nowadays known as "Herzegovina", would fall in 1482.

The Ottoman conquest of Bosnia marked a new era in the country's history and introduced significant changes in the political and cultural landscape of the region. Although the kingdom had been crushed and its nobility executed, the Ottomans allowed for the preservation of Bosnia's identity by incorporating it as an integral province of the Ottoman Empire with its historical name and territorial integrity, unique among subjugated states in the Balkans.

The centuries of Ottoman rule also had a radical impact on Bosnia's population make-up, which shifted and changed many times because of frequent wars with European powers, migrations, and epidemics. Notedly, a native Slavic-speaking Muslim community emerged in this period, eventually becoming the second largest ethno-religious group.

The Bosnian Christians also experienced changes, with the Bosnian Franciscans and the Catholic population as a whole, being protected by an official imperial decree. The Orthodox community in Bosnia, initially confined to Herzegovina and Podrinje, spread throughout the country during this period and went on to experience relative prosperity until the 19th century.

As the Ottoman Empire thrived and expanded into central Europe, Bosnia was relieved of the pressures of being a frontier province and therefore experienced less warfare, but a prolonged period of growing prosperity. Several cities, such as Sarajevo and Mostar, were established and grew into major regional centres of trade.

17th and 18th Centuries

The Ottoman Empire's military misfortunes caught up with the country, and the conclusion of the Great Turkish War with the Treaty of Karlowitz in 1699 once again made Bosnia the empire's westernmost province. The following one hundred years were marked by military failures, numerous revolts within Bosnia, and several outbreaks of plague.

19th Century

The efforts of the Porte (Ottoman government) at modernising the state were met with great hostility in Bosnia. This, combined with frustrations over political concessions to nascent Christian states in the east, culminated in a famous and unsuccessful revolt by Husein Gradaščević in 1831. Related rebellions would be extinguished by 1850. Later, agrarian unrest eventually sparked the Herzegovinian rebellion, a peasant uprising in 1875. This fed further discontent, which eventually forced the Ottomans to cede administration of the country to Austria–Hungary.

A state of relative stability was reached with the imposition of Austro–Hungarian rule, as it embarked on several social and administrative reforms intended to make Bosnia and Herzegovina into a "model colony".

Although successful economically, Austro–Hungarian policy, which focused on promoting the ideal of a pluralist and multi-confessional Bosnian nation, failed to limit the rising tides of nationalism. The concept of Croat and Serb nationhood had already spread to Bosnia and Herzegovina's Catholics and Orthodox communities from neighbouring Croatia and Serbia in the mid-19th century and was too well-entrenched to allow for the acceptance of the concept of Bosnian nationhood.

20th Century

1914 Serb Nationalist Gavrilo Princip Assassinates the Heir to the Austro–Hungarian Throne, Archduke Franz Ferdinand.

By the turn of the century, nationalism was intertwined with Bosnian politics, with national political parties aligning themselves to the three groups dominating elections.

The idea of a unified south Slavic state became a popular political ideology in the region, including in Bosnia and Herzegovina. The Austro–Hungarian government's decision to formally annex Bosnia–Herzegovina in 1908 (the Bosnian Crisis) added to a sense of urgency among these nationalists. The political tensions caused by all this culminated on 28 June 1914, when Serb nationalist youth Gavrilo Princip assassinated the heir to the Austro–Hungarian throne, Archduke Franz Ferdinand, in Sarajevo; an event that proved to be the spark that many believe set off the First World War.

A Political Migration Towards the Spirit of Bosnian Independence.
Following the First World War, Bosnia was incorporated into the South Slav
Kingdom of Serbs, Croats and Slovenes. Political life in Bosnia now was marked
by two major trends:

(a)   Social and economic unrest over agrarian reform between 1918 and
      1919 established through mass colonisation and property confiscation, and
      the formation of several political parties that commonly changed allegiance
      with parties in other Yugoslav regions.
(b)   The dominant ideological conflict of the Yugoslav state, between Croatian
      regionalism and Serbian centralisation, was approached differently by Bosnia's
      major ethnic groups and was dependent on the overall political atmosphere.
      Although the initial split of the country into thirty-three oblasts (districts)
      erased the presence of traditional geographic entities from the map, the efforts
      of Bosnian politicians such as Mehmed Spaho ensured that the six oblasts
      carved up from Bosnia and Herzegovina corresponded to the six sanjaks from
      Ottoman times and, thus, matched the country's traditional boundary as a
      whole.

Emerging in the 17th century and gaining prominence in the 19th century,
Yugoslavia was the vision of a single state for the southern Slavic people. The
name itself was coined from the Slavic words jug (south) and Slaveni (Slavs).

1918–29 The Formation of Yugoslavia
The country was formed in 1918 immediately after the First World War as the
Kingdom of Serbs, Croats and Slovenes by union of the State of Slovenes,
Croats and Serbs and the Kingdom of Serbs. At this time, it was more commonly
called a "Versailles' state", after the Versailles Treaty. It was officially renamed
in 1929 with the official name of Yugoslavia being implemented for use on the
international and home fronts, although it was used in regional and political
parlance from the signing of the treaty in 1921.

   This change was in line with Yugoslavia's monarch, King Alexander I, banning
national political parties in the same year, assuming executive power and renaming
the country Yugoslavia. In doing so he hoped to curb separatist tendencies and
mitigate nationalist passions. However, his policies later encountered opposition
from other European powers stemming from developments in Italy and Germany,
where fascists and Nazis rose to power, and the Soviet Union, where Stalin became
absolute ruler. None of these three regimes favoured the policy pursued by
Alexander. In fact, Italy and Germany wanted to revise the international treaties

signed after the First World War, and the Soviets were determined to regain their position in Europe and pursue a more active international policy.

However, Alexander persisted and attempted to create a centralised Yugoslavia. To do so he decided to abolish Yugoslavia's historic regions, and new internal boundaries were drawn for provinces, known as banovinas, named after rivers that offered natural boundaries. At this time many politicians were jailed or kept under police surveillance, and a period of controlled repression had been established.

Formation of Yugoslavia
1918–20

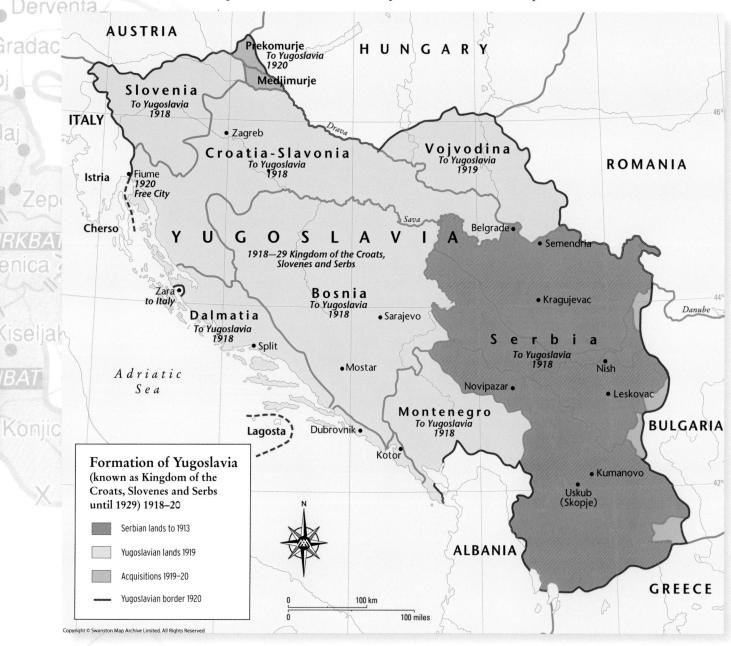

66

The effect of these policies and Alexander's dictatorship was to further alienate the non-Serbs from the idea of unity. Notably during his reign, the flags of the Yugoslav nations were banned, alongside communist ideas, doctrines and activity. This led ultimately to the king's assassination in Marseille during an official visit to France in 1934 by an experienced marksman from Ivan Mihailov's Internal Macedonian Revolutionary Organisation. This assassination was with the co-operation of the Ustaše, a Croatian fascist revolutionary organisation. The direct and short-term consequence was that Alexander was succeeded by his eleven year-old son, Peter ll, and a regency council headed by his cousin, Prince Paul. By all accounts this was unsatisfactory and appeared a monarchist reversion to mid to late 19th century monarchist doctrine and social divide.

These events were alongside the international political scene of the late 1930s, which was marked by growing intolerance between the people and the principal political figures and the aggressive attitude of the totalitarian regimes. What was unquestionable was the certainty that the order set up after the First World War was losing its strongholds and its sponsors were losing their strength.

1929 The Establishment of the Kingdom of Yugoslavia in 1929

The formation brought the redrawing of administrative regions into banates (regions) that purposely avoided all historical and ethnic lines, removing any trace of a Bosnian entity.

Serbo–Croat tensions over the structuring of the Yugoslav state continued, with the concept of a separate Bosnian division receiving little or no consideration. The famous Cvetković–Maček agreement that created the Croatian banate in 1939 encouraged what was essentially a partition of Bosnia between Croatia and Serbia.

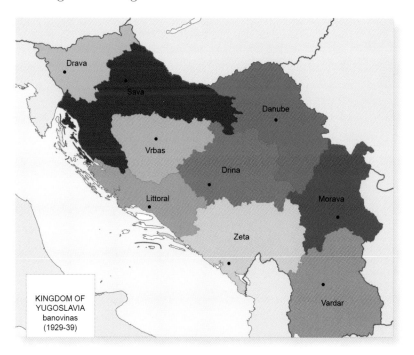

The Kingdom of Yugoslavia 1929–1939

1941 German Invasion

Outside political circumstances forced Yugoslav politicians to shift their attention to the rising threat posed by Adolf Hitler's Nazi Germany. Following a period of appeasement, the signing of the Tripartite Treaty, and a coup d'état, Yugoslavia was finally invaded by Germany on 6 April 1941.

Once the kingdom of Yugoslavia was conquered by Nazi forces in the Second

World War, all of Bosnia was ceded to the independent state of Croatia. The Nazi rule over Bosnia led to widespread persecution. The Jewish population was nearly exterminated. Tens of thousands of Serbs died in Croatian concentration camps. Many Serbs in the area took up arms and joined the Chetniks; a Serb nationalist and royalist movement that collaborated with the Nazis and committed numerous atrocities against chiefly Bosnian Muslim civilians in regions, which were under Serb domination and control.

1943 The Rise of the Partisan – the Ustaše
Starting in 1941, Yugoslav communists under the leadership of Josip Broz Tito organised their own multi-ethnic resistance group, the Partisans, who fought against Axis, Ustaše, and Chetnik forces. On 25 November 1943, the Anti-Fascist Council of National Liberation of Yugoslavia with Tito at its helm held a founding conference in Jajce where Bosnia and Herzegovina was re-established as a republic within the Yugoslavian federation within its Ottoman borders. Military success eventually prompted the Allies to support the Partisans, and the end of the war resulted in the establishment of the Federal People's Republic of Yugoslavia, with the constitution of 1946 officially making Bosnia and Herzegovina one of six constituent republics in the new state.

Importantly, repression of a different order had set in and from 1941–45, the Croatian Ustaše regime murdered around 500,000 people, 250,000 were expelled, and another 200,000 were forced to convert to Catholicism; the victims were predominantly Serbs, but also included 37,000 Jews.

The Yugoslavian people, with many inherent differences, found themselves commonly repressed and tortured, and not surprisingly the people of the federation found common ground through this repression and it bound them in a common purpose. The rise of resistance in this context was inevitable.

From the start, the Yugoslav resistance forces consisted of two factions: the communist-led Yugoslav Partisans and the royalist Chetniks, with the former receiving Allied recognition only at the Tehran conference (1943). The heavily pro-Serbian Chetniks were led by Draza Mihajlovic, while the pan-Yugoslav oriented Partisans were led by Josip Broz Tito.

"Death to fascism, freedom to the People." The slogan became popular after the death of Croatian Partisan Stjepan Filipović. As the rope was put around his neck on 22 May 1942, he defiantly thrust his hands out and denounced the Germans and their Axis allies as murderers, shouting the words. At this moment, a subsequently famous photograph was taken from which a statue was cast.

With remarkable efficiency, the Partisans initiated a guerrilla campaign that developed into the largest resistance army in occupied western and central Europe. The Chetniks, initially supported by the exiled royal government as well as the Allies, soon had to focus their efforts on combating the Partisans rather than the occupying Axis forces. By the end of the war, the Chetnik movement transformed into a collaborationist Serb nationalist militia, which was completely dependent on accessing Axis supplies. The highly mobile Partisans, however, carried on their guerrilla warfare with great success. Most notable of the victories against the occupying forces were the battles of Neretva and Sutjeska.

Through their endeavour the Yugoslav Partisans were able to expel the Axis from Serbia in 1944 and the rest of Yugoslavia in 1945. Aligned to this effort, the Red Army provided limited assistance with the liberation of Belgrade and withdrew after the war was over. Post victory, and largely manufactured by themselves, in May 1945 the Partisans met with allied forces outside former Yugoslav borders. This followed them also taking over Trieste and parts of the southern Austrian provinces of Styria and Carinthia, although the Partisans withdrew from Trieste in June of the same year.

Above: Josip Broz Tito during the Second World War, as commander of the Partisans

At this point the Allies attempted to reunite the Partisans, who denied the supremacy of the old government of the Kingdom of Yugoslavia, and the émigrés loyal to the king, leading to the Tito–Šubašić Agreement in June 1944. However, internal dynamics had taken precedence regarding international intent and Tito, seen as a national hero by the citizens of Yugoslavia, was elected by referendum to lead the new independent communist state, initially as its prime minister.

Above: Marshal Josip Broz Tito reviewing the Partisan 1st Proletarian Brigade, June 1943

1946 Onwards, the Federal People's Republic of Yugoslavia

Because of its central geographic position within the Yugoslavian federation, post-war Bosnia was strategically selected as a base for the development of the military defence industry. This contributed to a large concentration of arms and military personnel in Bosnia; a significant factor in the war that followed the break-up of Yugoslavia in the 1990s. However, Bosnia's existence within Yugoslavia, for the large part, was peaceful and prosperous. Being one of the poorer republics in the early 1950s, it quickly recovered economically, taking advantage of its extensive natural resources to stimulate industrial development.

69

The Yugoslavian communist doctrine of "brotherhood and unity" particularly suited Bosnia's diverse and multi-ethnic society that, because of such an imposed system of tolerance, thrived culturally and socially.

Though considered a political backwater of the federation for much of the 1950s and 1960s, the 1970s saw the ascension of a strong Bosnian political elite. While working within the communist system, politicians such as Džemal Bijedić, Branko Mikulić and Hamdija Pozderac reinforced and protected the sovereignty of Bosnia and Herzegovina. Their efforts proved key during the turbulent period following Tito's death in 1980 and are today considered some of the early steps towards Bosnian independence. However, the republic hardly escaped the increasingly nationalistic climate of the time unscathed. With the fall of communism and the start of the break-up of Yugoslavia, the old communist doctrine of tolerance began to lose its potency, creating an opportunity for nationalist elements in the society to spread their influence.

What Cost for Independence?

The route to independence had a bloody cost, with the official Yugoslav post-war estimate of deaths in Yugoslavia during the conflict being 1,704,000. Subsequent data gathering in the 1980s by historians Vladimir Žerjavić and Bogoljub Kočović showed that the actual number of dead was about one million.

On 31 January 1946, the new constitution of Federal People's Republic of Yugoslavia, modelled after the Soviet Union, established six republics, an autonomous province, and an autonomous district that were part of SR Serbia. The federal capital was Belgrade. Republics and provinces were:

- Socialist Republic of Bosnia and Herzegovina
- Socialist Republic of Croatia
- Socialist Republic of Macedonia
- Socialist Republic of Montenegro
- Socialist Republic of Serbia
- Socialist Autonomous Province of Kosovo
- Socialist Autonomous Province of Vojvodina
- Socialist Republic of Slovenia

There were still some key regional issues to resolve and in 1947 negotiations between Yugoslavia and Bulgaria led to the Bled Agreement. The aim of the negotiations was to include Bulgaria in Yugoslavia or to form a new union of two independent countries. After the intervention of Stalin this agreement was never realised.

Within the former federation, Yugoslavia solved the national issue of nations and nationalities (national minorities) within a structure that all nations and nationalities had the same rights. The flags of the republics used versions of the red flag and/or Slavic tricolor, with a red star in the centre or in the canton. This united all under a common flag with regional nuances.

Socialist Federal Republic of Yugoslavia

In 1974, the two provinces of Vojvodina and Kosovo–Metohija (for the latter had by then been upgraded to the status of a province), as well as the republics of Bosnia and Herzegovina, and Montenegro, were granted greater autonomy to the point that Albanian and Hungarian became nationally recognised minority languages and the Serbo–Croat of Bosnia and Montenegro altered to a form based on the speech of the local people and not on the standards of Zagreb and Belgrade. In Slovenia the recognised minorities were Hungarians and Italians.

Vojvodina and Kosovo–Metohija formed a part of the Republic of Serbia, but those provinces also formed part of the federation, which led to the unique situation that central Serbia did not have its own assembly but a joint assembly with its provinces represented in it. The country distanced itself from the Soviets in 1948 and started to build its own way to socialism under the strong political leadership of Tito. The country criticised both Eastern Bloc and NATO nations and, together with other countries, started the Non-Aligned Movement in 1961, which remained the official affiliation of the country until it dissolved.

Demographic Context and Influences 1920–95

It is important to put the historical events into demographic context. Yugoslavia had always been a home to a very diverse population, not only in terms of national affiliation, but also religious affiliation. Of the many religions, Islam, Catholicism, Judaism and Protestantism as well as various Orthodox faiths composed the religions of Yugoslavia, comprising more than forty in all. The religious demographics of Yugoslavia have changed dramatically since the Second World War. A census taken in 1921 and later in 1948 show that 99 per cent of the population appeared to be deeply involved with their religion and practices. With post-war government programmes of modernisation and urbanisation, the percentage of religious believers took a dramatic plunge. Connections between religious belief and nationality posed a serious threat to the post-war communist government's policies on national unity and state structure.

After the rise of communism, a survey taken in 1964 showed that just over 70 per cent of the total population of Yugoslavia considered themselves to be religious believers. The places of highest religious concentration were Kosovo with 91 per cent and Bosnia and Herzegovina with 83.8 per cent. The places of lowest religious concentration were Slovenia with 65.4 per cent, Serbia with 63.7 per cent and Croatia with 63.6 per cent. Religious differences between Orthodox Christian Serbs, Catholic Croats and Muslim Bosniaks. And the rise of nationalism, contributed to the collapse of Yugoslavia in 1991.

Similarly, the religious context is important as it is these esoteric differences that in part ultimately led to the political, social and national divides that led the region into civil war in the 1990s, just as the evolution of government and the political framework of Yugoslavia frames the migration in the political landscape.

7 April 1963 and the Birth of the Socialist Federal Republic of Yugoslavia (SFRY)

In 1963 the nation changed its official name to the Socialist Federal Republic of Yugoslavia (SFRY) and Tito was named President for Life. In the SFRY, each republic and province had its own constitution, supreme court, parliament, president and prime minister. At the top of the Yugoslav government were the president (Tito), the federal prime minister, and the federal parliament (although a collective presidency was formed after Tito's death in 1980). Also important were the Communist Party general secretaries for each republic and province, and the general secretary of Central Committee of the Communist Party.

Tito was without doubt the most powerful person in the country, followed by republican and provincial premiers and presidents, and Communist Party presidents. He was the glue that held the complicated constitution together and had credibility and support across most, if not all, nationalities and ethnicities to ensure he was also the lubricant to make it work. Tito's power and influence were in reality absolute and a good example of this was the dubious death of Slobodan Penezić Krcun, Tito's chief of secret police in Serbia, in a road traffic incident after he started to complain about Tito's politics. Similarly, the interior minister, Aleksandar Ranković, lost all his titles and rights after a major disagreement with Tito regarding state politics. Sometimes ministers in government, such as Edvard Kardelj or Stane Dolanc, finding Tito's favour, were rewarded with powers and influence equal to that of the prime minister.

Croatian Spring of 1970–71
However, despite ruling with an iron fist, regional and localised representation and discontent continued to rumble under the surface of hard-line suppression. Tito was all too aware of this undercurrent and with this recognition, suppression of national identities escalated with the so-called Croatian Spring of 1970–71, when students in Zagreb organised demonstrations for greater civil liberties and greater Croatian autonomy. The regime stifled the public protest and incarcerated the leaders. However, many key Croatian representatives in the Communist Party silently supported this cause, and this played out in the political arena. This culminated in a new constitution being ratified in 1974 that gave more rights to the individual republics in Yugoslavia and provinces in Serbia.

It was this pragmatic and on occasion retrospective flexibility in managing the diversity of the region that enabled Tito to retain region-wide command, supported by increasingly devolved responsibility.

As such, it has been argued that post-Second World War Yugoslavia was in many respects a model of how to build a multinational state. The federation was constructed against a challenging background: an inter-war Yugoslavia that had been dominated by the Serbian ruling class; and a war-time division of the country, as fascist Italy and Nazi Germany split the country apart and endorsed the Ustaše, which committed genocide against the Serbs. The internal line of conflict was well drawn and destructive, where a small fraction of Bosniak nationalists joined the Axis forces and attacked Serbs, while extreme Serb nationalists engaged in attacks on Bosniaks and Croats.

The possibilities of federal civil war were therefore almost uncountable. However, the common purpose of the Partisans bridged many of these possible lines of conflict and embodied a common purpose. The individual who embodied this purpose was Tito. It is not surprising therefore that when he died the power and influencing vacuum left by his departure was impossible to fill by one or even more people. Into this vacuum nationalist and religious lines of support found popularity, as the multi-faceted federation and Yugoslav nations sought to identify themselves with a common resolve.

During the mid-20th century and post-Second World War, ethnic violence was only ended when the multi-ethnic Yugoslav Partisans took over the country at the end of the war and banned nationalism from being promoted publicly. Overall, relative peace was retained under Tito's rule, though nationalist protests did occur, but these were usually repressed, and nationalist leaders were arrested, and some were executed by Yugoslav officials. As a portent of events to come, one protest in Croatia in the 1970s, called the Croatian Spring, was backed by large numbers of Croats who claimed that Yugoslavia remained a Serb hegemony and demanded that Serbia's powers be reduced. Twenty years later, such a protest escalated into region-wide war that tore Yugoslavia apart.

Throughout the rule of Tito, whose home republic was Croatia, he remained concerned over the stability of the country and responded in a manner to appease both Croats and Serbs, where he ordered the arrest of the Croat protestors, while at the same time conceding to some of their demands. Significantly for future events in 1974, Serbia's influence in the country was significantly reduced as autonomous provinces were created in ethnic Albanian-majority populated Kosovo and the mixed-population Vojvodina.

These autonomous provinces held the same voting power as the republics, but unlike the republics, they could not legally separate from Yugoslavia. This concession satisfied Croatia and Slovenia, but in Serbia and in the new autonomous province of Kosovo, reaction was different. Serbs saw the new constitution as conceding to Croat and ethnic Albanian nationalists. Ethnic Albanians in Kosovo saw the creation of an autonomous province as not being enough and demanded that Kosovo become a constituent republic with the right to separate from Yugoslavia. This created tensions within the communist leadership, particularly amongst communist Serb officials who resented the 1974 constitution as weakening Serbia's influence and jeopardising the unity of the country by allowing the republics the right to separate.

Consequently, an economic crisis erupted in the 1970s that was the product of disastrous errors by successive Yugoslav governments, such as borrowing vast amounts of western capital to fund growth through exports. Unfortunately, western economies entered recession, cutting the pipeline of economic oxygen to the struggling Yugoslav manufacturing base and its over-leveraged export-based strategy, creating a huge debt problem. The Yugoslav government had no alternative then but to accept an IMF loan. This represented a significant embarrassment for the political elite of Yugoslavia.

Statistically in 1989, according to official sources, 248 firms were declared bankrupt or were liquidated and 89,400 workers were laid off. During the first nine months of 1990 directly following the adoption of the IMF programme, another 889 enterprises with a combined workforce of 525,000 workers suffered the same fate. In other words, in less than two years "the trigger mechanism" (under the Financial Operations Act) had led to the layoff of more than 600,000 workers out of a total industrial workforce of the order of 2.7 million. An additional 20 per cent of the workforce, or half a million people, were not paid wages during the early months of 1990 as enterprises sought to avoid bankruptcy. The largest concentrations of bankrupt firms and layoffs were in Serbia, Bosnia and Herzegovina, Macedonia and Kosovo. Real earnings were in free fall and social programmes had collapsed, creating within the population an atmosphere of social despair and hopelessness. This was a critical turning point in the events to follow. Amid such austerity in earnings and economic turmoil, political and nationalistic fervor was given a stage and a voice to take advantage of region-wide discontent.

At this point in Yugoslav history, the journey turns quickly from despair into civil war and barbaric ethnic cleansing. It was if the jigsaw and patchwork puzzle of Yugoslavia walked expectantly towards distress and unlimited terror, even when put in context to its complex and often highly unethical history. Many argue this started in 1974, when the constitution dampened the institutional and material powers of the federal government. During this period, Tito substituted the structure and his unraveling weaknesses through an increasing willingness to compromise until his death in 1980. War, many argue, was an inevitability when you allow for history and the intensity of national and religious passion within the confines of the region.

These themes are recurring, repetitive and underpin any understanding of the route to the Bosnian War and the collapse of the united, federated Yugoslav state and its ideological dream.

1980–90 The death of Tito and the Creeping Inevitability of War

Not surprisingly, with the federal binding force of Tito removed with his death on 4 May 1980, ethnic tensions grew in Yugoslavia. With his passing the legacy of the constitution of 1974 was used to throw the system of decision-making into a state of paralysis, made all the more hopeless as the conflict of interests had become irreconcilable. The constitutional crisis that inevitably followed resulted in a rise of nationalism in all republics: Slovenia and Croatia made demands for looser ties within the Federation, the Albanian majority in Kosovo demanded the status of a republic, Serbia sought absolute, not only relative, dominion over Yugoslavia. Added to this, the Croat quest for independence led to large Serb communities within Croatia rebelling and trying to secede from the Croat republic.

The question of fair Serb representation and retention of influence across the former Yugoslavia created a melting pot of potential issues. The Serbs were widely spread, which created possible cross-border and national issues. Increasingly those of Serbian heritage felt isolated and ostracised, some more so, depending where they were located.

In 1986, the Serbian Academy of Sciences and Arts drafted a memorandum addressing some burning issues concerning the position of the Serbs as the most numerous people in Yugoslavia. Also, the largest Yugoslav republic in territory and population, Serbia's influence over the regions of Kosovo and Vojvodina had been reduced by the 1974 constitution. Here, because its two autonomous provinces had de facto prerogatives of full-fledged republics, Serbia found that its hands were tied, for the republican government was restricted in making and carrying out decisions that would apply to the provinces.

Since the provinces had a vote in the Federal Presidency Council (an eight-member council composed of representatives from six republics and two autonomous provinces), they sometimes entered a coalition with other republics, thus outvoting Serbia. Serbia's political impotence made it possible for others to exert pressure on the two million Serbs (20 per cent of the total Serbian population) living outside Serbia. Unsurprisingly, this exertion did not sit well with the Serbs.

To overcome and outmanoeuvre this increasingly difficult situation for the Serbian people, their communist leader, Slobodan Milošević, sought to restore pre-1974 Serbian sovereignty. In attempting to do so, other republics, especially Slovenia and Croatia, denounced this move as a revival of great Serbian hegemonies.

However, Milošević still succeeded in reducing the autonomy of Vojvodina and of Kosovo and Metohija, but both entities retained a vote in the Yugoslav Presidency Council. Significantly, the very instrument that reduced Serbian influence before was now used to increase it: in the eight-member council, Serbia could now count on four votes minimum – Serbia proper, the then-loyal Montenegro, and Vojvodina and Kosovo.

As a result of these events, the ethnic Albanian miners in Kosovo organised strikes, which dovetailed into ethnic conflict between the Albanians and the non-Albanians in the province. At around 80 per cent of the population of Kosovo in the 1980s, ethnic Albanians were the majority. The number of Slavs in Kosovo (mainly Serbs) was quickly declining for several reasons, among them the ever-increasing ethnic tensions and subsequent emigration from the area. By 1999 the Slavs formed as little as 10 per cent of the total population in Kosovo. Meanwhile,

Slovenia, under the presidency of Milan Kučan, and Croatia supported Albanian miners and their struggle for formal recognition. Initial strikes turned into widespread demonstrations demanding a Kosovan republic. This angered Serbia's leadership, which proceeded to use police force, and later even the Federal Army was sent to the province by the order of the Serbia-held majority in the Yugoslav Presidency Council.

Serbian Communist Party Leader Slobodan Milošević addresses the Serbian people in Belgrade (19 November 1988)

1990–92 A Loss of Hope and the Fragilities of Civilisation Exposed

In January 1990, the extraordinary 14th Congress of the League of Communists of Yugoslavia was convened. For most of the time, the Slovenian and Serbian delegations were arguing over the future of the League of Communists and Yugoslavia. The Serbian delegation, led by Milošević, insisted on a policy of "one person, one vote", which would empower the plurality population, the Serbs. In turn, the Slovenes, supported by Croats, sought to reform Yugoslavia by devolving even more power to republics, but were voted down. As a result, the Slovenian, and eventually Croatian delegations left the congress, and the all-Yugoslav Communist party was dissolved.

In line with the fall of communism in the rest of Eastern Europe, each of the republics held multi-party elections in 1990. Slovenia and Croatia held the elections in April since their communist parties chose to cede power peacefully. Other Yugoslav republics – especially Serbia – were less dissatisfied with the democratisation in two of the republics and proposed different sanctions, such as the Serbian "customs tax" on Slovenian products against the two of the union. However, as the year passed other republics' communist parties saw the inevitability of the democratisation process and in December, as the last member of the federation, Serbia held parliamentary elections that confirmed the (former) communists' rule in this republic.

However, significant unresolved issues remained. In particular, Slovenia and Croatia elected governments oriented towards greater autonomy of the republics (under Milan Kučan and Franjo Tuđman, respectively), since it became clear that Serbian domination attempts and increasingly different levels of democratic standards were becoming increasingly incompatible. Serbia and Montenegro elected candidates who favoured Yugoslav unity. Elsewhere the problem for representation and influence for non-majority Serbs within some regions was coming to a head. For example, the Serbs in Croatia would not accept a status of a national minority in a sovereign Croatia, since they would be demoted from being a constituent nation of Croatia and this would consequently diminish their rights.

Many had seen the outbreak of war as being inevitable in line with the fractious and increasingly open show of disunity and lack of trust between the key parties in managing the break-up of Yugoslavia. This then linked to the historical context of religious and national tensions that run across its former federated borders. War eventually broke out when the new regimes tried to replace Yugoslav civilian and military forces with secessionist forces.

Milan Kučan and Franjo Tuđman (Photo courtesy of Igor Modic)

When in August 1990 Croatia attempted to replace police in the Serb-populated Croat Krajina by force, the population first looked for refuge in the JNA caserns, while the army remained passive. The civilians then organised armed resistance. These armed conflicts between the Croatian armed forces ("police") and civilians mark the beginning of the Yugoslav war that inflamed the region. Similarly, the attempt to replace Yugoslav frontier police by the Slovenian police provoked regional armed conflicts that finished with a minimal number of victims.

A similar attempt in Bosnia and Herzegovina led to a war that lasted more than three years. The results of all these conflicts were almost complete emigration of the Serbs from all three regions, massive displacement of the populations in Bosnia and Herzegovina and establishment of the three new independent states. The separation of Macedonia was peaceful, although tension did exist with the Yugoslav Army occupying the peak of Straža Mountain on Macedonian soil.

Returning to the start point of the Serbian uprisings in Croatia, beginning in August 1990 by the blocking of roads leading from the Dalmatian coast towards the interior, this was almost a year before the Croatian leadership made any move towards independence. These uprisings were discreetly backed up by the Serbian-dominated federal army. At this stage the Serbs proclaimed the emergence of Serbian Autonomous Areas (known later as the Republic of Serb Krajina) in Croatia. In response, the federal army tried to disarm the territorial defence forces of Slovenia (republics had by then their local defence forces similar to the US Home Guard) in 1990, but were not completely successful. Running parallel with this, Slovenia began to covertly import arms to replenish its armed forces.

Similarly, Croatia also embarked upon the illegal import of arms, (following the disarmament of the republics' armed forces by the federal JNA), mainly from Hungary, and were under constant surveillance, which produced an infamous video of a secret meeting between the Croatian Defence minister, Martin Špegelj, and two men, known to be heavily involved with illegal arms trading and trafficking. This was filmed by the Yugoslav Counter Intelligence (KOS, Kontra-obavještajna Služba) and used effectively for propaganda purposes by Serbia and the JNA. Tensions continued to grow, with shooting incidents and shots being fired from army bases becoming commonplace.

In the same month, the Yugoslav People's Army (Jugoslovenska Narodna Armija, JNA) met the Presidency of Yugoslavia in an attempt to get them to declare a state of emergency, which would allow for the army to take control of the country. The army was seen as a Serbian service by that time, so the consequence feared by the other republics was to be under total Serbian domination across the union. The representatives of Serbia, Montenegro, Kosovo, and Vojvodina voted for the decision, while all other republics, Croatia (Stipe Mesić), Slovenia (Janez Drnovšek), Macedonia (Vasil Tupurkovski) and Bosnia and Herzegovina (Bogić Bogićević), voted against. The tied vote delayed an escalation of the conflict, but not for long. Slobodan Milošević took the initiative and installed his proponents in Vojvodina, Kosovo and Montenegro during what became known as the Yogurt Revolutions.

Following the first multi-party election results, in the autumn of 1990, the republics of Slovenia and Croatia proposed transforming Yugoslavia into a loose confederation of six republics. With this proposal all republics would have the right to self-determination. However, Milošević rejected all such proposals, arguing that like the Slovenes and Croats, Serbs (having in mind the Croatian Serbs) should also have a right to self-determination.

9 March 1991 Belgrade Demonstrations
In an atmosphere of escalation, on 9 March 1991, demonstrations were held against Milošević in Belgrade, with the police and the military being deployed

on to the streets to restore order, demonstrating a clear intent of a hardening of policy with the killing of two demonstrators. Later in March, the Plitvice Lakes incident was one of the first sparks of open war in Croatia and marked a symbolic increase in aggression and open conflict. Throughout this course of events, the Yugoslav People's Army, whose senior officers were mainly of Serbian ethnicity, maintained an impression of being neutral, but as time went on, they became increasingly involved in the state politics, losing the trust of the population they were there to protect.

Opposition demonstration in Belgrade, 9 March 1991

The Bosnian War (1992–95)

15 October 1991
Bosnia and Herzegovina declaration of sovereignty.

29 February and 1 March 1992
Referendum for independence from Yugoslavia, which was boycotted by most Bosnian Serbs. Ninety-eight per cent (64% turnout) voted in favour of the proposal.

3 March 1992
Bosnia and Herzegovina became an independent state.

March 1992

Following a period of escalating tension, Serbian offensives began in in eastern and northern Bosnia. The opening engagements in the Bosnian conflict were fired when Serb paramilitary forces attacked Bosniak villages around Capljina on 7 March 1992 and around Bosanski Brod and Goražde on 15 March. These initial attacks were followed by much more serious Serb artillery attacks on Neum on 19 March and on Bosanski Brod on 24 March.

It is widely regarded that the killing of a Bosniak civilian woman on 5 April 1992 by a sniper, while she was demonstrating in Sarajevo against the raising of barricades by Bosnian Serbs, marks the start of warfare between the three major communities of the federation.

6 April 1992 Open warfare began in Sarajevo

International recognition of Bosnia and Herzegovina had meant that the Yugoslav People's Army had to officially withdraw from the republic's territory, with their Bosnian Serb members quickly joining the Army of Republika Srpska.

Republika Srpska's offensives in 1992 managed to place much of the country under its control, being armed and equipped from JNA stockpiles in Bosnia and heavily supported by volunteers. By 1993, when an armed conflict erupted between the Sarajevo government and the Croat statelet of Herzeg–Bosnia, about 70 per cent of the country was controlled by the Serbs.

The Siege of Sarajevo

After being initially besieged by the forces of the Yugoslav People's Army, Sarajevo was besieged by the Army of Republika Srpska from 5 April 1992 to 29 February 1996 (1,425 days) during the Bosnian War.

"The possibilities of federal civil war were therefore almost uncountable. However, the common purpose of the Partisans bridged many of these possible lines of conflict and embodied a common purpose. The individual who embodied this purpose was Tito. It is not surprising therefore that when he died the power and influencing vacuum left by his departure was impossible to fill by one or even more people. Into this vacuum nationalist and religious lines of support found popularity, as the multi-faceted federation and Yugoslav nations sought to identify themselves with a common resolve."

Above: A Bosnian special forces soldier returns fire in downtown Sarajevo as he and civilians come under fire from Serbian snipers on 6 April, 1992

SARAJEVO - OLYMPIC CITY 1984
- SURROUNDED CITY 1992-1995
Almost 4 years under siege - Over 11000 killed people

FREE BOSNIAN TERITORY

SERBIAN FORCES

SERBIAN FORCES

SARAJEVO
BOSNIAN TERITORY

SERBIAN FORCES

UNION INVEST

Left: People look for wounded outside of the indoor market at the site of a mortar blast in the centre of Sarajevo that killed some 40 people, 28 August, 1995. (Photo by: Peter Andrews/ Reuters)

Above: Civilians wounded by a mortar bomb in Sarajevo's central market wait for treatment in a hospital corridor, 5 February, 1994. The woman at left died while waiting for treatment. (Photo by: Corinne Dufka/Reuters)

Below: An aid worker carries badly wounded 11-year old girl into the Kosevo hospital in Sarajevo after she was injured by a shell, July 1995. (Photo by: Reuters)

A British UN observer and a Jordanian colleague keep watch on Sarajevo yesterday after fighting between Muslims and Se

Sarajevo flare-up may kill ceasefi

By Robert Fox in Split

FIGHTING erupted at several points around Sarajevo yesterday, bringing fears that the seven-month ceasefire around the city may collapse.

Lieutenant-General Sir Michael Rose, the United Nations commander, blamed Bosnian government forces for starting the fighting on Sunday night. The crash of their heavy mortars being fired from the centre of the city sent people scurrying to the shelters once more.

The Bosnians were attacking a Serb supply road to the north of Sarajevo and the Serbs retaliated with anti-aircraft guns and heavy mortars, which struck in the old downtown area, killing two people and injuring 30.

Lt-Gen Rose threatened Nato air strikes on both sides if they did not stop their attacks. "It is a sad thing to see people enjoying the sunshine grabbing their children and running for cover," he said. "They must have thought the hell of the past two years had returned."

Serb and Bosnian Muslim leaders agreed last night to stop fighting to the north of the capital and to allow a UN observation post to be set up at the scene of Sunday's clashes.

President Alija Izetbegovic of Bosnia, and General Rasim Delic, his commander-in-chief, were later reported to have given a personal pledge to Lt-Gen Rose that their forces would cease all hostilities in Sarajevo.

There are growing fears that the Bosnian Serbs may be planning an offensive before an American move to have the international arms embargo on the Bosnian forces lifted on Oct 15.

Dr Radovan Karadzic, the Bosnian Serb leader, has sent a clear warning that the Serbs are about to strike because they believe the lifting of the arms embargo is inevitable, diplomatic sources said yesterday.

He told the Russian Itar-Tass news agency at the weekend that if the arms embargo was lifted the Bosnian Serb "state" would

Sarajevo faces up to snipers amid the snow

by Michael Montgomery in Pale

THE United Nations will attempt to step up Sarajevo's urgent winter aid operation today despite rising tensions and a big military build-up that could jeopardise the fragile peace around the Bosnian capital. Yesterday one person was killed and at least 12 were wounded when a city tram was hit by sniper fire.

In the aftermath of a rocky week in which the UN barely averted a major conflagration on Mount Igman, just south of Sarajevo, the humanitarian air bridge remained shut yesterday.

But the UN hopes to resume flights today to replenish the city's storehouses with food and medicines. Blockaded Sarajevo relies on the airport for nearly 80 per cent of its supplies.

With the first snow coating the foothills around the city, the UN believes it has at most

bilise "for a tota its enemies". He peace map whic the Serb requir single "unite vided" territory

The Bosnia intentionally t pose a strangle jevo, which s triggered Sur by Bosnian arm

The city's worse conditio time during t past two win believed the S

ays after re killed los near n zone, e airlift le turn nd the in the r Mus l bom aging

nging ulent begin ere e. for rav erb he ery ed ur he re it re

ing worse by the day. This is in stunning contrast to a growing mood of triumph across the border in Serbia, which is reaping the first benefits of its *rapprochement* with the international community. International flights have resumed to Belgrade and its football teams will soon be back on the European circuit. The siege mentality is disappearing.

This has prompted resentment among Belgrade's one-time proxies in Pale. UN staff who followed Thursday's stormy talks between Bosnian Serb leaders and the UN special envoy to ex-Yugoslavia, Mr Yasushi Akashi, described sharp tensions between civilian and military leaders over the blockade and course of the war.

"The Bosnian Serbs are angry and bitter about almost everything right now ... but they don't know what to do," he said.

UN officials said the Serbs' grudging consent to the resumption of aid operations and their muted response so far to the fighting around the demilitarised zone — sources say they have lost as many as 50 men in the past week — suggests they cannot afford being drawn into a guerrilla-style war in the rugged mountains south of Sarajevo.

Another explanation is that the Serbian blockade has made the Bosnian Serbs heavily dependent on UN food aid. Mr Akashi suggested this was why the Serbs have maintained relations with the UN despite repeated threats to cut them and expel all UN troops.

The UN is quick to point out that the Bosnian Serb leadership remains united against the UN peace plan, which would oblige them to hand over vast holdings. And the unpredictable Bosnian Serb commander, Gen Ratko Mladic, remains the focus of constant speculation.

But there is little doubt that Pale is feeling the cold isolation that it has brought upon itself. "It may be that our only lever on the Serbs is their dependency on us. This is a direct product of their isolation," the UN official said. "Perhaps the very best we can hope for right now is a war of attrition."

Nato planes quell Sarajevo flare-up

By Patrick Bishop in Sarajevo

THE agreement to halt the use of heavy weapons around Sarajevo suffered its worst setback when government forces and Bosnian Serbs bombarded each other on the southern edge of the city.

The artillery duels prompted the United Nations Protection Force (Unprofor) to call in Nato aircraft, which flew overhead until the situation calmed.

The flare-up was being interpreted as an ominous sign that full-scale fighting elsewhere in Bosnia could spill over into the capital.

Lt-Gen Sir Michael Rose, the Unprofor commander in Bosnia, said last night that such incidents could "cause the unravelling of the whole peace process".

Yesterday afternoon there were numerous exchanges of machine-gun and rocket-propelled grenade fire on the front line by the Holiday Inn, near the town centre.

The UN blamed the Muslim-led government forces for provoking Saturday

night's artillery battle by firing four mortars from the suburb of Hrasnica, on the city's south side, into neighbouring Serb-held Ilidza.

Gen Rose met the Bosnian Vice President, Mr Ejup Ganic, who has denied government forces fired first, and urged him to stop mounting attacks from inside the Sarajevo enclave.

"He agreed that he would halt all further military action," Gen Rose said.

The UN hopes to arrange a meeting of commanders from both sides at Sarajevo airport today to try to create a demilitarisation agreement for the Sarajevo area.

The UN said the Serbs, reeling from setbacks all over the country, were bound to respond rapidly to any provocation within the 12-mile exclusion zone around Sarajevo agreed in February.

Both sides undertook then to remove all heavy weapons from the area or put them under UN control at collection points. The Serbs responded to the mortar attack by breaking into the collection area at Ilidza and firing 120mm mortars back at government positions. They threatened UN Ukrainian troops, who tried to stop them by shooting in the air.

Government forces fired back, prompting the Serbs to break into a French UN-guarded collection point at Osijek, west of the city, and launch another artillery attack. They also tried to remove an anti-tank gun for use against a government tank which they claimed wa advancing on the area.

The situation only calme after two F-15 and two F-1 fighters flew over both sides positions.

Fighting continued in th north west of the countr

Editorial Comment: Page 22

CROATIA

Bihac

Gradacac

New fighting

BOSNIA-HERCEGOVINA

SERBIA

Bugojno

Srebrenica

Kupres

Sarajevo

Zepa

CROATIA

New fighting

Gorazde

Tijovo

MONTENEGRO

30 miles

CURRENT SITUATION
Control in Bosnia
- Serb
- Croat/Muslim
- ★ Territories under UN protection

1992–1995 The Siege of Goražde

On 4 May 1992, Goražde was besieged by the VRS. Goražde was one of six Bosniak enclaves, along with Srebrenica and Žepa, surrounded and besieged by the Bosnian Serb Army. VRS began a campaign of indiscriminate shelling, often hitting civilian buildings and inflicting mass casualties.

In return, the local units of the Bosnian Ministry of the Interior (MUP) began a campaign of retribution against the Bosnian Serb civilians who were still living in the city. Dozens of local Serbs were arrested and executed in the local school; hundreds more, including women and children, were forcibly held as human shields to protect the police station from shelling.

In August 1992, the 1st and 31st Drina Strike Brigades of the Army of the Republic of Bosnia and Herzegovina (ARBiH) successfully accomplished Operation Circle, thereby pushing the VRS forces out of the eastern suburbs. However, the siege continued. In April 1993 the town was made into a United Nations Safe Area in which the United Nations was supposed to deter attacks on the civilian population.

Between 30 March and 23 April , 1994, the Serbs launched a major offensive against the town. After air strikes against Serb tanks and outposts and a NATO ultimatum, Serb forces agreed to withdraw their artillery and armoured vehicles 20 km (12 miles) from the town.

On April 23rd, 1994 the British Army entered Goražde as part of the United Nations Protection Force (UNPROFOR), under Operation Grapple. The 1st Battalion The Duke of Wellington's Regiment was the first of three British infantry battalions to act as protecting force for the town, being followed by The Royal Gloucestershire, Berkshire and Wiltshire Regiment and The Royal Welch Fusiliers.

In 1995 the town was again targeted by the VRS, who ignored UN ultimatums and launched an attack on UN guard posts. Around 350 UN servicemen were taken hostage but the remaining men from the Royal Welch Fusiliers, who were already stationed there, and reinforcement Bosniak troops prevented the VRS from taking over the town.

It is broadly agreed that the contribution of the three battalions in this period helped avoid Goražde following the fate of Srebrenica, where the Bosnian Serbs continued on to after the failed attempt to take Goražde.

"*I woke up to a most eerie sound: the sound of complete silence. One would think that this sound would be welcome after twenty-five days of bombardment and carnage, but all I could think was, this is the end.*"

CHAPTER 5

GORAŽDE UNDER SIEGE, BY NIHAD GLUSCIC

BOYHOOD MEMORIES, 1992–1995

In 1992 Nihad was a young boy in war-torn Goražde, who had until this time watched TV, listened to the radio and self-trained himself to speak English in doing so. This was to prove useful in the coming years as he would talk regularly to the British soldiers as they patrolled the streets or at their OPs on UN duty in 1994 and 1995. Seventeen years later, having been introduced to him on the 2012 return trip to Goražde, I asked him to tell his tale. He now lives in Sarajevo and works as an Assistant Defence Attache at the Defence Section Sarajevo, British Embassy.

> "I was fourteen years old on the 4th of May 1992 when the war arrived in Goražde. Personally, it came as a surprise when I woke up to the sound of distant gunfire, with no idea who was shooting at whom. For the older members of our society, this came as no surprise, the war had broken out in Sarajevo the month previously and it was only a question of time before the torrent of warfare and its terror was to reach Goražde.
>
> Despite the water, electricity and the telephone lines being cut on the first day, people refused to believe the drama and trauma to come. Some declared that it would only go on for days, weeks, or a month perhaps, others proclaimed that it might last for years. For most this was a laughable idea, little did we know.
>
> I quickly came to realise and feel that we were under siege, with battle lines drawn a stone's throw away. My home happened to be underneath the Povrsnica Hill, where Bosnian Serbs were entrenched, and set up their mortar batteries. I also realised that this was not the kind of war I had seen in the movies, where soldiers shoot other soldiers to make military advances. In this war, everyone was a target, and no one was safe.
>
> Life got increasingly more difficult during the first months of the war, with homemade lamps and candles replacing the electric light and no TVs, radios or newspapers. We were

completely in the dark with what was happening and desperately waiting to hear there was an end in sight. Food was not a problem initially; the stores were well-stocked and there was plenty to go around, but as the winters passed, food reserves were belittled, and the town's stocks were used.

From May to September 1992, we dodged sniper bullets and mortar grenades, neither of which were particularly dangerous, providing you were vigilant enough and walked along the designated safe paths. Mortar batteries gave a solid forty-five second announcement, which gave people plenty of time to seek shelter. Moving from one river bank to another was a challenge as the connecting bridge was under constant fire by anti-aircraft guns perched on the hills around the town. Some smart and brave men ingeniously designed and constructed the improvised suspension bridge which they hung between the bridge supports' metal pillars, under the bridge above. Despite this, it did not make the experience of going over or under it any less scary!

The first good news came on the 18th of September 1992, when Goražde was "liberated", which basically meant that Bosnian Serb forces on the left side of the river were outflanked and ran away in panic towards Pale. This gave Goražde a much-needed break, but more importantly, hope. The siege hadn't ended, it just meant it was managed from afar. Though the snipers had ceased, the artillery shells increased in intensity and

Old washing machines in the River Drina reused to generate power

gave no warning of their imminent arrival. From this point forward, we had periods when shelling got stronger, then periods of peace when the forces were regrouping, and people were able to relax. The shelling at these times were the most dangerous and claimed the most lives.

Winter came sooner than we expected and brought a new player to the table, famine. I quickly understood the feeling of not knowing where your next meal is coming from and not taking food as being guaranteed. All convoys into Goražde were stopped, meaning Goražde quickly became a humanitarian crisis. With this the town lost its image from being somewhat colourful into something that appeared dire, desperate, with all the colour drained from it, casting grey clouds across the sky.

They only way to get food was to walk on foot to a peak close to Sarajevo, Grebak, where the Federation Army had set up a camp with food, and here Goraždans could take as much as they like. However, this was easier said than done. It involved travelling through the night between enemy lines and through minefields, with temperatures of minus 30 degrees centigrade. There were no stops or opportunities to warm up. Once you eventually reached the food, it was excessively heavy and awkward to carry, resulting in dropping items as you struggled to make your way back. I saw adult men returning with as much as twenty kilos of food or more after several days' excursion.

Fortunately, Goražde was then sent a lifeline by the rest of the world, as it had been decided that we were to be provided with food every night with airdrops. It became our daily routine and an adventure I became increasingly fond of due to its exciting nature. As boys, young men, we were carefree of the dangers involved and didn't quite appreciate the gravity of the situation.

However, hope was short lived as it didn't take long before people started to lose this optimism, realising that they could not see an end to the war. We became used to the death and horrors, facing the fact that every day was a fight for survival, although it didn't stop us from having fun and keeping our spirits high. We had many bands and many concerts; we swam in the river in summer despite the police chasing us away, as we could be killed by rifle shots or artillery, whilst in the pursuit of simple enjoyment.

The siege went on eternally, with quiet periods swapping

Above: Excerpt from Safe Area Goražde by Joe Sacco (2000)

Below: The hanging walkway under the central bridge in Goražde, Bridge Bravo to the British soldiers

89

with the offensives and periods of intense shelling. In April 1994 there came an offensive like no other. It raged on for twenty-five days, failing to stop not once, much to our disbelief and horror. The shooting was non-stop, unlike anything we had experienced to that point. The pressure was on Goražde as the Bosnian Serbs were determined to overrun the town. We witnessed an entire generation of young men, the defenders of Goražde, being annihilated with the death toll being devastating for all. The ring was tightening, and the Goražde townsfolk started to understand that soon we would be forced to evacuate. We were under no illusion as to what would happen to us if we didn't or indeed the dangers involved in doing so. I remember filling a small backpack and coming to the harsh realisation that these belongings may well become the entirety of my world and what I own. A more harrowing thought I recall was that these might be the last days of my life.

On the morning of the 25th of April 1994, I woke up to a most eerie sound, the sound of complete silence. One would think that this sound would be welcome after twenty-five days of bombardment and carnage, but all I could think was "this is the end". I thought we'd been overrun and soon someone would blast our doors and take us God knows where. I was terrified as I looked through the window where the streets were unnervingly empty. I was no longer terrified, I was petrified.

It was at this moment that I spotted a military patrol, spread on both sides of the street. They wore identical uniforms (which was not common for the warring sides) and most importantly, blue helmets. I was overwhelmed with the sense of relief. This is it! It is over! We have been saved! People started flocking to the streets, visiting friends and families and counting casualties. We, the children, swarmed around the British soldiers and held tightly to the fence around their camp, which was set up next to and within the local athletics stadium.

From this point for the next year or so, I spent a fair amount of time chatting to soldiers manning the gates of their OPs. Most of them were friendly and kind and gave us chocolates and sweets. At the time, I was obsessed with learning the English language and speaking to British soldiers was the first time to test my limited knowledge. Admittedly, it didn't go very well, I struggled with the British accent and barely understood what the soldiers were saying, but it was still a blessing.

While the other kids were asking for cigarettes (if only to trade them for something else) and sweets, I collected paperback books and very quickly built up a collection of fifty or so, most of which were very easy to read. Initially, I could barely understand them, but my vocabulary quickly expanded with the quality and quantity of books I digested, and eventually I was able to speak English with far more confidence.

Once a day, I would climb the Povrsnica Hill and visit an OP manned always by four soldiers and a Saxon. They didn't mind us being around and they were happy and chatty. They told us about things that were happening in the outside world, which made me realise the rest of the world would keep on living their lives, ignorant of the pain and *suffering we were going through. It also made me realise that we, the inhabitants of Goražde, and these soldiers, were in two different dimensions, but brought together in the same location for a short time. We were in it and had no route to escape, this was our home, they were amidst it temporarily and would be gone to the outer world and their own homes within months.*

Though the war and the siege went on for another year and a half, the 25th of April 1994 will always remain the date when everything changed, the day I saw a blue beret on the streets of Goražde. This is the day I was born again and was gifted to live to tell the tale, and not to become, like so many other young men of my town, just a name on a cold headstone resting in the valleys that run from the River Drina and into the hills around Goražde."

Nihad's notes: "The black and white photo below is the only photo I have from the period under siege. The photo was taken on the balcony of our flat in Goražde, in September 1994. We asked a photo reporter to take a photo and develop it so we could send it to our family in Sarajevo, attached to the Red Cross message (the Red Cross had a template distributed to all people so they could get in touch with their families). This was the first and only photo we managed to send to our family."

Left: Nihad with his mother, Fazila, and father, Zuhdo.

Below: Nihad with his family in 2017: his wife Merima, daughter Ella (aged 8), and son Deni (aged 5).

The back of the photo reads:

"Dear Auntie, we had this photo taken on our balcony because Mum could not make it down the stairs. The photo is of poor quality, but I do hope it will show you what we look like. Don't think we look as bad as this, it is summer after all. If you have a chance, send us your photo. Nihad"

91

Above: Goražde in flames

Right: A Bosnian soldier cradles a baby rescued during the bombardment of Goražde

Left: a Ukrainian
soldier with
UNPROFOR comforts
a wounded women
during the siege of
Goražde

Below: civilians on
route to the food
resupply at Grebak
from Goražde

HELP
BOSNIA
NOW

Above: In order to survive the Bosnian Serb Army siege of Goražde, Bosniak civilians had to make a daring journey to Grebak, a Bosnian Army outpost near Sarajevo, where they bought much-needed food and supplies and brought it back to Goražde on foot. The journey took several days and it was through Bosnian Serb Army territory. The columns consisting of several hundred, sometimes more than a 1,000 people, took place mostly during night. The journey was filled with ambushes, landmines and freezing temperatures. Dozens of people were killed, injured or froze to death. Their only aim was to survive!

Bridging the gap, The Duke of Wellington's Regiment First into Goražde 25 April 1994

Whilst this book is focused almost wholeheartedly on the deployment of 1RGBW into Goražde (August 1994–March 1995), it is important to remember it was not the first British regiment or UN forces to enter the town. The 1st Battalion, The Duke of Wellington's Regiment was deployed in April 1994, and established the UN operation in and around Goražde and handed over operations to 1RGBW. Whilst 1DWR will have its own stories to tell, below is a short, but relevant and highly impressive summary taken from the website of DWR's Regimental Association (www.dwr.org) that outlines the key points of 1DWR's deployment. For the purposes of this book, it successfully bridges the background offered by Nihad, ensuring 1DWR's service is recognised and 1RGBW's deployment contextualised, with the handover of operations to 1RGBW undertaken in August 1994.

In March 1994 the 'Dukes' deployed to Bosnia, with an area of responsibility covering Bugojno, Vitez, Travnik and the besieged enclave of Goražde. The latter was under siege for much of the war. It was declared a UN Safe Zone in that year. On April 25th The 'Dukes' were the first British unit operating under UNPROFOR to enter Goražde. The Regiment pushed the Bosnian-Serb Army from their positions around the town to a distance of over one mile. Their objective in doing this was to create a safe zone for the town. While at Goražde, Private Shaun Taylor of C Company was killed during an engagement with Bosnian-Serb forces while manning an observation post. The engagement lasted fifteen minutes, with over 2,000 rounds of ammunition being expended by the 'Dukes'. Several of the Bosnian-Serb soldiers were killed in the fire-fight.

Corporal Wayne Mills of the 1st Battalion became the first recipient of the Conspicuous Gallantry Cross, which is second only to the Victoria Cross.

On the 29th of April, 1994, a patrol led by Corporal Mills came under heavy small-arms fire from a group of Bosnian-Serbs. The patrol returned fire, killing two of the attackers. The patrol then withdrew, but the attackers persisted in firing on the patrol. The patrol soon reached an open clearing, where it was obvious they would be highly vulnerable to fire from the attackers. Corporal Mills then performed an astonishing feat of bravery. He turned back and engaged the group in a fire-fight, delaying the attackers long enough to allow the rest of his patrol to cross the clearing. During the fire-fight, Corporal Mills shot the leader of the group and the rest scattered into the woods. Due to that action he returned to his patrol safely.

Lt Col David Santa-Olalla (1DWR Commanding Officer) received the Distinguished Service Order for his inspirational leadership and courage during the 'Dukes' deployment to Bosnia. He personally arranged for the mutual withdrawal of Serbian and Muslim forces from the besieged town of Goražde, just as the Geneva talks were being held on the town. He was a truly competent leader during the Bosnia deployment, being first on the scene whenever an incident occurred."

Corporal Wayne Mills, awarded the Conspicuous Gallantry Cross

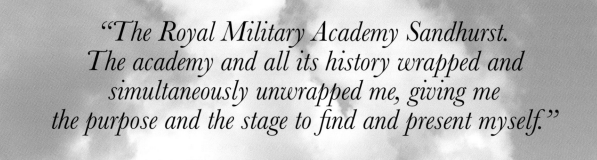

*"The Royal Military Academy Sandhurst.
The academy and all its history wrapped and
simultaneously unwrapped me, giving me
the purpose and the stage to find and present myself."*

CHAPTER 6

GORAŽDE –
A CATHEDRAL OF
THE SOUL

Goražde is a small municipal town of 20,000 people found astride the banks of the River Drina in central Bosnia. I have arrived there four times: summer 1994, spring 1995, summer 2012 and spring 2015. These arrivals had been pre-bound by excitement, resolution, nostalgia and charitable purpose.

Four arrivals, two by armed troop carrier, one by minibus and the last by rented car. Twice my journey started in Split, once in Sarajevo and once in Dubrovnik. Once I was accompanied by a couple of hundred or more soldiers, once with forty or so, once with twenty old comrades and finally with my immediate family.

Goražde is one of the cathedrals of my soul. Beyond those who live there, grow old and die there, it will mean little or nothing. Even to those who served with me I doubt many have as deep-rooted an affection for it, where its ramshackle streets, turquoise blue river and high valley mountain sides remain a reference point in my life I will not forget.

Cathedrals of the soul are metaphysical, spiritual homes, made from moments in time and memories of locations that have shaped your life. They have fashioned who I am and set the path of my existence. I have a half a dozen places that I can call home.

They were late coming, as my childhood passed as a loving one, but certainly with no academic merit. My time at school and university was notable more for my lack of application and success than for it. I did enjoy some limited success in sport, rugby and particularly cross-country, but my school did not foster or take advantage of whatever talents I may have been given. These childhood and youthful days shaped me but did not make me.

It was 1990 and I was already twenty-two by the time I found my first spiritual home, its foundations laid the moment I drove through the iron gates of the Royal

Above: The second cathedral of my soul: Sandhurst

Below from the left: Up high in the Alps; down from the mountains with Ian Anderson; happy landing after a paraglide from the summit of Mont Blanc to raise money for Sightsavers

Military Academy Sandhurst. The academy and all its history wrapped and simultaneously unwrapped me, giving me the purpose and the stage to find and present myself. I passed out from Sandhurst with some memorable praise and in good order, as one of the top cadets (a junior under officer, JUO), but sadly not quite the top cadet (SUO). As JUO I was one of eight holding swords that led the parade to the front of Old College, to be commissioned into the Gloucestershire Regiment. I had at last found myself, a career, a vocation and a life to follow.

The second cathedral is the Alps. Its high mountains, cragged peaks, deep green valleys and blue skies will remain a spiritual home until my days have passed. Over countless winters and summers, I have climbed to its highest summits and skied its slopes. I have played the rascal and the raconteur when young in Chamonix; the family man laterally, hoping my sons will find these mountains an inspiration as they have been to me. The Alps were gifted and introduced to me by Ian Anderson, a follow Gloster officer, a lifetime friend and the godfather to my son Alfie.

The third cathedral is Goražde, that I will return to momentarily, whereas the fourth is Gloucester Cathedral, both physical and metaphysical. Throughout its hallowed walls there are reminders of my military connection and to that of The Gloucestershire Regiment, the Glorious Glosters. These reminders vary from the celebrated poet Ivor Gurney to the County War Memorial Chapel. As you walk through its corridors, above your head you will find the aging and yet ageless colours of The Gloucestershire Regiment. Here is my military spiritual home and the home of my Christian faith well met in one place.

Above: The fourth cathedral of my soul: Gloucester Cathedral

The fifth cathedral of my soul: Slad Valley in Gloucestershire.

The fifth is the Slad Valley of Laurie Lee and Cider with Rosie fame, located in the heart of Gloucestershire, my home for five years. While here I discovered my love for the rolling Cotswold hills, dry stone walls and everything that is quintessentially English.

My sixth may well be my last, St Mary's Church, Cowley. Here I married my wife, Joanna, and our first-born, Montgomery, was baptised. We were married, and Monty was christened by the Reverend Andrew Grant, an ex-Gloster soldier,

known to me as the Rev, and one with whom I reconnected in 2012 en route to the little-known Bosnian market town called Goražde.

This reconnection would be tied to the third time I had visited the town of Goražde, my first time for seventeen years. This time would confirm my feelings towards it as a cathedral that would hold my attention and affection.

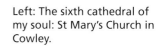

Left: The sixth cathedral of my soul: St Mary's Church in Cowley.

The town became famous momentarily in the early 1990s, being little known until its unfortunate rise to short-term infamy. In the spring of 1994 it found itself on the precipice of disaster, surrounded by the advancing Serb Army. Humanitarian disaster and human catastrophe appeared to be an inevitability as the world sat by and watched. Goražde before and after the war had 20,000 citizens, but by early 1994 had grown to more than 60,000 as the displaced Muslims retreated to the comparative safety of the town, running from the advancing Serb Army. Here they gathered in rooms, shelters and trenches, collectively standing on the steps of hell.

At this time, ill-equipped and under-resourced, the Bosnian Army (BiH) knew tragedy was probably days, not weeks, away. Many argue Goražde would have heartbreakingly competed with Srebrenica or Žepa in European history for brutality and inhumane loss of life if not for the late intervention of the United Nations, and specifically the arrival of the British Army. This is probably too much of an exaggeration, but certainly there is some credibility in the statement that the British Army's contribution in Goražde influenced, if it did not determine, the result.

In 1994, John Major's government and Whitehall defence chiefs responded to growing international condemnation of the deteriorating situation in central Bosnia and specifically to the unfolding situation in Goražde, by sending hundreds of British soldiers as peacekeepers to the UN-declared "safe area". The UN had

THE EAST (RIGHT) BANK - GORAZDE
B COMPANY'S AOR

GRADINA

SANAC

GAJ
VALLEY

BRDO

KOLIJEYKA

BISERNA

TOYANICA

OPIA

OP3

SAMARI

OP2

PARGANI

CEMETERY
VALLEY

OP2A
BARE

KAZAGICI

CP1

RIVER DRINA

BRIDGE 'A'

COTSWOLD CAMP

GORAZDE
TOWN

SERB VILLAGE

Above: A view of Goražde;
the third cathedral of my
soul.
Left: Etching, September
1994

established six of these areas in Bosnia in 1993, but the security resolutions 819, 824 and 826, which governed them, were ambiguous. The peacekeepers were to "deter" attacks on the town (the UN avoided the more explicit terms "defend" or "protect") and the use of force was authorised but linked to "self-defence".

Into this world of conflict, tension and ambiguity stepped the British Army. The officers and their troops were left to translate and interpret this unclear language into action on the ground, in the face of Serb hostilities. The UN front line and total exclusion zone was a 3km circle, its centre being the middle of three bridges that crossed the River Drina in the town. The outer exclusion zone of 20km for heavy weaponry was purely theoretical and largely unmanageable.

As it happened, the outcome at Goražde was a relative success story. In contrast to the terrible fate that befell Srebrenica and Žepa, the other Bosnian "safe areas", the Bosnian Army ultimately held the town. And, crucially, Goražde proved a turning point from the point of view of UN peacekeeping. It is now viewed as a rare and generally neglected example of effective, robust peacekeeping.

With this context it was initially the 1st Battalion, The Duke of Wellington's Regiment that took up the operational station, then replaced by my battalion, the recently amalgamated and named 1st Battalion, The Royal Gloucestershire, Berkshire and Wiltshire Regiment, more readily known as 1RGBW.

I was twenty-seven when we landed in Split. Earlier that year I had resigned my commission and was intent on leaving the Army. However, with the unexpected announcement of a United Nations operational tour for my battalion, my plans changed, as I was enthusiastic to be part of this adventure. I was the aide de camp to the regiment's colonel, Major-General Robin Grist, throughout the tercentenary celebrations of the Gloucestershire Regiment and was able to leverage his goodwill with what I considered a good and reliable reputation within the battalion to secure an extension to my service. Delighted with this result, I was appointed second in command (2IC) to B Company, and more specifically to Major Patrick Tomlinson.

The author in conversation with Martin Bell from the BBC, wearing his trademark white suit

"At last," I recall thinking, "I can be a soldier and test myself accordingly." It sounds clichéd all these years later, but it is a truthful and clear memory. Goražde awaited; I was excited, delighted, exhilarated to be given this opportunity.

Weeks and months passed with pre-deployment training. Our fear at one stage was that we would not be deployed, that all our hopes to be men at arms would be snatched away, but our time did arrive, and we deployed in late summer 1994. My foremost memories of arriving in Goražde were captured in the first of many letters sent to my parents:

The time is 0130, Friday 2nd September 1994.

I am sitting in the B Company operational headquarters, BRITFOR, Goražde, Central Bosnia. The day has been eventful, insightful, rewarding. I am sat on my canvas chair listening to the crackling radios, keeping us in contact with our boys in the UN observation posts (OPs) high above the town on the hills surrounding the town. The soldiers of B Company 1RGBW are presently adapting and aligning themselves to their new surroundings.

I have chosen the watch keeper duty to take me from 2200 to 0300 daily, which will allow me to undertake daily tasks within our area of responsibility, east of the River Drina. I am led to believe these will be varied, not least Patrick has promised me freedom of movement to take daily patrols into the hills and to the OPs, alongside other 'errands of need'. We are fortunate to have two Company Sergeant Majors, allowing me to support Patrick in a more proactive and far more interesting way. The next six months seem pretty set as to my role and I am excited by the thought of it.

It is only six days since we last spoke, when I left the UK on Monday past (August 29th, 1994), but how different our worlds will be. I also wonder how long before this letter finds its way home to Shropshire. As you know, the battalion flew into Split early on that morning, August 30th. The heat as we dropped from the plane was oppressive – 80°F and perhaps worse, the intense humidity engulfed you, wrapping your chest like a bear hugging tight. As we drove from the airport, littered with debris from the conflict, UN vehicles, resplendent in their white paint, could be seen everywhere.

Split, as part of Croatia, has been out of the conflict for two years, bringing a sense of normality amidst the ruin. 'Normality' in that people were trying to rebuild their lives amidst the destruction. 'Normality' in that there was no rifle fire, machine gun shots or the pounding of artillery that had obviously been resident here when Croatia was at war. There were few if any Croatian soldiers seen en route, there were no road blocks, no shooting, just the silence of the ruins surrounding us.

We stayed in a hotel the first night, The Palace, with my bedroom overlooking the Adriatic. Soldiers swam in the pool below, appearing oblivious to and detached from the reality of why they were here. Rifles, helmets and bullet proof vests lay casually against the walls and a liberal sprinkling of Union Jack boxer shorts could be seen swimming fore and aft in the blue pool. If it were not for the cold metal of my rifle resting against my bed, as I looked out from my window, I could very well be on holiday. The Adriatic, with its perfect blue seas, its islands dotted off the coast line, appeared to be welcoming and restful.

At 0300 hours the next morning B Company mounted its vehicles - 14 of them, 124 men, and we drove south, then south-west leaving Croatia and finally entering Bosnia. At one point in the distance I could see the puff of smoke as shells landed on the terracotta roofs of Dubrovnik. I am told Dubrovnik is or maybe was, a beautiful place.

As the second in command, I led the convoy, aided by an interpreter and liaison officer. An enormous sense of responsibility and one that made me feel alive, with purpose and animated. As animated as I was, it remained a surreal feeling throughout the journey. Surreal as if I was in a dreamlike state, as we passed through villages and towns broken by war, distant images I had seen in the TV were now very real and immediate.

This feeling was no more felt then when we entered Sarajevo. Here the unrefuted evidence of the carnage of war surrounded you. The roads, streets and airport were heavily armed by either French UN troops or BIH (Bosnian) soldiers. Not one building appeared to have escaped the hail of gun, artillery and mortar fire that had been sent down into the city from the hills above, occupied by the Serbs. They were being held at bay by the thinness of paper, a UN resolution and signatures within it, empowering the UN to do its duty. The co-location of UN and Bosnian soldiers suggested the latter knew how fragile any peace was, when based upon an international will that had let them down repeatedly in the months and years beforehand.

As we rested momentarily at the airport you will be delighted to hear I was interviewed by Martin Bell for the BBC. According to the boys I gave a good account of myself, ensuring I threw in the right comments about duty, purpose, doing the right thing in the face of adversity etc. Funnily enough, as clichéd as they sound, I believe what I said. As fame had found me for 60 seconds to be interviewed, it was the journalistic fame of that white linen jacket that I will remember!

Leaving the airport, we climbed up from the valley and through the now crumbling and derelict site of the 1984 Winter Olympics. There was something unerring about this part of the journey, as it seemed to demonstrate how delicate, tenuous, unstable the line that on which humanity and civilisation rests. Bizarrely all I could hear as we drove through these hills, beside the regular sound of gunshots, was the tune of Bolero. This was accompanied by flashing images of Torvill and Dean gliding around the ring as they skated their way to gold in the Sarajevo Olympics. The image of a man in a one-piece, purple leotard, dancing to classical music on ice was as far from reality as my or any mind could take you at that moment I would have thought!

It was not long before we were in to Serbian heartland and territory. The Serbians, stern faced and emotionless, possessing war beaten, hollow eyes, manned a series of check points on route. That night we were prevented from going into Goražde due to a 'Serbian administration error', non-existent I may add as they

Then: The winter Olympics in Sarajevo, 1984

Now: The ruins of Sarajevo's 1984 winter Olympics today

merely wished to impose their administrative will upon us. It was of course mind games, and one we were told to expect.

We were rested on a roadside in a small town called Rogatica, alongside and in the shadows of an old industrial mill. Rogatica has its own shadows, as I had read previously of the town being the stopping off point in 1992 for fifty Bosniak prisoners, who were executed in a local ravine. The local Serbs had a desperate reputation and had other crimes hanging over them, being suspects of further persecution, murder, rape, and sexual abuse, illegal detention, torture and other crimes too evil to think about. It was unnerving to think that possibly, probably, the Serb soldiers at the checkpoint where we were resting had been involved in such atrocities. You hope that time, judgement and retribution will catch up with them.

Our role is quite simply to ensure future crimes cannot be committed.

With the long night ahead of me in Rogatica it gave me time to think. As part of the UN we appear and feel largely powerless, more so the confusion over our mandate makes you feel vulnerable. It rattled me that these irregular soldiers, misfits of society and criminals dressed as soldiers could impose such a restriction on us, proud, professional British soldiers.

Everyone, all of us, have been trained, engrained to believe in doing the right thing for a just cause, to serve your Queen and country and that we are the most professional army on Earth. We are a Christian army by code and practice, but not one where religion (as we found in Northern Ireland and here in Bosnia) is used as a face for nationalism and a justification of very unreligious acts. We use religion as a guide stick to ensure moral conduct. Whatever religion, ethnic origin or other you may be, we are taught to play a fair hand and a straight bat, this is the British code of practice and is complementary to the International code of law outlined in the Geneva Convention.

I understand we are duty bound to protect those that are under threat from those that do not follow this code. Therefore, the UN mandate and its ambiguity are going to be our greatest challenge, weighing up what is morally the right course of action against the letter of the law as outlined as our instructions under the UN resolution.

Irregular and criminal they may be, but I cannot let my sense of moral purpose get the better of me. A moment of reflection has me remembering these 'irregulars' have been at war for some years, irregular they may be, proven in war they most certainly are. They have no moral compass, no sense of right or wrong and it is this we must always have at the forefront of our minds as we go through our daily business, knowing the blue beret we wear offers notional protection. This sounds all very grandiose, although I wonder what the reality of its application will be in the fields of play?

Next morning, we entered Goražde. The town, pre-war some 15 to 20 thousand, has grown with internal migration to 60,000. It is in a state of disrepair and despair. It reminds me of the black and white photographs you see of bomb torn and beaten cities of London and Coventry of the Second World War, the blackened and vacant windows staring out at you. Amidst these ruins, however, the people of Goražde, many thousands of them, are doing their best to continue life. More will follow on the town itself as and when I find time, which I will, to write.

As parents you will of course worry, but don't, we are well settled, and all is well.

Your son, Mart

Shell damaged building, Goražde, southern bank

"*The Olympic movement is one of hope, unity and peace and for Yugoslavia in 1984 this was its embodiment and yet ten years later the crowds of a people united cheering the sport before them had been replaced by battalions of armed men committed to their slaughter.*"

CHAPTER 7

SARAJEVO: 1984 WINTER OLYMPICS – 1994 CITY UNDER SIEGE

As outlined, it was in September 1994 that I found myself onboard and head out of a Saxon armoured personnel carrier, climbing slowly the mountainous roads that led from Sarajevo below us. Towards the upper reaches, the ground flattened and as it did we drove through what was the remnants of the 1984 Olympics village, toboggan run and the crumbling edifice that was once the epitome of this great sporting festival, the majestic ski-jump.

The 1984 Sarajevo Olympics brought the world to Yugoslavia in a celebration that was to be an expression of the Federation's thriving unity and success

As I wrote to my parents, I had the strangeness of the distant echoes of Bolero in my head, the tune played when the British ice skating pair Jayne Torvill and Christopher Dean danced their way to gold in the 1984 Winter Olympics. They remain the only duo to ever score 6.0 by all the judges, although the inappropriateness of the image of them, adorned in purple, gliding across the ice was incongruous, absurd in context to my situation. Ten years had passed and how this country demonstrated the hope for a better world in the 1984 Olympics seemed a lifetime and more away:

> *"February of 1984, a divided world set aside its rhetoric and took its differences to the ski slopes. The occasion was the XIV Winter Olympics, held in Sarajevo, Yugoslavia.*
>
> *Despite the death of Soviet president Yuri Andropov and the ongoing violence in Beirut, reporters remarked that "the scene in Sarajevo was a kind of Balkan Oz — sweet and surreal and dreamlike in its detachment from all other places and all other happenings on the rest of the planet."*
>
> *Indeed, more than one observer remarked on the "powerful irony in the fact that Sarajevo, the hotbed of political intrigue that touched off World War I, should be so laid back when it came to the volatile events of 1984." Optimism ran high.*
>
> *Even U.S. News & World Report commented that the games signalled "a brighter future for this grimy industrial city in the mountains of Yugoslavia" and forecasted that "when the Olympic torch will be extinguished, Sarajevo will be among the winners." Given its strategic location between East and West, its leadership role in the Non-Aligned Movement, and the way that it had apparently managed to suppress the deep ethnoreligious divisions afflicting the country, Yugoslavia seemed poised for even greater success.*
>
> *Seven years later, Sarajevo was the scene of the most harrowing European siege since Leningrad's 900-day ordeal during World War II.*
>
> *The comparisons to an Oz-like fairyland were abruptly supplanted by apt descriptions of war-torn Sarajevo as a hell on earth".*

RELIGION IN THE BOSNIAN CONFLICT, BY DOUGLAS JOHNSTON AND JONATHAN EASTVOLD 2004

Torville and Dean performed to perfection in the 1984 Olympics

My own thoughts at the time that held ice skating greatness for Britain as a reference point for Yugoslavia, were to resonate with others, as I soon discovered when I started to interview solders of my battalion (1RGBW) in 2012 for this book:

> *"Apart from Torvill and Dean and the 1984 winter Olympics, and a recollection of a history lesson and an iconic image of a uniformed general with an iron fist and*

bulled boots called Tito, I didn't have a clue where Yugoslavia was or an interest to be honest, but it was an operational tour and this was what we had joined the Army to do, to be a soldier and to soldier on. I simply couldn't wait."
Andy Paddon, former Corporal of B Company

This moment in time and vision before me, more than any other, spoke of how mankind and the civilisation he has created rests on thin ice, a knife edge, and that man and his humanity can so easily be unbalanced. Here joy and tragedy could be found in equal measures within less than a decade, hope and darkness could be referenced; where in Bosnia we find and see man's fragility and desperate plight. More than twenty years later the world is a far more dangerous place, and you could argue in the microcosm of central Bosnia, where the great religions of Christianity and Islam meet and found conflict in the early 1990s, it was a sounding bell for future troubles.

The iconic image of Tito dressed ceremoniously as the head of the Yugoslavian Army

There is hope in this darkness as at its heart both these great religions find commonality and in Bosnia, as in many other conflicts, religion was hijacked, ambushed and falsely carried as a banner to justify another cause, nationalism, which manifested itself in barbarism.

More recently, Pope Francis has worked purposefully on bringing together religions to find resolve to defeat evil. On his 2016 visit to Azerbaijan, he referenced the Muslim poetry of the Sufi, its author Nizami Ganjavi, to make this point (ref: *Catholic Herald*, October 2016):

The Pope said: "A great poet, a son of this land, wrote: 'If you are human, mix with humans, because people go well with each other.'" Francis quoted another of Ganjavi's lines: "The fruits of this world are not eternal; do not adore that which perishes!" Explaining the passage, the Pope told the leaders, "Religions are called to help us understand that the centre of each person is outside of himself, that we are oriented toward the Most High and toward the other, who is our neighbour."

Sheik Allahshukur Pashazade, the region's chief imam, told the Pope in return that as "head of Vatican state and of the world's Catholics, your activity is of great interest to us." The sheik praised the Pope's defence of immigrants and particularly "your protest of connecting the name of Islam to terrorism, while harshly condemning the real causes of terrorism, and your incisive speeches against xenophobia."

In addition to leaders of the country's majority Shiite Muslim community, representatives of the Jewish community, the Russian Orthodox Church and the Lutheran Church attended the gathering. In the country of more than 9.4 million people there are only about 570 Catholics, and most of them are foreigners. Still, the Pope said, the Catholic Church has found a place in the nation, which proves

111

that "it is not opposition, but cooperation that helps to build better and more peaceful societies".

In every religion, he said, there are people who oppose tolerance toward and any sign of collaboration with people of other faiths.

"Religions have an enormous task: to accompany men and women looking for the meaning of life, helping them to understand that the limited capacities of the human being and the goods of this world must never become absolutes."

Religions must never "lend support to, or approve of, conflicts and disagreements," the Pope said. "God cannot be used for personal interests and selfish ends; he cannot be used to justify any form of fundamentalism, imperialism or colonialism."

There are words in here that could as easily have found credibility and purpose in 1994 in addressing the multi-religious society and population of central Bosnia. These words could be given a stage throughout history, but perhaps are more needed than ever today.

With reflection, time passing and with age, you see that religion plays its part. Nationalists, politicians, and obviously, the people of Bosnia played their central part, but so did the international community, represented by the United Nations. When I returned to the remnants of the Sarajevo Winter Olympics site in 2012, it was not the distant echoes of Bolero I heard, but the chit chatter of old comrades and then of silence. There are few places that capture the futility of the war so simply, where the message of the Olympic movement is one of hope, unity and peace, and for Yugoslavia in 1984 this was its embodiment. And yet ten years later the crowds of a people united cheering the sport before them had been replaced by battalions of armed men committed to their slaughter.

The former site of the 1984 Olympics above Sarajevo have become a tombstone to war, suffering and the loss of hope

Ten years had changed this city from being the host of the Winter Olympics to be a city under siege. Seventeen years later, when I came back again, it had a sadness and yet hopefulness about it. As I drove out of Sarajevo in September 1994, I recall thinking I must write a diary, to record such moments and thoughts, so impactful had the images of Sarajevo and its aged Olympic Village been, but soon gave up this onerous task. Many years later I mentioned to my mother my sadness in doing so. Some days later she handed me a file with all my letters home from Goražde, sorted in chronological order. "Here is your diary", she said. How grateful I am she kept them! This unintended diary finds itself in this book and unless otherwise noted, all the letters were sent to my parents and span the six months of my deployment in Goražde whilst on Operation Grapple.

The distinctive light blue British Forces Mail (MOD Form 674) letter was commonly used by most soldiers to write home to friends and family.

10th September 1994 first to my brother Roger

Week two ends in Bosnia-Herzegovina. Today has been a day of great sadness for the battalion, and indeed for the regiment. En route to one of the Observation Posts, high up on the hills surrounding the Muslim and Bosniak town of Goražde, one of A Company's Saxons (an armoured personnel carrier) slipped from the treacherous tracks and plummeted 400 feet down the hillside. It finally came to rest at the root of a stubborn tree that refused to be bowled over by the twelve tons of cascading metal. The driver, Private "Ben" Hinton, was killed during the fall. God only knows how the remainder of the Section sixteen in total) were not fatally injured, being thrown out as it fell to earth. It has been a sobering afternoon for all.

Strangely, if Ben had died at the hands of a gun, bayonet or mortar, we could have accepted it more readily. To die in a RTA (Road Traffic Accident) makes his loss seem hollow or does not do justice to his service or to the man, but he died a serving soldier, that we must remember. I will not dwell further on this travesty.

As for the town, my home for the next 6 months, it has a sadness also, a desperation and yet hope resides. Goražde has a population of 60,000 today, but I am told it was 20,000 before the war, it has gathered Bosnians as they have fled from the advancing Serbs. Predominantly the town is populated by Bosnian Muslims, but I am unsure religion is at the heart of the problem, much as in Northern Ireland where the Catholic-Protestant divide is a mask for nationalism. We are resident here, a blue beret as our shield, surrounded by the beautiful hills of Yugoslavia and on them the Bosnian Serbs (BSA) wait. Having spoken to the Serbs on numerous occasions, as I patrol within the exclusion zone, I believe if we, the UN, were to leave Goražde, then genocide would shortly follow. What is not clear to us is how the apparently unguided and understandably desperate state of the Bosnian and predominantly Muslim army (BIH) would handle a UN withdrawal and a Serb offensive. This uncertainty, or rather certainty of disaster, reinforces our sense of purpose, but I wonder if in six months my view will be the same, in retaining such objectivity or will I find myself firmly aligned to one side or other?

Do you remember the TV programme we used to watch on a Saturday morning of French Cavaliers, The Flashing Blade, with the song that bellowed out, much to Mum's annoyance, "It is better to have fought and lost than not have fought at all"? There may well be no other option for the ill-equipped BiH to fight and to lose this fight, although if hope resides and seeks and finds a resolution this may be the town's salvation.

It is a strange, wondrous, mystical and beautiful place, Yugoslavia, but it is tragic, terribly sad, forlorn and lost.

Cemetery Valley, September 1994

114

DUST TO DUST

The earthen shadows of graves stacked high
Are encased with a sun burnt crust
Hold tight the memories of those that die
From flesh, to earth, to crumbling dust
That lifts with every gentle breeze
To valley, tree top and rugged peak
Where nook and cranny hands do seize
The fading fragments of the weak

As those that fall on dusty tracks
Are trampled down by leathered feet
That shuffle into half-filled cracks
Drawn open by the summer's heat
Seek the hollows of eternal sleep
Wind-blown memories, scattered, roam
Above the Drina river running deep
Down the valleys and beyond to home

Where rising mountains touch the sky
An earth below in shattered parts
The heavenly voices begin to cry
For those lost souls and broken hearts
That wander meadows of wetted grass
Unforgotten and not lost upon the seas
That tip-tap the surface as they pass
Left whispering on the summer breeze

They offer shade to sparkling streams
Where restless they do creep
They shelter a moment begot of dreams
Reprieved and now to fall asleep
Yesterday's voices are heard today
The river's rocks washed by their tears
Once blue water now washed grey
Released from this war's cursed fears

OP3 looking down into
Cemetery Valley

Note: Written following the first visit to the main cemetery in September 1994, and experiencing rows upon rows of freshly filled graves and more so, open pre-dug graves awaiting the bodies of the fallen.

11th September 1994

Week two day 1 ends - no mail, no packages, no contact with the outside world and, to be honest, neither am I sure how our mail and letters are getting out. The Serbs are blocking our convoys now, so "that" morale-boosting injection of the friendly letter, has not found its way into Goražde. We wait, and we will wait!

As you are no doubt aware from the news, television, Ceefax or whatever media you have at your fingertips, the battalion suffered its first fatality yesterday in what can loosely be called a road traffic accident (RTA). I say "loosely", because to compare the roads of Goražde, the real-time situation and the vehicles to the A5 in Shropshire, a Sunday morning and behind the seat of a Ford or Land Rover is inappropriate.

One of our Saxons (armoured personnel carrier) was on route to an Observation Post along a treacherous dusty track when it lost its footing, slipping from the roadway and tumbling 400 feet down the valley. The driver, Private Hinton, was killed instantaneously, with five others being thrown from the vehicle. As tragic an event as this is, it is also remarkable that only one man was killed as 14 tonnes of hardened metal tumbled down into the valley below. Naturally, to have a loss so early in the tour has been a tragedy sobering for all, although if a bullet had killed Ben it would, strangely, be easier to accept, as an RTA seems a simple waste of life.

My role is evolving, and I am making an intellectually non-demanding job as interesting and challenging as possible. Yesterday I led a UNHCR humanitarian convoy south-east up the Drina valley to a Bosnian outpost - it's very interesting to meet the people of the enclave in situation and to see at first-hand what the images of television struggles to portray. Amidst the devastation these people, the Bosniaks, seek to carry on life as normal as possible, as much as their limited resources and food will allow them to do so. The threat of being overrun by the Serbs must be ever present and if this did happen, you fear the consequences for these isolated families would be dire.

In advance, but most likely delivered late, happy birthday Dad for the 16th!

Memorial to Private Ben Hinton, with the Saxon number plate he was driving sitting at the foot of the cross. This temporary memorial became a permanent structure in 2012.

FOOTSTEPS OF A SOLDIER

Vinyl silk grass polished silver with the morning dew
Raise their drooping heads towards the red dawn sky
Crushed under foot, leaving a shallow trail of history
Grass touched by moving beast, both wandering ox and man
As they passed lonely through these wind-swept peaks
Through silent villages veiled in mist with silhouetted view
Then from this foot trodden path through trees and orchards
A furrow to hollow windows staring as if a face of mystery
Ransacked charcoal home, ram shackled for a greedy feast
A sieged city for two years, five months and solitary weeks

(3 October 1994. Note: A foot patrol to Gaj Valley)

Left: The author leading a patrol above OP1 and the Samari ridgeline towards Gaj Valley

Below left: OP1, situated at the top of the Samari ridgeline and overlooking the town from its high vantage point

Below right: OP1 on Samari under construction, September 1994

13th September 1994

No doubt you are aware of the second tragedy that has been befallen us. The battalion was shocked, but we carry on. To be honest, I could not believe it when I heard "I can confirm three fatalities" crackle over the radio net. I can say little more than I said in my letter dated 11th September and hope to ring you this evening to let you know, quite selflessly, that all is well. Although you will appreciate the queue of those hoping to grab a single moment to speak to family to say "all is well" is long now. Regardless and understandably, A Company (both tragedies have fallen on this rifle company) quite rightly carries priority in calls. It is a sadder thought still of the duty officer making the heart-rending journey somewhere back in the U.K. to attend to the homes of the lost and for the parents, wives and friends to be told of their loss.

I will not dwell upon the deaths of the soldiers, but to say that by the grace of God, and it can be by nothing else, ten soldiers survived the two incidents, when quite simply there should have been none. I found myself for the first time in a long time praying to God, our Father and hope he can forgive me for turning to him at this moment, only when I need him. I prayed for the families of the lost soldiers and I prayed for the safety of those left to serve in the coming months, and found myself praying for all those amongst us, the townspeople of Goražde and especially the children that line the streets daily, hoping for a simple gesture, a gift of a sweet or chocolate ("Bon bon, bon bon," they cry).

There will be questions asked about the choice of the Saxon on these hills, just as there will be questions over redeploying it on the same tracks so soon after the first incident, but we have a mission and responsibilities and cannot dwell on such matters. Some may find the decision of the Commanding Officer to brush it aside, learn from the mistakes and make good for the future a hardened, a dispassionate course of action, but it is the only course we can and should follow. The only alternative is to do all patrolling by foot and this would leave us exposed to small arms fire. I am concerned, however, as to a loss in confidence in the Saxon by the boys and especially the drivers, as she is all we have got to protect us as we carry out our duties and she is woefully inadequate. We appear to be damned if we do and damned if we don't, neither option being perfect or preferred.

Regarding my own employment, I have taken the bull by the horns, grabbed hard and am determined to make my stay as challenging and interesting as possible. Two days ago, I commanded and led a UNHCR convoy up the Drina valley, hugging the riverside road much of the way, passing a fading hillside monument dedicated to Tito and then turning into the Ostranica valley to the village of Llavaca. On arrival, we distributed food, clothes, medicine and all the material goods that have been donated by the people of Britain. It rather puts our own material desires and wants in perspective when you see the delight and excitement of a young child trying on a worn, second-hand pair of shoes and showing them proudly to his friends and family. It is a privilege to be given such an opportunity to bring joy into a child's life. I revisited the valley today and hopefully have claimed this biweekly adventure to be my own.

Coming back into the town, I sat amidst the ruin of what would have been the town square. You could easily imagine it when it would be market day, bustling and vibrant, but it is deathly silent now. I had time to spend with the Community Representative, a legacy title of the communist era. Our equivalent would be the mayor and I daresay, unlike our own in their refinery, this one earns the few pennies he earns!

We spoke at length through the interpreter, who is patient, excellent and as interested in increasing her vocabulary as to translate! I was trying to understand through our conversation what it must feel like to be under siege and comprehend the fear of the unfolding travesty if the siege was broken. We talked for almost an hour and we concluded our conversation with a handshake and mutual compliments. I thanked her for her insights and honesty and she thanked me for mine. I returned to the relative security of the barracks, she to her home over-looking the square.

The sun continues to shine, although the nights are getting colder, as darkness creeps in a little earlier each day and winter's freshness can be felt, especially on clear nights. They tell us the winters here are white, cold and brutal, I am looking forward to this change. Send my love to all at home, to the two of you especially and to my loyal hound Tess.

Below, left and right: The last post was played as the guard of honour stood silently as the coffins of Privates Chris Turner, Philip Dowdell and Philip Armstrong were taken by helicopter to Sarajevo and then to the UK

Below, middle: Memorial to the fallen, replaced with a permanent memorial in 2012

17th September 1994

Tomorrow the Serbians have graciously allowed a convoy to leave Goražde and as a direct consequence the boys, all of us, are frantically putting pen to paper, grabbing the opportunity to send news to the outside world. This practice of hasty, pre-convoy scribbling has become a well-practised art, when the notification is confirmed, the equation is simple: convoy out = pen to paper!

The summer, an overwhelming and overpowering heat when we arrived only seventeen days ago, is slipping away quickly. What were hot humid evenings with burning hot afternoons have become crisp nights with pleasant afternoons, the same as a high England summer. If we could hold this moment, this temperature and mix of blue skies, windless afternoons and loose jumper-clad evenings it would be perfect, but winter will soon be upon us.

I spoke briefly on the phone about the shooting incident outside Goražde, what good fortune and fame the regiment enjoys being mentioned in The Shropshire Star! To be honest, such incidents are commonplace, where the rattle of gunfire near and far is ever present. Yes, we are under threat, but we are well trained and prepared, and at least half of the shooting incidents are playful posturing, distant and not close by, around and amidst us and with intent.

Four days ago, I was again the convoy commander escorting humanitarian aid to Llovaca, ten to twelve miles from Goražde, upstream. The route is simple, beautiful and inspiring, following the river road up the Drina valley. Why UNHCR convoys require an escort is because the river also marks the confrontation line between the warring factions, north of the river is the Bosnian Muslims, south the Bosnian Serbs (I stress Bosnian Serbs as opposed to Serbians).

The valley is deep, with the hills rising steeply on each side from the river's edge. The fields along the river are caressed by the river below them and woodland above them, where the trees hold on tight to the hillsides, which are steeper still. It reminds me of the Wye Valley and particularly the painting above the fireplace in the sitting room of Breighten Springs. In military language, far from the image at home, we would say this is the vital ground with line of sight for the enemy and, in this case, excellent sniper opportunities. Mother would say in her colourful vernacular that this is "ideal bandit country"!

On returning from a successful drop-off at Llovaca we turned eastwards into sniper alley and back into the Drina valley. It was a peaceful day, you could feel the fresh air against your face, when suddenly a definitive sound of a "crack-thump" above my head and then five times more. This noise is not commonplace, but in training you are taught to identify and react against it, this reaction is to be commonplace.

120

The "crack" is the noise the high velocity bullet makes as it passes over your head, or rather the vacuum it creates being filled by the air. The "thump" is the round leaving the rifle itself. This comes afterwards, as the sound of the weapon travels slower than the bullet itself. They say that the time between the two distinctive sounds offers the chance, if you concentrate, to calculate approximately how far away the shot was fired, and if you concentrate a little more, in approximately what direction, which gives you the opportunity to return accurate fire. To estimate the range, you start a quick count (5 counts per second), then multiply the count by 100 to get the distance. Example, "Crack" 1, 2, 3, 4 "Thump" equals 400 metres. As you can imagine, even for the most assured person, it is a very rough calculation and estimate. The alternative practice is to get your head down, look for cover and then offer a passing thought to "where the hell did that come from?"

UNHCR convoy en route to Llovaca, running through sniper alley, with a Tito memorial emblazoned on the hillside behind. It was on this spot days later that a convoy was ambushed and a UNHCR driver was killed by a Serbian sniper positioned in the hills above the River Drina, which flows below and right in the photo above

"Bennett, get ready to put your bloody foot down," was my immediate reaction, ensuring the convoy trucks behind were in good order, my own thoughts awaiting further shots. "Zero, contact, wait out," followed immediately, as I sent the incident report back to HQ. Our mandate under fire is to extract ourselves from the area of threat, poetically called the killing zone, this title alone concentrates the mind, although this course of action rests uneasily for us as we are trained to advance to contact, not extract ourselves from it! The convoy rumbled behind us, we drove up front, before we could blink, the danger was behind us and Goražde in the distance rushed towards us.

Anyway, here I am tip-tapping a letter to you, obviously safe and sound as we safely extricated ourselves from this skirmish. The Serbs, probably proud of their display, found this short-lived, as soon afterwards they received a bloody nose. One of our Saxons broke down in the same area. The Serbs in the hills above, most likely the same, attacked with 15-20 shots, and B Company boys, held in their position awaiting relief, retaliated with c.1,000 rounds of middle-weight machine gun. Minor casualties for us (one shot in the arse) and the Serbs several fatalities, we have been told. We have positively demonstrated our intent to fight fire with fire, when in these early days we had been told the Serbs would seek to test our resolve, determining our understanding and steadfastness in relation to the UN peace mandate.

I am invigorated and enlivened by this work, this challenge gives you a sense of purpose. All is well under the Yugoslavian skies and, with Sunday upon us, we will speak soon.

121

TRUST IN GOD

In Goražde, a mother cries for food and fresh water
For fruit and God's apple for her dying daughter

Be not worried, trust in the Lord, Luke preached
Fear not to ask for God's tenderness and love
As children grow old before youth is reached
Their mothers' husbands bereft and lost thereof
For fields no longer grow soft yellowed corn
Where a chorus of girls are torn with loathing
Touched with anguish on the day they're born
Their memories well bloodied by tortured things
Of duplicity and of sinful men appearing liars
To be turned away their time at heaven's gate
Lest Luke forgets to tell what will transpire
The guilty and the damned to be lain prostrate

Jesus had spoken to the twelve disciples
Preaching not to worry for water or food
To do so would surely turn all men to fools
Such concerns and desires are basic and crude
Then look at the hills and the meadows of green
Surrounding the town to where they have fled
Such beautiful countryside is so rarely seen
Hiding the shadows of headstones of the dead
Luke, why will the corn not grow in this clay?
Found in hilltop meadows and hallowed ground
They're bloody scarred and topped with decay
Where a farmer harvesting is a missing sound

What royal clothes did King Solomon wear,
furnished in rich silk and new satin stitches?
Had not Solomon in his pomp a fortune to share,
to portion these treasures from his dungeon riches?
The poor do not care for gold and empty graces

Or for stitched patterns cross woven in pretence
Colours and displays that shine in their faces
Bearing material desires beyond their expense
They seek simplicity and not in the extreme
Basics to warm them as a poor man's array
New clothes are a high and misplaced dream
A distant horizon for thoughts of yesterday

Let me dream of the mountain flowers that will grow
Colouring fields with petals like out stretched hands
Fields of grass and corn and winter fields of snow
Covering this enriched clay and blood-filled sands
Should man persist and hold to a belief in God?
Why does he not deliver these people from strife?
Has he not witnessed the devil riding roughshod?
Over wind swept flowered meadows full of life
I've shared my feelings and my thoughts perverse
Walked unploughed spiritual pastures never seen
Luke in you and the Lord I fall and am immersed
Wash my heart of hatred and leave my soul clean

Note: inspired by Luke 12 v.22–31, read one night after an extended day's patrolling and visits to various detached and isolated homes.

The author distributing Christmas gifts provided by the children of Gloucestershire to the children of Llovaca. Visits to this hamlet deep in the pocket were routine and a welcomed task.

20th September 1994: first letter to my sister Hannah

It's 10 o'clock in the evening, 2200 hours in military parlance! I'm sitting in the operations room in Cotswold Camp listening to the crackle of the radio, occasionally being disturbed by one of the observation posts, perched high on the hills above us.

"Hello zero this is OP1, sighting as at 2145 hours, one times vehicle seen moving south, south-west." In the background, you occasionally hear the distinctive ripple of rifle and machine gun fire. My radio operator turns to make another cup of coffee, the second-hand ticks, ticks and life goes on.

I have not written since I arrived, so now I can look back and bring you up to date.

After months of speculation, "You're going, no you're not. Yes, you're going, probably, might, no, wait, yes now you are going!", we finally flew from Brize Norton on the 30th August. Two and a half hours later we, 75 members of B Company, landed in sunny (80+ degrees F) Split. We scuttled smartly in line through the airport, amusingly with rifles and ammunition in hand, through the "nothing to declare" aisle, into the sunshine of Croatia. Our transport awaited and from here we were driven to British Forces Headquarters (BRITFOR HQ) just outside Split.

The British Army is fascinated by administration and we were to become willing victims of its all-encompassing system for the next 3-4 hours. Sign here, sign there, take this, take that and so on. The remainder of the Company arrived later that evening and on completion of their administration, we left Split at 0300 hours.

Below right: Goražde looking down into Cotswold Camp

Below left: the entrance to Cotswold Camp

It has always been a source of bemusement to me, the Army's determination to travel at the most inhospitable hours of the day. It would have been appreciated by all to have reveille at, let us say, 1130 hours, followed by a light brunch, an episode of Neighbours and away at 1430 hours (ish). A drive down the Adriatic, afternoon tea in Mostar, watch the rugby, a game of darts perhaps, a beer and then bed at sunset. This would be perfection, or have I just read today's detail for the French Army? If I added the daily white napkin waving and practising of the art of surrendering, we would indeed be the French force of freedom! I know, I know, they are our comrades in arms (here in Bosnia), but 1,000 years of jostling between our great nations cannot be lost for the sake of political correctness! Anyway, not a bloody hope in HMF, it's: "Up you get lads, don't wake the sparrows and here's your bully beef!"

Children playing with the weapons of war by one of the OPs

Split, being in Croatia, has been out of the war for 2-3 years and there is evidence of the ongoing attempt to return to normality. I use this term reservedly as everywhere there remains the evidence of this bloody conflict.

We set off in our white-painted Saxons, travelling south and following the stunning coastline of the Adriatic, before turning south-east into Bosnia-Herzegovina. Before doing so, in the far distance I could see the terracotta-tiled roofs of Dubrovnik and recall thinking of its beauty, depicted in so many photographs, and my hope to go there in the future. It had been under siege in 1991-1992 and had largely avoided destruction, I understand.

On turning into Bosnia, we had the privilege of meeting Bosnian-Serb soldiers for the first time, (abbreviation BSA), and what a pleasure it was! Throughout Bosnia the BSA occupy a series of checkpoints to ensure the United Nations Protection Force (UNPROFOR) do not smuggle weapons or supplies into the Bosniak/Muslim enclaves. Consequently, each convoy, for example the B Company convoy I was commanding, is obliged to manifest all items for inspection by the BSA. They take this as the perfect opportunity to impose their will over the UN. It's a way of them saying that they are accommodating us, not us controlling them.

Systematically they check all items on the manifest and have more recently taken to petty theft from UN convoys: cameras, film, clothing, etc. with their priority being weapons. The British refuse to accept this situation and pay for this obstinacy by being held at BSA checkpoints for anything up to five to six days. We were lucky being held for only 18 hours, although at the time I didn't think so as every hour that passes by without incident is painfully slow.

125

The Siege of Mostar was fought during the Bosnian War first in 1992 and then again later in 1993 to 1994. Initially lasting between April 1992 and June 1992, it involved the Croatian Defence Council (HVO) and the Army of the Republic of Bosnia and Herzegovina (ARBiH) fighting against the Serb-dominated Yugoslav People's Army(JNA) after Bosnia and Herzegovina declared its independence from Yugoslavia.

We drove into Bosnia, climbing into the Yugoslavian mountains on tracks freshly made by the Royal Engineers, the sort of tracks you would normally associate with Emmerdale Farm. I even have affectionate memories of the never-ending A1 from Catterick to London after this little jaunt! Two years of intensive media coverage should have prepared us for most of what was to come, but as we climbed the hills surrounding Mostar you could see that we were collectively appalled by what we saw, many looking disbelievingly at the destruction that lay before and around them.

Mostar lay prostrate before us and within it, a city's people were going about their daily chores; the scene of wanton destruction is hard to put into words. Every building carries pock marks, shell marks, evidence of rifle and machine gun fire. The streets were worn and potholed and the windows emptied of glass, as if hollow, like darkened eyes looking out in hope. If this is man's work, these men must meet their maker and pay for their work, as it is not the work of good, or God, but of evil.

Leaving Mostar, we travelled to Kiseljak and on to Sarajevo. At its airport I had my chance for fame when introduced to Martin Bell (of ITN and white jacket fame). He was resident at Sarajevo Airport and obviously bored with no top brass to interview, so he came wandering towards us, looking for opportunities to talk to and interview arriving soldiers. I was full of thought and enthusiasm, bluffed my way into an advantageous position and eventually got myself interviewed. He was concerned about the situation in Goražde (our destination), as this was seemingly a "hotspot" in Bosnia.

"Umm, yes, a fine question (and a fine white coat I may add). A very difficult and yes, an oh so, so difficult question and yet, in one way so, well simple. It's ironic that something so complicated is so, well simple, yes that's the word, simple. The British Army, la de da and hurrah, wearing pith helmets and being led by a brass band, has always got itself in difficult positions and got themselves out of it with a smattering, a modicum of glory. That's what we do and will always do and anyway, blah, blah, blah and so on, Goražde did you say, where's that, do you mind me asking?"

If the truth be known, I had a general chat, offered an insight and did my best to say the right things with a spirit of uppermost positivity. And, anyway, I'm only a buckshee captain who, if it be known, carries no weight, but if I got on TV and managed to advertise myself as a brave and hardened warrior, open to letters from the gals in the UK, then discussing the political situation in Bosnia with Martin Bell served me well! However, I understand after all my best endeavours, we failed to get TV coverage because the IRA announced its unilateral ceasefire on the same day and stole my thunder!

From Sarajevo, we drove on to Goražde, arriving mid-morning on 31st August. Within 24 hours we had taken over from the outgoing battalion, The Duke of Wellington's Regiment. I don't think that they could have got on to their transport any quicker, as they set off on the long trip back to Blighty, leaving us a well-wrapped and prepared package, the town of Goražde.

"Here you are IRBGW, your very own gathering of lunatics on the loose: the Muslims/BiH and the Serbs/BSA, and by the way, see that wondrous sunshine above you and those infinite blue skies, look well and remember them, as a cold winter is in its ascendency. Wrap up well boys, we're off to England!"

This to be our pleasure, and what a bloody pleasure it is turning out to be!

As a little insight and summary: Goražde is a Bosnian Muslim enclave/pocket of approximately 60,000 people (it was 20,000 before internal migration driven by the war). It is, however, important not to directly associate these Muslims with the view we have of Islam as we see it in the Middle East. They are far less orthodox in its following, nor do they do they dress like them and, to date, since

127

Goražde late summer, 1994. Bridge Charlie can be seen in the centre of the photo, with the lower slopes of the Biserna beyond it.

our arrival we have not had the echo of the morning chorus and calling to prayer as you would experience in the more traditional Islamic countries.

These are your westernised and late twentieth century, ex-communist Muslims, from a time when this and all religions were played down or even quashed. Just as we have seen the degradation of deep-rooted Christianity at home in recent years, we need to understand the people of Goražde may be Muslim by faith, but hundreds of years of religious persecution, some recent, has diluted their traditional religious doctrine, and whilst in practice it may be reduced, they do see themselves as Muslims.

Importantly, the Serbs (Orthodox Christians), see the Bosniaks as the remnants of the Islamic Ottoman Empire (and therefore Muslim). Whether they practice matters not, for upon their and similarly the Serbs' faith and these differences, this conflict was born and continues.

There is a sense of untrustworthiness with our dealings with the Bosniaks. This is understandable when you consider they are fighting for their lives, but this mistrust is disconcerting and makes our job harder. As one of the lads pointed out: "Everyone round here, both sides, appear to lie through their teeth" he quipped, adding immediately "or would do if they had any!" I anticipate such reservations and untrustworthiness will be found in our dealings with the Serbs also.

Goražde had been subjected to three years of intense warfare and was on the verge of collapse and defeat when the UN stepped in, fearing genocide and atrocities would follow. At this stage, tipping on the verge of catastrophe, the UN, BSA and the Bosniaks/BiH secured agreement: UN Security Council Resolution 903 for Goražde. This agreement was based upon a 3km exclusion zone taken from the middle of three bridges in Goražde (situated on the River Drina). The BSA are restricted from carrying weapons within this area and are further restricted of using heavy weapons (artillery, etc.) up to 20km. It is our job to enforce this agreement.

GORAZDE 20km EXCLUSION ZONE

Standard exclusion zone map distributed to all soldiers

What do we do? B Company, my rifle company, occupies the right bank of the river, manning observation posts overlooking the town. To enforce the UN mandate, we patrol the confrontation line between the two factions, resplendent in our very smart and easy to see blue berets! We additionally escort UN humanitarian aid convoys into the wilderness and the rest of the Bosnian pocket, working with the UNHCR.

I am pleased to tell you my job is very rewarding and increasingly interesting. This is in part due to having the luxury of two very accomplished WO2s [senior non-commissioned officers] within B Company, which allows me to undertake other duties. I have established a very good working relationship with my company commander, Major Patrick Tomlinson, which helps my desire to be out and about and doing things aplenty.

Patrick has a simple, clear-cut leadership style and has a strong sense of purpose. He most certainly possesses self-belief, but not an arrogance, and is willing to listen to his team, once you have gained his trust. He commands, rather demands, respect and this I like, as I know I am a difficult person to work with (perhaps it is my strength that I know my weakness!). He's that good he could almost be a Gloster! Supporting Patrick and helping him achieve his mission is my mission, and whilst doing so I seek to retain a sense of humour and search out a little banter with the boys! Not a bad job, not a bad job at all and what I joined the army to do.

I'm what is known as an area operations officer. Sounds impressive and probably is except I don't know what this means! No, I jest. On behalf of Patrick I control all the Company assets (125 men and 25 armoured personnel carriers called Saxon), tasking them to the ground within our area of responsibility as directed by Patrick of the MBE variety!

I undertake a variety of other tasks, including on the ground liaison between the warring factions, using two interpreters attached to our rifle company. This is excellent fun, fascinating and thought provoking, if you take much of what is said with a bucket of salt. The BSA are all too willing to offer you their equivalent of whiskey, slivovitz, when in discussions. This is fermented plums that tastes like meths. To be polite one drinks, when in Rome, but invariably it is tossed to the floor when they are not looking as drinking it on duty is, of course, prohibited and, more so, it's blinking 'orrible!

Daily routine is set and starts with the duty bugler outside my Portacabin sounding off reveille at 0630. It is a wonderful start to the day and can be heard in the OPs above the town. Daily tasks will include manning the operations room, a patrol into the town and up into the hills, and bespoke tasks as given by Patrick.

At 1630-1800 hours, each day we can run through the town, including a detour through a marked mine field over one of the bridges. I am keeping myself busy, and by night time (it gets dark about 1945 hours presently) there is time for rest, apart from the continual "crack-thump" of gunfire in the surrounding hills and the bugler playing Last Post at 2200 hours.

To help us through this boredom the Company Sergeant Major and I have built a club to go to each night, The Toucan Club, so called due to the alcohol limit over here is two cans per day. I attempted to paint a toucan on the wall next to the entrance, but unfortunately, being limited to red, white and yellow, it looks like a welcoming sign for a London back street acid house rave or the logo for the Goražde Gentlemen's Club, not that of a civilised soldiers' bar for a tipple or (max of) two!

This is all in a day's work for a young thrusting army officer, who resigned two months ago, although Patrick may well persuade me otherwise yet! I even managed to find myself in a little shoot and scoot escapade last week. All I can say is: "Thank goodness for GKN Sankey and my driver," who fortunately sees himself as the reincarnation of Ayrton Senna!

Pausing whilst on patrol above Goražde, en route to OP1

I have told Mum and Dad to not trust the media and to await my letters or Sunday call for clarification on matters, as sadly you cannot trust in the media to give an accurate depiction of life in Goražde. If there is no news they will make it.

As you are aware, recently we lost four soldiers in two accidents on the high mountainous tracks. The media promised not to release details of these incidents until the next of kin had been informed, yet sixty minutes later, sprawled across the television screen "Three soldiers from The Royal Gloucestershire, Berkshire and Wiltshire Regiment have been killed in Goražde". No further explanation. I think Mother is probably a fair representation of all mothers and no doubt spent two days waiting for clarification and worrying "was it her little boy?" before I could ring her.

My call must have been a blessing, but I can imagine the knock on the door of one of the boys' families that died, to be opened to see uniformed military officers standing before them, knowing before they spoke that they would be bearing tragic news. Most of the boys are not in such an advantageous position as

131

me vis-à-vis access to telephones and still haven't had the chance to ring home. Many parents will be left with "no news is good news" to rely on, until the families of the fallen have been told. The media's self-interest in pursuit of headlines has no appreciation regarding the sensitivity of dealing with such matters or handling such travesties whilst the military is on operations. I wish they could try to understand and appreciate the situation the families find themselves in at home, restless and without information. Their actions are irresponsible, but also blameworthy is the MOD for failing to control the release of this most sensitive information.

I will write again and considering that I have six months of this Godforsaken and yet strangely endearing place, I find this fact quite reassuring, as I can set my stall and look to make the most of this adventure. I daresay six months of army tinned rations, "Good morning, this is the BBC World News", wearing green day in and day out, outside toilets, wind between the legs, the coming of winter, would send many barmy. However, my role excites me, the town and its situation excite me, and I feel alive and with purpose.

At least being in Bosnia I have an acceptable and valid excuse for being a single man, although I understand the Goražde postman is having considerable difficulty delivering the lorry loads of letters from passionate, and eager admirers writing in hope from the UK! I strongly believe the women of Britain need a rest from my overflowing and limitless charisma and my Ferrari-fuelled rampant libido. It is best I give a chance to the other men of England to seek out love and affection!

I've wittered on for too long and have no doubt that you must be bored rigid by this monologue. More importantly, the corner of my duvet is winking at me. It would do if I had one, and now I will close my dispatch from Goražde.

UNPROFOR
ID card

132

20th September 1994

Here I am again, so soon after the last letter. The reason for this missive is that our address has changed from BFPO 548 to 543. Obviously, letters sent to 548 will still reach us, but the 543 number will hopefully accelerate the process of delivery as its mail will fly directly into Sarajevo, rather than travelling through Split.

The last two days have been particularly interesting, as yesterday we took part in the first BiH/BSA body exchange. Negotiations had been in motion for many months prior to agreement, consequently the bodies were in a state of decay, "rather ripe" one of the boys declared. The primary purpose for this exchange is not just some heartfelt desire to bury the dead, but to gather information on mutilations, interrogations and evidence of ethnic cleansing and brutality.

Naturally, for the families it brings closure, but it is the dark side of this war that such exchanges reveal untold and unmanageable brutality. Not surprisingly, both the Bosniaks and Serbians have been accused of conveniently losing bodies or hiding evidence. Standing between these two groups is like being fixed between two heavyweight boxers in round 12, both exhausted and you as the referee wanting to close the bout as a well-earned draw to prevent further injury, but neither is willing to take this option. It is a bleak and sorry task.

Being involved in such unnatural situations brings home the reality of the place in which we find ourselves. As much as you try to find humour in the darkness to mask or trivialise your involvement to cope, it is a sobering reality.

Running in parallel there is routine and the continuation of our patrolling the 3km total exclusion zone. Our mandate is to prevent the Serbians or the Bosnians using, and even having, any/small arms (rifles) within the restricted area. Over the past two weeks we have confiscated several weapons (12) from the Serbians, being carried within open sight in our area of responsibility. Under the UN resolution they are also restricted from wearing uniforms and we now find ourselves observing the absurdity of small pockets of men, naturally unarmed, wandering the paths of the exclusion zone, soldiers camouflaged as civilians, soldiers in mufti, and apparently not armed, but almost certainly carrying concealed weapons.

Technically speaking, the total exclusion zone is equally applied to the townsfolk and Bosniaks, but they are not our main concern.

Confiscations have become a sport for us and a league table of seizures has been established. I am not sure the Serbs are willing participants, but they are in the game, and indeed are the game! It keeps the boys entertained amidst the boredom, ensures the Serbs are aware of our purpose and appeases the townsfolk, showing we are upholding the UN mandate.

Right: the author with B company interpreter Haris, discusses the contents of a mule's baggage

As I've entered the league I am keen to be playing for the trophy, as are all of us, but how do such events unfold, here's an example:

One of our foot patrols confronted a uniformed and armed 5-man patrol just south of OP (Observation Post) 1 on the Samari ridgeline, overlooking the town to the north-west and Serbian territory to the south-east. Apparently, bless them, they were lost! As such they were adamant they would not give their weapons over and the situation had quickly become a stand-off. Whatever the outcome, it would involve an embarrassing climb down for one party. You should put this in context to a British soldier losing his weapon, as this is a court martial offence, so one can understand the resilience to release or hand over your weapon to us, as one expects a court martial would be a preferred outcome to the punishment by the Serbs for loss of weapon.

You also need to understand that what I am giving as an example, the boys are doing daily and regularly as they seek to enforce a loosely configured mandate. They do so with fortitude, professionalism and good humour. I do it momentarily, they do it routinely.

On this occasion, I arrived with my Interpreter. The situation was clear cut; irrespective of their reasoning or excuses the resolution is black and white: (a) they were uniformed (b) they were armed, there was quite simply no room for negotiation. We had been given a very clear directive from Patrick, our OC, that we had to be robust and manage our responsibilities exactly in line with the UN mandate. If we waivered, an inch would become a mile and our reputation with the Serbs and Bosniaks would be worth nothing.

It's a strange thing demanding rifles from a group of armed men. Despite knowing you were doing so with the authority of the United Nations, being on a hillside many miles from nowhere, such authority feels worthless. Many of the boys have similar stories to be told and will do so, I have no doubt, today, tomorrow and as they grow old. After twenty minutes the Serbians handed over their weapons and were escorted to the limit of the 3km zone. If only I had had a camera to record them disappearing. We were all exhilarated by the result, what a thrill, but not a game to be played too often!

Below: The author with members of B Company

134

ODE TO IVOR GURNEY

2nd/5th Gloucesters 1915–17

I have wandered across Severn washed fields
Which flow with hedge born sparrows
I hear your music and a tribute yield
From ploughed pastures and muddy harrows

Songs of pain and beauty you did cherish
Your eager charity sustained in grief
You lie silent in stone in Cotswold parish
A tuneful history holds fast your beliefs

Ivor Gurney in Gloucester's regimental dress after the war

What strange service binds us in sacrifice
Brushed primrose metal worn fore and aft
Your words, not mine, eloquent, precise
War's lost tears found in a writers' craft

You're walk no more on western plain
Nor Cotswold hill or Severn sea
Remember the shire and Glosters slain
Brave soldiers' spirits your songs set free

I'll lose my sickness and grow strong
Dear Ivor I'll happily write of you
I'll write of meadows where you belong
Remembered by many and the few

21st January 1995

Note: Ivor Gurney was born in Gloucester in 1890. He lived his life in Gloucestershire and served in the county Regiment 1915–17. He returned to the county and to Twigworth where he died and was buried in 1937.

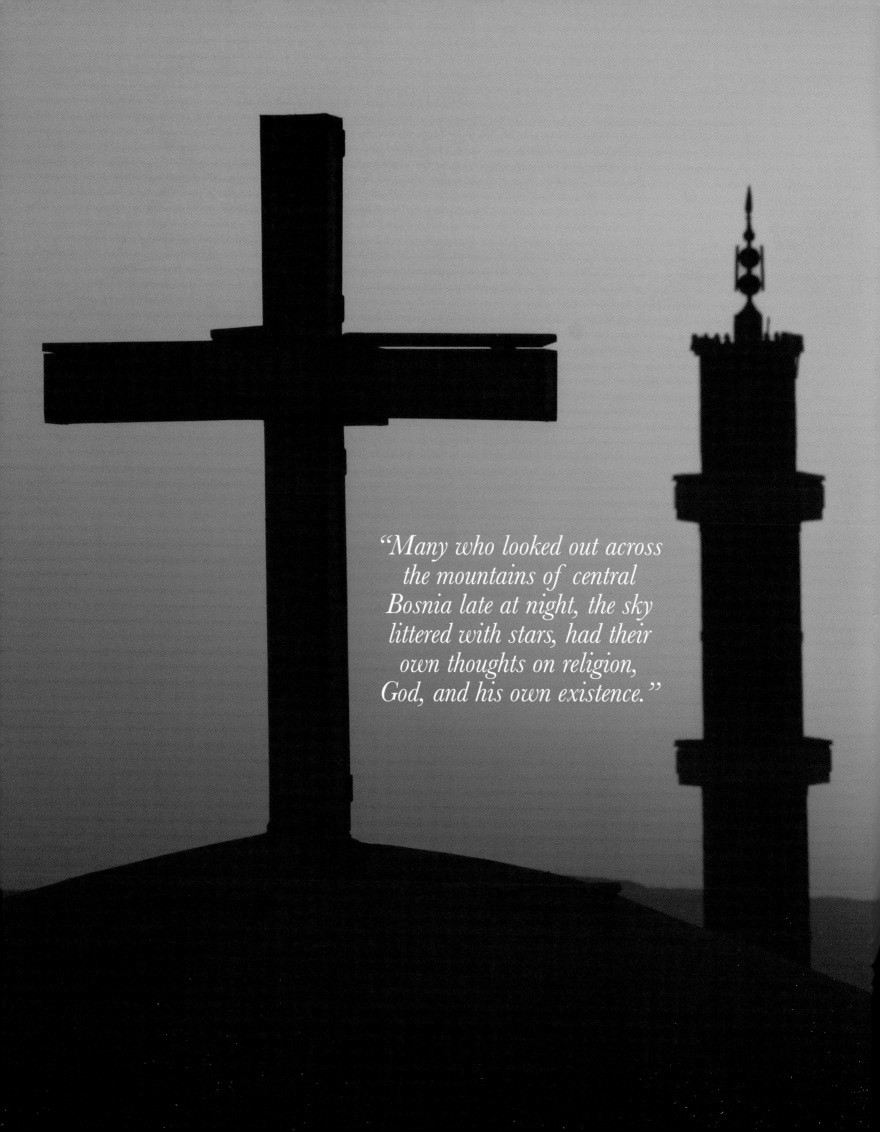

"Many who looked out across the mountains of central Bosnia late at night, the sky littered with stars, had their own thoughts on religion, God, and his own existence."

CHAPTER 8

RELIGION – THE BALKAN DILEMMA

I arrived in Goražde understanding that the role of religion in the conflict was a defining factor. In my letters home I invariably defined the warring factions as 'Muslim' and 'Serb'. Why was it that I did not define them as Bosnian–Muslim and Bosnian–Orthodox, or more correctly, the Bosniaks and Serbs? At the time my simplified view was that the Bosniaks were defined by their religion, whereas the Serbs were defined by their sense of nationhood and allegiance to Serbia.

We had entered Goražde with an understanding that our mandate was to protect the Muslim population of Bosnia from being brutalised by the Serbians. 'Serbs' was a generic term, capturing those of Bosnian or greater Serbia geographical heritage: Serbians, who were and are an ethnic grouping. We had no other point of reference to frame our opinion, only that the Muslims were facing annihilation and slaughter by the Serbs. A civil war justified by those seeking independent nationhood had become one of religious and racial hatred. Our moral compass, our joint purpose, was guided by this consideration; it was a simple case of right versus wrong.

Unlike today, in 1994 I had no understanding about Islam, much as I had no appreciation of the Orthodox Church. At the time, I had thought the situation comparable to that found in Northern Ireland. Broadly speaking, in Northern Ireland religion had been used as front to nationalism. Protestant verses Catholic and those wishing to retain their British identity and rule from Westminster and those seeking a united Ireland, a desire for nationhood fronted and framed by religious allegiance and a deep-rooted divide born from an imperialistic history. The British had brought the Protestant faith to Ireland, much as the Ottomans had brought Islam into the Balkans. Hundreds of years had passed in both cases, but in each a subconscious awareness of a distant inheritance remained, where the essential and defining link to the past and your identity was your religion. In Ireland, the lines of political and social demarcation are somewhat easier to determine, a desire for a united Ireland versus a desire for the seven provinces of Northern Ireland to stay as part of the United Kingdom, Catholicism verses Protestantism, race against race. In central Bosnia there existed a boiling pot of provocations, where lines were not so simply drawn, where the Yugoslavian Federation and Tito had scrambled the nationalities and sought to squash religious allegiance, thwarting nationalistic ambitions and ideals that lay dormant, but not extinct, and held the potential of future conflict. When the oppressive hand of Tito waivered and disappeared, these powerful embedded beliefs and emotions found new breath and at their heart religion defined them. The warring factions that evolved were branded in part by their religious background, just as much as their identities of race being Bosnian or Serbian.

These were and largely remain my opinions and views, although I researched the question of the role of religion in the Yugoslavian conflict to corroborate my understandings with those that analyse and have assessed the Yugoslavian situation as a profession and are known authorities.

Jennifer Kayongo outlined her thoughts in a Stanford University research paper (Chapter 1: Religion's Role in Yugoslavia During and Following the Communist Era, The History and Analysis of the Conflict in the Former Yugoslavia) as follows:

"The role of religion has throughout the Yugoslavian communist rule and throughout religious nationalistic rule, been shaped by those in power. The treatment of religion by the Yugoslavian communist government shifted with the pressure of the West. The treatment also changed as Tito enforced Yugoslavian unity. Tito was very careful to repress religious nationalism, whenever it emerged, and to use other calculated tactics to keep religious nationalism from becoming a major problem for the communist government.

However, these tactics, to build unity and end religious nationalism, may have actually worsened the situation in Yugoslavia by increasing the religious tension. When communism collapsed in Yugoslavia these tensions escalated into the Bosnian conflict."

My views on nationhood and its marriage with religion as one of its defining principles appear to be supported when Kayongo further states: "The role of religion in post-communist Yugoslavia has been, for the most part, to link itself with religious nationalism, the two most prominent examples of this being the Roman Catholic Church of Croatia and the Serbian Orthodox Church. This collaboration with religious nationalism can also be viewed as the offspring of communist Yugoslavia's initial harsh repression of religion and its subsequent control of religious expression and freedoms."

Most importantly, my view that Tito's emphatic leadership worked as a repressive lid on the boiling pot of nationalistic and religious temperament, in preventing it in overheating, appears to be upheld when she summarises: "Yugoslavia was unified under a charismatic leader, outside threats to their independence, and self-management and the communist regime's repression of religious tensions, with little recurrences of religious nationalism. With the rise of religious nationalism following the collapse of communism and the ensuing Yugoslavian conflict, in the words of Paul Mojzes: '[the] Communists were able to dispose neither of nationalism nor of religion despite their efforts in each [of these] directions.'

Further reinforcing my comparison to the situation in Northern Ireland, Douglas Johnston and Jonathan Eastvold (International Center for Religion and Diplomacy, Religion in the Bosnian Conflict) assert, as one of three views on the subject: "A third alternative emphasizes the long history of coexistence between religious and ethnic groups in cities like Sarajevo, [arguing] that the conflict was not inevitable but was rather fanned into flame by political opportunists like Slobodan Milosevic who, foreseeing Communism's demise, made a 'compact with nationalism' as a means of staying in power."

This perspective is also summarised well by Richard Holbrooke, architect of the Dayton Peace Accord:

"Yugoslavia's tragedy was not foreordained. It was the product of bad, even criminal, political leaders who encouraged ethnic confrontation for personal political and financial gain. Rather than tackle the concrete problems of governance in the post-Tito era, they led their people into a war."

From a British or UN soldier's perspective, arriving as an independent arbitrator amidst such insanity, it is the impact of war in the name of, or justified by, religion that leaves its mark:

"Having served in Northern Ireland, Bosnia, Kosovo, Afghanistan and Iraq, I have no time for religion in my life, having seen how it has caused so much damage and distress. I may occasionally ask God to look after my children, which I suppose is some tacit recognition of a superior being, but if there is, he or she has much to answer, as man has been burdened with the possibility of death and much more for far too long because of religion." (Corporal Taff Davies, A Company 1RGBW)

Corporal Taff Davies on board a Saxon 1994

However, in Bosnia, where religion framed each party, calling on this call to arms in the name of your religion or god can create differing dynamics, as Mitja Velakonja, a sociologist at the University of Ljubljana, explains:

"The Serbian nationalist tendency to invoke religion in support of its war aims essentially backfired. Rather than curbing whatever Islamist threat was posed by a mostly secularised, nominally Muslim population, the religious rhetoric provoked a reaction from throughout the Muslim world. Fresh from dealing the now-defunct Soviet Union a humiliating defeat in Afghanistan, scores of foreign mujahedeen flooded into Bosnia, their noses attuned to the scent of Muslim–Christian bloodshed. Within Bosnia, moreover, religion-based violence radicalized the nominal Muslims."

Velakonja further underpins the credibility of this statement by recalling the reaction of the Muslims at the rank-and-file level, which is typified by this statement from a young Bosnian Muslim soldier:

"I never thought of myself as a Muslim. I don't know how to pray, I never went to mosque, I'm European, like you. I do not want the Arab world to help us, I want Europe to help us. But now, I do have to think about myself as a Muslim, not in a religious way, but as a member of a people. Now we are faced with obliteration, I have to understand what it is about me and my people they wish to obliterate."

As someone arriving from a racially integrated and tolerant society (which Britain can say it is), I would often struggle to comprehend how anyone could turn on neighbours, friends or family (where marital cross and inter-religious families were not unusual in Bosnia), as Velakonja refers to when saying:

"In certain parts of the former federal state, the population was so integrated that their nationality was not distinguishable, and in such places former brothers became 'eternal' enemies. By way of this, Croats became 'genocidal Ustasha', Bosnians are 'Islamic mujahedin' fighting a 'jihad', the Serbs are born Chetniks, and the Slovenes, Austria's stable-hands. The principal community needs an enemy against which it can establish itself as the radical opposition and, by way of this, define its complementary imaginative mythical order. For the enemy to play its role effectively, it also has to assume some metaphysical dimensions."

Even when trying to comprehend the situation and contextualise the boundaries through and by any perceptions or established understanding of any religious creed, this often came into conflict with our limited understanding of the faiths being promoted and supported in Bosnia and Goražde:

"As much as the Serbs did not appear Christian in their actions, neither were the BIH what I considered to be true or traditional Muslims. Most drank Slivo* or beer, or both, and did not keep to the dietary restrictions that I understood to be the mainstay of the Islamic faith, eating pork and so on, nor did daily prayer play its part. In both cases religion appeared to be a veil for other purposes and mischief." (Private Danny Ashton, A Company, 1RGBW)

This view was echoed by Gary Morley (Corporal B Company, 1RGBW) when asked about his views on the role religion played in Bosnia and directly in Goražde, where he spent many months: "I have many memories of that tour and like most, at times, found it difficult to understand the deep-rooted hatred that was dished out in the name of religion and nationalistic beliefs."

*Šljivovica, Śliwowica, Slivovitza, Schlivowitz, or Slivovitsa is a fruit brandy made from damson plums, often referred to as plum brandy. Slivovitz is produced in east-central and south-east Europe. It was consumed daily by both sides and often offered to the British soldiers in their regular interaction with the Bosniaks, or more regularly with the Serbs. The homemade product drank in and around Goražde was agreed by most to be one of the most memorably putrid liquids to ever be fermented in the pursuit of alcohol and many soldiers shiver and can taste its legacy when it is mentioned today, so uniquely repulsive was it.

141

Similarly, when looking back and assessing the role of religion (as I saw it) in Goražde, it was the dark and inhumane side of it that frames my memories, as the Bosnian War showed how religion can be used to cultivate hatred, foster division and lead to ethnic cleansing. The question you are left asking is, how can anyone do serious harm to another person in the name of their faith, where every meaningful faith, as far as I know, denounces such crimes and preaches peace?

Ethical killing and the pursuit of killing is a contradiction to the holiness and pursuit of most true religions. However, it has been resident in man's history for so long, religion has almost become defined by wars in its name throughout history. Indeed, the first holy war was probably in October 312 CE when the Roman emperor Constantine saw a vision of the cross in the sky with this inscription "*in hoc signo vinces*" (in this sign you will win).

Constantine trusted the vision and had the cross inscribed on his soldiers' armour. Even though his forces were outnumbered, he won the battle against an army that was using pagan enchantment. Historians regard this as a turning point in Christianity's fortune.

This is all very well, although armchair warriors that sit at home many hundreds or thousands of miles away from the situation about which they articulate their opinions or make unfounded suppositions and write their version of history from a distant classroom, have often not seen the events or even been to the place that created this history. This book in no small part has been written to capture the thoughts and memories of those that were there, adorned with a United Nations blue beret as they would have been. Men, such as 'Taff' Davies:

"I remember seeing an unedited news video during the beat-up training (pre-deployment training) of an old woman in her seventies demonstrating unbelievable hatred, a loss of humanity and a madness when stabbing a captured man to death with a pitchfork. How could this happen, you ask yourself? No doubt she had experienced trauma on an horrific scale, possibly the loss of some or all her family, the rape of her daughters, the mutilation of her friends, bearing witness to horror that drove her hatred and madness. This is not to justify her actions, but to suggest a reason for them.

The Balkan War showed on what a fine line civilisation rests and how easy it is for man to fall into barbaric ways, and here I was to be witness to it. What made this more the confusing and worrying was that this happening on Europe's doorstep. Bosnia was the borderland between Islam and Christianity and where these two great religions met this religious divide was to frame the war and its purpose, even justification.

I recall one occasion that struck me as showing how this war had stripped man of any sense of civilisation. I accompanied my OC (Major Ian Harris (IVK)) to evaluate a sniper task to the south, down the river valley at the village of Vitkovići. It had been recorded that a Serbian

142

The Serbian Orthodox Church dedicated to St. George on the outskirts of Goražde

sniper was taking pot-shots at civilians, including children, from a high vantage point to the east.

The proposed task was to identify a way within the terms of the UN mandate that we could eliminate the threat and thus protect the civilians in the area. This was made more difficult as under UN rules of engagement we could only return fire if fired upon. How I ironically prayed for us to fall under NATO and its more direct rules of engagement and not to be restricted by the UN and its own limited terms, as being party of a NATO deployment would have allowed us to have been far more proactive in our role in protecting the people of Goražde.

Sadly, the sniper location was too elevated and out of range for the L96 (the standard UK sniper rifle). My recommendation was therefore to allow our own snipers to stalk the Serbian location to get sufficiently close and achieve the task or, failing that, deploy a couple of SF GPMG (Sustained Fire provided by the General-Purpose Machine Gun, the iconic heavyweight and reliable machine gun of the British Army) in an overt OP, draw their fire and allow us to eliminate the Serbian snipers by doing so. Sadly, whilst a moral and correct course of action, this would have fallen outside our UN mandate and was rejected.

What I remember thinking, however, and still reflect on this today, is: How could a man lie there calmly, without emotion and make a calculated decision to aim at and shoot innocent and unarmed civilians, more so children? Justification would appear to be linked to religion, which

RESTRICTED

RULES OF ENGAGEMENT
(To be carried by all Officers and Warrant Officers)

1. RULE No 01: AUTHORITY TO CARRY WEAPONS

OPTION A: NO AUTHORITY

OPTION B: AUTHORITY GRANTED TO CARRY PERSONAL WEAPONS (PISTOLS, RIFLES AND LIGHT MACHINE GUNS).

OPTION C: AUTHORITY GRANTED TO CARRY PERSONAL WEAPONS AND DEPLOY VEHICLE MOUNTED, CREW SERVED WEAPON SYSTEMS (MGs, GUNS AND CANONS UP TO 90mm)

OPTION D: AUTHORITY GRANTED TO CARRY PERSONAL WEAPONS, DEPLOY VEHICLE MOUNTED, CREW SERVED WEAPON SYSTEMS AND DESIGNATED SUPPORT WEAPONS (LAW, HEAVY MGs AND MORTARS UP TO 82mm)

OPTION E: AUTHORITY GRANTED TO CARRY PERSONAL WEAPONS, DEPLOY VEHICLE MOUNTED, CREW SERVED WEAPON SYSTEMS, SUPPORT WEAPONS AND ARTILLERY (MEDIUM AND HEAVY ANTI-TANK WEAPON SYSTEMS, HEAVY MORTARS AND ARTILLERY)

2. RULE No 02: STATUS OF WEAPONS

OPTION A: WEAPONS ARE TO BE CARRIED UNLOADED AND MAGAZINES OR ROUNDS ARE TO BE IN POUCHES OR AMMUNITION RACKS. THE CIRCUMSTANCES UNDER WHICH SOLDIERS MAY LOAD AND FIRE WEAPONS ARE GOVERNED BY THE "ORANGE CARD"

OPTION B: AUTHORITY IS GRANTED FOR PERSONAL WEAPONS TO BE CARRIED IN A "MADE SAFE" CONDITION. ALL OTHER SUPPORT AND VEHICLE, CREW SERVED WEAPON SYSTEMS ARE TO REMAIN IN AN "UNLOADED" CONDITION. THE CIRCUMSTANCES UNDER WHICH SOLDIERS MAY LOAD/COCK AND FIRE WEAPONS ARE GOVERNED BY THE "ORANGE CARD".

OPTION C: AUTHORITY IS GRANTED FOR WEAPONS TO BE CARRIED IN A "MADE SAFE/ HALF LOAD/CHAMBER EMPTY" CONDITION. THE CIRCUMSTANCES UNDER WHICH SOLDIERS MAY COCK AND FIRE WEAPONS ARE GOVERNED BY THE "ORANGE CARD"

OPTION D: AUTHORITY IS GRANTED FOR WEAPONS TO BE CARRIED IN A "MADE READY/ ROUNDS CHAMBERED" CONDITION. THE CIRCUMSTANCES UNDER WHICH SOLDIERS MAY FIRE WEAPONS ARE GOVERNED BY THE "ORANGE CARD"

3. RULE No 03: RESPONSE TO HOSTILE INTENT OR HOSTILE ACT (WITHOUT USE OF FIRE)

OPTION A: OBSERVE AND REPORT, WITHDRAW IN ORDER TO PRESERVE OWN FORCE

OPTION B: STAY IN PLACE, MAKE CONTACT AND ESTABLISH LIAISON WITH OPPOSING FORCE(S) AND/OR LOCAL AUTHORITIES CONCERNED

OPTION C: OBSERVE AND REPORT, STAY IN PLACE, WARN AGGRESSOR OF INTENT TO USE FORCE AND DEMONSTRATE RESOLVE BY APPROPRIATE MEANS WITHOUT OPENING FIRE

OPTION D: OBSERVE AND REPORT, STAY IN PLACE, WARN AGGRESSOR OF INTENT TO USE FORCE AND DEMONSTRATE RESOLVE BY APPROPRIATE MEANS. DEMONSTRATIVE USE OF FIRE POWER IS AUTHORISED

4. RULE No 04: DISARMAMENT OF PARAMILITARY CIVILIAN AND SOLDIERS

OPTION A: NO AUTHORIZATION GRANTED

OPTION B: AUTHORIZATION IS GRANTED IF FAILURE TO DO SO PREVENTS THE UNPROFOR (BHC) FROM CARRYING OUT ITS TASK. IN DOING SO, USE MINIMUM NECESSARY AND PROPORTIONAL FORCE UP TO AND INCLUDING USE OF FIRE, IF HOSTILE INTENT SO WARRANTS, OR A HOSTILE ACT IS COMMITTED. HAND OVER TO APPROPRIATE UN AUTHORITIES AT THE EARLIEST OPPORTUNITY.

PTO

RESTRICTED

RESTRICTED

RULES OF ENGAGEMENT FOR UNPROFOR OPERATIONS IN BH

FOR ISSUE TO ALL PERSONNEL AUTHORISED TO CARRY ARMS OR DEPLOY VEHICLE MOUNTED, CREW SERVED WEAPONS AND SUPPORT WEAPONS AND AMMUNITION

GENERAL RULES

1. YOU HAVE THE RIGHT TO USE FORCE IN SELF DEFENCE, AND TO PROTECT SPECIFIC PROPERTY OR INSTALLATIONS SPECIFIED BY YOUR SUPERIOR.

2. IN ALL SITUATIONS YOU ARE TO USE THE MINIMUM FORCE NECESSARY. FIREARMS, VEHICLE-MOUNTED, CREW-SERVED WEAPON SYSTEMS AND SUPPORT WEAPONS MUST ONLY BE USED AS A LAST RESORT.

3. YOU ARE TO ACT UNDER THE ORDERS OF THE SENIOR OFFICER - SAILOR/ SOLDIER/AIRMAN AT THE SCENE.

CHALLENGING

4. A CHALLENGE MUST BE GIVEN BEFORE OPENING FIRE UNLESS:

A. TO DO SO WOULD INCREASE THE RISK OF DEATH OR GRAVE INJURY TO YOU OR ANY OTHER PERSON

B. YOU OR OTHERS IN THE IMMEDIATE VICINITY ARE UNDER ARMED ATTACK

5. YOU ARE TO CHALLENGE IN ENGLISH BY SHOUTING:

"UNITED NATIONS HALT HANDS UP"
FOLLOWED BY
"UNITED NATIONS STOP OR I FIRE"

OR IN SERBO-CROAT BY SHOUTING:

"UJEDINJENE NACIJE STANI ILI PUCAM"
(PRONOUNCED PHONETICALLY)
"UYEDINYENE NATSYEI STANI ILI PUTSAM"

* REPEAT THE WARNING AS NECESSARY TO ENSURE UNDERSTANDING.

* THEN COCK YOUR WEAPON

* THEN FIRE WARNING SHOTS IN THE AIR IF THERE IS TIME TO DO SO AND THE USE OF LETHAL FORCE WOULD ALREADY BE JUSTIFIED

PTO

RESTRICTED

---

had been misinterpreted to such an extent that he would kill and slaughter the innocent in [his] god's name. If I had a faith beforehand, I believe I would have lost it at that moment.

On another occasion, a rumour came from the south bank (B Coy) that a young woman had been seen walking across one of the bridges over the Drina, carrying a new-born baby. When she got to the middle she paused, looked to the river below and dropped her child into the rushing waters underneath. Apparently, she was brutally raped and impregnated by a Serb soldier and had been so traumatised by this event that she found it difficult to deal with living and felt wholly detached from her child, which was the living memory and incarnation of the rape.

More than twenty years later, as I walk my dog, I sometimes pass the local church or a place of worship in Two Locks, Cwmbran (where I live), and see happy people of all ages having fun with an obvious sense of belonging, brought together by Christianity, and I think how lucky they are to have such a sense of belonging.

I find myself reflecting on this perfect image of harmony and see that aging woman in her seventies taking a pitchfork in hand and wonder if circumstances changed here, in the UK, could one of these most gentle people before me be carried to such lengths by hatred and desire for revenge? It appears ludicrous to think so, but it happened, it happened and more in Bosnia, where in no small part the church and the mosque played their parts in homing this hatred."

Perhaps one who has an inimitable insight to the question of religion is Andrew Grant, a private in 1RGBW in 1994 and later, as we will discover, one who found faith and more in the September of that year. Having experienced an epiphany in its true religious context, whilst in Goražde and writing this more than twenty years later, now as the Reverend Andrew Grant, he recalls his emotions as follows:

"Looking back, the religious landscape was complex, and we found ourselves as an essentially Christian force, in a context where we felt more of an affiliation with Muslim forces on the ground. Their generosity was remarkable despite their adverse living conditions. They treated us like friends, and their warmth and hospitality remain engraved on my memory.

From a personal perspective, it was Muslim soldiers who came to the aid of Stephen Johnston and I immediately after the accident we were involved in (see later).

"The abiding irony was that in Goražde the Serb forces (supposedly Christian), were generally viewed by us as the aggressor. I heard that some Serb soldiers had challenged some of our guys, saying that they couldn't understand why the Christian

Corporal Taff Davies at OP7

British Army were not siding with them, fellow Christians from the Bosnian Serb Army.

"It was clear to me back then that the label 'Christian' meant very little. 'You can identify them by their fruit, that is, by the way they act. Can you pick grapes from thorn bushes, or figs from thistles?' (Matthew 7.16, Living Bible).

"I also realise the following is an acute generalisation, and that atrocities had been committed on all sides within the conflict yet, where there had been unwarranted Serb aggression and merciless acts, it seemed that the only Christian thing about them was in name only. For anyone claiming to be a Christian, the measure of that claim must be judged against a person's actions and behaviour. The apostle Paul said: "But the fruit of the Spirit is love, joy, peace, forbearance, kindness, goodness, faithfulness, gentleness and self-control. Against such things there is no law." Galatians 5:22–23 (NIV).

History shows that the Serb forces often behaved in completely the opposite manner. (The Reverend Andrew Grant, former private 1RGBW)

Far left: Andy Grant in his Army days

Left: Andy Grant as the newly appointed vicar for St Cuthbert's in Marton, Middlesborough

Andrew's more poetic and insightful views are complemented by those of Private 'Clarence' Heal (Mortar Platoon, 1RGBW), who captured what many soldiers thought more succinctly:

"My understanding of the role of religion in the conflict and personal faith was pretty simple. During the tour, I was in a unique position, being mobile and behind the wheel throughout the country. My job was to be the supply convoy leader's driver and radio operator, or as colour sergeant Mick Hopgood christened it, Driving Miss Daisy! My boss was Captain Paul Sulyok (Light Infantry), he was bilingual and a good bloke for a Rupert (the term used for a graduate from the Royal Military Academy Sandhurst, a young officer).

As a Bristolion and a half caste or 'Mocha' (as I was then known in the non-PC Army of the early Nineties), and having already served in Northern Ireland, I thought I would be ready for the ethic and religious mix of Bosnia and lines of hatred. How wrong I was!

Having been lucky enough to drive throughout most of the country, meet and experience hundreds of people of all ages and from all sides, I formed the following views of the role of religion in central Bosnia:

It was a means to an end. Whatever caste or creed you were, it was merely used as an excuse and a smokescreen. Everything was justified and dressed up in self-righteous religious indignation. From my understanding of history, gathered on my travels, it appeared the situation had been on the boil since the fall of the Ottoman Empire, only more recently being kept in check by Tito and the hard line of Communism.

The Serbs, schoolyard bullies that would make the Crusaders look like Sunday school teachers.

The Croats, sly and always out to make a few bob, would make Gerry Adams look like a saint.

The Reverend Andrew Grant and the Padre, Patrick Irwin, on the return visit and dedication of the memorial stones June 2012

The Bosniaks and Muslims, getting the short end of the wedge, but had become adept (had no choice) at playing the victim (I wouldn't play poker with them, as they would have the shirt off my back).

Whilst categorising, we should also mention us, the good ol' Brits: sarcastic, blunt and doing their best to not getting involved, despite a desire to do so."

However, as difficult as it may have appeared to be amidst this complex and ever-changing landscape, where religion and your own belief (for those who had it) would be tested, we did not define our purpose on these lines. Our role as UN peacekeepers was marked by what was needed to be done to prevent a capitulation to inhumanity, ethnic cleansing and chaos. Our understanding and appreciation of the situation became clearer when we deployed into Goražde. More than twenty years later upon returning to the town, my view that religion was a principal factor in defining the Bosnian War remained the same.

Left: Danny Ashton, Julian 'Clarence' Heal and Rifleman Steve Kent during a lull on operations. Support Company 1Rifles Nawa, Helmand Province, Afghanistan, 2009

Below: Private Clarence Heal, Sarajevo 1994

Religion – Individual Faith in Adversity

What of our religion? The British Army remains an armed force principally based on Christian values, whilst warmly welcoming all faiths. It is the armed forces of Her Majesty and she remains the Head of the Army, State and the Church of England.

General Francis Richard Dannatt, the former Head of the Army 2006–9, wrote about this subject:

We operate within the moral code of the Geneva Convention, but also as a Christian force for good. Our own moral compass is the duty we undertake and the framework of social acceptability that is enshrined in our religion. This is not to the exclusion, but inclusion of all religions and this tolerance and acceptability is important to remember. Christianity as I understand it, as part of the Armed Forces understand it, is a framework to work within, not a doctrine to impose on others. Commonality exists between all religions and our learning was to adopt and portray the virtues and values of our religion, not to suggest it was any better [or worse] than any other belief.

Richard Dannatt had commanded 4 Brigade, which in 1995 was responsible for UN Sector South West in Bosnia. His performance, negotiating with the leaders of the warring factions prior to implantation of the Dayton Accords, was inspirational.

He is now General Francis Richard Dannatt, Baron Dannatt, GCB, CBE, MC, DL. As Vice President of the Armed Forces Christian Union and President of the Soldiers' and Airmen's Scripture Readers Association, he is a man of strong faith.

My generation (as a whole) is possibly the last one where childhood education had Christianity at its centre, as a fundamental, immovable part of our schooling. I attended services at school five times a week, I was an enforced recruit into Sunday school, my parents were Christian, and I was brought up as one. I add that I was unceremoniously expelled from Sunday school in a village in Shropshire, as from the high reaches of the choir stalls I had aimed and hit the Bishop's hat, Kenneth Skelton's mitre, with a perfectly executed shot. A dry pea had been propelled across the church by an eight year old's best puff through a single straw.

Despite this early expulsion from the church and as a child, a soldier and throughout life, I have believed in God and try to run my life within the expectations set by the Christian doctrine. I believe in a time when being Christian is perhaps slightly peculiar as opposed to normal, where you are more likely to keep your faith to yourself than talk openly about it, as it is not commonplace to do so. Do I believe that a Heaven and Earth and a Devil, Hell and Holy Spirit exist? In a

literal sense, no, but in a metaphorical one, yes. I do not advertise my faith, just as I would not judge those with no faith or those who are dedicated to another.

In Goražde, away from the hurly-burly of modern life, I found silent partnership with the Padre, as eccentric as he may have been. I found moments of silent prayer and I retained my faith. It served a purpose, it gave me hope and acted as my moral compass. Since leaving the Army I have retained my faith, advertised on a limited basis on Christmas Eve, Easter and Remembrance Sunday and sometimes in-between. I lost my faith with the loss of my Father, as I was angry with God for my father's passing, but rediscovered it because of this loss, as I eventually turned to God to help me understand it. My faith has given me strength and it has found my weaknesses, and in Goražde it was a silent partner that was always with me.

My question about faith is: "Why do I seek God when I need him?" Always in time of loss, in confusion or need. It appears a narrow, one-sided relationship and one that I felt ultimately interrogated the meaning of my religious belief and found it wanting. I know many more devoted Christians that have an answer for this, but I questioned the depth and meaning of my faith when I appeared to take and not give when in my hour of need.

I would think about this at night when on radio duty in Goražde, reflecting on the day's events. Many of my poems written in these hours capture my internal ongoing debate, where God, hope, resurrection and the afterlife run through my words. Padre Patrick was unknowingly influential in many ways. Not least, he gave me confidence to write, he was patient in my learning and anonymous in his teaching. His eccentricity made religion approachable, enjoyable and believable. He was a figure in the shadows but offered a point of contact with no allegiance and outside the framework of rank and order of Army life, and one the soldiers needed.

With the fatalities, the subjects of God, mortality and life were present and more openly discussed, and therefore Remembrance Sunday and Christmas Day adopted a greater significance. Throughout, Patrick was the reliable, amiable point of contact. It was not 'him' or religion that bound us, but something he embodied, although his character added a little magnetism to Christianity. When confronted with the possibility of death, mankind as a race struggles to accept his or her mortality and seeks answers to the eternal question as to the purpose of our existence. The Padre could not offer definitive answers, no one can, but he offered something to believe in, he listened with unwavering patience and gave counsel and warm, considered words and allowed you to look to the future, as opaque as it may have been.

It is with these thoughts and my own understanding of how religion had played its part when I was in Goražde that I sought out other considerations. Of those

The RTAs that killed the four young private soldiers of 1RGBW happened when in two separate incidents the Saxons they were on board slipped from the treacherous mountain muddied roadways.
In one Private Ben Hinton was killed, in the other Privates Phillip Armstrong, Martin Dowdell and Chris Turner

who had listened to the Padre, many would have looked out across the mountains of central Bosnia late at night, the sky littered with stars, and may have had their own thoughts on religion, God and his existence.

It seemed appropriate to ask Ian Harris first, the officer commanding A Company, the company that experienced the two fatal accidents only a few days apart at the beginning of the tour in Goražde.

"Having been brought up in a Christian household, as the son of a minister, I recall drawing on my own belief and faith. As a result, I believe I sensed a blanket of calmness and order descending on me which helped me to tackle the challenges of this testing period for A Company. However, this did not remove the frustrations and challenges that I experienced. For example, I remember my personal frustration with 'the system' for failing to provide a battalion padre at this early stage of the tour. Just when I felt that I and my soldiers needed one, where was he? Although these were private thoughts, it seemed right to be thinking about what I should or could do to provide spiritual assistance in addition to leadership and operational command to my soldiers.

I also recall the intense experiences of the incidents themselves. The reality that death and injury had found A Company, leaving shattered soldiers and vehicles strewn down the sunlit hillside of a distant valley in a distant land. I remember talking with and observing the injured soldiers, lying on stretchers before me, awaiting evacuation, wondering if more would die, silently praying that none would do so. None did.

I remember the hours of delay in the evacuation of the injured and the dead, complicated by our remote location and the bureaucracy of the Bosnian Serb Army (BSA). I also remember thinking about how those A Company soldiers who were deployed in the remote OPs could pay their respects to the dead and the injured soldiers being evacuated. Therefore, it was satisfying that each of the several casualty evacuation helicopters, responded to my request and flew low and slow over each of the OPs on their departure, allowing some level of acknowledgement and

GORAZDE FORCE

REMEMBRANCE SUNDAY SERVICE

13 NOVEMBER 1994

ORDER OF SERVICE

HYMN

All people that on earth do dwell,
Sing to the Lord with cheerful voice;
Him serve with fear, his praise forth tell,
Come ye before him, and rejoice.

The Lord, ye know, is God indeed;
Without our aid he did us make;
We are his folk, he doth us feed,
And for his sheep he doth us take.

O enter then his gates with praise,
Approach with joy his courts unto;
Praise, laud, and bless his name always,
For it is seemly so to do.

For why? the Lord our God is good;
His mercy is for ever sure;
His truth at all times firmly stood,
And shall from age to age endure.

To Father, Son, and Holy Ghost,
The God whom heaven and earth adore,
From men and from the angel-host
Be praise and glory evermore. Amen.

THE LESSON: Ezekiel 37.1-14

HYMN

O God, our help in ages past,
Our hope for years to come,
Our shelter from the stormy blast,
And our eternal home;

Beneath the shadow of thy throne
Thy saints have dwelt secure;
Sufficient is thine arm alone,
And our defence is sure.

Before the hills in order stood,
Or earth received her frame,
From everlasting thou art God,
To endless years the same.

A thousand ages in thy sight
Are like an evening gone;
Short as the watch that ends the night
Before the rising sun.

O God, our help in ages past,
Our hope for years to come,
Be thou our guard while troubles last,
And our eternal home.

ACT OF REMEMBRANCE

Let us remember before God, and commend to his sure keeping:
those who have died for their country in war;
those whom we knew, and whose memory we treasure;
and all who have lived and died in the service of mankind.

They shall grow not old as we that are left grow old:
Age shall not weary them, nor the years condemn.
At the going down of the sun and in the morning
We will remember them. ALL: WE WILL REMEMBER THEM.

THE TWO MINUTES SILENCE

The Last Post and the Reveille will be sounded.

THE ADDRESS

HYMN

1. Onward, Christian soldiers!
Marching as to war,
With the Cross of Jesus
Going on before.
Christ the royal Master
Leads against the foe;
Forward into battle,
See, his banners go!
Onward, Christian soldiers!
Marching as to war,
With the Cross of Jesus
Going on before.

2. At the sign of triumph
Satan's host doth flee;
On then, Christian soldiers,
On to victory!
Hell's foundations quiver
At the shout of praise;
Brothers, lift your voices,
Loud your anthems raise.
Onward, Christian soldiers!
Marching as to war,
With the Cross of Jesus
Going on before.

3. Crowns and thrones may perish,
Kingdoms rise and wane,
But the Cross of Jesus
Constant will remain:
Gates of hell can never
'Gainst that Church prevail
We have Christ's own promise,
And that cannot fail.
Onward, Christian soldiers!
Marching as to war,
With the Cross of Jesus
Going on before.

4. Onward, then, ye people,
Join our happy throng,
Blend with ours your voices
In the triumph song;
Glory, laud, and honour
Unto Christ the King,
This through countless ages
Men and angels sing.
Onward, Christian soldiers!
Marching as to war,
With the Cross of Jesus
Going on before.

The original service sheet of 11 November 1994, where sheets were copied and roughly folded for a service that had a true sense of purpose allowing for the recent deaths in the battalion and the intensity of the surroundings

farewell to take place. It was my desire to show respect in death and acknowledge the impact and importance of involving the living.

In the aftermath, the company drew itself together. We closed ranks. I remember worrying about the absence of the padre and wondered whether I should try to offer some form of religious support. Perhaps a service of some sort? But no, nothing formal at this early stage, only hours after the incidents, we gathered together, bonded by tragedy, grieving and remembering Ben, Phil, Martin and Chris with a mix of prayers, silence, stories, humour, memories and tears. It seemed to help us all.

These memories and other things drove me to getting something visible to remember those killed and I was determined to have them in place before I departed (three months later). It therefore somehow seemed right and appropriate that during a patrol within a few days of the incidents, my Company Sergeant Major and I found a Muslim refugee stone mason and two marble slabs that had come from nearby Montenegro. These were carved by him for us with appropriate inscriptions, then commemorated and placed in situ in short services several weeks later. These memorials survived in place for many years until they were 'mistakenly' removed and returned to the UK in the mid-2000s. However, these were returned by a group of Goražde RGBW veterans in 2012. They are now resting in their original and rightful locations of 1994. During their return in 2012, they were re-dedicated by the Rev Patrick Irwin, our battalion Padre who joined us shortly after the incidents in 1994, and Rev Andrew Grant, one of the soldiers who had been seriously injured in one of the vehicle accidents of

151

1994. The return of these memorials 'home to Goražde' and their re-dedication in this manner seemed to me to be pertinent and lasting, which in a way was my original objective; that Ben, Phil, Martin and Chris, and those who were injured, should never be forgotten." (Major Ian Harris, OC A Company in 1994.)

Above: The repatriation of the bodies of Privates Ben Hinton, Phillip Armstrong, Martin Dowdell and Christopher Turner.

Above right: Padre Patrick Irwin conducts a brief service on the arrival of the bodies.

Danny Ashton, one of Ian's private soldiers in A Company noted:

As a non-religious person, it was very hard to understand how important faith was to others. I was not brought up in a religious household and tolerated RE at school as it was one of the easier subjects, no other reason!

However, religion as an influencing tour de force was made clear to me in Goražde, where both the Serbs and BiH went to extremes to try and justify what they were doing in the name of (their) religion. Frequently the Serb soldiers asked if I was a Christian and then would seek to use this new-found commonality to build a relationship with me, which seemed futile and meaningless.

Early enforced and childhood exposure to religion was echoed by Taff Davies, also of A company:

When I was growing up, religion only came into play when at school or weddings. At school, like most, we had assemblies and learnt the Lord's prayer, sang hymns and took part reluctantly in nativity plays. Senior school was learning about the Bible and Christianity, although I can never remember learning about other faiths (other than there was a Jehovah's Witness in our form and every time we had an RE lesson she would go somewhere else and we would have Christmas presents and she wouldn't).

On joining the Army at sixteen we paraded every Sunday in our best kit for the church service, but at least in the Army the padres were generally humorous and could relate a lesson to real life, which made it more interesting."

It appeared to me that a large minority of those soldiers interviewed for this book had no meaningful faith they had carried beyond childhood. For those that had no faith, their experiences in the Army seemed to reaffirm their lack of belief; for those with wavering faith, such experiences tested it to the extreme. However, running through all was a common belief in human nature and its ability to offer strength at moments when man or woman can be most tested.

As for my own faith, having gone on to serve a full career in the Army and having travelled extensively, I do not consider myself a religious man. 'Live and let live' is my view. However, twenty years later, when we revisited Goražde, seeing Rev Grant and Mick Stacy walking down the hill where they had suffered terribly, reaffirmed my faith in human nature. The strength they showed in confronting their demons, made the return trip for me worthwhile.

It was perhaps the travesty of the two Saxon accidents that have come to define this operational tour. It was the unnecessary waste of young British lives that have echoed down the years that took some of us back to Goražde in 2012 and started my own journey to reflection and to writing this book. It is, however,

The laying of the memorial stones and setting the crosses in remembrance for three of the fallen, A Company soldiers gather to commemorate their loss late in 1994

from those who survived the incident and all that lived through the bitterly cold winter of 1994 that we can learn so much: The Reverend Andrew Grant

As I cast my memories back, I recall the accident, of course. The shock setting in as the vehicle toppled over off the track, before building up momentum as it began to spin through the air. Suddenly I am sat on my backside on the side of the hill, with the vehicle lifting off me and leaving me behind.

I cry tears of relief and say, 'Thank you Jesus'. He was there, intervening. I cannot, of course, explain why, when I think of the other guys who didn't survive. I was no better man than any of them, no more deserving of survival. This to me remains a mystery.

I am thankful to God for what I truly believe was an act of physical deliverance, but this is not to be a reason for personal triumphalism; but instead, a reason for quiet humility, always aware that our friends died that day, bringing with it unimaginable grief to their families.

Martin, Christopher and Phil were not abandoned by Jesus that day (nor Ben a few days before in the first accident). I believe they moved into his fuller presence, and in doing so, said their own thank you as they entered his loving eternal rest.

Faith is often found at such moments and it has been recorded throughout history, where men at arms and soldiers, when facing their own mortality, find time for religious reflection and, for some, self-hope. For most, however, they ask for help, hope and understanding for others:

"On the night of the second accident my section was tasked with guarding the crash site. I recall very clearly Corporal Errol Flynn, Danny Nield (KIA Afghanistan), Sid Hart, Daz Cole and myself sitting around a fire we had made to keep us warm from the early winter winds.

The night was washed with the reality of the tragic events of the day and I remember us discussing quite readily death, God and the afterlife. The sense of mortality brought on by the day's events made the evening very emotional and bought religion to the heart of the conversation. (Danny Ashton)

Perhaps the complexity of the Bosnia situation was added to by the intervention of the UN's multi-cultural and multi-religious peacekeeping force, and this addition is best captured by the unfortunate series of events experienced by Clarence Heal, which he recalled some twenty years on with amusement. It never ceased to amaze me how the soldiers could find humour amidst the darkest of events and times, when adversity and physical challenge were a daily routine:

The highlight of the tour, where I was the sorrowful victim of my race and religion, was a week appropriately from hell.

It started with a lorry load of abuse from a Croat traffic cop trying it on with me and Captain Sulyok for speeding outside Visoko. Things got worse as the uniformed protagonist thought I was a Malaysian 'Malbat' Muslim. Eventually we got him to see sense and reason. However, this respite was short-lived as a little further down the same road a couple of days later, at the infamous Rogatica

(Rogo-tits-ups) checkpoint, whilst I was witnessing Captain Sulyok having a god almighty row with the Serbs over a can of OMD 80 oil, along comes Lance Corporal 'Embo' Emberson (Recce Platoon, 1RGBW), thinking it a good idea to tell the Serbs I'm a Muslim!

"When considering the reason why we were in Bosnia was in no small part religious hatred and I was in the heart of Serbian (Orthodox) territory, not surprisingly, an altercation ensued. After a bit of a ding-dong punch up between a huge Serb and me, where I quickly started to look like a giant panda, and the Serb similarly with a healthy black eye, Captain Sulyok managed to calm

Saxons lined up pre-prepared for patrols, Cotswold Camp, Goražde, 1994

155

the situation and in my mind should have been awarded a medal for UN peacemaker of the year!

Battered and in need of a rest, we finally got to the Bosniak And Muslim checkpoint on the outskirts of Goražde, to then be further humiliated by them trying to wipe my face because they thought I was African and had a 'chocolate face'! It was a torrid journey, where I had been exposed to differing views as to my colour, race and religion, by all warring factions, ironic when my role was as an arbitrator of peace amid them!

No more could go wrong; the week was done, and the lights of Cotswold Camp welcomed. I jumped from the Land Rover, haggard and battered and straight into a royal bollocking from for the RSM for being, as he quaintly put it, 'in shit state'.

Heal, look at you for god's sake, you look a mess. Where's your sense of personal pride? You look like you've been on a journey through hell, as opposed to a road journey inside a well warmed Land Rover. Get yourself in good order by the time I next see you. You're in shit state.

Since this day, I leave the role of faith within my life to my long-suffering Filipino and Catholic wife!

The Saxon was used to provide protected mobile patrols and in static duty on the observation posts

BISERNA SERVICE

I vowed to thee my country
To serve at my request
To be loyal to men of county
This honour I am blessed

I heard the soldiers singing
Old hymn books in their hands
Amidst the valleys ringing
Above battle-weary lands

High service to our Lord
In deep vacated trenches
The fading echoes of accord
Where death's aroma stenches

Such English songs do render
Of chariots and fields on fire
An English heart so tender
Found in mosque and spire

In Padre's hand is broken
Crisp bread of Jesus' soul
His blood as wine bespoken
Our hope his deathly toll.

Once more we lift our voices
To sing out to the Lord
The hope for peace rejoices
For these Englishmen abroad

Note: Recalling impromptu services held on
Bisena by Padre Patrick Irwin.

Padre Patrick Irwin was not warmly received by all!

B Company soldiers relax and await a Sunday service high above Goražde

22nd September 1994

I have no doubt that you have been watching the news and will be aware the Serbs attacked and destroyed a French armoured personnel carrier today. In retaliation UNPROFOR requested an air strike, this mission being named "Blue Sword".

At least one Serbian tank was destroyed, probably a T-54/T-55, this is an old 1954-55 Soviet tank, of which the Yugoslavian Army had many. The result of this reaction is that UNPROFOR fears further retaliation and consequently UN forces in Bosnia go to what is known as state RED.

There are three colourful stages of readiness, you will be delighted to know:

Black – normal activity, no direct threat, wearing berets and bulletproof jackets outside camp.

Amber – possibility of an attack, jackets worn, helmets carried.

Red – a direct attack is likely, helmets and jackets on, into hard cover.

At state RED I find myself inside the Saxon, our own armoured personnel carrier, listening to the continuous crackle of the radio, as I man the Company operational radio net from its command vehicle. The likelihood of retaliation is, of course, a real one, as the Serbs are predictably unpredictable. Indeed, their behaviour is becoming increasingly unreliable and inconsistent as October 15th (and the possibility of the lifting of the arms embargo), approaches.

I believe President Clinton has little regard or rather comprehension of what effect this would have on the ground for UN troops. Maybe this disregard is fostered and made more the easier as there are no US troops deployed on the ground, and therefore the October date does not have the same impact for the U.S., with none of its armed personnel readily exposed to its consequences.

For Goražde, the end to the embargo would make little difference as the enclave is under siege and its people have adopted an appropriate defensive mentality. It is clear and worthy of note that the BiH are preparing as if we, the UN and/or British Army, will not be there at their hour of need, despite our very visible presence on the ground today. Surely, we would not let the town's people down at the exact moment they need us?

To be honest, I am a little confused as to the exactness of our mandate, or rather I would like to find some grey areas and ambiguity that would allow us to stand firm, if such a scenario unfolded. I fear, however, the preparations of the BiH are well thought out and therefore our presence is merely a gift of an interim period, a respite, to allow them to prepare for the inevitable, a time when the UN and its resolve will be found valueless and our own purpose disregarded.

Some argue the direct consequence of Clinton's strategy, enforcement through air superiority, would most likely lead to the UN (the British and the French

Corporal Slug Southern give a reading and a lesson at the unrehearsed service at OP2, on the Biserna ridgeline

Padre Patrick Irwin

forces) withdrawing and this in turn would lead to the fall of Goražde and all that we have achieved dissolving into nothing. More so, the town and its people would be sacrificial lambs of this strategy. It is ironic that Clinton's primary political motivation and those of the UN is to protect the Bosniaks and the minority Muslim population, where such air strikes if continued would make our position on the ground untenable and would therefore inevitably harm the Muslims through our enforced withdrawal.

I am no politician and but a soldier on the ground at the end of the political food chain, but to me this strategy appears an insight into the lack of consideration by the Americans of the Balkans, its history and its geopolitical situation. We appear as if we are playing God with hundreds, even thousands, of years of ingrained tribalism, be this wrapped up in a religious cover or not, which produces a deep-rooted sense of identity, one that can breed the opportunity of conflict as these roots and their identities breathe again and become freed or challenged. I believe American interventionism and international policy frequently lacks this understanding and situational empathy.

Certainly, here in the Balkans its foreign policy and approach for resolving the issues in the region fall short of the required thoughtfulness. Specifically, the Americans do not appear to understand the manner of the men they are dealing with amongst the leadership of the Serbs. They underestimate or misunderstand them to our peril and to the peril of the Bosnian people, as unimaginable terror and brutality are resident tools of their evil trade, are characteristic of this Slavic race and tenants at the Serbian leaders' table.

Amidst this turmoil, political posturing and high-brow geo-politick, you seek moments of solitude and my own sense of being seems best captured by my attempts to frame moments or images in the written word. Whilst my heart rests in the fields of Gloucestershire, I have moments that I can see Shropshire, the county of my birth and much of my childhood and your home for many years. I tried to capture my thoughts of both in words scribbled late at night, firstly I wrote of F W Harvey, a famous World War One poet of The Gloucestershire Regiment, who loved the county of his birth and then of Shropshire, the county of my own. It is perhaps sitting on top of Lilleshall Hill that embodies such moments and allowed me to write words that gave me comfort. They are just thoughts, as I have no pretence to consider myself a poet, as my attempts will demonstrate! Maybe I am more a thinker that writes his thoughts down on occasion.

Left: Staff Dunn and RSM (WO1) RSM Wood, State Red, on board and locked down in a Saxon, November 1994, Cotswold Camp, Goražde

Below left: The Daily Telegraph, winter 1994. U.S. policy was an ongoing concern to the British soldiers on the ground, the recipients of any Serb reaction to what they saw as a provocative U.S. policy towards them

16 THURSDAY, SEPTEMBER 22, 1994 ★ ★ ★

US warned not to lift Bosnia arms embargo

By John Kampfner, Diplomatic Correspondent

THE United Nations Secretary General, Mr Boutros Boutros Ghali, called yesterday for plans for an immediate withdrawal of UN troops from Bosnia to be finalised in case the Americans lift the arms embargo on the government.

The report to the Security Council was the sternest warning yet that the UN Protection Force would effectively cease to exist in the event of unilateral American action.

But, with growing optimism in New York and European capitals that the issue is unlikely to come to a Transatlantic showdown, Mr Boutros Ghali said that for the moment he was recommending a six-month renewal of Unprofor's mandate.

The issue will be at the forefront of a flurry of diplomatic activity over the next week, starting with President Boris Yeltsin's talks at the weekend with Mr Major at Chequers.

They will be followed by discussions between members of the Contact Group — Britain, France, Germany, Russia and the United States — on the sidelines of the UN General Assembly, at which President Bill Clinton, Mr Yeltsin and Mr Douglas Hurd, Foreign Secretary, will make keynote speeches.

Washington has found itself out of line with the UN and most of its partners on Bosnia, a rift that all sides are seeking to heal. Much will depend on Mr Clinton's strength of will in taking on a determined lobby which wants to see the Muslims given active military help.

The US administration has set Oct 15 as the deadline for the Bosnian Serbs to accept the peace plan. But there is no sign that the Serbs will change their line, leaving Mr Clinton virtually no choice, but to ask the Security Council to lift the embargo.

He would need the support of nine out of the 15 members. But that is highly unlikely. In addition, Russia is threatening to use its veto, a move that would not be lamented in Paris or London.

Assuming he failed to gain the support he needs, Mr Clinton would either risk antagonising Capitol Hill, in the run-up to congressional elections, or his European allies. If he dithers, Congress would need a two-thirds majority to force him into action.

● The 1st Bn The Royal Highland Fusiliers will replace the 2nd Bn The Royal Anglian Regiment when it ends its six-month deployment in Bosnia late next month, the Ministry of Defence said yesterday.

Above: OP14 (from left) Sergeant Roberts, Private Coleman, Corporal McDermin, Sergeant Morris, Corporal Lay, Corporal Bloodworth, Captain Collier, Colour Sergeant Griffiths

161

Summit hugs fail to hide rift over Bosnia

By Stephen Robinson in Washington

THE Bosnian crisis loomed over the first day of the summit between President Bill Clinton and President Boris Yeltsin in Washington yesterday as the Russians sought backing for a conference of the main parties trying to stop the war.

Russian officials credited Mr Yeltsin with making the original suggestion for a conference, an idea which Washington has previously opposed, suggesting the Americans were more supportive this time.

Despite their best efforts to patch up their differences on the issue, with Mr Clinton greeting his visitor with a warm bear hug, the two leaders sparred lightly about the Bosnian arms embargo.

immediately talks began.

Both leaders make much of the warmth of their personal relationship, but there was a flash of old Russian superpower steel when, in the course of brief remarks during a photo-call, Mr Yeltsin let it be known Moscow's response would be "negative" should the United States press to lift the Bosnian arms embargo.

Mr Clinton tried to defuse any disagreement by saying the issue might be "a lovely academic discussion" given that Bosnian leaders favoured a delay of up to six months in implementing any United Nations vote to lift the embargo. "We have been

together every step of the way, and we're going to do our best to stay together," Mr Clinton said, papering over what have been very clear differences in the two governments' policies.

Mr Yeltsin said: "The United States is a strong partner, and not an easy one to deal with, just like Russia." Mr Yeltsin had set the tone for the meeting the day before in a combative address to the UN General Assembly, asserting Russia's enduring "great power" status and her right to conduct "peacekeeping" on her borders.

In keeping with the tone of recent meetings the talk yes-

terday was of two partners of equal status. The two men do get along well, in part as Mr Clinton recalled, because they first met when he was seeking the Democratic nomination in 1992 and the encounter boosted his campaign.

Immediately after a formal welcoming ceremony at the White House, Mr Clinton and Mr Yeltsin began talking in the Oval Office, principally about Bosnia and then wider security issues.

US officials reacted coolly to Mr Yeltsin's call for substantial new cuts in strategic weapons arsenals. Instead, the Americans wanted to address the control of nuclear material and missile components in the former Soviet Union. An agreement to work together to curb "loose nukes" will be signed today and hailed as one of the summit's achievements.

The *Washington Times* reported a leaked CIA analysis prepared for the summit questioning Mr Yeltsin's ability to enforce any agreement to control nuclear material.

The CIA reports that orders from the president's office are not obeyed by the Russian Ministry of Atomic Energy and other agencies which resent US involvement in dismantling Moscow's nuclear weapons.

This two-day meeting lacks the drama of past Washington superpower summits, and few Americans would have even noticed Mr Yeltsin's presence. Most people's attention was turned to the jury selection in the OJ Simpson trial.

Editorial Comment: Page 18

Rose hails U-turn on embargo

THE United Nations commander in Bosnia, Lt-Gen Sir Michael Rose, yesterday hailed a Bosnian government climbdown over lifting the arms embargo. He said the authorities had heeded his warnings that they could lose the eastern enclaves and provoke a UN departure from Bosnia. Neither the Muslim-dominated Bosnian army nor the Bosnian Serbs were yet ready for a return to full-scale war, he said, adding that the Bosnian government had signalled it was ready to give peace a chance — for another six months at least. His comments came a day after the Muslim-led government indicated in New York that it was no longer insisting that the

lifting of the UN embargo on weapons sales to former Yugoslavia be effective immediately. "I think that decision to postpone further moves toward lifting the embargo is tremendous news for the people of this country and for the peace process," Gen Rose said. "Having an artificially imposed time line on a peace process undoubtedly creates difficulties because peace is drawn out and never proceeds smoothly, but if you are patient and persistent, in the end you get there."

The Bosnian army was not yet strong enough to defeat the Serbs if the country was plunged back into full-scale war, he said. "I have always said, and this is why I was

not surprised by their decision, that the consequences would be dire and incalculable.

"First of all, they are not in a position to defend the enclaves. I have had many discussions with military commanders in those enclaves and they are as aware as I am that if Unprofor (UN Protection Force) withdrew ... then those enclaves would be overrun.

"Sarajevo is an enclave. I am not saying Sarajevo would be overrun, but certainly the Bosnian Serb army control all the high ground around Sarajevo and therefore the utilities. And life in Sarajevo would return to the hell it was two years ago if we withdrew." — AFP

Private Meek writing home in the sunshine, high on the hill at OP6

F. W. HARVEY ("WILL")

The Gloucestershire Regiment 1914–19

In Hartpury, a Gloucester village, where coddled he was born
A fulsome nest of birds sings beautifully at early misty dawn
Above tilled fields of Redlands the darting swallows fly
Past shire horses and haybarns where farmyard animals lie

Above the playful chatter of a springtide of love lost birds
Dreamlike flows and spills through grazing flocks and herds
Of cattle and western ewe gathering as a Cotswold crowd
Whose bleating sounds and joyful banter echo soft and loud

Listen to the singing and the playing of the orchestra
Warbling tunes and laughter heard both near and far
This bustling sound of bird and beast a happy harmony
Drowning in Severn waters as a cathedral's symphony

As a boy Will played between those hallowed walls
Divine pleasures of choristers singing as their duty calls
Drew him from mellowing hills and western hazy land
To sound of booming guns and the rattling of the band

Through byways and rustic lanes shadowed with leafy trees
Across the wind-swept channel blown onto battled seas
Fallen trees and stump to trenches of Ploegsteert Wood
Gloucestershire at his heart he wrote about the good

Inspired amid German trenches they took him from the free
Venturing forward from British lines at lonely Laventie
Entrapped and turned a prisoner held at Gutersloh
Where hindered by captivity poetic words did flow

And with this time to reflect his prose made full amends
From this deep-felt art came his Gloucestershire Friends
Years past before to his county with freedom he returned
To vales and the cock crowed farms he had always yearned

In England he would walk on the hills of dreams he'd seen
Hill covered meadowed fields running to Forest of Dean
At last content as a rescued soul time past in valleys sweet
In forest towns and forest trees his happiness complete

A dedicated life to the people of his beloved county
Whose love and lasting thanks became his only bounty
Then finally the choristers sung the Dream of Gorontius
That settled an anguished life with Elgar's happy flush

17th January 1995

Frederick Harvey in regimental dress, serving with The Gloucesters throughout the First World War and, right, pictured, after the war.

Note: F. W. Harvey was born in Hartpury in 1888. He served in his county regiment during the First World War One before moving to the Forest of Dean, where he worked fastidiously for the lower classes. A memorial tablet was unveiled in 1980 in Gloucester Cathedral that read: "He loved the vision of this world and found it good."

SHROPSHIRE

On Shropshire's softened rolling plain
Of ancient fields of corn and rape
Wind sweeps o'er the fallen remains
Of heaving oak blown out of shape

From emerald hills of Wales it glides
The Severn chestnut waters stare
Its foaming bore where history rides
O'er meadows washed with Marches air

Great surging waters pare deep gorge
A teeming stream through blackened arch
Past church spire that flies St. George
Like fluttering footsteps on the march

Below the Wrekin's clinging wood
Above and o'er Wroxeter spheres
Stones echo from where Romans stood
Well washed and worn by English tears

Fox hunting to the poacher's beat
Long Mynd thunders to horse's hooves
Clee Hills covered by snow white sleet
Wenlock Edge and valley grooves

Below the castle and market town
Each westward look to Celtic towers
Black mountains appear misty brown
Offa's Dyke lies blushed with flowers

Hamlets pucker at fresh run streams
Much Wenlock, Acton, Stretton stone
Above buzzards fly with opened wings
No movement as they are gently blown

In valleys marked with steam and smoke
Canals are edged with drooping willow
That casts shadows on barge with coke
Still waters run through pastures mellow

Shropshire's plain is etched in history
Its hills and heaths do make this shire
Of whispering oak and medieval mysteries
O'er its rivers, villages and fields of mire

Lilleshall Hill and memorial,
Shropshire

22nd September 1994

Thank you for your letter and in anticipation of more to come, thank you for the books and stamps.

Dad – today is pay day, I have reason to believe I'm back in credit! Wonders will never cease.

Having become laptop literate and embracing the new world we are entering of computers, evolutionary software and the unknown, I thought I'd jot down tonight's edition of 'Life in Goražde' on the ever-fluorescent screen of the Company's computer. Therefore, my apologies for the impersonality of a typed letter, but let us begin:

Once more I find myself listening to the crackle of the radio, watching the second-hand crawl round the face of my metal grey Army issue watch (known in hardened Army circles as 'GIO for men'). A few days have passed since I last scribbled a note to you, not that my last attempt was not a significant event, it's merely with mail going out and not coming in you tend to lose track of who and when you last wrote a letter.

No post since the last mail drop on September 14th, good old Johnny Serb has seen to that. So here I am, another day drifting by, quite happy to sit and thump the key pads for a while as I try and paint a picture of life in the UN holiday camp 'Costa del Bosnia'.

It's just past ten o'clock on Sunday evening, the end of another week in Bosnia. The Regimental bugler, silhouetted this evening by a full moon, has just played the Last Post. In the clear night the crisp notes ring out, echoing down the Drina valley, up her gulley's and re-entrants before fading to a whisper and finally to nothing. High above us, perched on the surrounding mountains, our soldiers are tucked away in their Observation Posts. From these isolated positions you can hear the bugler announcing the arrival of night and to them this eerie, yet reassuring tune symbolises the end of another day.

Having been on the mountains at trumpet hour, I can picture the town in the valley below, the only light coming from the United Nations camp, recently christened Cotswold Camp, and the silver shine on the roads and the walls of buildings provided by the reflection of the moonlight. In the town no movement, no light, no noise, just the simple emotive, indicative melody of the bugler.

Have you ever heard of the song 'I've been dreaming of a moon shadow' by Cat Stevens? The tune and not so much the words are in my head tonight.

Today is an anniversary of sorts, for it is one month today we arrived in Bosnia. Is reflection after one month of a six-month tour appropriate? I think I'll call it a short-term assessment as opposed to reflection.

After the months of continual speculation before our departure on whether we would or indeed whether we should be sent, we now live under daunting clouds of the possibilities that could unfold and the questions that remain unanswered as to the exactness of our mandate. We take the high command of the UN's mandate, extrapolate it and then add our interpretation at Battalion, Company, Platoon and soldier level, this is the essence of the British Army's command and orders structure , to ensure at all levels, whilst you retain an absolute alignment to the overall objective, you have freedom of movement to make decisions independently at each level. What is our duty, what is our level of exposure and how are the politics being handled that ultimately impact the British soldier on the ground are three questions that are interlinked. Our duty we do not question, our exposure is ever present, and we do what we can to mitigate risk. The politics that have brought us here are out of our hands, but the purpose as to why we are here is clear every day.

Politicians pontificating on this matter have an adverse effect on the morale of the soldier on the ground, not that this is a consideration for a Whitehall bureaucrat, an armchair warrior who would find him or herself ill at ease in the conditions the soldiers accommodate as part of their duty. Such uncertainty erodes morale and blurs our focus, but the boys simply get on with it and as they are still in the honeymoon period of this deployment, such grumblings are momentary.

Here is food for thought. A private soldier earns about, or just shy of £10,000 per year before tax. This works out at about £27 per day or as we are on duty 24/7, about £1.10 per hour! If you are married, after being away for thirty days (so they have just arrived into this land of plentiful and bounty!), they will get an extra £3.50 a day. Service is not financially motivated, but the soldiers being paid fairly for their duty is surely a reasonable request?

Our perception is that the U.K. government and the United Nations are unsure what to do at this moment, whilst appearing to accept and be waiting for the inevitable, with President Clinton seeking to push forward with his proposal to lift the arms embargo and re-arm the Muslims and its likely consequences being well understood. Although only today the Muslims have requested a stay of execution on this embargo, as they feel it would not (yet) be beneficial. Oh! How Clinton must despair! It's important to remember that this action would be a recognition that the peace process has failed, and inter-factional war would reignite and suggest that civil war and its conclusions are the only way a solution to the Balkans' inter-territorial issues can be found.

Consequently, in this scenario our position as peace keepers becomes untenable. Personally, I feel the Clinton will succumb to the reality of the situation and to the pressures of the international community and be forced to swallow humble pie and show restraint over rearmament. There again he may say "sod 'em" and lift it unilaterally and that is the rub and basis of much of the uncertainty.

If the 'good ol' Yankee boy from the west' does lift the embargo the timing would be crucial. The problem would remain on how to extract the ten thousand UN soldiers from the war zone without serious incident or confrontation. Furthermore, both warring factions have stated they would attempt to thwart any such withdrawal. In the short term it is not in the Muslims' interests for us to make a hasty withdrawal before they have re-armed. Similarly, it is not in the Serbs' long-term interests for us to withdraw, as any solution to the Balkans will undoubtedly involve UN cooperation and involvement at some stage. There is an inevitability about all of this, but the journey to this inevitability appears shackled with problems.

It appears the Serbian people are increasingly and particularly concerned about world opinion, when considering worldwide condemnation of war crimes and atrocities. Having crossed the divide of brutality and genocide already, operating outside the moral parameters of the Geneva Convention, you can only presume the warring factions would fall quite easily into barbaric actions once again if war resumed. Therefore, it is not just the fear of return to warfare, but it is the type of warfare that would unfold that creates a sense of urgency in ensuring peace can and must be maintained at any cost. In this light you can understand the absolute fear the people of Goražde must feel daily, where the thin blue line of the UN offers some hope of lasting salvation.

Naturally any decision for the U.S. is made easier because there are no U.S. troops on the ground. There is no possibility that Bill's decision could be judged in the context of American servicemen losing their lives. I very much doubt that he would be judged at home on the loss of British, French, Turkish or Ukrainian lives. Our position and consequently our safety depends upon the incongruous and uncertain genius of those collectively involved in geopolitics and foreign policy.

So, what do we do? As British soldiers have always done – 'Mine is not to reason why, mine is but to do or die', putting it simply we, soldier on! We do our bit, we ensure we mitigate risk and we protect our own and we operate within the mandate as required and as we interpret. We wait and wait and wait to see how the world outside Bosnia decides our and more so, the Bosnian people's fate.

We are here for the duration of six months, this I feel certain and must drive and underpin all that we do. Of course, this is what we want to do and would do far better without ill-informed, often ill-judged interference and if we had some greater flexibility to manage the situation in the ground.

I close my eyes and I can imagine and hear the echo of a grey, pallid, inconsequential man wearing a similarly grey suit working in a grey office in Whitehall bewailing the requests from IRGBW in Goražde for food, ammunition, diesel and so on. In a typically arrogant and detached manner, his voice bellows "I bloody well don't see why they don't just get on with it, that's what they're paid to do for god's sake. Of course if I was there ....."

Getting on with it is exactly what we're doing and in so doing, daily life on operations becomes tolerable, interesting and rewarding.

I would have a delight in pulling these bureaucrats from their leather-clad, tax-paid arm chairs and making them do a week or two of what the boys are doing. They lord themselves, tell others what to do from the safe zone in central London. I am not the first and will not be the last to bemoan the Ministry of Defence and the detachment that exists between those that make policy and the soldiers that execute it.

The reality is we are under and poorly armed, without a clearly defined mandate, without resources and in an exposed and detached location and environment. I personally feel the U.K. Government has failed us comprehensively and by the grace of God hope this precarious position does not crumble, for all the parties: Bosnians, Serbs, the UN soldiers and the charity workers here of their own volition.

We are however where we are and do get on with it and, despite my moaning and concerns listed above, all in all it is thoroughly enjoyable and rewarding.

I will not labour this point or convince myself that life in Goražde is better than a tour down King's Road on a hot Saturday afternoon, admiring the best that London has to offer, but I will however attempt to give you an insight into life in Goražde on a day in day basis by looking at the last forty-eight hours.

It is now, having taken a coffee break mid-letter, ten to twelve (2350) and I have three hours and ten minutes left on stag (radio op duty). It is likely therefore this note will become extended as I look to fill the next 190 minutes! This is a constructive way to pass the time as opposed to reading the boxes of Jackie Collins novels donated to the soldiers from the discerning and well-meaning British public.

You now have a choice:

Option one - continue to plough your way through the mire of this self-pitying diatribe

Option two - move to 'Advance to Go', read the final paragraph and hope by my return in March I have forgotten that I even sent you this letter

As the RSM would say "At your own time go on!"

I believe I told you previously the threat of attack from the Serbs is real. Indeed, as is the threat of attack by the Muslims. An example of this threat occurred last night, with two attacks on one of our observation posts (OP).

A Company's loyal hound Jasper was a permanent resident at the Company's OPs throughout the tour and accompanied the soldiers on many patrols

This OP is situated on the Samari Ridge, dominating the town of Goražde to the North-West. Immediately below it the Serb positions of Cemetery Valley oversee the main route from the east into Goražde. To the South-East the rolling countryside of Bosnia extend deep into Serb territory. The main Serb position in the Cemetery Valley is called the Red House, so called because well, it's red.

There are usually 20-25 Serb soldiers in this location, recently reinforced to 40 since the NATO air strike in Sarajevo last weekend. The Serbians retaliated to this air strike with an open-ended threat to all UN forces in Bosnia. Our local Serb boys obviously took this to heart and with courage, no doubt augmented by slivovitz, decided to test our resolve.

At ten to eight last night two shots were fired above the OP from the Red House. The sentry clearly identified the firing point from the flash of the weapon's barrel as the rounds cleared its chamber.

On this occasion no response was offered from our OP, as the rounds appeared to be shot without intent, being high above the OP. Additionally, such firing incidents frequently happen when the Serbs have partaken in too much essence of plum, and as the nights draw on, they get bored, probably with their own company and feel a need to fire a round or two!

At ten o'clock the Serbs, now very drunk and I have no doubt very bored, opened fire once again, but this time with automatic fire. The rounds winged their way into, over and around the sentry position. Private Stratton, only 19 but as cool as a cucumber, retaliated immediately with two short sharp bursts from his heavy machine gun (GPMG).

The 'thud-rud-da-da-thud' echoed down the valley. It was rather well-timed as it coincided as an accompanying crescendo to the bugler's Last Post. I must add, the bugler leapt into the air and the last three to four notes jumped a couple of octaves! Not only could you hear this crescendo, but you could clearly see the phosphorus on the tips of the machine gun bullets burning straight lines of red light in the night sky. The phosphorus continued to burn on impact before sizzling to nothing. OP1 immediately sent a Contact Report, ensuring in doing so that the airway was kept clear for communication between it and the headquarters, in this case Sergeant Major Johnny Yemm, Private Robinson and me in the control room.

Across the valley OP3, slightly below on the Kolijevka Ridge, responded to my command "Hello OP3 this is D22A switch Sierra Foxtrot to X-Ray 104 – wait figures three – over" the radio crackled into life as OP3 responded OP3 "Roger Out". I think a quick explanation is warranted. Sierra Foxtrot = Sustained Fire, a heavy machine gun. Secondly with a combination of lenses (that many have tried and failed to understand) you can have a series of pre-set targets that you can turn the weapon onto as required, each of these are numbered and therefore as

171

easily done in darkness as in daylight. The Serb house had the dubious honour of being one of these pre-fixed targets, namely X-Ray 104.

It is in such times that you realise the repetitive nature of your training enables you to work, respond, articulate yourself with little additional thought. Each part of the engine in tune with the other. OP1 responding as required and without hesitation, the control room coordinating aligned activity and OP3 responding and taking the necessary actions upon demand. It all seems such fine-tuned routine and so it is.

We waited in the cool night for the next retort, OP1 and 3 were ready, expectant. None came, the Serb had tested our willingness to respond and our response had been immediate, robust and accurate.

The night passed with no further activity. By morning, in discussions with Patrick, it was clear that someone had to visit the Serb position to discuss this incident. This had clearly been in contradiction of the UN Exclusion Zone agreement, signed by all factions, both in firing at UN soldiers (or any) and that the Serbs were doing so with weapons not allowed within this restricted area.

Patrick was happy for me to deal with it and similarly made it very clear to me our message had to be sharp and unequivocal. He also insisted a foot patrol into the position should be taken as an open show of purpose. A weapon had to be confiscated and shown to be as we patrolled back into Goražde. Why? The Muslims and townsfolk would be waiting and watching our actions, as this was a clear breach of the agreement and protocol and they would be looking to see how or if we were going to deal with this flagrant breach.

As an option there is a quick route down to the Red House we use in line with the UN mandate for unconcealed patrolling, namely being as open in our activities and as visible as possible. If we took this route today, the Serbs would see us coming and enable them to move men, weapons or both before we entered their position. This would make our job far more difficult.

Allowing also that these playful fellas had used us as their source of entertainment and target practice the night before, I decided the normal patrol route would be inappropriate. Anyway, I wanted to use this opportunity to prove a point to the Serbs. I briefed Patrick on my thoughts, he liked the approach and told me to 'crack on'.

My story is of course no more than the boys of A and B Company do routinely and daily. Patrol, monitor, control, intercept, hearts and minds and so on. This is our daily routine, but hopefully in telling one incident from my own experience, it will give you an insight to what the boys are doing day in and day out and the life of the soldiers on duty here in Goražde.

Accompanied by six soldiers and a rather anxious interpreter, we headed from camp up to OP3 and took the long route via OP2 and passing Poser's Rock, which looks down into the town with wonderful views, to arrive at OP1. This sits at the top of the valley and looks down into the Red House a few hundred metres away.

After a quick brew and a catch up with Stratton, to ensure I had all the facts at hand, we left OP1 and headed south-east and away from the Red House. In so doing this took us into dead ground and well out of sight of the Serbs. From here we climbed up a ridge covered in trees and for all the world we could have been deep in the Forest of Dean. Crossing over a track, we stumbled across some wire, it looked like communication cord. Corporal Southern had a field telephone with him. Teething into this line he rang it and was amused to find it being answered by two perplexed Serbs. A couple more times he called and then Slug (his nick name) cut the cord, leaving a hand-written message in Serbo-Croat 'Have you lost communication? I think so! Kind regards UNPROFOR'.

Continuing down the track, the ground fell away to our right. Another kilometre of dusty track, in the shadows of trees and below us (about five hundred metres) we could see the Red House. Crawling forward in the sun-burnt grass I could see Topalovic, the positions commander, playing cards to the rear of the building. Leaning against the back wall and sitting out the front were two sentries, who were passing a bottle of slivovitz to each other, it was mid-morning and alcohol was at hand! This of course was a continual worry for all of us, as it made the Serbs unpredictable. It was of course the partner to boredom and a way to pass the hours for these men many miles from their homes.

We continued for a further two to three hundred metres until we were out of sight from their position. Slipping through the fence the meadow fell away into a small gulley before levelling out onto a plateau, not more than twenty-five feet wide, overlooking the house and the battered remnants of its dusty garden. It would make my back yard at university look like the gardens of Versailles!

Reaching the plateau, I left two of my patrol to crawl forward onto its ridgeline, leaving them with specific instructions that will shortly become apparent. The gulley petered out as it reached the white house to the rear of the main position and enabled us to close to within ten metres before I decided that enough fun had been had. At this point I stood up, walked (with heart in mouth) into the Serb position, followed by Corporal Slug Southern and the interpreter in hot pursuit. Stratton and Hall held a position slightly to the rear but were easily visible.

"Dobro jutro" - Good morning, I used in full my extensive Serbo-Croat vocabulary. The sentry shook his head, his eyes appearing as if golf balls, as he saw us for the first time. His sentry duty had been poorly serviced! On gathering himself he gave a limp wristed attempt to challenge us. There was an air of embarrassment and uncertainty as to what should be done, what he should do. Walking past and ignoring the sentry I walked towards Topalovic*, putting my hand out as a gesture of intent that this entry was not to be a provocative action. I had met him before on several occasions, finding him to be both hospitable and charming.

He shook my hand, but at the same time shouted some harshly spoken words at the sentry, who simultaneously took a fist to the side of his head from a giant of a man, who appeared to be exercising immediate punishment on behalf of Topalovic. I think the sentry had had sufficient slivovitz in the minutes prior to impact to act as a pain killer and appeared to not notice his punishment!

Hands were shaken, and we were offered seats. There was an attempt to shift the conversation back to the same old rhetoric and away from the obvious reason for our visit. We had, I know, already pushed our luck. I took a seat at the table, with my back to the hillside, Stratton and Hall beckoned Topalovic to sit down. In so doing he was left looking up the hillside. As he sat down the two members of the patrol left on the ridge line above the house made their presence obvious, kneeling with their rifles clearly in hand. It was a simple but apparently effective gesture. Topalovic smiled and waved his hand to his men, as they were obviously flustered by this turn of events. They calmed themselves and momentarily coffee arrived.

Through the interpreter I passed on the feelings of both the OC and CO regarding the firing incident. I made it clear that the weapon [or at least a representative weapon] had to be released. To be honest there was adrenalin running through me, this was exciting stuff, but I was fully aware of the unpredictability of the situation. Topalovic made motion as if to say no weapon would be released, my reply was to threaten to cordon off his location., further informing him that each house would be turned upside down to locate this weapon. Any weapon found in this search would therefore be open to confiscation. I knew this would be exactly the line Patrick would have taken and expected me to take on his behalf.

There ensued a pregnant pause that appeared to last an eternity. Corporal Southern glanced at me as if to say, "interesting situation, his play". I wondered how many times this week a similar standoff would be played out between the UN and the Serbs. Many, I thought.

So, there we were, six of us, surrounded by upwards of thirty unstable battle-hardened, mostly drunk, Serb soldiers of the lunatic variety demanding that they give us their weapons! My protection, a blue beret.

Topalovic looked at me through crystal blue eyes and scratched his black beard.

Can you remember Fiddler on the Roof? His beard is identical to Topol's, in fact he is reminiscent of Topol in many ways.

"The weather is fine today, winter is on its way" my translator offered Topalovic's words. 'Weather, frigging weather, I want a weapon not a weather forecast' I thought. I stopped and thought briefly, had he heard of the British fascination about the weather and that this, therefore, would be common ground for negotiation?!

My own courage was now bolstered by a single sip of slivovitz, even this repugnant sip leaving a long-lasting taste burning my throat. Curtailing the conversation on clouds, sunshine and forecast I said "Topalovic, I know you have weapons here, we know, they know [I pointed to the town] and we cannot tolerate it. Contrary to what your soldiers may believe this is not a game, it may have seemed so last night, but you know the conclusion to this conversation, it is not negotiable. Give one weapon that will represent the weapon used last night and that will be the end of this matter. No search, no further repercussions." Corporal Southern looked at me again "Checkmate" he appeared to suggest, although I was unsure whether I had Topalovic at check or him me! A second pause, a flick of the wrist and a M70 B2 (automatic rifle) appeared.

Passing the weapon over to me, Topalovic smoothly un-cocked it, a round dropped from the barrel and he removed the magazine. "Weapon only, you did not say ammunition Captain." He smiled and added "I enjoy a good hearty conversation, now we drink." and so, we did. One moment we are shooting at them in self-defence, the next a war of words and a minute later we find ourselves drinking to old times. We left half an hour later with Topalovic promising that this will be the last time I will have to pay such a visit. If only I could believe him!

I returned to the company headquarters, my home, where after a hard day's work you should have hoped for the familiar greeting from your beloved, "Good day at the office darling?" "Yes sweetheart, popped in to see the boys at The Red House, they send their regards and I have a present for you." My home-bound conversations and evening's relaxation are somewhat distant of such dreams!

My rest of the day was administrative routine: reports, returns, debriefs and so on.

What other news and duties?

1. Humanitarian Convoys: distribution of clothing and food. A favourite subject and topic of mine for several reasons. It puts your own material desires into perspective when you see the smile of a five-year-old child when they put on a pair of 'second-hand' shoes for the first time, very new to them! I don't get involved as much as I would like to do with this as Battalion Headquarters manages most of the internally facing duties within the town, but when given

the chance to do so it allows you to see the good we are doing in many different and simple ways.

2. Liaison: by far the most entertaining. You listen, nod politely and promise nothing as each side tries to buy your affection through slivovitz, fresh bread or whatever means they believe appropriate.

3. Free time: you do get some. I generally try to do some extra exercise, which usually includes running through a marked mine field towards the other end of town. Slightly bizarre, but what isn't in this place. Other hobbies to fill your spare time? Writing letters, one a day to family and friends.

4. Reading: a must. There was an American flavour at the beginning of the tour with F. Scott Fitzgerald, Mark Twain and AD Salinger. English writers are now making a comeback with John Le Carre, Iain Banks, TS Eliot and even Wordsworth. Would I have read this collection back at home? I may even come back an educated man!

5. Patrolling: I've said enough on this for this letter or indeed all subsequent letters!

So here you have it, if you are wondering what your son is up to any day soon, his life goes on; reveille and the bugler starting the day; breakfast; briefing; patrol; lunch; liaison or humanitarian convoy; a run; some supper; a beer; read and write; last post and the bugler ending the day; Ops duty and bed in Portakabin; ad infinitum.

That is about it, my life in Goražde, although my R and R is now on the distant horizon and January 10th is not that far away!

Before I forget and to close, I have been in discussions with my translator and decided I needed to have at hand and ready some useful sayings to help me whilst engaging the Serbs on patrol and add to my extensive vocabulary, which is presently good morning, Dobro jutro. I requested tuition and four useful sayings, to be tested upon tomorrow and I believe may be useful, not sure you will agree:

1. Debeli ljudi su cesto veseli! – fat people are always cheerful
2. Slonovi ne mogu igrati košarku – elephants cannot play basketball
3. u mojoj supi je lopta za golf – there is a golf ball in my soup
4. ogledajte leteĐu banana – look a flying banana

Hope all is well at home, give 'Tess' a pat or ten from me.

Original typed words and poem about Topalovic, 22 November 1994

TOPALOVIC

Dapple gray whisps drift and curl, rising from Gornje Kolijevka
Then turning white to be absorbed by the fields of Samari,
While below red and white houses are blackened by their pillage
Reaching out their existence, creating warmth amidst the gloom.
From where these houses rest, as the cotton of a spider's web
The paths of Kolijevka are marked by the steps of time
And silvered by the morning dew that strokes the woods beyond
Caressing the contours and slipping to where soldiers lie
Where once their families had fed and children played
In scattered orchards of apples, pears and leafless trees.
These orchards are now littered with shining rifle brass
That reveals the desperate state of mans' desire
Which dampens the greeting of hardened burning oak
That dances with orange sparks that leap from fire red embers
Flickering a welcome as though a reflection in his eyes.
Then from this bristling face a glowing smile gives way
Expressing emotions no longer distant or duty bound
More welcoming than the burning fire beneath his sodden feet.
His heart gives way to mirth that receives us with open arms
That beckons us to disarm and sit at benches cut anew.
Shuffling into comfort smoke is drawn through tarnished hands.
Such hands that hold deathly keen steel now offer keen assistance
Passing small cupped kava that clips the lips with sweetness.
We talk and lift the dusts of time with unwrapped photographs.
With frayed edges and images our dreams fade and disappear
And I see Topalovic the soldier to be more than a man in green
I see Topalovic as a father, a brother, an uncle and a friend
Just as me or Tom or Dick he is but another man.

22nd November 1994

Note: Topalovic was the local BSA commander for the hillside
hamlet of Gornje Kolijevka, known as the Red House. After a
firing incident by one of his soldiers, involving OP1, a weapon
confiscation ensued that led to Topalovic's demotion. We became
good friends in the following six months of the tour.

Topalovic reminded the author of Tevye the dairyman and lead character played by Chaim Topol in the 1971 film, Fiddler on the Roof.

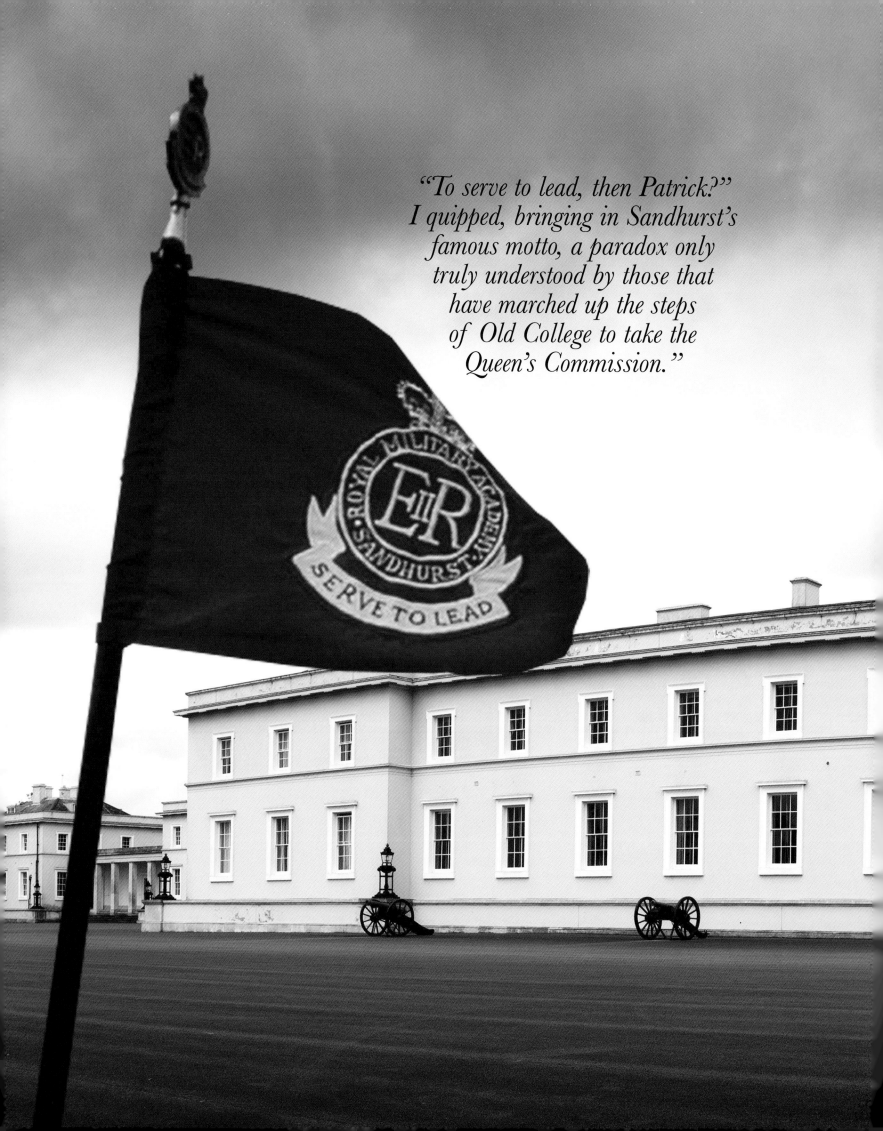

*"To serve to lead, then Patrick?"
I quipped, bringing in Sandhurst's
famous motto, a paradox only
truly understood by those that
have marched up the steps
of Old College to take the
Queen's Commission."*

CHAPTER 9

WE SERVE TO LEAD

THE BATTALION'S HIGH COMMAND

Whilst most of the content of this book is focused on my memories and the reflections of soldiers on the ground, it is equally important to balance these views with those burdened with the responsibility of leadership.

I needed to secure the views of those I felt to be key to steering the battalion through its six-month deployment. There will be positions some feel I should have included, such as the Adjutant or the seasoned Quartermaster, but I have not done so, believing these roles to be more about management, as opposed to leadership. Those commanding, the commanding officer (CO) and his rifle company commanders, held central roles within the battalion's leadership spectrum. I also include the CO's 2IC, the hand on the CO's shoulder and the CO's right-hand man, the regimental sergeant major (RSM). Whilst all these positions have managerial aspects to their roles and daily tasks, it is the responsibility of leadership, be it executive (the CO), direct on the ground (the rifle company commanders), or giving leadership in depth (the 2IC and RSM), that I have included.

The Commanding Officer, Lieutenant Colonel (later Brigadier) Patrick Davidson-Houston

There could have been no finer setting for my final meeting related to the writing of this book than the hallowed grounds of Whitehall and The Foreign and Commonwealth Office (FCO), more commonly called the Foreign Office.

It was a late summer's evening in mid-September 2017, when I turned right into Whitehall with Admiralty Arch behind me. I walked with increasing purpose as the great street opened out before me, the time was 17:30. My meeting was set at 17:30, I would be arriving five minutes before, which in military parlance would be on time. I was due to meet Brigadier Patrick Davidson-Houston, who retired from the Army in 2009 and was working as a senior adviser for the Stabilisation Unit based in the Foreign Office.

I had met Patrick five years earlier, during my first attempt to bring my memories together, then meeting in the shadows of nearby Buckingham Palace. He had been courteous and upbeat then and would prove to be the same this time. Patrick had been the inaugural commanding officer of the 1st Battalion, The Royal Gloucestershire, Berkshire and Wiltshire Regiment (1RGBW), when the regiment was formed on 27 April 1994. He then led the battalion, placed under UN high command, into Bosnia four months later. At our first meeting my notes recall him mentioning the final phase of the deployment from Sarajevo into the Drina Valley in August 1994, a convoy that included B Company: "When we entered the Goražde corridor and the valley that would take us up into the town, there was a surreal silence; the beauty of our surroundings caught me for a moment, masking the reality of the situation and the threat around us; it passed quickly to be replaced with excitement and anticipation."

Additionally, Patrick had been my last commanding officer before I left the Army and had, I recall, spoken kind words about me at my dining out night. It was therefore appropriate, in many ways, that conversation with Patrick would conclude my investigations and research into 1RGBW's deployment into Goražde in the late summer of 1994, following it through its six-month deployment and departure from the war-torn town in the spring of 1995.

With my thoughts focused on the pending meeting, my footsteps appeared to echo loudly on the surprisingly empty walkway. In military mode once again, I found myself subconsciously 'getting on the heel' and could hear the distant echoes of the RSM bellowing these words. As I ventured further down Whitehall, I passed Downing Street and the many statues of the bold and the great, until I was alongside the Cenotaph.

A fleeting thought registered as I looked across to the monument. The very reason I was meeting Patrick was, in no small part, due to remembrance. Remembrance of the four young men from 1RGBW that gave their lives on its operational tour (Op Grapple) in 1994–95: Privates Phillip Armstrong, Martin Dowdell, Chris Turner and Ben Hinton. Four young men, four of over 7,000 men and women of the British Armed Services that have lost their lives on operations since the end of the Second World War.*

*Since the end of the Second World War II, 7,185 UK Armed Forces personnel have died on operations in medal-earning theatres. The largest number of deaths among UK Armed Forces personnel in one Operation was the loss of 1,443 lives in Malaya between 16 June 1948 *and 31 July 1960. NATO - and United Nations - led Operations in Cyprus, the Balkans and Afghanistan are ongoing. As at 17 February 2016, thirteen UK Armed Forces personnel have died as a result of Operations in Cyprus, seventy-two the Balkans and 456 as a result of Operations in Afghanistan. (Ministry of Defence paper: UK Armed Forces Deaths: Operational deaths post World War II 3 September 1945 to 17 February 2016).*

Moments later I was showing my ID at the reception and waited for Patrick to arrive, which he did so as Big Ben rang out its eight rhymical tolls for the half hour, it was 17:30 precisely. "Maurice, my dear chap, how are you?" Patrick was as immaculately dressed as he was immaculately on time; it was good to see him.

Pleasantries done, we walked into the square beyond the reception. Patrick looked up and pointed, his arm rounding as he outlined where we were, turning almost a full circle. "This building, magnificent as it is, is the home of the Foreign and Commonwealth Office. It occupies a group of buildings which originally provided the headquarters for four separate government departments: The Foreign Office, the India Office, the Colonial Office, and the Home Office. From here the British Empire was administered and run, it is a place steeped in history and an inspiring place to work."

As an avid historian and one with a deep-rooted interest in the days of the British Empire, it was not hard to imagine the great engine of the state and its empire being run from within the walls of these awe-inspiring buildings. My thoughts were easily attuned to be able to imagine dignitaries being hustled through the corridors and to hear the echoes of chit-chattering staff as they discussed the great events that have shaped our history; the many thousands of them over the hundreds of years that have been privileged to work here.

As we strolled through the marbled and ornately carved hallways, adorned with historic events and people, set in the classical style ordered by Lord Palmerston, the Prime Minister at the time of its development, we stopped momentarily to take in a point of interest or two. Against such an enriched tapestry the fleeting moments the British Army had spent in Bosnia in the early 1990s appeared insignificant, but a stitch or two it had added, and it was these I had come to discuss.

Coffee in hand, I started by asking Patrick about his memories on taking command of the battalion and specifically the challenges in managing and leading a recently amalgamated regiment. I suggested that the amalgamation of The Gloucestershire Regiment and The Duke of Edinburgh's Royal Regiment (Berkshire and Wiltshire) had perhaps been more challenging due to the events running up to it, being the highly charged and often emotional tercentenary celebrations of The Gloucestershire Regiment, which had been undertaken in the weeks immediately before the amalgamation.

"The tercentenary celebrations and amalgamation were unfortunate in timing, being a month or so apart in spring 1994, but you could conversely say it added to the strength of the overall regimental identity. I don't feel it made it any more difficult than it could have been, we simply had to get on with it. For over four years we had been in the same brigades – 24 Airmobile Brigade and then 19 Infantry Brigade, many of the officers and senior NCOs were well known to each other, the foundations were already in place in many ways.

About eighteen months earlier I had been second-in-command of 1 DERR, before being posted on promotion to HQ Allied Rapid Reaction Corps in Germany, and with Mike Motum as my opposite number in 1 Glosters, we jointly chaired the working group for the amalgamation. Mike was an old friend from the days when he had been captain of cricket and I was vice-captain at prep school, which probably made some quite emotive discussions about 'badges, bands and dress' a bit easier! The key was forging a new identity and there was no better way to do this and to focus minds, than an operational tour. We were fully aware of the possibility of a deployment to Bosnia, as we approached the amalgamation, and were hopeful this would come to fruition to give extra impetus to the new battalion.

We were scheduled to deploy to Kenya on Exercise Grand Prix in autumn 1994 but told that there was an option to deploy us to Bosnia as Britbat 2, if required. The intensity of training when working towards such a purpose had always been a focal point in developing team identity in my experiences, be it at section, platoon, company or battalion level."

"Can you recall your thoughts after receiving confirmation of our deployment?" I asked.

"Very much so. We had been told to undertake UN pre-deployment training as a contingency and as part of this we deployed to Salisbury Plain in May 1994 for a Battalion Group exercise. As the exercise progressed, I was anticipating or rather hoping we might receive some positive news. As the days passed, the anticipation grew that a decision was imminent on whether we would, or we would not deploy. On the evening of the last day of the exercise the RSM, WO1 Ivor Wood, brought me the news. In the days before email, such communications came through via a tele-printer, direct from HQ United Kingdom Land Forces. Personally, I was exhilarated, and asked the RSM to gather the battalion in a hollow square on the parade square. An hour later, as the sun was setting over the plain, I had the battalion before me, and gave notice of our deployment to Goražde. The level of excitement was palatable from that point on and for me it was the moment that the foundations of the battalion's identity were truly cemented. I was also enormously relieved, I would have dreaded announcing we were not deploying!"

Private Ben Hinton receives the guard of honour, before his coffin is flown to Sarajevo and on to the UK

Patrick paused, then added: "It was the subsequent operational training, the preparation and the presentation of New Colours at Windsor Castle in June, the deployment to Bosnia in late August and then the dual tragedies in early September 1994 that all brought the battalion closer together."

I had meant to come on to the tragedies later but took the opportunity to do so. "It would be good to have your thoughts on the two Saxon armoured vehicle incidents, as in many ways, for many of the battalion, especially those of Goražde Force, these tragedies defined or rather have subsequently become to define the legacy of the deployment. It must have been a point where your own leadership and the leadership of those around you, was tested in an untimely and unforeseen way?"

"I can recall exactly where I was when the first accident occurred. I was with the acting RSM, WO2 Pete Tait deep into the rural area of the so called Safe Haven, known as the Goražde pocket, at OP12 with the recce platoon. The radio crackled, and I recall the tone and tempo of the voice, giving me advanced warning, be it momentarily, of the first accident. It was without doubt one of the worst moments in my life, it was also a moment when you realise the weight and responsibility of leadership, which then felt a very lonely place – as had often been alluded to in lectures at Sandhurst and the Staff College at Camberley by former commanding officers. I just knew I had to get on with it."

183

"There was of course the immediacy of the second accident a few days later on 12 September 1994," I added, "Which could have been a tipping point in confidence in the battalion's leadership, let alone an immediate loss of confidence in the Saxon itself?" Patrick explained how the inner core of his leadership team worked together at a most difficult time for all.

"Ian (Harris) was obviously at the heart of these tragedies, dealing with the impact on his company with a number of severe challenges; I offered support and compassion, but needed to give him space to lead his team in dealing with the tragedies. In effect, he had lost 10% of his company (four soldiers killed and nine injured) in the first two weeks of the deployment, and yet, he had still to deliver on the UN mission in his company's operational area. Without a doubt, his task was a really demanding one, which he handled with confidence and great professionalism. At headquarters level, the experience of the acting RSM and my second-in-command (Major Stephen Oxlade) was invaluable and the interface with the family's officer (Captain John Dineen), back in the UK, was crucial to the morale at home.

'Because of the recent amalgamation, I had a group of company commanders who were all very capable, healthily competitive and had years of operational experience. Many of my young battalion HQ staff also had recent operational experience, and I used them as a sounding board in decision-making." It was a military leadership structure, I thought, designed and tested over many years and at this time, its component parts were falling into place to deal with the tragedy of loss of life, whilst continuing to face very challenging operational situations on a daily basis.

Patrick concluded on this point: "They never failed to deliver even in the darkest moments," before continuing: "One of the most difficult decisions was the question of how to use the Saxon armoured personnel carriers, following the two fatal accidents, and minimise the risk of future ones occurring. For a time, it felt as if the weight of the world was upon my shoulders, with this key assessment and decision needing to be made quickly and based on evidence we had from our investigations. We could have stopped using Saxons in the mountains, which would have meant doing all patrols, deployments of Quick Reaction Forces and resupplies on foot, as we did not have spare Land Rovers or trucks to replace the Saxons. This would have severely limited our operational effectiveness, as a key factor was the daily risk we faced from small arms fire and occasional mortar and shellfire – nearly ninety engagements in our first 110 days in Goražde – which could be mitigated by using Saxons for appropriate tasks that did not require foot patrols. At least they offered some reasonable under-armour protection and had a very effective turret-mounted machine gun.

"In the days after the accidents, I walked and drove up and down most of the key tracks with my patrol team and Royal Engineers troop commander. Rather unusually for an infantry officer, I had studied for a degree in civil and structural engineering, which helped considerably in looking at the condition of tracks, as well as assessing the Royal Engineers' recommendations. Having consulted my company commanders, we agreed that we should continue to use the Saxons, but of course needed to consider and implement procedural changes and policies to mitigate the risk of further accidents. No doubt, there may have been a few who questioned the soundness of the decision, but the Saxons proved throughout the tour to give us an operational advantage over the warring factions."

It was clear in talking to Patrick how difficult this situation was, and how the travesty and tragedy had different impacts on many people. It also demonstrated how the privilege of leadership comes with the burden of responsibility. My own understanding and appreciation of these specific events had been given much clarity through this discussion.

Patrick did not state directly, but alluded, that with these deaths, there was a sense of waste. Lives given under fire in warfare, whilst tragic, were to some extent, to be expected. Lives lost in an unanticipated way, through an RTA for example, seemed unnecessary. This point I had spoken about in my letters home at the time and my thoughts then were like echoes carried down through the years. My research and interviews suggested the overriding feeling of the soldiers on the ground, with the years that have passed, was that such losses were not due to poor decision-making but more so to inappropriate tools, or vehicles to be specific, to do the job at hand. Many comments have been made on this point, but at its core, the Saxon was a vehicle designed to transport troops at speed down the Autobahn and across the undulating fields of the North German plains, to face the Russian threat on the Inner German Border between West and East Germany in the 1980s and not designed for use on muddied, unstable tracks high up in the Yugoslavian mountains.

In his concluding comments on this point, Patrick reflected on the lack of a padre being at his and the battalion's side at the time of the tragedies (Padre Patrick Irwin arriving a week or two later in the tour; the padre had coincidentally been at the same school and in the same house, but a year below Patrick, the CO, and they were old friends). "Such a voice and presence wasdefinitely missed," he added thoughtfully. He explained, being a Christian had helped him cope with these most difficult times on operations, particularly with the loss of such young lives. "Often those with faith find themselves leaning on it more so in adverse times. I also think, when testing circumstances arrive, those on the margins of religion often find themselves seeking support from the padre and asking the question why?" It was why, he suspected, the padre was so well received and respected by the soldiers and regarded as a key team member of the leadership team during the Bosnia tour.

Personally, I believe whilst the padre has rank (being commissioned as a captain), it is as if the padre is equally without rank. He carries authority, but assures confidentiality and objectivity, and his allegiance, as many soldiers will tell you tongue in cheek, is to a much higher command to that of the battalion, brigade or division! In barracks the padre's voice and presence are invariably found in the shadows, but when on operations the padre comes into focus and is visible. Even those beyond the margins, from what I experienced, became a little inquisitive as to the role of religion and questioned the existence of was a God, when facing their own mortality. Even being angry or disillusioned with God, as many were occasionally or permanently, suggested that there was a God to be angry with in the first place, or certainly something yet to be explained.

Patrick concluded: "The padre occupies a unique position within the leadership structure of a battalion, where the influence of this position is also defined by his

The commanding officer, Patrick Davidson-Houston briefing the media, Goražde, 1994

186

or her personality. In this context, we were particularly lucky to have Patrick Irwin amongst us", referring to Padre Patrick's uniqueness, tall physical presence and engaging personality.

On the broader subject of the tour in its entirety, we had joint experiences to share, discussing the intensity of the first 100 days and the level of significant engagements resulting in several soldiers being wounded. "What impressed me," Patrick said with obvious pride, "was the level of understanding demonstrated by the soldiers on the ground. When severely challenged they dealt robustly with hostile situations, whether returning fire or negotiating their way through illegal checkpoints. This was balanced by their level of compassion supporting the war-weary people of Goražde, regardless of their ethnic origins. I was confident that our individual and collective operational experiences from the Northern Ireland campaign, coupled with our pre-deployment training for Bosnia, would serve us well. They proved to be a strong foundation for the UN peace support operations we were to conduct under very different rules of engagement in Bosnia. The intensity of the activity was only matched by the consistent professionalism of the soldiers facing unknown circumstance and striving daily to be 'A Force for Good' – the UN Protection Force (UNPROFOR) strapline." I could only concur with this statement, bearing witness to the performance of the soldiers of B Company.

We delved further into the preciseness of the UN mandate and our own mission with it, "Our mandate was reasonably clear as far as it went, be it the facilitation of humanitarian aid or other immediately aligned activities, but less appropriate to the situation in the so called 'Safe Haven' of Goražde, that we had been deployed into as a 'protection force'. It was apparent from day one in Goražde that my leadership team and I would not be content to sit and watch the days and months pass idly by just manning the line of confrontation around the town and the rural area known as the 'pocket'. There was an unspoken calling for all of us to do what we could for the beleaguered townsfolk. My Company commanders', initially Patrick (Tomlinson), Ian (Harris), followed by Simon (Gray) and Ed (Brown), set their minds on doing everything they could reasonably do within the UN mandate to help improve the lives of the population of Goražde, who had suffered two and half years of siege and wartime austerity. This austerity was most apparent in the faces of the children who lined the streets daily, calling on our soldiers' charity."

"It appeared to me," I told my former commanding officer "a strange command as CO? Not least one third of your battalion was detached and to be found in another part of Bosnia. In Goražde, where your battalion's core resided, the daily operational effectiveness and decision making was very much devolved to your company commanders?" "That is true," Patrick said, "I would say my role as

187

War-torn Goražde shows the impact of intense artillery shelling, with the front line trench running between the houses

the commander of the UN Goražde Force was more to give direction, guide and support my company commanders as much of the activity was occurring at the company, platoon and patrol level – 'mission command'.

"My command also included a number of supporting elements from the British Army, not least a Royal Engineers troop, Royal Signals satellite communications section and logistic detachments, including for the second half of the tour a mobile bath unit! In addition, we had a Norwegian medical company with a Finnish armoured ambulance platoon, Ukrainian mechanised company and French reconnaissance detachment, so a broad international command, which posed some leadership challenges!

"As you mentioned, about a third of the battalion were elsewhere in Bosnia – our logistic base in Kiseljak with a small detachment in Sarajevo, and C Company under Major Farren Drury attached to Britbat 1 in Burgojno. Of course, I still had responsibility for the 1 RGBW rear party in the UK who were responsible for looking after our barracks, and most importantly, our families in Catterick Garrison.

"Inevitably, part of my time was dealing with UN Bosnia–Herzegovina Command (BH) in Sarajevo and HQ United Kingdom Land Forces back in the UK, who were both very supportive but nevertheless demanding. Goražde Force was not under one of the UN sector commanders, unlike other similar-sized battalion groups, but directly under the Commander BHC, Lieutenant General Sir Michael Rose, probably the UK's most experienced operational commander and highly respected by the UN troops."

Patrick added: "It would have been very easy to have got tied down in Goražde Force HQ running day-to-day operations, but I was very lucky to have a strong team in the second-in-command, initially Major Stephen Oxlade and then Major Mark Lavender, and the operations officer Captain David Brown, whom I justifiably trusted enormously. This meant that I was able to get out every day and visit all the troop locations in Goražde, normally over a three- or four-day cycle. I also made several road trips out of the Goražde Pocket through Bosnian-Serb held territory to visit other elements of 1RGBW across Bosnia and report into HQ BHC, which would take several days depending on the mood of the warring factions on their illegal checkpoints. Much time was spent in meetings with commanders and civic officials from both the Bosnian-Muslim and Bosnian-Serb sides, often in long negotiations and discussions about ceasefire violations, prisoner releases, and the evacuation of civilian sick and injured. These were often frustrating and exhausting, but when they succeeded highly rewarding. For example, facilitating for the first time in two and half years, extracting 250 critically ill and injured Bosnian-Muslims to Sarajevo for treatment. Much of this success was down to our UN civilian adviser, Graham Day, who was an old Balkans hand and former Royal Navy and Royal Canadian Navy submariner!"

It appeared that as the commanding officer with his battalion group spread across Bosnia, Patrick may have felt upon occasions, more like an experienced team manager on the sidelines, as opposed to the team captain on the pitch. This is a somewhat unfair comparison, as managers have people working for them, whereas leaders have people that follow them. To be an effective CO in peacetimes, you could possibly get away with being an effective manager, to be one on operations you would need to have both leadership and managerial capabilities. When I first met Patrick, I thought him the manager, not the leader. Time has proven me wrong, and whilst some may disagree, you cannot underestimate his pride in service, his passion for those that served with and for him and an earnest felt belief he did his best in a trying and unique deployment; one that has passed into history as a speed bump in the Army's glorious past.

"What are your overriding memories?" I asked, seeking to draw the conversation to its natural conclusion. "It was the collective ingenuity and resourcefulness

Helping the critically ill into a Saxon to be extracted to Sarajevo for treatment

of the soldiers under my command, their limitless sense of humour and ability to face the most arduous of tests, robustly when required and with compassion when the situation called for it. This was no better illustrated then by the reaction to being cut off for twenty-eight days in November/December 1994 without any supplies coming into Goražde, living off emergency ration packs and finding imaginative ways to carry on operating with very limited fuel, and the temperature in the higher patrol bases dropping to minus 20 degrees centigrade. Not one soldier complained; they all appreciated that they were still much better off than those they were seeking to protect, which was very humbling.

"In the final analysis, when we handed over our responsibilities on 2nd March 1995 and left the war-ravaged land of Bosnia–Hercegovina to return to the UK, we all felt that we had done our best in trying to protect the people in and around Goražde and Borgojno. We had in one way or another improved their lives in dire circumstances, under a less than appropriate UN mandate, with very limited resources, being cut-off from the normal military support a battalion group might expect."

Patrick paused and made a wider point, "There is no doubt in my mind that deploying to Bosnia on Operation Grapple for six months so soon after the formation of the 1st Battalion, The Royal Gloucestershire, Berkshire and Wiltshire Regiment, contributed enormously to the early success of the new Regiment".

High-level visitors to Goražde were rare with only six or seven over the six-month tour due to the often-hostile tactical situation and difficulties getting into and out of the 'Safe Haven'. One of these was General Sir Charles Guthrie, the Chief of the General Staff, who was most welcome as head of the British Army. He complimented us on our steadfastness and professionalism and on his return to London he reported that 1RGBW were the most outstanding battalion he had recently seen on operations.

"Looking back, has it, the Army, been enjoyable, a life well spent?" This was a sweeping and perhaps a little too intrusive a question to ask, "My twin brother, who is no stranger to the Army having spent seventeen years in the TA, also asked me that question recently, 'Have you enjoyed your career?'. It appeared a strange, even rhetorical question, 'Why, have you?' I asked him, 'It's a job, a profession,' he answered referring to his time in the aircraft industry, and that, I thought, is where we are different. I have thoroughly enjoyed my military career, but don't

Resourcefulness of the soldiers left a lasting impression. Here preparing for winter on OP1.

misrepresent this as enjoying every moment. There have been many high points and inevitably low points, frustrations and some doubts and failures along the way. Too often, it has been very tough on my family, but their support has been unwavering. On reflection, I feel that I have been pretty lucky in thirty-five years of service to Crown and country."

"And the high point?" I asked. His response was immediate, "The privilege of command at battalion level. To be the first commanding officer of 1RGBW on amalgamation of our very fine antecedent regiments was a huge honour, but also quite a daunting and humbling challenge. I was supported by a very strong team of officers, warrant officers, NCOs and soldiers, which is why I believe the amalgamation worked so well and our first operational tour was judged as being such a success. I recall during officer training at Sandhurst, the commandant often referring to commanding one's regiment as the high point in any military career. At that time, it was beyond my thoughts, but as I found out nearly twenty years later, he was without a doubt right!"

"To serve to lead, then Patrick?" I quipped, bringing in Sandhurst's famous motto, a paradox only truly understood by those that have marched up the steps of Old College to take the Queen's Commission. "Indeed EB, I believe we all strived 'To Serve to Lead' in the finest traditions of the British Army, not least we owed it to our soldiers."

191

The wind was fresh when I walked across Westminster Square, Patrick fading into the distance as he walked in the other direction. As Churchill looked down on me from his plinth in Parliament Square, I stopped and hailed a cab. "That," I said to myself "was a worthy conclusion to my research and investigations into Goražde, the leadership under which I served and my personal journey of rediscovery."

Newspaper cutting, winter 1994

Glosters help ease plight of Bosnians

THE MAN commanding the Glosters' mission in war-torn Bosnia says his men have made a real difference to the people of the shattered state.

Lieutenant Colonel Patrick Davidson-Houston was speaking as members of the Royal Gloucestershire, Berkshire and Wiltshire Regiment prepared to return home after their six-month humanitarian mission to the former Yugoslavia.

Soldiers, who flew out to Bosnia in August, will have about six weeks back in Britain before leaving for their next foreign posting in Cyprus.

"One thing that I feel here is that you can see some progress. You can see how you are really affecting the lives of some people here," Lt Col Davidson-Houston said.

"I feel that in a lot of Bosnia there has been a lot of success – despite what the international Press may say with talk about withdrawal and ceasefires failing.

"The fact is that if the UN was not here then things would be a lot worse than they are now.

"People would not only be dying in the fighting, but they would be dying due to exposure to the severe weather and lack of aid getting through.

"I think we go back older, wiser, more mature and inevitably I will go back with great optimism, still hopeful that there will be a solution in this country."

Members of the regiment have had to endure temperatures as low as minus 32 degrees C.

"This has been a very demanding tour," Lt Col Davidson-Houston added.

"We go back to England for six to eight weeks, of which three weeks will be leave and then I think that people really will look forward to the new challenge of going to Cyprus.

"There is the opportunity of overseas exercises from Cyprus, indeed we have got a Falkland Islands tour next year, so I think everyone is looking forward to it.

"It will be something completely different."

■ An armoured car on patrol in Bosnia. ★

■ In charge... Lt Col Patrick Davidson-Houston. ★

The Second in Command, Major Stephen Oxlade, Battalion 2IC, Goražde Force (retired Colonel)

"I was the Battalion Second-In-Command for the first three to four months of the tour and I was delighted to be asked by the author for my thoughts and personal recollections.

I was involved in the initial reccess with the commanding officer and deployed with the advance party into theatre. The first few weeks were spent with the dynamic Major Farren Drury, OC C Company, and our diligent adjutant Captain Simon Bailey in Bugojno. Our logistic base was in Kiseljak, which was very ably led by our quartermaster Captain Algy Turner. Under him and latterly the very experienced Captain Mike Godwin, his team had the hard task of resupplying

192

two separate locations – Bugojno and Goražde, which were many miles apart in opposite directions. The quartermaster's team worked tirelessly throughout the tour and his team, without which we could not function, must not be forgotten. We are in their debt.

It was there that I learnt of our Saxon accidents. I visited the injured, who were dispersed in a variety of military hospitals. To have two vehicle accidents only a few days apart and with the loss of the lives of four of our soldiers and many with injuries was a huge blow that hit the battalion hard.

I represented the commanding officer at the four funerals in the UK. Naturally there was concern about the perceived futility of their deaths by relatives and close friends at the funerals. I spent time with many groups repeatedly explaining that without our presence in Goražde, and the contribution that their loved ones had made, there would be the deaths of many thousands

Major Stephen Oxlade at peace with his pipe after another demanding day in Goražde

of men, women and children. We were the filling in the sandwich between two warring factions and were preventing genocide and further bloodshed. The battalion was conducting one of the most important peace support operations that the British Army had been involved in for many years – and it was working. Afterwards, I visited the rear party in Catterick and spoke to the wives, highlighting the exemplary work being done by their husbands and that they should be very proud of what they were achieving. I made the point on countless occasions and earnestly meant it, that many lives were being saved due to their presence.

On moving to Goražde, time was spent managing the security and day-to-day running of the camp, forming an extraction plan should it ever be required and ensuring there was sufficient logistic supplies to conduct operations. There were many excursions to see the local Muslim and Serbian battalion commanders to resolve issues that had percolated up from the companies. The very proficient Major Mark Chynoweth working alongside other agencies, developed a number of contingency plans for the extraction of the Goražde Force should we ever have to. All of them were quite risky. I laboured over the most preferred option, trying to think of everything that could go wrong and what we could do about it. The deduction was not much but it was of some comfort to know that should the worst ever happen, that there was a plan and some of it had been rehearsed in England.

Much will be said in this book about the day-to-day life for the Goražde Force. An additional reflection is of a young dentist who had arrived on a resupply convoy the previous night and was filling the tooth of a soldier in a Portakabin. There was a call for us to take to our battle positions, which was a regular occurrence when there were NATO air strikes elsewhere or a period of high tension throughout the region. The dentist, just out of training, had little option but to continue to treat soldiers in a trench for most of the day. The regular sound of firing between the adversaries was just background noise to us, as we had become used to it, but not so for the dentist, who hurriedly departed for Split that evening. A day later I received an irate phone call from her superior saying that the visiting dentist had been traumatized by the experience. You can imagine my response!

Interpreters Alisa and Haris on the steps by B Company operating HQ, Cotswold Camp

As we were in the Bosniak enclave of Goražde, and our interpreters were mainly female Muslims, although when visiting the local Serb battalion commander, they provided interpreters for us. The courage of the Muslim interpreters was humbling. When accompanying patrols near the Serbs front line, which was most of the time, they were regarded as spies by the Serbians and often loudly abused by the soldiers. There were a number occasions when they tried to capture my own interpreter, which resulted on one occasion in a robust response from my accompanying patrol, cocking their weapons to make their point.

In November the temperature plummeted and day-to-day life, especially for the townsfolk of Goražde, became tougher. Refugees flooded the town dressed in nothing but rags, looking sullen and gaunt. There was no electricity for the town and food was scarce. The hospital had their own generator but little if any fuel. I met several Médecins Sans Frontières surgeons and nurses who were working in the most horrific conditions and I greatly admired them for what they were doing.

Parts of Goražde were like pictures of towns that had been destroyed in the Second World War. Rows of shells of buildings with rubble and house debris everywhere. Walking through these parts of the town on a dark night with no moon and roads lined with the ghostly silhouettes of building hulks and rubble was an eerie experience. One heard the occasional shuffling of a passer-by but no sound other than distant firing. Chris Rea's song "The Road to Hell" was popular at the time and I remember thinking how very apt that was for Goražde.

Our resupply convoys were then prevented from reaching us by the Serbian Army. The implications of this were delays to us leaving and returning from rest and recuperation (leave), no post, no visitors, but more importantly, no fuel for our generators and vehicles. There was no fuel for vehicles to resupply the observation posts, so we used teams of donkeys to make good and where patrols successfully walked back and forth laden with supplies. This continued for some weeks and culminated in the commanding officer and the regimental sergeant major leaving on a convoy for Sarajevo, only to be detained by the Serbian Army. They were not allowed to continue their journey, and their vehicles were prevented from moving.

I visited the local Serbian Army commander and a heated discussion followed. I made him aware of the implications and we both spoke louder and louder in our native tongues, which was

Above: 14th April 1994. French UN troops await medical evacuees from Goražde at the Olympic Stadium, Sarajevo

not getting either of us anywhere. I changed tack and, through their interpreter, slowly but forcibly suggested the possibility of an NATO air strike unless I could speak to them, so I knew they were safe. I will never forget the look in the interpreter's flickering eyes, who could clearly see that the stakes were rising. After much unintelligible shouting between themselves, the radio call was eventually made, and I learnt they were all in good order.

I thanked them, saying that as second-in-command I was now promoted to the commander of Goražde Force and I was going to make the most of it. More so, that I had been waiting many years for this and now I truly thanked them for giving me this opportunity! The tension broke, there were guffaws of laughter, drinks were poured and timings and frequencies of our daily call, which lasted for as long as we wished, was brokered. Though the world was listening in on our conversation, it was refreshing to hear that those on the detained convoy were being well treated, they could keep their weapons, and all were in good heart. Confrontation isn't always the best way to achieve your aim!

Left: UN donkey delivery of rations and mail became a common sight throughout 1RGBW's six-month deployment into Goražde

There was then a sustained period of no resupply convoys getting into Goražde. Fuel was becoming critical. We needed sufficient for the generator to provide electricity for the camp, including the Royal Signals communications centre, which provided secure comminutions with our brigade headquarters and London. We had sufficient composite rations, ammunition and water, so we remained operational but diesel fuel was the issue, as it was for the whole enclave.

Vehicle fuel tanks were dipped daily to ensure each vehicle had at least half a tank of fuel, which I assessed was the minimum needed for the extraction plan. There was no heating in the camp despite the temperature being between minus 10 to minus 20 degrees Celsius at night. As the days wore on stricter measures were taken, which culminated in there being no power for anything except for the communications centre. Exercise bikes were quickly adapted so that fevered pedalling would recharge the radio batteries. At night, battalion and company operations rooms were in semi-darkness with signallers pedalling to recharge the radio batteries so they could communicate with their observation posts and to keep warm. In true soldiering spirit, the level of consequent banter aligned to this activity was memorable!

The local and county newspapers drew attention to the plight of the battalion and the impact of frustrated convoys and poor lines of supply into Goražde

Times are tough for UN in Gorazde
s Serbs restrict convoy movements

...her letter from local soldier **Private Calvin Fuller** ...news of the UN troops currently on a tour of duty ...the Bosnian city of Gorazde. They are now on ...ve rations and have no fresh food at all, he says

THE UN here in Gorazde are having a bad time of things with the Bosnian Serb Army restricting the movement of convoys into the city.

This means that we are not getting the supplies we need to do our job as well as we have been.

We are very low on diesel and so movements in our Saxons armoured personnel carriers have been reduced so we can't do as many patrols as we would like.

We are now on reserve rations and have no fresh food whatsoever.

Many members of the company, myself included, have been ill with a mystery bug.

Our rooms have no electricity or heating and none of us have permanent rooms because there aren't enough Portacabins to go round.

Mail usually comes with the convoys but because they are not getting through we have no letters to read.

Most other places in Bosnia are getting supplies but we are not even getting cigarettes – a real luxury when we can get them.

Mines are still a big threat here.

A member of our battalion was unfortunate enough to stand on one the other day, fortunately it was only a home-made one so he is being sent back to England with nothing more serious than a broken foot.

The warring factions are usually friendly towards us but we have learned not to trust them – they will chat to us one minute but think nothing of having a pot shot at us the next.

We have to stay neutral so that we can get information from both the Serbs and the Muslims through the translators who are attached to our battalion.

There's talk of an increase in fighting, a sort of last push before the winter sets in, so we have taken added precautions just to be on the safe side.

Things are definitely not peaceful over here, some people might think it is settling down because there has been less coverage on TV.

Gorazde seems to be very tense and we are all aware that the dangers here are still great.

According to the locals the snow should fall soon so we are expecting a white Christmas which should make a change to the ones in England.

e Calvin Fuller (centre) with other members of his unit ZWGS2105H94

...uller makes friends with some local youngsters in Gorazde ZWGS 2107H94

● Ready for action – Calvin Fuller in front of a Saxon armoured personnel carrier with the town of Gorazde in the background ZWGS2106H94

The Saxons were left idle with enough diesel to allow for an extraction from Goražde, but not sufficient to enable localised armoured patrols to continue within the enclave

As fuel supplies dwindled, I gave the order to close the communication centre at night to the Royal Signals detachment commander, only to be told that this was not for me to close, but only on orders from the commander in chief of the Army in London. Detailed daily fuel records were kept on my handheld Psion computer and so it was easy to extrapolate how many days of fuel we had left depending on various options. After providing these options, permission was given; HF communications were established with Brigade Headquarters 200 km away and life went on.

Our brigade commander was keen to help, and we discussed what he could do, which frankly was nothing that did not risk a serious loss of life both to us and to those who would resupply us. Fuel could be dropped in large rubber pods at night, but the town of Goražde was in a deep valley. The threat from both protagonists on either side of the valley to any aircraft, in addition to the direct threat to ourselves trying to collect the fuel pods and return to camp safely, made this option unviable. There were plans to reinforce or help extract us, but we remained operational and were in a far better state than most of the inhabitants of the township, so I declined any external offers of help. The company observation posts and patrols continued and life without electricity in Cotswold Camp and what it provided became the norm.

We tuned in to the BBC World Service and learnt that our plight in Goražde was headline news. I remember when the sky was clear seeing the contrails of the

197

Right: Private Fedrick (A Company) on duty in the back sangar, Cotswold Camp

NATO jets making a large white cross in the sky with the centre of the cross being high above our heads. The aircraft had a flight level below which they could not patrol, and though it was set quite high, it was comforting to know the aircraft were there if required. I don't think those pilots ever knew how reassuring it was to us to know they were there.

After a period of weeks, we received notice that a resupply convoy that has been held at the border was going to be allowed through the Serbian checkpoints to reach us. The convoy was cheered on arrival, we had fuel for the generators, some fresh rations and about fifty sacks of post. Many from home had heard of our plight and had written or sent small parcels just addressed to – A British Soldier, Goražde, Bosnia. There were handwritten letters wishing us well and parcels containing knitted socks or gloves and sweets. The company sergeant majors ensured those soldiers who had not received many or any letters from home had at least something to open. I learnt afterwards that many relationships were formed because of hopeful letters being sent by young women, back in the UK, to the soldiers on the front line, some of which resulted in marriages.

Below: Goražde mid-winter 1994–95, taken from OP1 looking. Its deep valley location frustrated radio linkage, leaving Goražde Force isolated when shortages demanded minimal fuel to be used for the generators to support communications

Our time in Goražde was undoubtedly a huge success and it provided the politicians of all nationalities the time to try and find a solution. To what or whom did we owe this success? We were a newly amalgamated battalion and though many individuals had served operationally before in other areas of the world, we had not fought collectively together as a cohesive unit.

The amalgamation of two proud infantry regiments worked and one of the many reasons why it did, was largely due to the detailed planning of the previous commanding officers and the then Captain (now Brigadier) James Daniel Adjutant 1 Glosters. His task was to plan the ORBAT of the new battalion by individual names, down to every private soldier, determining where in the companies of the new battalion everyone would be placed. He ensured there was an equal divide between both regiments in every section, platoon, company and an even distribution of the key posts. This success was the format that other regiments adopted who amalgamated after us. The Royal Gloucestershire, Berkshire and Wiltshire Regiment consisted of the very best from both regiments and there is no better way to bond a new unit together than to send them on an operational tour.

The pre-training had been excellent, as was the very detailed handover we had received from the Duke of Wellington's Regiment. Add to this, the indomitable spirt of the british soldier which shone through, most of whom were living in semi arctic conditions in the UN observations posts high in the hills.

It must not be forgotten that the Goražde Force in Cotswold Camp also consisted of soldiers from a forward air control team, Royal Engineers, the Royal Army Medical Corps, Royal Signals, Royal Electrical and Mechanical Engineers and the Royal Logistic Corps, as well as a Norwegian medical unit, and a small French liaison team.

We were united together in one common purpose. All of us were proud to have served in the Goražde Force.

Above: The Battalion 2IC takes on the chef's responsibilities

Left: Patrolling continued throughout the cold winter. A four man foot patrol leaves OP1 to traverse around to OP2, which occupied the Biserna ridgeline above the town

The Regimental Sergeant Major, RSM Ivor Wood (retired Major) August - December 1994

I was the last RSM of the Gloucestershire Regiment and the first of the newly formed and amalgamated battalion, 1RGBW. I changed cap badges in April 1994, oversaw the inception parade that, although a low-key affair, was an important parade as the first serious act of the RGBW. This was followed by the battalion being issued its regimental colours in June that year and then moving straight into an operational deployment in August. As part of this, I was deployed to Bosnia and was relieved in post by my successor, RSM Ian Tate, in December 1994.

Prior to RGBW, I had been a Gloster for twenty years and had the privilege of preparing the 1st Battalion and the regiment for its 300th anniversary parades, freedom marches and the final parade held in Gloucester Docks, March 1994.

As a field soldier I would consider myself up with the very best of them, but I also felt drill and the wider aspects of soldiering were as important in shaping soldiers for operations, as the grittier operational training had to take place before any battalion entered the operational theatre. I would often be heard telling those complaining about drill or other mundane tasks that take up a soldier's day, "There is more to soldiering than muddy boots", and that is as true today as it was then. The parades we did prior to deployment were as much a part of shaping the battalion as was the specific training.

From left to right: RSM Ivor Wood tucks into baked beans with the commanding officer, accompanied by Captain Jerry Collier (liaison officer), Major Mark Chynoweth, Ian Savage (liaison officer) and David Brown (operations officer)

I don't really remember deploying to Bosnia but do remember arriving in theatre. We were initially based in Bugojno, before moving to Goražde. Whilst at Bugojno, we took over an old and disused factory, which later became C Company's home for the duration for their six month tour. Planning started immediately for our first operation, which was the relief in place of The Duke of Wellington's Regiment, to allow them to make their way home to the UK. They had set up a base in an old sports stadium in Goražde, one of three Muslim enclaves in the east of the country; we were to leave C Company in Bugojno.

The main body of the battalion mounted its vehicles and drove on to Goražde, where it had been agreed we would hand over responsibilities at a Serbian checkpoint in the little town of Rogatica. There were many stories told of Rogatica that it had hosted some of the most violent scenes in the war and more recently, clashes between British soldiers and Serbs, which were to continue throughout our time whilst on UN operations in Bosnia.

Rogatica was the checkpoint at the east of the Muslim-held areas and was the gateway to Goražde and Pale, both of great interest to the Serbs for very different reasons. The Serbs took this checkpoint a good deal more seriously than we did and this was often the cause of many fist fights between our soldiers and Serb guards. Most of these were fueled by slivovitz, which was a mainstay of the Serb daily diet, but fights nevertheless. It's reassuring to know that we acquitted ourselves well and lost very little equipment, although I am aware it was the scene of a god almighty fist fight between the Serbs and DWR, as the former had tried to remove much of their personal equipment. I personally felt the Serbs had far more respect for the Union Jack than the UN or its blue beret, which became apparent once we arrived at the enclave.

Life in the sports stadium was frantic at times, but never boring. I spent most of the time out and about and when in the camp, strolling around with purpose to visit those within it. I rarely felt threatened in the camp, although we would be sniped at from the over looking Senokas mountain range, but did our best to not take any meaningful notice; the odd zing, zap here and there or a dirt spurting upwards as a bullet hit the ground near you was all there was to tell.

Life was austere, rough and ready and, as far as most were concerned, bearable. Supplies into the base, including mail, were very limited, to the point that for weeks they did not come at all. This was a deliberate ploy of the Serbs to squeeze us as much as possible without breaking the UN rules. Food became limited. Although we had mountains of composite boxed rations, fresh vegetables were non-existent and the camp itself became a dust bowl in the high summer, a mudbath in the early winter and a frozen pond mid-winter.

There were few buildings in the camp's perimeter, but those that did exist were in a bombed-out state of disrepair. A Company and the vehicle workshops were in an old bus depot within the perimeter and battalion headquarters and was used primarily for the drivers and interpreters. The core of the accommodation was flat-packed, prefabricated huts that housed between four and six soldiers. When there were not enough of these at points of high demand, canvas army tents were used. It wasn't until I was leaving in December that the Serbs let more flat-pack accommodation units into the enclave.

As the RSM, I accompanied the commanding officer everywhere. I attended meetings with him in and out of camp, visited all the locations in our area of responsibility and played the age-old role of barrack RSM when within the camp. A further responsibility of mine was to monitor and ration the fuel, particularly petrol. The primary vehicles ran on diesel and, in comparison, to diesel reserves, petrol was in abundant supply, but of little use to us. The use of vehicles daily was limited to key vehicles, being the command vehicles and their supporting escorts. We had a fuel supply once every six weeks or so, which meant the Saxons were used only for key patrols and to support the OPs. It was precarious, but manageable.

The cookhouse in action, Cotswold Camp, Goražde 1994

At one point, we were down to 50 litres of diesel per vehicle, this reserve being required to facilitate our exit from the enclave should the need arise (a Saxon's full capacity was 150 litres with a range at this capacity of 480km). The petrol was required by the SIGINT (signals) unit and was a strategic asset and important for camp morale, and the chefs who used petrol-fired burners. Whenever vehicles left the enclave they were under clear instructions to bring petrol back in on their return. For a perspective to be gained by the reader, one jerry can of petrol, 5 gallons, would last the chef for a week if managed properly. Our entire stocks fluctuated between eight to ten jerry cans at any one time. On top of this demand we had to supply and support the local hospital, which was always our priority and this is where the bulk of our petrol reserves went upon resupply.

The SIGINT was a strategic asset and needed to run their radios and charge batteries twenty-four hours per day. The companies and myself often clashed regarding the petrol they used and generally they got short shrift from me on this specific point. Imagine my disappointment when B Company smuggled in eight jerry cans of petrol, and they only declared four. Imagine my further surprise to find the B Company CQMS was running a petrol generator to power company tools to help improve their lot at the expense of the collective. I fell out with the OC B Company (Patrick Tomlinson) in a very public way over this, no one was surprised!

Other than this event and a minor disagreement with OC A Company over

202

high-octane tourism, I believe I got on well with the company commanders.

I recall the health and hygiene medical officer flying in for a two-day inspection, a visit planned to validate their existence, I imagine. It was possibly divine intervention that he went down with salmonella poisoning and stayed with us, moaning and whining every day for six weeks. No matter how much he did so, the Serbs wouldn't let his return journey happen, so we had to put up with him until heaven and earth were moved to rid ourselves of him.

Similarly speaking, a small convoy of rations and mail was delivered by a young one-pip (lieutenant) RLC officer. He'd been detained at Rogatica, abused at other checkpoints en route, only to be topped and tailed by our cook doing the same. Justifiably so, as he found that one of the containers he had managed to get through contained nothing but pineapple chunks and oyster sauce! The operations officer commandeered his containers, one of which was the air-conditioned refrigeration container (apparently there were only three in the country) and the removable beds from his trucks, which he protested that he had to take back, but needs must when in such situations and he departed lighter than he had arrived!

Conditions in the camp were austere to say the least, and showering was a luxury. The operations officer and the intelligence officer were in competition to see who would stand in the unheated shower longest, which was outside their flat-pack accommodation. It is credit to them both that they got under it to shower every day until the water ceased to flow due to ice. I can tell you, with amusement, some very odd noises came from the shower as we drew nearer to winter!

To me the pioneer section were the unsung heroes. They were tasked to help where ever they could and WO2 Johnny Yemm, the pioneer warrant officer, should have been officially commended for his outstanding efforts and tireless commitment to his duties, his ingenuity and professionalism. Alas, awards and honours were few and far between and it is a disappointment that many I considered the real champions of that tour were not recognised.

On more meaningful matters, I knew from my position of having the ear of most, that the commanding officer was not overly popular with all the men. This was a shame, as in my opinion, he was genuinely a good guy, which was reconfirmed when I met him in later life. During the tour, my relationship with him could have been better and, upon reflection, I could and should have made a greater effort to ensure this was the case.

It was a comment by the operations officer, David Brown, who would later go on to be the commanding officer himself, that shook me to the core and woke me up to the fact that my poor interaction and relationship with the CO was not lost on others. Whilst standing near the sandbag wall, a place where one generally let off steam and put the world to rights, David told me that when I had been the

RSM, 1 Glosters he thought I had been superb and the best he had experienced in his career. He followed by telling me that post-amalgamation I was probably the worst he had worked with, that had an immediate impact. It was the awakening I needed, and I certainly took his comments on board. I would like to think that my game and performance from that point improved and I did my best, as any RSM must do, to support his commanding officer. I have met up with Patrick Davidson-Houston (the CO) a couple of times since leaving the Army, notably in Afghanistan, where he was with the FCO for a period. We shared many brews and hours together, it being quickly apparent he had mellowed with time, had become warm and approachable and I similarly warmed to him greatly. Perhaps also I had mellowed with time.

I was an old Glosters and the CO was an old DERR (Duke of Edinburgh's Royal Regiment) and that mix was reflected through most of the senior management within 1 RGBW. The DERR was formed from the Berkshire and Wiltshire regiments and within their lineage they had the 99th Regiment of Foot. The 99th were famed for their turnout, whatever the conditions, hence the term "dressed to the nines". The DERR were known throughout the infantry for being a "bullshit" regiment regarding perfection and smartness; by contrast the Glosters were most certainly not! The Glosters view was that belts were used for holding trousers up and putting pouches on to carry ammunition and water, whilst the DERR view was that they were used for blousing the jacket when worn in camp and fighting equipment wasn't worn. Most soldiers deployed in full fighting gear, so their belts were part of their fighting equipment. The CO turned to me one day and noted, about a month into the tour, that the troops were not wearing their green belts when walking around the camp. I gave him my view as to the obvious, but nonetheless, he insisted that belts were to be worn. It was my role as his RSM to make good on his command.

I spoke to the CSMs of A and B Company and the SNCOs running the attachments and asked them to parade their blokes so that I could have a quick word. We generally avoided doing this as it presented a target for the drunken Serbs perched on the overlooking mountains. With all lined up and formalities done, I simply told the gathered masses that: "The wearing of green belts is an operational necessity and therefore will be worn always, when not in fighting order". That went down like a bucket of cold sick and for a while, green belts were worn (by those that had them), but within a week these belts became scarce and then the policy appeared to die a death, by its own accord. I must admit, I never wore one, as I was always dressed in fighting order or had it close to hand. I was presented with a candle holder on return to the UK, made from the tail fins of two mortar rounds brought into camp. In-between the two tail fins was a brass

204

plaque that read, in Serbo–Croat, "Green belts are an operational necessity". I use it to this day!

More on the 99th! When my replacement arrived in December, I kindly put him up in my flat-pack accommodation. A big mistake! On the first morning, it was minus many degrees inside (let alone outside), and I was in my bag with my bobble hat on. As I lay there I saw the pending RSM take out an iron (yes, he'd brought an iron with him). I watched with amusement and horror as he started to iron his clothes for the day and the handover. I couldn't believe it! The moment he hit that steam button, it was so cold, it raced to the roof and condensation soon rained down on me. For the next hour I lay in my sleeping bag with the drip, drip of the water from above. That was indeed a low moment, one amusing in hindsight, but you can guess which his parent regiment was: yes, he was the full embodiment of the 99th of Foot! Roll forward the years and now we are good mates and laugh about it now, but then, amidst the cold of Goražde, I lacked a sense of humour and was aghast at what was found before me, ironed trousers and green belts galore!

One evening, the CO heard a ruckus in the camp and asked what was going on. I casually mentioned that the Royal Engineers were hosting a strip show and that no doubt the ruckus was the blokes that had gone to watch it. With this he stood and, in his clipped and sharp way, sternly, stated, "Come with me RSM, this will end now". The CO made his way into the tent, expecting what I did not know, to indeed find a show going on. Two pair of hands came through a curtain and dancing fingers made their way along a makeshift stage, removing paper garments as lingerie they had attached to their hands. I knew this beforehand, but really wanted the CO going in blind, for full amusing impact, which indeed he found similarly amusing. There were certainly plenty of locals, both male and female, that would have been very happy to have provided a real show for the troops, but if that did happen, I never got wind of it and believe it never happened.

However, there are many other things that happened, and I have stories aplenty that could fill a book, but one final one note will be saved for when we left Goražde. I thought my time was done, only to be taken hostage along with the CO, his adjutant and CSM B Company, alongside many others from Goražde Force. En route to Sarajevo, we were surrounded by a well-armed Serb rifle company and escorted to a school playground at Ustapracha, where we were 'detained' for eight days. We listened to the BBC world news every night, being referred to as being 'detained'. It was with much joy that we raised a cheer when a news reader finally referred to us as 'hostages'. More joy, as I won the 82 Deutschmark sweepstake for accurately picking our release date and time!

By and large it was uneventful, we were well treated, knew our guards and

205

captors well by the end and pretty much had control over them rather than they over us. The Serbs liked their booze and every meeting entailed a lot of slivovitz being drunk. The CO would not touch the stuff and to his credit he made that clear to them from the outset, attending meetings with guns, knives and other items dangling from your belt, to be met by Serbs, throat-cutting henchmen, similarly dressed, as this was their currency, with a bottle in hand.

Personally, I had a good deal of respect for the Serbs that we dealt with, as they were professional, overall straight talking, if not a little ruthless and never belligerent towards us. There were exceptions and they were dealt with accordingly, but in general most meetings were cordial. Helping our cause was that the CO was a straight-talking, no-nonsense negotiator and always won the day. Well done sir! The same was not the case with all the other warring factions and I often felt that the hand that was feeding them was being bitten.

Did I enjoy it? Absolutely yes, as indeed I have for all my operational deployments, both as a soldier and as a civilian, when laterally I have worked in the security sector. Upon leaving the Army I worked throughout the Middle East and Africa and I have bumped into many folks that served with us in Goražde, including the CO as already mentioned. The feedback regarding the tour of 1RGBW has always been good, exemplary even, always positive. I have never been back to Goražde, despite having been invited to do so. Such invitations always seem to clash with other commitments. I would love to go back someday, but I fear that time may have passed".

The RSM with the Commanding Officer.

5th October 1994

Today we mastered and controlled a civilian/P.O.W. exchange. Did you see any of this on the news? What a nonsense and potential circus! There were so many fingers, hands in the pot, all with authorisation to do this, to do that, whose responsibility was x, y and z. It was hard for us to keep control and it could have been potentially full of incident, but with good military order we completed what was an exchange of people, many of which were elderly, and further accompanied by women and children.

Many of the Serbs were over 70, some 80 years of age and were therefore loaded with due care and attention into trucks and escorted out of Goražde by my Saxon and a couple of others, resplendent painted in white and blazoned with UN letters, shown boldly in black. It was a strange event, with some very aged folk bidding farewell to their homes since their birth, even hugging and offering a heart-rending parting to some of their Bosnian friends.

It was as if their tears represented the sorrowful state this once great and united nation had fallen into. They were born in Goražde before the Second World War, had lived alongside their Muslim countrymen and women for a lifetime and now were being forced in their twilight years from their homes due to their distant ethnic origin.

It was in a way a controlled and authorised ethnic cleansing, for given the choice many would have stayed. What was supposed to be an achievement felt more like a reinforcement of what this war had become to represent. These people were forced to move after 60, 70, 80 years of contentment, of having years of relative happiness in their homes, living with, and not in fear of, their neighbouring Bosnians and Muslims. They were citizens of Goražde, who had grown up and lived happily alongside each other, whatever religion or national identity. It was their sons and grandsons that had taken the country into war and it was their families that were now shepherding them into a new largely unwanted and not desirable life.

Equally, at journey's end, the images of reuniting friends were moving, but you do feel for the elderly generation and those who have been commoditised and branded by their faith or nationality. As we herded these people, shuffling them in and out of wagons, lorries and buses, there was a great sadness in the air. We called out names and numbers, to the echoes of shouting and occasional tearful or screaming children and to the sobbing old.

I sat on top of my Saxon, looking down on this frantic scene and reflected on an image I held of the days of Nazism, a black and white image as clear as day follows night in my mind. Such frantic scenes have haunted Europe since the end of World War II, as we know how sinister the final conclusions of such enforced gatherings, segregation and exchanges could be. This thought brought a new sense of purpose, as I thought how easily man can tip from civilisation into barbarism and, there below me, how saddening and frightening that life can be easily devalued. What purpose did it serve these elderly Bosnians in swapping them like cards? Their safety perhaps is now guaranteed amongst their own, but at what cost? Their homes and friends, and a lifetime and patchwork of memories attached to this town, have all been torn asunder. There was something tragic and deeply worrying about the scene unfolding below me.

I sat this evening, scribbled a poem and finished my last book. Reading and writing helps you either hide and take you away from the day-to-day, or helps you order your thoughts. Therefore, reading and more reading and these hours I will fill by reading.

I need help to fill my literary gaps and have a list of books I have set as my target to read by tour close, I enclose a cheque to cover cost. Could you possibly send me (a) Jane Austen, Sense and Sensibility (b) Emily Bronte, Wuthering Heights (c) Edgar Allan Poe, Selected Tales (d) Any Joseph Conrad, The Secret Agent. In addition 30 x 1st class stamps, stamps for the USA and Korea, envelopes and writing paper, a hot water bottle and, oh yes, Chaucer's Canterbury Tales and like The Generation Game, as teddy passes by, a SW radio ('Yacht Boy Type' 203 or 230), so I can pick up "Good morning, this is the BBC World News", white chocolate (loads) and, of course, if possible one of Mum's infamous fruit cakes (it will last the journey and age perfectly with time and the journey!

BRDO

Rattling sounds from Brdo
Are reported by OP1
Gradina capped in snow
Shadows the Serbian gun

Echoes down Gaj Valley
Are heard by OP2
The Serbian soldiers rally
To where the bullets flew

A flock of birds in trees
Are seen by OP3
Leap on winter breeze
To safer perch they flee

Soldiers freshly shaven
Report a foot patrol
Blackened hair like raven
Such men to be consoled

Rifle shots on the hour
From muddied tracks below
Distant chimes of bell tower
Soft sounds on falling snow

Bleak houses we do pass
Seen by naked eye
Where litter covers grass
Death daily multiplies

Ice paths soldiers tread
A fire report returned
Walls red with bloodshed
Emptied homes left burned

The author with Corporal
Slug Southern made
frequent visits to the Serb
forward position on Brdo.

White walled in OP hide
You hear a trooper's voice
New found mountain guide
High peaks and skies rejoice

Serbian voices left behind
Their darkest shadows past
Leaving images in the mind
Such memories born to last

Note: Brdo was a BSA position outside the 3km TEZ. It was manned by twenty to fifty soldiers with two .50 calibre HMG, one pointing down Gaj and the second down Biosoka Valley. It was infrequently visited by patrols, but their confidence was gained over the cold winter months by delivering token supplies.

7th October 1994

Dad, I have been lent a book by Sergeant Rumble (Military information SNCO for our Company), "Wilfred Owen, A Biography" by John Stallworthy (Oxford University Press 1974, reprint 1989), quite superb. Similarly, "On the Psychology of Military Incompetence" by Norman F. Dixon, both worthy of your attention.

Everything is well, except for the cold, bitter cold winds and the driving rain. I volunteered to do an extra radio stag this evening as the operations room is one of the only places that is (a) warm (b) has light (c) has semi-comfortable chairs. I will soon make the short, sharp dash to my freezing Portakabin to strip and slip into my ever-welcoming sleeping bag. Is it Thursday? I think so. One day fades into the next. I can only say with some confidence that today is October! Sunday Reveille is put back one hour, no operational reason, but will signify the end to another week. I do hope all is well in Brooklyn, love to Mum and Tess, your soldier-son in haste Maurice

TO A GLOSTER SOLDIER

Washed pastures below can be seen
Of windy fields dressed finely green
And further still Gloucester town
Bathed in mist with fields of brown

Well-shaped and joined by sandy lanes
That shimmer wet with springtime rains
Reach out to the vales and hills ahead
Whispering to tombstones of the dead

Place names and named places women knew
Lists the deceased of war for their review
Where from this seat and high place of rest
Souls of the fallen are found compressed

I see soldiers marching from every quarter
Bid farewell to wife and son and daughter
For loyalty and love for shilling and crown
Drew young men from western towns

The dreams of home in hearts did burn
An impassioned desire to live and return
Such memories are held of those that die
Across muddied fields of Europe lie

Here on ancient aged battlements
On the wind I hear soft sad repents
Listen and be humbled and fear to weep
History of shire and soldiers that sleep

The 28th! The 28th! of Cheltenham Spa
Tewkesbury and men of Gloucestershire
Was the wind the tapping of a soldier's feet
Or was it the cries of a drummer's beat?

Now listen and hear of the honours afar
Quebec, Alexandria and Quatra Bras
Then stumbling to chimes of cathedral tower
The sound of clapping hands made me cower

The 61st! The 61st! shouts the lonely crier
Bringing men to the streets across the shire
Or was it the wind or the rustling of a soldier's feet
The fading notes and echoes of the drummer's beat?

Now listen to the echoes of honours fought afar
Salamanca, Alma and heroic Chillianwallah
Now alone I lifted my feet from sodden soil
Muddied boots dragged with a soldier's toil

The Glosters! The Glosters! From the Vale of Stroud
West countrymen of Gloucestershire shall cry aloud
From French fields where eight thousand poppies grow
To ill drained trenches where their blood did flow

To Dunkirk and D-Day and the road to Mandalay
Two thousand poppy petals sadly blown away
Echoes of young men calling with a hungry thirst
Reaffirms a saddened history that tells the worst

To Korea and Imjin River famous they were led
Wearing blue beret and a citation to the dead
This harmony of whispers rang clear on the wind
Such a noble history no man can rescind

In solitude and loneliness our grief cannot afford
To allow us to forget these men forgive them Lord
For exposed I stood with wind blowing in my hair
Having scaled limestone hills from Gloucester fair

Winds took me to the lonely Beacon
With driven resolve no man to weaken
I close my eyes and hear voices of the past
Softened tones of soldier's names to last

Note: Late night duty in the operations room afforded the author time to reflect, and often his thoughts would take him back to Gloucestershire and the association he and his regiment had to the county.

12th October 1994

Six weeks today, time is slipping by. The first soldiers left four days ago for "R & R" (Rest and Recuperation), the long trip back home via Rogatica, Sarajevo, Mostar, Split and finally on to Birmingham. Although all were pleased to be leaving, when they return in two weeks it will be a long haul to the end of the tour in March. I am fortunate, although saddened to be missing Christmas and New Year, as I have it the right way around. By the time I have flown home, enjoyed my leave and returned to Split and back to Goražde, it will only be five weeks to tour end.

The strain on those that are married is obvious, accentuated by the lack of convoys in/out and therefore the lack of mail and contact with family. No doubt this is mirrored at home, where the postman is probably welcomed each morning with a hopeful smile. What makes it harder is the short-lived weekly 10-minute phone call, often delayed and framed by staccato, satellite conversions and hurried goodbyes at 9 minutes 57, 58, 59, 60 seconds. You see the boys waiting patiently, watching the time anxiously, as it draws to their time, then a soft and polite tap on the window hurries the occupant into their goodbyes and then it's one man out and one man in.

I look at my Company Commander, Patrick, two years married, and he has just had his first child. During those two years, he has completed a six-month unaccompanied tour in Northern Ireland and now six months in Bosnia. His child was christened 7 days before he flew to Bosnia. You then account for the days out of bed and away from home in the training that leads up to an operational deployment and you can see how personal relationships are continuously under stress in the armed services. In this context I feel positively relieved that I am a single man at this moment, as I am too much an emotional soul to cope with such distant heartfelt distractions.

The weather, which I previously reported to be apparently racing towards winter, has taken a turn for the better. We are told our initial two-week cold patch was a cold front and the temperature will be milder until mid-November. "Milder" is used as a relative term as the daytime temperatures are reminiscent of a sunny spring day in the Cotswolds, but the clear skies give way to bitterly cold evenings, nights and early mornings. Warmed by the good and faithful army sleeping bag, it is the first challenge each day to peel yourself from its warmth and face the chilled air of the day. The boys agree it is more warming and comforting to be in an OP than in one of the Portacabins and portable fridges in camp. It does breed a quickness in step from bed to washing area to wash and dressed. I'm in/out in approximately six minutes, shaved and on route to work (12 yards away!).

My fitness campaign has continued with enthusiasm. Accompanying my almost daily patrols, I am also running four miles a day. The gates open at 1600 hours. The course takes you into town, through crowds of rag-tag men and women and ever hopeful kids shouting "bon, bon mister, bon, bon". Navigating yourself through the crowds, you drop down to the third bridge, known as Bridge Charlie, skip through its marked minefield and back along the banks of the River Drina. After the run, which acts as little more than a warm-up, I visit the Colour Sergeant's new creation, his gymnasium.

Dispel any images of modern day racquet centres or gymnasiums. Our gym consists of weights made from parts taken from cars, lorries etc., taken from the local scrap heap. Benches for sit-ups, with the cushions taken from a deserted bus outside camp and two body length mirrors "borrowed" from a derelict house. Crude but effective. There is a rustic charm about our gymnasium.

August had rounded my physique, but six weeks here with a conscious effort to eat no puddings, drink no beer (2 ciders/2 Boddingtons to date) and limit chocolate intake, has seen a trimming ½ stone and a welcomed reduction to the waist. My feet, rarely seen this year, have made a return to the front seats and can be seen every day! While on the subject, could you please get hold of two London Marathon entry forms for me. You can get them from some sports shops, alternatively you can ring their office in London (Nutra-Sweet London Marathon). I'm hatching a plan to run a marathon here on Christmas Day, for Sight Savers and hope to get the Commanding Officer to support it. If my training continues a pace, I should comfortably beat my best time of 2 hours 54 minutes.

I have also enclosed a few poorly written poems, scribbled in the silent hours when all is quiet and the crackling on the radio dies to nothing, bar the occasional weather report, sporadic firing incident or radio check. I am of mixed opinion as to their quality or lack of quality, to be honest. They are more poetry attempts (and poor ones at that) as opposed to being poetry in quality!

(a) The Politics of Peace Keeping

(b) Eroded History

(c) Footsteps of a Soldier

(d) Sentry on Samari

Lastly, my dog. How is she? What a champion decision to rescue her from Battersea. Remember to groom her and take no nonsense, as she will have you under her spell shortly, as she held the whole battalion in Catterick Garrison. She is adorable, as I hope Mum is finding with the passage of time and through gritted teeth ("I knew we'd end up looking after your dog!").

Note: The Gloucestershire Regiment was founded on 5th March 1694 as the 28th Foot (North Gloucestershire). The 61st Foot (South Gloucestershire) was founded in 1756. In 1881 they became The 1st and 2nd Battalions The Gloucestershire Regiment. After celebrating their Tercentenary in 1994 the Regiment were amalgamated with The Duke of Edinburgh s Royal Regiment (Berkshire and Wiltshire) on 27th April 1994 to form The Royal Gloucestershire, Berkshire and Wiltshire Regiment.

The badges of the conflict, as collected by Major Simon Gray

215

"A back-against-the-wall attitude; it was all about survival."

CHAPTER 10

THE RIFLE COMPANIES AND THEIR COMMANDERS

"My Company commanders, initially Patrick Tomlinson and Ian Harris, followed by Simon Gray and Ed Brown, set their minds on doing everything they could reasonably do within the UN mandate to help improve the lives of the population of Goražde."

(Brigadier Patrick Davidson-Houston reflecting on the role played by his company commanders in 2017)

The end of tour battalion newsletter

At the end of each tour the battalion would produce a newsletter, offering a light-hearted insight into what had happened. Although there was always a serious undertone, its distribution was for the members of the battalion and their immediate families. The following are the key extracts taken directly and unchanged from A and B Company's end of tour notes.

A Company Group 1 RGBW on Operation Grapple by Lieutenant Simon Ross

Having managed to fit Op Grapple training in among all the other commitments, following formation, it was with something approaching relief that A Company donned their pale blue berets and boarded the transport to RAF Brize Norton in late August 1994. The Company left tearful, cheque-book waving wives and girlfriends behind to bravely 'soldier on'. The Company flew to Split with Excalibur Airline, and the stewardesses gave as good as they got from the soldiers all the way.

Right: WO2 (CSM A Company) Sumner and Major IVK Harris on board a Saxon, December 1994 Goražde

Below: Goražde's children

On arrival in sunny Split the general feeling was, 'if this is peace-keeping, I can get used to it!'. All too soon, baggage was being loaded and the Company boarded its 'economy class' transport for the long and bumpy journey to Goražde, stopping briefly at Kiseljak, or Bugonjo, and for some an 'overnighter' at Rogatica.

On arrival at the then unnamed 'Cotswold Camp' (did RSM Wood really get a free Gortex jacket for this free advertising?), the Company was quickly thrust into the business of handover/takeover with the deeply suntanned and happily smiling men of Corunna Company, 1 DWR.

Our knowledge of Goražde on arrival was minimal, apart from the few shots of the town seen on television back in April 1994. First impressions were of a community cut off from the outside world and exposed to extensive fighting. The street scenes were somehow like those of an OBUA [Operations in Built Up Areas] village, the only difference was that 60,000 people were still living there. All windows had been blown out and all houses were covered with small arms and tank round strike marks. Several were completely gutted (signs of ethnic cleansing?), some had partially collapsed or were weakened by fire, but in a clear majority of homes the owners remained, continuing to live as best they could amidst their meagre possessions. Those homes not occupied were either too close to the BSA frontline or had been destroyed by the fire. Some 30,000 refugees sought shelter in any 'container' to which they could fashion a roof.

It was against this backdrop that A Company moved into Cotswold Camp beside the River Drina, centring themselves on a derelict bus station. The soldiers were housed in Portacabins. Meals were shared with wasps and everybody soon lost weight through a combination of hot, humid temperatures and the local drinking water (the 'Drina Diet'). Almost everybody was affected with 'Drina Bottom' to some degree or other.

Fortification and building robust Ops was a key task on arrival. This provided protection against armed attacks and helped to get the soldiers through the bitterly cold Yugoslavian winter.

Extensive foot patrols of the Company AOR quickly built a clear picture of the warring factions' strengths and dispositions. It also gave us a chance to appreciate the strength of the BSA positions from the Senokos Feature, which rose 600m above the camp and Goražde. The upper slopes of Senokos were covered with oak and pine woods, whilst the lower ones by fields and plum orchards. The locals made plum brandy or 'slivo' out of these plums. The River Drina runs through the town and was both the inter-company boundary and sewer system.

The Company was tasked with liaison between the warring factions, manning of six Ops, as well as patrolling the areas between and along the warring factions' front lines. Access to these Ops was from the valley bottom up steep and narrow tracks. Two of these Ops, eight and nine, were only accessible along particularly narrow tracks which clung to the steep hillside. It was on these tracks that the worst accidents of the tour took place. On Friday 9th September 1994, only five days after taking command, Corporal Stacey's Saxon slipped off the track after the surface collapsed. The vehicle rolled on its side for about 300m down the hillside. A wood cutting party in the area, commanded by Colour Sergeant Apperley, was soon on the scene. Due to the severity of his injuries, Private Ben Hinton was killed in the accident. Only three days later, another Saxon rolled off another track near OP 8. Again, reactions by all involved were swift, but tragically Privates Martin Dowdell, Christopher Turner and Phillip Armstrong died. All are commemorated by memorials, the former at OP 9 and the other in a Factory

Valley, by the hillside where the second vehicle came to rest. Nine other soldiers were injured in the accidents but are making steady recoveries. The Company soldiers rallied around each other and despite the great loss, pushed on with the job in hand.

The destruction of most of the houses of Goražde during the siege left thousands living in desperate conditions and relying on harvesting wood from the surrounding mountains to keep warm, cook and wash.

The situation between the warring factions was extremely tense. The BSA positions, on the Senokos, the Biserna and Pargani Hills, overlooked Goražde. From Senokos, the BSA soldiers had clear line of sight from their trenches into the centre of Goražde. Five of the Company Ops had regular liaison with the BSA. OP 7 was located on the BSA front line and had a good neighbourly relationship; the nearest BSA position was only 50m away. The BSA were friendly towards A Company soldiers. They could afford to be, they were in the strongest positions and A Company patrols were regularly given a cigarette and a cup of the local coffee when they stopped at BSA positions. This did not stop the Serbs occasionally targeting UN patrols. A Company patrols deployed with blue berets and small flags, 'hard to distinguish from BiH soldiers at ranges above a few hundred metres' so the BSA said. However, in several of the contacts there could be no question that it was an A Company patrol. On one occasion the QRF were visiting a BiH strong point when the BSA fired three rounds. The first struck Sergeant Lewis' SUSAT, grazing his leg. The second landed close to the QRF Saxon and the third passed through the material of Private Temme's trousers, having arrived with the OC to give assistance. There could be no mistake about UNPROFOR being directly targeted, since there were two white UN vehicles in the immediate area.

These incidents demonstrated two points. Firstly, A Company were lucky to escape without casualties in these shooting incidents. Between September and January there were a total of seventeen shooting incidents involving A Company soldiers. On many occasions patrols escaped injury by only a few centimetres. Secondly, unless in a major contact, rounds were not returned. Returning fire, in many circumstances, would only have escalated the problem, increasing the risk to the patrols and threatening the fragile peace. Indeed, A Company soldiers might have been increasingly targeted and drawn into the fight. On most of the contacts the safest and easiest option was to withdraw out of the contact point and continue with the tasking.

220

In one incident, covering fire and instinctive fire and movement drills were necessary to extract a patrol from a BSA contact. Lance Corporal Linker's patrol was contacted on an exposed track 200m up Factory Valley just after a vehicle drop off. The Saxon returned and gave effective fire to cover the patrol's extraction back down the track. The BSA were very apologetic following the incident and yet again an A Company patrol was lucky to have escaped without any casualties.

The Bosnian Muslim Army (BiH) did not generally target UNPROFOR soldiers.

Major IVK Harris above Goražde, A Company sector

However, on one occasion, a soldier stepped on and detonated an improvised anti-personnel mine laid by the BiH without notice to UNPROFOR. The EOD had previously cleared an emergency evacuation route from OP 9 down the Factory Valley through BiH front lines. Lt Ross was commanding a foot patrol to mark this route, which had been cleared 48 hours earlier. Moving up to a natural choke point the lead man, Private Evans 34, detonated the mine, breaking his foot. Thankfully he was not wounded too severely and has made a complete recovery.

Relations with both warring factions varied considerably, one moment they were your best friends and the next they would refuse to talk or allow foot or vehicle movement due to 'orders from above'. This made a difficult job all the more frustrating and on many occasions, it was a case of counting to ten very slowly and starting again – Balkan hospitality!

The Ops A Company took over were designed for summer. Consequently, our priority was the winterisation of these locations, in order that soldiers could continue to work in the expected winter conditions of -20 degrees and several feet of snow. The soldiers of A Company soon became overnight do-it-yourself experts, having weatherproofed all company locations. Much thought and effort went into this work, indeed any visiting DWR soldier would be hard pressed to recognise the place he left in September. Along with the nuts and bolts of conversion work on the OPs, the camp also became more comfortable. A Company soon boasted the Tropicana Club, which doubled as a briefing room and a tastefully decorated TV room. You could not turn a corner without seeing someone sawing or chopping wood to feed the wood burning fires, these being the only source of heating for the OPs and camp alike. The job of winterisation was a logistical battle and much initiative and imagination was displayed prior to the arrival of the snow towards

Lieutenants Mark Spandler and Simon Ross on patrol mid-winter, A Company sector

the end of December. The Company worked against the backdrop of fuel shortages and increasing restrictions on its freedom of movement, imposed by both warring factions. These combined to make conditions spartan throughout Goražde Force.

January and February saw heavy snowfalls and freezing temperatures. Consequently, vehicle movement became almost impossible. At one point the Company employed the services of a mule-jockey and his cart to resupply the OPs. January also saw a gradual decrease in firing incidents as Cessation of Hostilities Agreement took hold. With this the Company prepared to redeploy into other areas to widen its monitoring tasks.

As the tour came to an end everyone in the Company looked forward to the sun of Cyprus and was able to take great satisfaction in the fact that the West Bank of Goražde was a quieter and more peaceful area than it had been on their arrival.

Oh! One final point – Corporal Boyd looks forward to Wales 2010, as the Welsh rugby team commence genetic experiments to compete with the mentally and physically stronger Englishmen!

When there was spare fuel, some was allocated to wood cutting, which made light work of the task compared to logging and sawing by hand when fuel was sparse

222

Left: A Company, Operation Grapple

Below Left: A Company Nominal Roll, ORBAT 25/08/1994

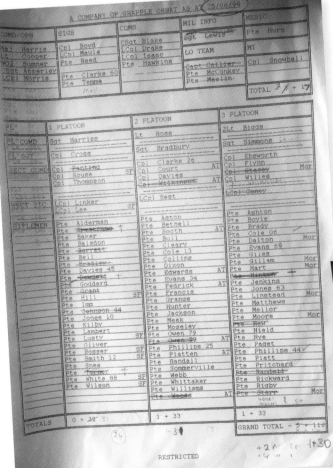

Pte Bishop L/Cpl Beetson Pte Hawkins Pte Cull Pte Lyons L/Cpl Morris Pte Loach
Pte Brown L/Cpl Drake L/Cpl Maule L/Cpl Isaac Cpl Taylor Pte Clarke 60 Pte Parkin
Cpl Snowball Sgt Chimiczewski WO2 Sumner (CSM) Maj Harris (OC) Lt Muspratt ("IC) CSGT Blake (CQMS) Cpl Boyd

Above: A Company, Headquarters

Below: A Company 1 Platoon

Pte Lowe Pte Mann Pte Balsdon Pte Dowdell Pte Barrett Pte Snee Pte Goddard Pte Kilby Pte Alderman
Pte Grant Pte Armstrong Pte Oliver Pte Johnson Pte Lake Pte Pedley Pte Imm Pte Jones 10 Pte Collister Pte Davies Pte Bell
Cpl Cross Cpl Thompson Sgt Harris 72 2Lt Spandler Cpl Hart L/Cpl Shepherd L/Cpl Linker

1st Battalion The Royal Gloucestershire, Berkshire And Wiltshire Regiment
2 Platoon A Company
27 April 1994

1st Battalion The Royal Gloucestershire, Berkshire And Wiltshire Regiment
3 Platoon A Company
27 April 1994

Pte Williams Pte Somerville Pte Grange Pte Randall 14 Pte Reed Pte Jackson Pte Aston Pte Clearly Pte Jennings Pte Moseley Pte Bethhell
Pte Webb Pte McConkon Pte Dutton Pte Phillips Pte Whittaker Pte Bruton Pte Dixon Pte Hunter Pte Cole 13 Pte Owen Pte Meek
L/Cpl Clarke 28 L/Cpl Barley Cpl Davies 64 Lt Ross Sgt Bradbury L/Cpl Best L/Cpl Ash

Pte Jameson Pte Phillips Pte Hinton Pte Evans Pte Garlick Pte Jenkins Pte Mellor Pte Brady
Pte New Pte Matthews Pte Nye Pte Murphy Pte Jones 93 Pte Rigby Pte Pritchard Pte Neild
Pte Cole Cpl Franklin Cpl Ebsworth Sgt Keating Cpl Sayer L/Cpl Coney L/Cpl Blackmore

Above left: A Company 2 Platoon

Above right: A Company 3 Platoon

Looking back, my personal musings. Goražde Force, 1RGBW A Company Commander (August 1994 - December 1994) Major I V K Harris (retired Colonel).

I was asked by the author of this book to contribute some personal thoughts on my experiences of commanding A Company 1 RGBW in Goražde in 1994, and to put them in context of my wider Army career. I was delighted to do so.

My initial years as a young officer in the Glosters in the very early 1980s in Germany during the Cold War saw endless military exercises and training for the Third World War, punctuated by plenty of adventurous training and sport. We experienced a comfortable standard of living, even on exercise. I recall there were only occasional disruptions, including the restrictions imposed on military fuel and training ammunition due to the Government's defence moratorium in 1980–81.

Throughout my postings to Northern Ireland, with the Glosters and The Light Infantry in the 1980s, the RGBW in the 1990s and commanding a Royal Irish battalion in the early 2000s, I experienced the extraordinary complexities of soldiering and the demands placed upon our soldiers and leaders: the rules of engagement, the potential immediate

Left: Lieutenant Mark Spandler (middle), A Company. The group of lieutenants had all graduated from The Royal Military Academy within the last twelve months and were set real-time leadership challenges that the Academy had prepared them for. They proved to be a competent and popular group of young officers.

Major Ian Harris in discussion with Serbs in the A Company sector

strategic impact of an individual's actions; the long hours of boredom; the watching and monitoring of the 'pattern of life' from observation posts. All have their parallels with Goražde.

My deployment to Afghanistan in 2011–2 highlighted to me how sophisticated and technical our operations had become: the use of advanced technologies; the almost guaranteed resupply of logistics and the delivery of air-delivered weapons; superb and timely medical support with helicopter casevac; the coordination of multiple intelligence and information collecting assets and the fast and timely delivery of the associated data to the soldier on the ground. All so very different from Goražde in 1994.

In my view, it was the collective effect of so many new challenges and unusual circumstances that makes the Goražde 1994 tour unique. Some low-level tactical examples of this extraordinary operation include:

The placing of our Saxon armoured vehicles (equipped with a coaxial machine gun) in areas of civilian population to prevent Serb snipers from targeting children; an extremely unreliable and unpredictable resupply route, resulting in a frequent lack of rations and mail, due to the 'hijacking' of supplies by the Serbs; the moral dilemma of having to decide whether UNHCR heating and cooking stoves being brought in for the desperately exposed and vulnerable civilian refugees, whom we were protecting, should be taken by us for our exposed, freezing and rudimentary observation posts up on the snow clad hills; the initial lack of winter clothing; the almost medieval existence imposed on our soldiers – including the need for them to collect firewood using homemade improvised trolleys constructed from scavenged materials, whilst swathed in blankets as protection

225

Right above and below: A Company hearts and minds with the children in their sector

against the cold; the closeness of our remote observation posts to the opposing front lines of the Serbs and the Muslims – at times, less than ten yards; the use of mules for resupply; our casualties being evacuated by helicopter subjected to enforced inspection by the Serbs due to the Serbian suspicions that we might be smuggling Muslim refugees out of the enclave; the Serbs holding our soldiers on leave convoys for hours or days whilst en route to Sarajevo; the frequent 'confiscation' of personal items during these same convoys; controlling the rats and mice; the attached Norwegian Army medical team shooting the starving stray dogs and cats to avoid the spread of disease; the conversion of gym cycling machines to enable the charging of our military radio batteries; the paddle wheels made from old washing machine motors placed in the nearby fast-flowing River Drina to generate modest levels of electricity; the making of a mortar and artillery troop shelter from the vehicle inspection pit in the coach garage in which we were based; the unreliable satellite communications during the weekly call home; the locals' homemade plum brandy – slivovitz, and its generous provision to us during our rural patrols around the hills; the knowledge that General Mladic was visiting the area observing us and directing his local Serb Commanders to be more ruthless and less accommodating towards us.

Below: Ablutions and showering facilities were at best rudimentary

In addition to these unusual and unfamiliar challenges, we should not forget that the battalion had been formed only four months previously on the amalgamation of the Glosters and the DERR. This brought additional dimensions to the command and leadership teams, both in training and deployment.

Right: A Company checklist card, carried always

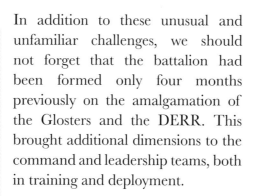

UN CHECK LIST

A COY 1 RGBW

ALL COMMANDERS MUST:

Have - **KNOWLEDGE**
BRIEF - Their Teams
CHECK - Their Teams

EVERY PATROL/TASK - REMEMBER!

BATTLE PROCEDURE - (Wng O)
TASK DETAILS - (What is ME?)
MIL INFO - (What is new?)
ACTIONS ON - (Mines, Sniper, VCP, Arty, Cas, Lost, etc - Has every man been briefed?)
COMMS - (Radios Working? - C/S's known?)
VEHICLE - (First Parade, POL, etc.)
FIRST AID - (Kit Complete? - Location?)
MAPS - (Safe routes - Cleared routes)
WEAPON/ROE - State

REMEMBER BE:

PROFESSIONAL
ROBUST
IMPARTIAL

Since 1994, I have revisited Goražde many times – during NATO (IFOR and SFOR) operations in 1995–96, during EU operations in 2004–05 and in 2012. In 2012, I travelled with twelve fellow veterans, who had served in Bosnia in 1RGBW during 1994-95, including some whom had been injured. We took with us the original 1994 memorials commemorating the losses of Privates Philip Armstrong, Martin Dowdell, Ben Hinton, and Chris Turner. These memorials, along with other Regiments' memorials from around Bosnia, had been removed and returned to the UK because of an Army-wide decision in 2007. On this trip, we replaced these memorials at their two original locations at the sites of the September 1994 incidents. A service of dedication took place at each site conducted by Rev Patrick Irwin, our 1994 Goražde Padre, and Rev Andy Grant, a veteran RGBW soldier, who had been injured in one of the incidents. The

Above: Children of Goražde were ever-present throughout the daily duties of the soldiers as they patrolled through the streets of Goražde

visit and return of the memorials would not have been possible without significant help from the local community and the local Bosnian Muslim Army veterans. These were well represented at the services, along with the British Ambassador and his team from the British Embassy in Sarajevo.

Looking back, what can I conclude and take forward? I will always remember our soldiers, their resourcefulness, loyalty, fierce sense of comradeship and teamwork, their sense of humour and their ability to deliver despite all the challenges and often against all the odds. I also remember those who paid the ultimate price and those who were injured, including those still suffering today.

I am pleased that this book is highlighting the extraordinary role of the battalion during its Goražde tour. The positive contribution made by 1RGBW to the UNPROFOR mission in 1994–95 in Goražde should not be underestimated. Despite the widely recorded and perceived faults of the wider UNPROFOR mission and mandate, and the many awful tragedies throughout the conflict including Srebrenica, the soldiers of Goražde Force should hold their heads high at a job well done under extraordinarily testing circumstances.

Padre Patrick Irwin, Ian Harris, the Reverend Andrew Grant and Maurice Evlyn-Bufton above Goražde during the Old Comrade return visit in 2012

Major Ed Brown MBE (Retired Brigadier) Goražde Force 1RGBW
A Company Commander (December 1994 - March 1995).

I joined the tour midway through and came from an appointment as SO2 DS
at the Junior Division of the Staff College. It was during my second year there
that my former Battalion, 1 Glosters amalgamated with 1 DERR and formed 1
RGBW. I was short-toured in that appointment to re-join the Battalion, which
had recently amalgamated. I was desperate not to be 'left out' and thankfully the
Commandant of JDSC, Mark Elcomb LI sympathised and assisted, when at one
stage it appeared that mid-tour changeovers of key appointments were not going
to be allowed.

A great friend of mine was Operations Officer of 1 RGBW (David Brown)
and strongly encouraged the Commanding Officer at the time also. The CO
was from the DERR and did not know me, so David's input was timely and
important. I had completed by this stage two tours in Northern Ireland (one
as COP Commander and one as OC Support Company) and a UN tour with
UNFICYP (no real assistance or great preparation for a UN role, although I did
have a blue beret, which had already been shaped!)

A Company, which I took over, had had a torrid time in the early part of the
tour and had had four soldiers killed in two appalling accidents, where tracks gave
way under the weight of the Saxon armoured vehicles. Several wounded soldiers
were also evacuated to the UK.

As requested by the author, here are some random events and thoughts on the
tour from my perspective and in random order also:

In the first few days of my tour, I was taken by the Serb liaison officer (Captain
Ian Savage) to meet the Serbian commander, who commanded the encircling
forces. He was ex Yugoslavian Regular Army (a colonel I think) and was physically
small, rotund and I immediately did not trust him. Conversely, his 2IC was an
ex international basketball player and was a real character and a large physical
presence, who spoke excellent English.

On that visit we were to discuss a shooting incident and Ian told me that he
was going to read the commander the riot act. We met the commander in his
office and Ian began to berate him over the act and threatened him with a robust
response from our soldiers (likely, but against a force which had both artillery
and armour one thought was probably not taken seriously) and then airstrikes
(the challenge in us securing such support was minimal and therefore probably
highly unlikely). The two Serbs patronised us with listening and nodding, but
everyone in the room understood fully that we were in a difficult if not impossible
situation, being surrounded by a much more powerful force who could snuff us out

at whim, especially so that reinforcements for us were a long way away and not able to deploy in sufficient force or in time. I quickly realised the difficulty of our position and the challenge of our ROE (Rules of Engagement).

Some few weeks later, over the Christmas period, we were invited to have a meal at the Serb HQ. I attended with a few members of the Company, including CSM Chris Sumner; an excellent man who was steady and calm. A great feast had been laid on and there was much slivovitz, music and jollity. The lack of proper electricity, either

Serb soldiers adjacent to OP7

in Goražde or elsewhere, allowed slivovitz (which is utterly filthy and very potent) to be poured with apparent abandon on the floors. I can honestly say that in my whole time, the furthest it ever got was the tip of my tongue and that was enough!

The evening was very jolly, and everyone relaxed, and the Serbs became completely drunk and rowdy. As the evening came to an end and we were about to leave, the Serb 2IC and one or two others drew their pistols and I looked at CSM Sumner, both of us thinking we were about to be taken hostage or involved in some form of Mexican standoff, as such we both reached for our weapons. Our concerns were quickly allayed. Whilst singing at the top of their voices, the users proceeded to fire their pistols into the ceiling in celebration. We beat a hasty retreat and left them to their party. The powers of slivovitz had been proven!

Daily I tried to get to at least to two or three of the OPs under my command and to visit the soldiers on the ground. Mostly, this was done in our Land Rover, but sometimes we patrolled with our HQ Team; CSM Sumner, the Read brothers (60 and 67) and Private Temme, who later left to become a policeman in Bristol.

We decided to walk from the Camp out to the east and then up the ridge to one of the OPs. We carried day sacks with two UN flags attached. We informed Sergeant Danny Simmonds (OP Commander) that we were on the way up and started to cross a large field. We were suddenly fired upon by a medium machine gun from the ridge and thankfully were able to run forward to take cover beside a raised earthen bank. We made ready and prepared. The boys wanted to return fire, but our OP was on the same ridgeline and on hearing the MG they had already made progress down to the Serbs to get them to stop firing.

We did not return fire but waited for the OP to tell us that the Serbs had stopped. We then withdrew back across the field feeling extremely exposed and made our

OP5

way up the side of the field in cover to the OP and then down to the Serbs to remonstrate with them. The Serbs, who I think had all been drinking, made great show of being very apologetic and gave me an AK47 bayonet as a present (which I still have). It was clear that they knew exactly what they had done but were bored and probably just having fun at our expense. We tabbed back to the town to the town hall to find several of the boys assisting in preparing entertainment for a children's Christmas party. I remember Private Fedrick (whose father had been RSM DERR) singing a solo to these kids and thinking how incongruous this tour was; one minute taking cover from a hail of lethal bullets and now sitting listening to soldiers singing carols to children. The joys of interposing between opposing forces with a UN beret!

Boredom was a great threat to soldiers of every nationality; ours, Serbs and Bosnians. On one occasion, we received a call on the radio that one of the OP Commanders (Corporal Darren Coney) had been down visiting the Serb position and on the way back had collapsed in the snow and was not moving. We were close to the scene and rushed to the location in two Land Rovers. He was unconscious lying in the snow and the boys could not bring him around. It appeared that he had been drinking slivovitz and had drunk himself to a standstill (or this was my immediate thoughts). He was medevacked back to camp. I went to visit him in

230

the hospital and was informed that he had been fed Morphine in his slivovitz and that they had given him an overdose; he was lucky to be alive. It was then dark, but I was keen to make our way back up to the Serb position to find out who had done this and to address this most serious issue.

We drove up with all lights on and shining a light onto the Blue UN Flag. I was extremely angry, as we still did not know if Corporal Coney would see the night through and be alright come dawn. I admit I laid it on quite thickly at the Serb position and the situation became extremely tense as most of the Serb soldiers there had been drinking. Rifles were cocked by them, with us reacting in self-defence doing the same and as we did so, I gave the order to diffuse the situation and for my team to get back into the Land Rover and withdraw back to Goražde. I must similarly admit as we drove away, I could feel my head shrinking slightly into my shoulders, as we half expected a hail of shots to be delivered as we left; thankfully all passed peacefully. Thankfully also Corporal Coney made a full recovery and spent a great deal of the next few days having the mickey taken out of him for trying to short tour himself and lying down on the job!

Goražde sits in a deep valley between high mountain ridges. As there was no electricity in the town, other than that produced by the turbines in the River Drina, the main source of heating and cooking was wood-burning stoves. The smoke from these stoves and other open fires hung over the town in a dark haze. Thankfully most of the OPs that I had in my sector were on the high ground surrounding the town and driving up the Senokos to the OPs was rather like taking off from a UK airport with the towns below cloaked in mist and rain.

As we drove or walked up the hills, we would frequently and suddenly burst through a layer off fog to be taken into bright sunshine with snow-clad mountain tops appearing from the clouds in the distance. We would often sit looking down at Goražde wreathed in smoke coming from the home fires being burnt and make the most of the sun's rays before making our way back to camp. On occasions we would come across small outlying farm houses, where they would bake bread for the Bosnian soldiers manning the front line.

When offered, such mouthfuls of fresh bread were very welcomed, and the smell and taste of this fresh bread remains with me, as we would often be asked to sit, and chat and we would try and find out any information about the immediate situation. As we tried to familiarise ourselves with the whole of the sector we would make longer foot patrols into areas that were not covered by our OPs. One area called Podcovacic Dol was a high plateau high up in the mountains and we often patrolled out to the abandoned village that sat on its plateau.

We would drive to one of the most distant OPs and they would take us by Saxon to a drop-off point and we would patrol for several kilometres through thick

Right: Serbs were welcoming, although never to be trusted. Corporal Taff Davies befriending the Serbs within A Company's area of responsibility whilst on patrol

pine woods until we broke out into a large open bowl. It was a beautiful and completely silent area with an abandoned farm house in the middle. Over a period of weeks, we visited it many times and eventually established a temporary OP there. It was not one of the recognised OPs and as a result it obviously made the Serbs rather nervous since they started shooting and occasionally sniping at its location. It was extremely remote and impossible to reinforce other by than on foot and so eventually we gave up this distant

OP. The location was, however, handed over to the JCOs, General Rose's private army of SAS observers, and they continued to use it frequently.

Goražde had a small Christian Orthodox population who had always lived happily alongside their Muslim neighbours. They were mostly elderly people who had not been able or willing to leave. As the situation grew worse across the country and there were more and more incidents of trouble against them, the UN decided to mount an operation to take them out to safety. Mark Chynoweth as Head LO, was tasked with providing their liaison and I was to provide their

Below: A Company sector, below the town of Goražde is veiled in mist and hidden

security from a collection point in a school to the Serb check-point to the east of the town. The old people mustered in the school and Mark and I went down to brief them and then escort them out. We both entered the school room where they were gathered and were suddenly in the middle of a frenzied crowd of elderly people, all clearly very agitated, scared and uncertain of the future, all very sadly with their life's possessions to be carried with them. The smell of so many people who had clearly not be able to wash properly for weeks, if not months, and all confined in a small space was almost overpowering and this added to the sense of desperation.

232

As desperate as this may have been, my focus remained my soldiers. I had arrived in the Company to find one of the soldiers (Private Evans) had lost part of his heel in a mine strike whilst foot patrolling on the Senokos. He was confined to camp and the boys ragged him endlessly about his injury, giving him nicknames such as Peg, Crip, etc. He was however, being well-treated medically and enjoyed remaining with the Company. He was very much part of the operation. We received an edict that anyone who had been injured should travel out of the location to be seen by a psychiatric nurse to check for PTSD. I discussed this at length with Evans, who really did not want to go and wanted to stay where he could continue the tour and recover. After several discussions with the CO, I was overruled, and he was sent out to rear echelon. We never saw him again and he was sent back to UK. I understand PTSD and its effects, but this was a situation where I genuinely believe that the positive effect of being surrounded by his comrades in arms would have served the soldier much better than the treatment he received.

Together with us in Goražde was a detachment from Médecins Sans Frontières (MSF). At the nightly operations brief run by the CO, everyone was asked to update on their situation for the day and plans. At every brief, without fail, one of the Frenchmen in the team would brief that unfortunately they had not received any shipments of medicines, which of course impacted their ability to serve the sick, ailing and injured. This led the soldiers to referring to them as Sans Frontiere or SF, because, of course, they didn't have any medicines at all! However, the work they did was recognised and appropriately applauded by all, as they did what they could in a demanding situation and with limited resources to do so.

Similarly, and with us in Goražde, but housed in a separate location in the town centre, was a detachment of UN monitoring officers (UNMO), whose job was to monitor ceasefire violations. They were a mixture of Scandinavians and Africans mostly. They lived in the basement of a bombed-out house and some of them rarely came out from there.

One of the team, a Nigerian, started to display mental issues, and this came to such a point that their commander made the decision to have him taken out of Goražde for medical care. A Scandinavian was tasked to take the Nigerian in a Landrover to Sarajevo. Once they had gone some way down the riverside road towards Visegrád, they stopped to remove the snow chains from the Landrover. The Nigerian officer, who was obviously suffering from some sort of Schizophrenia, attacked the Scandinavian with a set of chains and tragically killed him. He then took off in the Land Rover and later crashed into the Serb checkpoint at Rogatica, running off across the fields on foot with the Serbs at the CP giving chase.

He was later apprehended and handed back to the UN. A detachment from 1 RGBW, led by Mark Lavender (Battalion 2IC) was dispatched to try and locate the body, which was found along the banks of the River Drina. It was an awful episode, especially as the Scandinavian had been one of the more proactive and very well-respected members of the UNMO detachment, was simply excellent and had been a frequent visitor to the camp. It was later reported, but not officially and unsubstantiated, that the Nigerian had been returned to Nigeria and had been executed after a trial by a military court martial.

Sometime later, one of the chefs in the cooks' detachment also went slightly mad and picked up a rifle from one of the troops and threatened to kill himself in the cookhouse. Our gallant Battalion 2IC, Mark Lavender, dispatched himself to take control of the situation and to talk the chef out of his intentions to take his own life. Word spread quickly around camp and most particularly in relation to the self-selection of the 2IC, as mediator, for he had a reputation for being tough and uncompromising and as such, expected the incident to end in either the death of the chef or the 2IC or even both! We were all greatly relieved, however, when some time later, Mark Lavender appeared at the door of the tent with rifle in hand and chef following looking a little embarrassed and meek. A brave and selfless deed by Mark that can and should be remembered.

A few closing observations looking back on the tour:

We were placed in an impossible position by the UN, but thankfully we did not face a Srebrenica-type assault in our time. I often reflect on how we would have reacted to such an appalling attack. Some years later, I worked alongside the commander of the JCO detachment in Srebrenica and he was completely traumatised by not only what he had witnessed, but also his sense of powerlessness. I am confident that we would have stood our ground and put up a determined defence of the town's people, but there would have been significant losses on our side. We were constantly trying to appear strong, resolute and determined in the face of huge odds and with little chance of any sort of sensible reinforcement; it was an extraordinary situation.

It is my observation that there is a type of soldier/NCO/officer who is entirely unsuited to complex UN peacekeeping operations. They find the restrictions, the ROE, the observing tasks, too difficult to cope with and they are not made up to adapt to such demands. This is what I learnt through observations on many tours. When entering Goražde and having commanded the COP some years earlier in 1 Glosters, I was keen to find some of them and to bring them into A Company, this I thought would add some steel and further professionalism. One JNCO was

234

one of the best soldiers in COP but proved to be just one of these unsuitable soldiers. At the time he was a disappointment to me and seemed unable to raise his energy or enthusiasm to lead his section in what were mundane and repetitive tasks, as this is where a certain type of leadership is needed. This did not make him a bad soldier, but a good one in the wrong place and I am pleased and not remotely surprised, to report that he went to Pathfinders (The Paratroopers) from the Goražde tour and then successfully to join the SAS.

The battalion returned to UK and after a few months we arms plotted to the Western Sovereign Base Area in Cyprus. Soon after we arrived, we were put through a base security exercise by our Garrison Commander. The battalion was hardened by all that it had been through in Bosnia and we did not perform very well in the exercise. We were accused of being arrogant and not taking the exercise seriously. I think he was right on both counts. However, the reputation of the CO, who eventually was promoted to command one of the Brigades in Northern Ireland, was saved by the presence of one Brigadier Arthur Denaro as DComd British Forces Cyprus, who had been part of the UNPROFOR HQ when we were in Bosnia. He knew the reputation of the battalion and became something of a mentor to it, knowing the performance on exercise in Cyprus did not reflect the battalion and its capability so well demonstrated in six long and hard months in Bosnia.

Finally, I would say and firmly believe, that the breakup of Yugoslavia and its slide into an awful ethnic war was a tragedy, but the efforts of the battalion certainly played a part in the transformation of the countries of Bosnia, Serbia and Croatia into the peaceful places that we see today. Every member of 1RGBW should take a pride in this deployment despite its many frustrations and the tragic losses we incurred".

The victorious Officer's Mess football team. From the left, rear row: Captain David Brown, Lieutenant Charlie McConachie, Major Mark Chynoweth, Major Ed Brown. Front row left to right: the author and Ian Savage

20th October 1994

October got off to a great start with the first ten days sliding past quickly and as if in a dash. The middle of the month has gradually drawn down to a go-slow, as life has found a pattern and has remained comparatively normal for the past week or so. Normal that is in context of daily expected activities and events. The daily firing incidents between the warring factions amount to over one hundred, none of these specifically targeted against UNPROFOR, but you can't trust either side and you must remain vigilant and understand we remain a possible target.

Across Central Bosnia, the BiH forces have adopted a policy of limited response in all areas as they continue to snipe, fire and feign daily attacks, thus preventing the Bosnian Serbs (BSA) from concentrating their efforts in one area, most likely Goražde, Srebrenica or Zepa.

In my opinion the political and military leaders of both factions no longer represent the feelings and opinions of their soldiers and, more importantly, their people on the ground. Having spent six to seven weeks with these people, they are weary, exhausted by the war and fearful of a return to total war and its consequences.

The soldiers of the BSA surrounding Goražde remain comparatively upbeat, relatively professional, but miss the normality of home life. They talk repetitively of wives, children and home life. They talk of the war ending but cannot articulate what it would take to get to this point. There is a creeping sense of travesty, a tragedy in waiting, as the possible calamity ahead becomes more likely or inevitable. It appears to have been accepted that war will eventually unfold once again and materialise as this interim stalemate and peace talks fail to work. What I mean by this is that amidst the fog of war and the rhetoric of politics, there appears no route forward and therefore the possibility of slipping back into war and carnage is evident.

On a morale-boosting point for us, yesterday General Rose visited Goražde, literally on a flying visit. In his operational brief to us he acknowledged and pointed to the reputation British forces have with the rest of UNPROFOR, the BSA and BiH.

In questions, the issue of convoy management and Serb intervention was bought up and was clearly resident in all our thoughts. It seems a recurring and seemingly everlasting problem. "I know, it's tough" he said. "but we must live with it, adjust to it and make best of it." What, of course, he meant [or I liked to think he did] is that it is bollocks that we are constrained and suffer humiliation due to an unworkable UN mandate. These bollocks also a recognition that the British Army should not be put in this position. His words were not said light-heartedly and there appeared a smattering of frustration coming from this very senior and accomplished soldier working with his hands tied behind his back and being dictated to by a United Nations, which appears set upon fostering a paralysis of inaction.

I have every sympathy with this view. Take, for example, the shooting of a UNHCR convoy driver just two days ago, just outside Goražde. It was being escorted by two of B Company's Saxons. The BSA claim they were fired at first and that they believed they were not UNHCR convoy trucks, despite, of course, having watched these trucks being loaded in camp with humanitarian supplies and drive out of camp.

Following an investigation of the event and the debrief from the sergeant convoy commander, it appears the BSA shooting may have been prompted by the BiH shooting over the convoy into BSA positions as they drove down the appropriately named sniper alley, along the River Drina. It appears the BiH may have been attempting to prompt a reaction from the BSA and get our convoy caught in the crossfire. Supposition, of course, but a possibility. If this is true, it shows what a thankless and impossible task it is in which we find ourselves, although I find it implausible the BiH would do this when we were escorting humanitarian aid for distribution to their people further into the enclave.

Sadly, implausibility is commonplace in Yugoslavia, where the only expected thing is the unexpected!

Saxon leading and guarding a UNHCR convoy down 'sniper alley'

The patrols deep into the Goražde pocket to deliver much-needed humanitarian aid, food and support were a welcome respite for many of the soldiers and warmly received by the inhabitants of isolated hamlets. Above a patrol takes in the sun in late September 1994 and is rewarded with finely-brewed Bosnian coffee.

21st October 1994

Austerity has set its stall at our gates, as we cannot get meaningful supplies into Goražde.

As a rifle company group, we have two days of fuel left and we are now on week three of compo rations, this is guaranteed to block you up! Of course, we can and will survive on compo rations, that is solely what they are designed to do, to keep the soldier fighting fit in testing, austere and challenging environments. The protein and calorie count has been worked out meticulously to ensure the soldier can march on a full stomach and fight with energy as the sun rises or falls!

Fuel, or lack of it, is another matter, as with our protective mobility, the Saxon, impaired, our capacity to do our job is also lessened, as is our ability to extract ourselves from Goražde if required.

The situation could be described as precarious and appears to be making little or no progress in finding a resolution. I wonder if the Prime Minister has any appreciation of the circumstance in which we now find ourselves? His daily update may or may not include us, he may not know of us, IRGBW, as he munches through his toast and marmalade, no doubt spooned from a very fine Fortnum and Mason hamper, with fresh tea soothing his delicate lips!

Naturally we will just get on with it, but I do reflect on the reality of the situation in which we have found ourselves. Here we are supporting a UN mandate and in a high-profile peacekeeping role, where you would have thought it would have been all well thought out. It is slightly alarming therefore, that we find ourselves outnumbered and surrounded by a large and relatively well-armed, battle-hardened Serbian force, a force that has a limited track record for demonstrating reason. Before it lies BRITBAT, Goražde, under-resourced, ill-equipped, inadequately armed and short of the most basic of supplies. A thin blue line of defence and purpose that is here to make this not-so-safe-haven of Goražde, safe.

On the positive side, and being very British, the weather has taken a turn for the better. Looking outside the operations room, the sunshine is bright, spirited and refreshing. The light casts long reaching shadows, and they bring a momentary peace to parts of the town and softens the hills and their valleys around us.

Yesterday I lay on a hillside alongside one of the OPs, staring upwards, into the light blue sky and beyond. I thought of Painswick Beacon and its vista over the Cotswolds and of Lilleshall Hill and its view of the plains of Shropshire and wished for home.

At such moments, I can close my eyes and see the rolling fields of Gloucestershire, its dry-stone walls and fields aplenty with sheep, cattle and roaming horses. I sat up and unrolled my map into my expectant hands. The 3km red circle on the chart, representing the Total Exclusion Zone, is slowly becoming an invisible and yet strangely tangible fence line that appears more like a line of imprisonment every day that passes.

I have found myself thinking on occasion that six months here is a futile waste of time, not for me personally or emotionally, but in relation to our stated purpose in supporting a confused and largely unsustainable mandate.

In many ways it does appear worthless, but as this thought takes hold, the thanks we receive from children, women and the elderly override it and help to nurture a feeling of purpose. I am, however, convinced of one thing: that extending my commission to be able to play my part on this tour was and will always be the right decision. A very good decision, possibly the best I have made in my topsy-turvy career and one I believe will prove itself to be a profoundly good one.

This I feel sure, this experience is something I will carry through my life and I believe, in part may well shape who I become.

Dad – it makes me understand why you refer to your service in Kenya in the 1950's as being so influential and rewarding and one that helped shape the person you have become. Not a bad influence at all and not a bad result found in you, I may say Dad!

25th October 1994

The ice cream van arrived in Goražde, Santa also and all our Christmases early in one white convoy! What presents indeed, the best and wrapped in steel, diesel! Yes, lovely cans and more cans of diesel! I shall never pass a Shell or BP garage again without full appreciation of those oh-so-lovely, full diesel pumps smiling at me!

I have no doubt after considerable UN, political and military pressure, the Serbs allowed a convoy into Goražde, or rather a fuel convoy, as food remains compo rations only, what joy!

A convoy of fuel means one other thing. One thing every man and mouse of any rank is happy to receive, MAIL! It is uplifting, astonishing the lift to morale that a letter, parcel or both can give to the "British Tommy" serving abroad. What can I say, but a tremendous and heartfelt thank you for the parcels that arrived today. I don't think I have had so many wrapped boxes and envelopes laid before me since Christmas as a small laddie in Sittingbourne, Sheriffhales, Cott Barn House or Brooklyn, thank you!

Padre Patrick and I are intending to load the donkeys tomorrow, a mule-mail convoy of two will head into the hills to distribute this bounty. Letters and parcels will be opened and a bully-beef tinned lunch will be cooked and served as soldiers catch up on home news. Some will resist the temptation to open all the chocolate and other luxuries that have been sent from England, others no doubt will have a sweet, sweet feeding frenzy!

What other news of Goražde? The bitter cold winds of a few weeks ago have been gently warmed by a late summer sun and partial cloud cover. On a long patrol today, we climbed from the village of Kazagici 500 metres to the peak of Sanac. From this vantage point you could see down the Gaj valley into the town of Goražde. The fields with recent rain have turned a wonderful, rich and verdurous green and soften the view.

Tess would love this countryside. From this high spot, the opening scene of "One Man and His Dog" could be perfectly shot. Unfortunately, in this episode it would be "One Man Missing His Dog"! How is my most loyal of hounds?

From Sanac's peak we contoured round the wood before climbing a further 700 metres to a little-known Serbian position high above. The climb was hearty exercise and I am developing elephant's lungs with this daily jaunt, feeling I could quite ably run a marathon or two this evening! As we climbed we paused momentarily below the Serb position, turning to look down the valley and canopy of the deciduous woodland below.

Since I was last here a couple of weeks ago, summer has parted and left us.

In its place the rich autumnal colours of golden browns, yellows and reds have arrived. The view was breath-taking. Autumn has lit its fire as the forest's canopy glows red and is further coloured with rusty orange and bronzed leaves, framed by the green near and in the distance and the grey-blue sky above. It reminded me of Symonds Yat and Wye Valley, more so the painting of Breinton Springs in the sitting room, where the two of you dated on hazy summer afternoons. I have mentally noted that upon my return I will walk the Wye Valley with Tess at my side.

It is now fifty days into the tour and I feel I have achieved much, allowing for limitations and restrictions imposed upon us. Half a stone lost, plenty of exercise, reading, letter writing (although a little disappointment in the return rates from certain friends) and some wonderful, if not demanding, experiences.

This is a wholesome experience and one that makes you feel complete in its passing.

Need I say, give my dog Tess a dozen pats and one for your own, Jeannie too!

Note: The Donkey Mail Service prepares for departure in Cotswold Camp

Left: The autumnal colours dominated the views throughout October

Above: Goražde and the B Company sector beyond the river, in the middle the athletics track and Cotswold Camp can be seen

Right: Cotswold Camp with the Senokos range and A Company sector rising into the distance

30th October 1994

It's Sunday the 30th October. Two months ago, today we arrived in theatre, not knowing what to expect or how long we were going to be here. When we arrived, we undertook initial operations with the threat of Clinton lifting the arms embargo on the Bosniaks and Muslims and lived with the uncertainty of the possible consequences of that potentially ill thought out policy.

The tension for the first few weeks, indeed up to when Clinton withdrew his offer of rearmament, was so strong you could almost touch it. His decision on withdrawal on this policy was to be announced on 15th October, however the day slipped by without a word on the streets or from the media. The presumption was therefore that the status quo would remain, no rearmament. From this point of interim clarity our relationship with the BSA and the Serbs and the BiH and the Muslims has steadily grown in strength, although I cannot bring myself to trust either partner and, whilst understanding their plight, I mistrust the short-term intent of both.

As I write, on the horizon we can see new tensions arising, as the BiH has undertaken offensive action in the BIMAC area and on Mount Igman, above Sarajevo. With these advances, the short-lived peace enjoyed, and the possibility of long-lasting peace have at least stuttered if not fallen.

They are, of course, within their rights to take this action, so when at the negotiation table they talk from a position of strength. It is however, a dangerous strategy, although the BiH and Bosnians have played things very well. They have won the attention and opinion of the world press and politicians and stroked the executive of the United Nations within Bosnia, enabling them to regroup, rearm, consolidate and concentrate their forces covered and behind the humanitarian mission of the United Nations. This is, of course, a simplistic view and I am sure some heavyweight politician can shoot holes in my supposition, but this is my perception and my reality. I am convinced we, the UN and aligned and supporting governments, are being played by the BiH and more so, the BSA who seeks to serve its own cause regardless.

This is not to remove or dilute the humanitarian justification for us being here in the first place, as the argument remains that if we had been given a firmer, more combative mandate, more lives may have been saved.

There is no doubt that the BSA leadership will and should be found accountable for atrocities and those responsible should feel the full international weight of The Hague Convention, but to say the BiH are entirely guiltless of any wrongdoing would be a mistake and a misrepresentation. There is evidence alone in Goražde as to Bosnian atrocities and stories of BiH sponsored executions of Serb civilians, young and old men. These executions I understand were undertaken in the school buildings earlier in the conflict and siege, and on both sides civilians, including women and children have been used as human shields. Guilt rests with both sides, but the greater burden by far with the Serbs.

At a personal level, I keep myself occupied and dedicate myself to fitness with one or two sessions a day. Although losing and having lost sufficient weight, being much fitter than on my arrival, I still feel tired, very tired, as do many of the soldiers. I believe it's the unbalanced diet, living on compo rations, lack of fresh water, drinking predominately chlorinated water, a mundane routine and living constantly with a degree of uncertainty. The hours are long but fulfilling and the Portakabin unwelcoming, where this must also be a contributing factor.

I don't want to sound as if I am not happy with my lot, I am, but it is a simple statement of fact; tiredness is catching up! Therefore, and not believing they work, but could you send me 60 days' worth of multivitamins (and iron) and vitamin C tablets, or something along these lines. Perhaps this might help? If not just mentally!

Thank you both so much for the parcels and letters that continue to bolster and hold up my morale. They are truly welcomed and more warmly used and shared with others. It sounds as if Dad is counting down to retirement in good order, a time for you both to dedicate proper time to each other. Before it arrives, I think you should list five things that you've always wanted to do, visit, see. This list should frame future journeys and adventures, although don't put Goražde on that list, one family member visiting this town will suffice!

1st November 1994 to my brother Roger

Many thanks for the letter and much appreciated chocolate, this was devoured by 0530 this morning as an early breakfast. It seemed so much easier to reach out of bed and unwrap a Toblerone than dress and crawl across the camp to the cookhouse!

It appears that Roger E-B is having an outstanding time in his new job, a renaissance is probably an appropriate term. What of you and Tina? Perhaps she will make a good man of you, if she is blind or daft or both!

As for me, I continue to train hard with two burning exercise sessions a day. My fear is that on joining Civvie Street, after such a protracted period without alcohol, little food and plenty of exercise, I will blossom like a balloon within a month. I must therefore take advantage of my newfound physical condition and mental confidence and capture some rich, blonde, short-sighted vision of perfection, committed to emotional diversity, to move us quickly into married bliss, before I capitulate to the temptations of London town, bloat, grow, blossom and turn into a doughnut, to rely solely on my character and not physique and then surely I will be left a lonely man!

In the interim I continue to patrol and lead patrols further into Serb-held territory on the Right Bank, quite exciting and hair-raising stuff, but good for the soul. Risk, after all, is a comparative term in this job and the situation I find myself. Nothing beyond saving life or protecting your comrades and soldiers is worth risking injury, and yet boredom and the desire to experiment makes me look for new adventures. I'm not wired to the moon and will keep within the boundaries of responsibility, but there is a shadow of temptation when on duty, an irresistible desire to go that one step further, to investigate and detect.

The patrols themselves are a form of tremendous exercise. From camp the surrounding hills climb to a thousand meters to the craggy peaks of Samari, Kolijevka, Vran Polok and Gradina. On these positions the Serbs wait patiently for the opportunity to finish off what they started. We usually use the Gaj valley to approach these positions. The valleys are tree-lined with oak and elm and remind me of the Forest of Dean in Gloucestershire, the county I consider my home. By the time you reach the top your legs are pleading for rest, your heart is pumping and the shirt on your back soaked from the endeavour, held tight to you by your body armour. The Serbs greet us with relaxed smiles, laughter, slivovitz and an offering of a stale cigarette, not the perfect drive through!

I hope all is well at home and Ma and Pa are enjoying the twilight years of Dad's career. You must encourage them to book/look ahead and undertake all the things they've always wanted to do. One thing being out here teaches you is that life is precious and must be lived, every moment.

9th November 1994

It can only be a few days since I wrote to you with an update from Goražde. How easy it has been to say previously "little changes in Goražde" and how easy it would be to say, "little has changed since my last letter". However, I do recall I previously expressed my concern regarding the growing sense of deterioration of the situation in Bosnia.

How do I explain this escalating tension between the warring factions without preaching? I don't believe I can, so forgive me if I sound like a pompous, opinionated history master talking to his pupils.

As you know the BiH, having rearmed and reorganised and largely supported by western nations, have been flexing their expansionist muscles throughout Bosnia. In Bihac, Bugojno, Sarajevo they have made territorial gains against the Serbs/ BSA. The Serbs, previously in the advantageous position of being better equipped, are now suffering from their principal shortcoming and disadvantage, a lack of manpower.

Consequently, the BiH attacking on so many fronts have stretched the BSA resources; this has been accentuated by the reduced mobility of the BSA because of lack of fuel, a direct result of the sanctions imposed upon them. Every BiH group of meaningful force or importance is presently involved in expansionist activity, except for "Goražde Force". It is a common belief that the BiH is executing a coordinated plan across Bosnia with the aim being to reunite the pockets of Goražde, Srebrenica and Zepa with mainland, central Bosnia. The three enclaves remain dangerously isolated and, despite the best efforts of the BiH, I fear for the poorly defended peoples of these towns.

Personally, I do not believe the BiH is capable of co-ordinating and executing such a broad-based and ambitious offensive, certainly independently. Whatever the reality, the BiH is undertaking hasty and extensive defensive preparations around Goražde. The town is obviously on a war footing and we are observers in this unfolding drama.

I can see from a BiH perspective that it would make sense to defend Goražde in the eastern part of the enclave while attacking from the west and driving towards Sarajevo. The aim being to widen the corridor and access to Sarajevo and seek to release the advantages of this unification.

The Serbs are naturally extremely concerned about this increased activity, so what's their reaction? They dig deep and build high to enhance their own defensive and offensive preparations. The BiH see this activity and take another step towards defence or military escalation within the town, leading to a spiralling in defensive activity linked to activity outside the enclave, they are most definitely on a collision course.

Amidst this bubbling pot of uncertainty, we sit with the hands of peace reaching out to both factions. They see us but decide when to hear us. We are peace keepers, but as we are here to protect innocent civilians we would be better mandated and armed as peace enforcement rather than peace keeping. We feel somewhat helpless but remain hopeful of resolution.

One of the most significant combat indicators for me is not the digging of trenches or the increase in activity, but that Samari (one of our female translators), suddenly got married two days ago. This was not a pre-prepared or rehearsed event, as it was only decided twenty-four hours beforehand. She's married a young soldier. It is reminiscent of World War One and Two, true love stories, young couples marrying in haste before he or she was sent to the front.

There is an increased sense of readiness on both sides and we sit between the two. What is our role in this situation? Morally, we could not and should not leave the town to defend itself, as I believe it is incapable of doing so. What potential cost would this incur in loss of life? Muslim, Bosniak, Serb, Orthodox, British, Christian? All sides go about their business working on the assumption that we would not stay if war returned. If we go, then what has been our role? Have we failed? We have sought to keep an equal hand of robustness and distance from each party, which allows us to play our role in keeping the peace. I believe both sides and especially the Serbs know we are resolute in our purpose and that if pushed we would defend the civilians [not the BiH] from wanton destruction. Whether we would be able to do this and the right thing is done by higher command and the UN is a different question.

Rest assured we are pre-warned, pre-armed. We are doing the right thing and it feels good to be at a moment in time when you have such purpose.

Samari on the steps before going on a routine patrol.

SENTRY ON SAMARI

Winter's cold hands cup his wind burnt face
As on each lonely peak, reaching, touching heaven's floor
God whispers on the breeze into cotton-covered ears
Starry, starry night, the crispness full and sweet
Of October, snow-topped mountains near
With soldiers, white watered sodden feet
The faint rustle of the Earth below
Anxious tapping, shuffling of the boots that move at night
The crisp clap, clap of mitten hands battling through the mists
Each timed, precious breath a cloud of human smoke
Those crystal eyes glistening in the light
With single frozen finger no man must provoke

Note: the image of the British soldier staring into the night throughout winter, the bitter cold winds and snow challenging their personal resolve, is one that most soldiers will be able to recall.

B Company Group 1RGBW on Operation Grapple by Captain Maurice Evlyn-Bufton

Within hours of returning from summer leave the decision that the 1st Battalion was going to Bosnia had been made. Army precedent dictates that when making decisions of this magnitude they allocate as little time for final preparation as possible! Consequently, thirty six hours later, Major Patrick Tomlinson MBE, bundled his loyal half-packed section commanders and his totally unpacked platoon commanders into a grey military bus and headed south to Brize Norton. The company second in command, Captain Maurice Evlyn-Bufton, and the ageing company sergeant major, WO2 BAD Phillips, waved to their officer commanding and watched the bus turn from the gates of Alma Barracks. Returning to the company office, B Company was dismissed, 'Fall out' came the command from the CSM. The 21C and CSM picked up their golf clubs and made their way to Catterick Golf Course for final training. Back in camp, under the command of Private 'George' Nyland, last-minute packing for the operational tour was taking place.

The South Bank, Goražde, B Company Sector

On 29 August the company landed in Split to be welcomed by sweltering heat. The soldiers' highly polished boots glimmered in the sun as they scuttled through passport control, led by OIC scuttling WO2 Hussey. That night they rested in a hotel, the last for Goražde Force and the first of many for those of Echelon. This was followed by the gruelling drive to Goražde, interrupted by a further night at the Rogitica checkpoint at the kind hospitality of the Bosnian Serbs. This impromptu hospitality was rewarded by the CSM donating two sniper rifles to the Bosnian Serb cause! He reasoned that their proposed use within Bosnia was limited as Private Sean Ridler, the late owner of the rifle, was unlikely to hit the, or indeed any, target!

On arriving in Goražde, Lieutenant Charlie Maconochie, in theatre for seven days and already convinced he was a war veteran, escorted the members of the company to their accommodation. This was to be the most successful piece of map reading he completed during the six-month tour. The joyful cries of 1 DWR

248

soldiers could be heard echoing down the Drina Valley as they made their way to Split and the UK for well-deserved leave. Back in Goražde, the B Company warriors set about their task with vigour and under the guidance of section commanders the observation posts (OP) and checkpoints (CP) were manned and the real work began.

The initial difficulty faced by all was the pronunciation of the various villages and features. Although well acquainted with these names after the first month, the introductory ground briefs were confusing for all: 'The Right Bank? Quite simple really. You have the high features of Bare, Kolijevka, Samari, Gradina, Mala Biserna, Pargani, Straza and not forgetting the Sanac, Prisoje and Toyarnica. These overlook several valleys: Gaj, Bioska, Cemetery and of course the Drina – that's the big one! I won't tell you all the village names, but the ones you need to know are Gornje Kolijevka, Kazagici, Zuzelj, Krsnica, Zupcici, Vran Potok and Causivici. However, I'll leave out Milanovici, Radijevici, Dobra Voda and Drijeznjak. Any questions?'

Having added these to their vocabulary, acclimatisation to the demanding patrol routes throughout the B Company area of responsibility became the priority. With the temperature in the mid-eighties and dressed in the Army issue portable sauna unit, cunningly disguised as CBA, the excess weight gathered over leave soon disappeared. Within three weeks Private 'the leek' Healey had reduced his clothing demand on the CQMS from a twelve by twelve to nine by nine-foot tent (he subsequently knocked two and a half minutes off his BFT time).

It was tempting to lie back in the Yugoslavian sun and enjoy the hazy days of summer. However, the OC, an expert in meteorological matters, had undertaken a weather assessment and concluded with two startling observations: firstly, winter invariably follows summer and secondly, winter tends to be colder and wetter than summer. Therefore, the locations, created in haste and in anticipation of a temporary deployment by 1 DWR, would have to be revamped in preparation for the winter.

The company was fortunate to have within its orbit Sergeant Major Yemm, 'the Yemminator', a legendary character from the Forest of Dean. Although trained in the Army as an assault pioneer, one arrow in his quiver, his experience as a scout in Cinderford's 4/7th Boys Brigade, where he spent many happy days wandering through the oak woodlands and swimming naked in the River Severn with his best friend 'Gurt Winterwhistle', would prove to be invaluable in the reconstruction of the OPs and CPs.

He was given the company allocation of thieves and vagabonds, whom in turn drew on the vast pillaging experience of Lance Corporal Eddy 'the fingers' Edwards. By the end of October all locations had been completed and the chief forester was two stone lighter, due to his dedicated physical routine and the noticeable lack of cider in Goražde.

Meanwhile, the company quarter master sergeant (CQMS) Steve Hanson displayed his own building talents within Cotswold Camp. Lance Corporal Edwards, on loan from Jonny White and the Seven Dwarves, delivered lorry loads of equipment from Kazagici and helped build the Toucan Club, sauna (enter Private Healey), gymnasium (enter Private Mark 'the muscles' Juggins), coffee corner, wash tent and drying room. The dwarves retaliated by digging the deepest long drop in British military history, affectionately known as the 'Two Turd Club', which the commanding officer christened during a private ceremony.

In early September the quarter master started preparing for handover and withdrew all equipment from the company, leaving each platoon with one Saxon, one SF gun (without tripod) and a broken axe (on demand). The CQMS

Private Price stands firm at CP1

continued to astonish all in Goražde Force with razor-sharp creases and polished boots of a standard last seen at the Trooping of the Colour. His over-enthusiasm affected the CSM and Corporal Wyatt, who immediately withdrew all ammunition and signals kit respectively. The company was now defenceless and incommunicado, but very smartly dressed.

Meanwhile, operations continued. The OC conducted liaison with both warring factions. Captain Kepic, the Bosnian Serb Army (BSA) Right Bank Commander, enthused at 1 RGBW's arrival and promised the full co-operation of his men within the 3km Total Exclusion Zone. Commander Salko, on behalf of the Bosnian Muslim Army, guaranteed UNPROFOR's safety, as his men had no weapons to threaten them. Within the BiH those that had rifles had no ammunition and those that had ammunition had no rifles. This was our first challenge, to ensure this equilibrium was maintained.

Acting on Captain Kepic's assurance, the OC called in the mortar section, under command of Lance Corporal Eddy Edwards 69, from OP 11. Driving down Oscanica Valley, their reliable Saxon broke down. As they attempted to identify the fault, machine gun rounds landed around their vehicle. In what Lance Corporal Edwards considered a reasonable use of force, 1,200 rounds were returned, and the section extracted safely. Although Private Jones 04 has

Colour Sergeant Hanson

never got to the bottom of this incident (*he was of course shot in the arse*), warring faction rumour suggests this firepower demonstration had fatal consequences for the BSA.

Next day, Monty Python's Flying Circus moved out to survey the site of this action. Unable to identify the strike marks, the BSA provided another crack and thump demonstration. Battle drills were actioned, and all took cover. Corporal 'Jessie Wyatt' proved, beyond doubt that the automatic on his rifle was in good working order. Fortunately, Morris McWerter was at hand to confirm a new record for rounds discharged in a non-battle environment. Initial reports had Colour Sergeant Griffith ahead with 72 rounds (a fine performance for OC Recce Platoon). However, Jessie came through triumphantly with just under three magazines. Although firing 85 rounds in 21 seconds, he was disappointed to have fumbled his second magazine change and firmly believes he can reduce this time by three to four seconds.

Captain Kepic (BSA) apologised profusely: 'Mayor Pratwick – you are a most good and honourable solicitor. Let me conserve you this will not stoppen again.'

Next day the BSA fired at OP 1. Unfortunately, Sharp Shooter Stratton was on duty and successfully drilled many GPMG rounds into the Red House at Gornje Kolijevka. At half time the score was: B Company 2 – BSA 0.

With routine well established it was time to undertake some adventure training. Lieutenant Matthew Vine was appointed the officer in charge of surfing and water

251

sports. Being a keen and competent surfer, he decided to give a demonstration of his talent to the people of Goražde. During this demonstration his trousers fell as he had foolishly forgotten to secure his green belt.

To the dismay of the locals this led to the immediate curtailing of surfing activities. Matthew assures us that further demonstrations and open-air performances will be undertaken in Cyprus this summer.

With the days drawing in it was time to participate in some traditional activities. Bonfire night offered the perfect opportunity for the Royal Engineers to exhibit their own firepower demonstration. The evening was supposed to have been a series of five-minute plays taken from within Goražde Force, accompanied by the soldiers warming themselves by the giant fire. In reality it turned out to be a series of five-minute plays.

After careful consultation between the international panel of judges, the compere for the evening, WO2 Bernard Yemm, announced that B Company's musical 'A Pants Production' (including the celebrated hit 'Sergeant Major Fetch my Rover') had run away victorious. Naturally, there were cries of 'fix', but video evidence later proved that this victory was warranted.

As November progressed the situation between the warring factions deteriorated in line with American diplomatic efforts. The BiH had been promised support and arms by President Clinton. In Goražde this had a remarkable effect on the attitude of the Muslim soldiers. Firstly, they no longer perceived their CPs as caravans, but as armoured personnel carriers. Secondly, Commander Salko had become increasingly confused over the limit of his responsibility and decided to mark his territory with a WW1 trench stretching from CP 1 to CP 3, approximately 2km. This was kindly dug by his mother and other close relations.

Understandably, the BSA took offence to this sudden gardening activity. At OP 2 Vlado, a Bosnian Serb resident of Pargani ridge, became inquisitive about the BiH drainage system. He questioned the OC about its purpose and threatened to undertake offensive action against the Chocolate Box, a BiH OP forward of the confrontation line. As Vlado was often full of bravado, the OC slapped him on the back, smiled and bid him good day. That night, and three bottles of slivovitz later, Vlado gave Goražde Force a free firework display. This included 350 AK 47 rounds, a 64mm rocket, an RLG and two grenades. This was sufficient to wake the hibernating Sergeant Desborough in OP 2, some ten metres away. With the entire UN force under the hard cover of collective protection (COLPRO), Vlado had successfully taken on the BiH and the UN, winning single-handedly. Next day the OC led 6 Platoon up through Pargani village to cordon the BSA location, Scabs 1 and 2, which led to the confiscation of many weapons. Vlado was mentioned in despatches and given three months in Foca Prison. On his return he was adamant that it had all been worth it, although only six rounds were confirmed strikes. Based upon this performance, the commanding officer guaranteed him a place in the 1st battalion's shooting team.

Not all the company was present to enjoy this spectacle, with the allocation of leave taking up to twenty-five soldiers from each company at any time. At the end of November, the CSM cheerfully climbed aboard the transport bound for Kiseljak. Unbeknown to the CSM, the company had collected 500 Deutsch Marks and paying it to Captain Kepic had guaranteed his temporary kidnapping at Ustipraca. That the commanding officer was there was purely coincidental. They were released to enjoy two weeks at home and returned refreshed to continue service throughout the bleak winter.

Corporal 'Ginge' Mather (B Company) supported the ongoing convoy effort from Kiseljak into Goražde throughout the tour.

Soon after their return, Major Patrick Tomlinson packed his bags and went AWOL, leaving Major Simon Gray to take hold of the reins. The company wished 'Tommo' well and prayed that England would experience a freak cold winter to remind him of his soldiers in Goražde, as he warmed his feet in his Scooby Doo slippers at The Royal Military Academy, Sandhurst.

Major Simon Gray launched himself into his position of command by announcing a series of initiatives. Under his direction the wood fire that heated the shower unit was surrounded by an insulating sheet. It worked exceptionally well, conserving the heat and burning through three water pipes within the first week of its application.

Immediately before Christmas ex-President Jimmy Carter persuaded the BSA to sign a four-month Cessation of Hostilities Agreement in return for an unlimited supply of peanuts, both ready salted and dry roasted. In Goražde, Commander Salko celebrated, and placed both of 43 Brigade's rounds safely into a locked box, next to a picture of a 105mm Howitzer.

Above: The children of Goražde celebrate and join in the Christmas celebrations and panto

The festive season arrived with a flourish. Christmas Eve saw further skits presented by all sub units. The compere was provided by the 'local community leader', Mohammed Mo He welcomed the crowd to the evening's activities with a traditional west country greeting, married to a Bosnian hill-top dancing routine, most peculiar. Later to be identified as the Coy 2IC, his fetish for dressing up was addressed by the regimental medical officer, Crazy Wee Jock McDiack, whom rumour has it wears nothing below his kilt less a tattoo of 'Rabbie Banns'.

Christmas Day had the OC and CSM conducting meals on wheels to all locations. CP 3, led by baritone Corporal Harry the Seacombe Southern, received everyone with an interesting interpretation of traditional carols. This included the limited-edition version of 'The Twelve Days of Goražde'. Unfortunately, by 5th March it was 192 days!

Below: Christmas Day on the Ops

The significance of New Year was, quite simply, that soldiers could say "We're going home this year". Soon afterwards the incoming OC, Major Richard Westley, from the 1st Battalion, The Royal Welsh Fusiliers, arrived for his recce. Not surprisingly he was warmly welcomed, even Sergeant Musto climbed from his sleeping bag to offer his advice on operations from within a cotton cover, although Corporal McGregor remained steadfastly attached to the inside of his.

Major Westley missed the rolling valleys of Wales and to remind himself of those valleys and hills he delivered snow, wind and rain. Fortunately for the sheep they were left on the farm and Private Jonny Parker 25, the company sex pest, was left disappointed with an empty pair of wellies. Within twenty-four hours OP 1 and 3 were covered by 12 to 18 inches of snow.

Fortuitously the Ministry of Defence had spared little in providing all that was possible in winter clothing. The section pair of Arctic socks was distributed, and time shared equally, being washed every fourteenth day. The day after it stopped snowing the CQMS withdrew them for handover.

The company hoped that the snow would stay until March, that time would drift by and that *The Sun* newspaper would supply another sackful of ever-hopeful girls from Blighty and England's shores to write to. Private Lennie Fitton's collection of letters and photographs have subsequently become of interest to the London Zoological Society. The Society believes that he has discovered a genetically proven throwback to pre-Neanderthal days. Two days later, Lennie announced his engagement to Gabrielle the Gorilla from Skegness. Incidentally, she is 36 (stone), divorced with four kids, but Lennie loves her – and we love you too Lennie!

Unfortunately, the commanding officer had different plans. To the alarm of the Company it had to plan a move to the Osanica Valley by 15 January. Another 500 Deutsch Marks and 200 Benson and Hedges convinced Captain Kepic to make life difficult for the proposed change in deployment until March. The company settled back into a well-established routine.

With six weeks to go the snow took a temporary leave of absence and left Cotswold Camp reminiscent of the Somme battlefields. Private Willie Wilson stepped from his Portakabin on 19th January, attempting to cross to the kitchen, and hasn't been seen since. Due to the battalion being over-manned, neither the OC nor the commanding officer minded this loss. Private Davy 'Gortex' Pagett was disheartened as Willie owed him £15 that could have been employed in the final Cotswold Camping order. Nevertheless, in the six months spent in Goražde he had successfully collected a full regimental issue of train spotting kit.

At the beginning of January General Rose made his second visit to Goražde accompanied by the BBC Panorama film crew. His visit had been well rehearsed and, arriving at CP 3, Sergeant Musto greeted him at the top of the steps as planned, the scenario would have been good material for a Blackadder sketch, with my imagination running riot on the subject:

Lieutenant-General Michael Rose, RSM Wood and Lieutenant Colonel Patrick Davidson-Houston

"Good morning your Highness, I mean General Sir. Sir, if you don't mind me saying, Rose is a most appropriate name, as you sir, are radiant and blossoming like no other rose I have seen. Please let me, sir, lick your boots, sir please."

The boys were in good form, not fazed by the General, who was similarly able to connect with them. I'd say the General thoroughly enjoyed the visit to the Right Bank.

The CQMS was horrified by the mud that surrounded him in every quarter. He found himself unable to withdraw this mud or put sunshine on demand. He optimistically approached the Padre in the hope that the Padre's higher formation could bring the summer forward. Alas, this was to no avail. Facing a dirty trek three times a day, he took to driving to meals from the hard standing at the B Company end of camp to save the shine of his boots. He had considered the high route along the camp battlements, but this had been quickly discounted when Uncle Johnny 'wings' Yemm took a tumble and fell into the depths of the mire below. It took Uncle Jonny two weeks to thoroughly clean his muddied moustache.

The CQMS's kind offer to turn the cook house into a drive-through was

turned down by the regimental sergeant major, as
he feared he would lose the weekly allocation of fuel
to wash the battalion's berets. Although, in principle,
he agreed wholeheartedly with the keep boots-shiny-
policy. The only people that kept their boots clean were
the evacuees that were carried across the swamp before
being shipped out to comparative safety. The CQMS
attempted to change his name to Akmed Hanson to benefit from this service but
changed his mind when he realised that being carried would ruin the creases in
his trousers.

Above: The cookhouse,
Cotswold Camp

So there you have it, B Company were first in and last out. Did we achieve our
mission?

"To establish the conditions of temporary peace on the right bank of Goražde
as part of the commanding officer's overall concept of operations in order that
both warring factions have a six-month period in which to totally reorganise
themselves prior to mounting offensive operations in the spring". The answer
would have to be "yes". Before closing B Company's account, one question that
needs to be asked for our loyal servants in Whitehall, whatever happened to our
UN pay? We will never know.

Left: Corporal Gary Morley,
the author and Company
Sergeant Major Jonny
Yemm in B Company
Headquarters, Cotswold
Camp

Major Patrick Tomlinson MBE (Retired Colonel), Goražde Force, 1RGBW B Company Commander (August 1994–December 1994)

Far better to rein in an enthusiast than kick an idle one.

One of the benefits of the recent amalgamation was that the company was full of very capable and well-motivated officers and soldiers. I was very lucky with B Company, I declared at the end of my tour in Goražde that there was only one soldier and one officer not yet ready for war-fighting, the rest capable and professional to the core. One of these enthusiasts and capable officers was my company operations officer, the author of this book, and anxious not to be categorised as idle I have finally agreed to put some thoughts on paper. I should have reined him in harder I think!

Married with a one-month old daughter, I left a wife very much wondering what she had let herself in for marrying a soldier, not least because the previous year I had spent six months deployed as company commander in Crossmaglen in Northern Ireland (NI) and on my return, I had made a big point about that being the operational tour out of the way, what could have been famous last words! Now, within a year, having spent the best part of it in an enclave effectively surrounded by the Irish border and the focus of terrorism, along with about 50% of the company also ex-Duke of Edinburgh's Royal Regiment (DERR), I was about to experience the sensation of being surrounded again, this time camped in another enclave with the townsfolk of Bosnia and surrounded by Serbs, and very much the core of battle-hardened Serbian Army.

The blend of Gloster, Berkshire and Wiltshire regiments and soldiers worked well and recent experience of operations in NI also proved to be valuable. Although we had recently re-rolled into Armoured (Saxon) Infantry, it was clear from the recce that it was going to be a good old foot-slogging enterprise as the terrain east of the River Drina was steep and hilly, with tracks too narrow for regular use by heavy wheeled armour. It was also clear that, despite our Saxons, my rifle company had a few more months to go as light infantrymen on foot.

There were many similarities to operations in South Armagh, half-platoon-sized OPs requiring a degree of independence and self-sufficiency but also rigorous discipline, especially in keeping things clean and tidy to help keep on top of important health and hygiene requirements. This may not have seemed important to some, but it was essential to keep the 'squits' at bay and, frankly, to maintain our reputation with the both Serbs and Bosnian for being overtly professional.

The other core skill and discipline from the NI experience was the company's confidence to engage and talk to people and particularly this was a useful experience

258

to have in place when private soldiers were being asked to confront battle-hardened Bosnian and Serb soldiers, asking and often demanding the confiscation of their personal weapons or to engage in broader, free-flowing conversation in the hope of gleaning information (about intentions, troop movements and so on).

There was one big difference: no Yellow Card (the rules of engagement card used in Northern Ireland by the British Army which defined when you could shoot whilst on operations). Setting the tone for Bosnia during training was a challenge and I remember briefing the company that this conflict was not worth the life of a single RGBW soldier, yet the risk of loss of life would arguably be much greater (and proved to be). We had to move from an environment where a soldier was used to being able to shoot only as an act of last resort (and be able to justify the fact in the law courts), in an environment where there was an inclination not to shoot at all, to one where the instinct to preserve life could flourish.

Fortunately for the success of our Bosnia operations, the rules of engagement for Goražde allowed a more aggressive response and B Company's clear willingness to respond to aggression was demonstrated on many occasions throughout the tour and undoubtedly prevented loss of life.

Recollections:
Goražde and its people

A back against the wall attitude, it was all about survival; this statement captures it all for the people of Goražde. The men fought, and the women did the rest; it was the women who chopped and collected the wood, who queued for and carried water, that dug and tended the vegetable patch in the garden, who cooked and fed the family. To be fair, I think the men did their best to provide electricity for their homes. This took the form of washing machines being floated in the River Drina tied to the main structures of the bridges that crossed over the river. Each of these platforms had homemade paddles that turned the dynamo and turbine within the washing machine itself and this action provided enough power to recharge the batteries linked by wire to the walkways along the bridge – ingenious. Sadly I don't think anyone ever took a photograph!

Overall and to many of the soldiers, the Bosnian men were idle and the community support projects to repair and repaint schools or other community buildings never rested easily with me, but I was very

"Homemade paddles that turned the dynamo and turbine within the washing machine itself and this action provided enough power to recharge the batteries linked by wire to the walkways along the bridge – ingenious". Photo taken by Major Simon Gray

259

Left: A soldier of 1RGBW responds to the children's call of 'bon-bon', where sweets taken from their boxed rations would be happily distributed

Right: CSM Brian Phillips distributes sweets to the children outside Cotswold Camp

happy to provide assault pioneer or other SME advice but not the manpower to do the actual work; at least not with the Bosnian soldiers looking on as they did with apparent amusement and disdain. Any decision was therefore balanced with the desire to help the needy, the women and especially the children.

Who indeed could forget the children clamouring for sweets? "Bon bon, bon bon". It made many of us realise how materialistic and spoiled our own society had become when simple things could mean so much. Certainly I remember returning to UK after the tour and being appalled by the excess that was available and wasted in our own superstores.

Operations:
Administration and Logistics

The company was split with half living in hill-top OPs and the rest with Company Headquarters in Cotswold Camp, located within the sports stadium on the edge of the town. The soldiers had a definite preference for life in the OPs, despite their true austerity, no doubt something to do with the critical mass and presence of the sergeant major community in the main operating base, the centre of inbuggerance many soldiers would say!

It took a lot of hard graft to get the OPs to be as warm and comfortable, as they proved to be in the bitter cold climate of winter. Thank goodness for the Battalion Assault Pioneers and Sergeant Major Yemm. The sergeant major master-minded, and with the help of the soldiers, constructed winter-proof OPs on the most vulnerable locations. Each dug down through 4ft of granite rock and reinforced with timber so that each site effectively blended into the hill. All OP sites had wood-burning stoves, and as winter came, they proved their worth being perfectly snug. Conversely, back in the main base we had to get up every morning and de-ice our towels, as the Portakabins proved to be pre-made freezers and wholly undesirable and useless for living and sleeping.

However, not all was so bad in headquarters. The B Company CQMS, Colour Sergeant Hansen, not wishing to be outdone by the hard work and ingenuity of Sergeant Major Yemm, was superb in building communal hot water showers. This was like water from heaven, collected in huge cleaned out oil barrels, heated by wood-burning fires, which kept it warm overnight. The water was sifted using the Saxon's NBC air-filtration piping and therefore whilst in camp and we had diesel, it was perfect, and each soldier had access to a shower every morning. Add the newly constructed Toucan Club (soldiers were limited to two cans of beer in any twenty-four hour period) and we had clean and happy soldiers being able to attend their very own and comfortable company club.

Above: Sergeant Major Johnny Yemm masterminded the build of the Observation Posts and much of the supporting infrastructure in Cotswold Camp

If we had one difficulty it was in the provision of wood for the stoves and although we had chain saws, there was a very limited supply of fuel. Hard work was required with routine hand sawing, cutting and logging. However, on occasion ingenuity and daring was called for and when one of our ingenious SNCOs managed to smuggle into Goražde eight jerry cans of fuel, passing through the Serbian checkpoints, I thought it just and fair to offer four of the cans to the RSM and the central effort. Sadly, the RSM did not

Below: Sergeant Rumbold relaxes in the Toucan Club, B Company

see it this way and a most inglorious argument took place between the RSM and me, when the former discovered that CSM Hansen also had four mysteriously unaccounted jerry cans and was using it to power his chain saws. I refused to surrender any more fuel, it appeared fair and square and an even distribution of the spoils, which probably contributed to a comment in my annual report about how on an occasion I appeared not to understand the big picture! However, I stand by my decision and most importantly my company appreciated the stand-off and more so the pile of logs that came from it!

"Military piece"

There was a solid foundation in place, with excellent logistical support. The soldiers were looked after, and the military response from my company was consistently first class.

Attitude

What I recall most and with some warmth is the competition between soldiers and sections, such as the innovation showed to make their OP the best, to have created something unique, where for example rumours of a new man-made oven in one of the OPs would spread like wild fire and lead to a desire to meet and better this innovation, and more so of weapon confiscation.

No Serb or Bosnian soldier could carry a weapon in the neutral 'de-militarised' zone. Any soldier found to be carrying one had their weapon confiscated. The ruling served a couple of purposes; firstly, it imposed RGBW/UNPROFOR authority over the combatants and secondly, it provided competition amongst the section commanders as to who could confiscate the most weapons. I do believe that Corporal Andy Padden finally tallied the most weapons, with an unscrupulous or innovative (depends which way you look at it), use of his Stanley knife to cut through rifle slings being key to his success!

Company Sergeant Major 'Bri' BAD Phillips on patrol and discovering a very empty bottle of slivovitz, evidence of a passing Serb patrol!

Search

On one occasion, amidst the Serb front line that over-looked the Bosnian houses, a drunken Serb had thrown grenades into these houses that were located directly below them. There were no casualties, but it prompted B Company to conduct a thorough search of the Serb positions; as this was a clear violation of the UN agreement. This search and follow on imposition of the letter of the law, probably represented the low point in British–Serb relations (in B Company's area), as the search was conducted in a rather hostile atmosphere, as the Serbs sought to make the operation difficult. No weapons were found (they had been spirited away during the night), but the Serb Commander (Kepic) did agree to post the culprit away from Goražde, he was never to be seen again. From our perspective, it was a good opportunity to establish authority over the combatants and demonstrate we were happy to play the role we had been charged to undertake.

Control

A directive emerged from the Bosnian Headquarters that all UNPROFOR patrols were to show their passes when patrolling during the day within the enclave. This did not go down well at all with the company, who had spent the previous few months protecting the Bosnian enclave from the surrounding Serb forces. It is no surprise that B Company decided to turn a 'Nelsonian Eye' to the Bosniak order. No surprises either that I decided to test this point when I took Company Headquarters on a local patrol to try-out the resolve of the Bosnian checkpoint commanders. I knew the route we were to take that I would be confronted by a Bosnian NCO commanding the checkpoint directly across the River Drina and would, as such, be covered by a turreted Saxon being used as a sentry point at the main base.

Some pre-planning had taken place and the turreted L37 GPMG had been made ready in anticipation of my patrol to the checkpoint in question and being only at 200m this firepower was more than adequate protection. What was key to the ensuing stand-off was my plan in pointing out that if the company sergeant major was to lower his raised arm before the patrol was allowed through unimpeded, then the Saxon gunner had orders to open fire on the check point. The NCO reported back to his superiors, and the patrol could proceed, and Company Sergeant Major BAD Philips could lower his now very tired arm and continue forward. I then visited my opposite number, the Bosniak leader of the troops in our area, Salko at the Bosnian Headquarters, and it was agreed they would not enforce the checking of passes on patrols east of the river and that B Company could continue as before.

Shooting: Winning the fire-fight

Sniper Alley 1 B Company had one dislocated OP position occupied by the mortar platoon. It rested the other end of 'Sniper Alley'; the same was suitably descriptive. A shooting incident did take place when a mortar vehicle broke down on changeover and as the soldiers were attempting repair it, they were ambushed, and one soldier was painfully and rather embarrassing wounded by a ricochet up his gluteus maximus, it was something of a flesh wound but it did require him to be evacuated.

More remarkable was the action carried out by the REME recovery corporal, who ignored the incoming fire and, with no regards to his own safety stuck his head into the engine compartment to effect repair. He was successful, the vehicle restarted, and they managed to extricate themselves out of the killing zone and he was duly awarded a Mention in Dispatches (MiD) for his very brave efforts.

UK papers reported the double contacts and incidents, drawing attention to the harsh reality of the task facing the isolated British force in Goražde

Sniper Alley two was a similar action in that, yet another ambush took place, this time with the focus on a joint patrol from both BHQ and HQ B Company tasked to review the site where the action had taken place the previous day. There was little surprise that when this review was taking place on the ground, the UNPROFOR gathering was fired on again, however, this time with a more aggressive reaction from the B Company soldiers.

Signs of activity at Belgrade Airport, where airliners are emerging from hangars in preparation for the end of sanctions against Serb

British units clash with Bosnian Serb

BRITISH soldiers have retaliated twice in two days after coming under attack in the besieged Bosnian enclave of Gorazde, a United Nations Protection Force spokesman said yesterday.

They fired more than 1,100 rounds near Mihovici on Wednesday after Bosnian Serb forces fired hundreds of rounds at a broken-down British armoured personnel carrier, said Major Dacre Holloway.

Early yesterday, another British unit returned more than 500 rounds after being attacked on three sides in the southwestern sector of the pocket, said Major Holloway.

It was not clear who had fired the first shots. Bosnian Serbs fired hundreds of rounds at the stricken Saxon when another British crew arrived to recover the vehicle, Unprofor spokesman Commander Eric Chaperon said.

Major Holloway said the British soldiers responded with 1,100 rounds from their automatic rifles, and the 7·62mm machine-guns mounted on the Saxons in an hour-long battle.

Both units returned safely. The spokesman said the question of calling in Nato air strikes against the Serbs on Wednesday had never been raised because the unit involved did not request air support.

"The first we knew about it was when they sent a report in," he said. Unprofor can call in Nato air strikes when its forces come under attack, though it appears increasingly reluctant to do so.

Another British unit was attacked in a separate attack early yesterday in the south-western sector of the Gorazde pocket, with 75-100 small arms rounds fired from three different positions, said Major Holloway.

He denied that the UN was deliberately playing down the incidents. "Both sides are trying something on now especially since they have lost a couple of people in the last few days," he said.

That was a reference to two road crashes in the Gorazde pocket last week which cost the lives of British soldiers. — AFP

● **Robert Fox** in Zagreb wr Serbs in the village of Ilica cut o main water supply to Sarajevo terday, virtually re-imposing siege which nearly brought the nian capital to its knees last win

For several weeks, electricity plies have been intermittent an gas supply is on for most hous the centre for only one day in th

Serb forces in Ilica have also firing on the only mountain s route for the Muslim population a 20mm anti-aircraft gun, in b of ceasefire terms.

There ensued a classic infantry response to coming under effective enemy fire; *take cover, suppress the enemy and win the fire-fight*. Both patrols were able to fire and move out of the killing area thanks mainly to the suppressive fire being laid down, whilst under fire himself, by Corporal Lewis and his pintle-mounted machine-gun.

The after-action review conducted by me was of interest: when I asked how many rounds the section had left following the firefight only my driver (Private Robinson) and I still had a full complement of ammunition; the total rounds for the rest of the patrol was three rounds left! When asked to explain, the section commander professed to be totally mortified by his apparent lack of control of the suppressive fire:

"Sir, I am mortified, I really am. Totally unprofessional, I am very sorry, but to be honest all my military life I have been praying to be involved in a firefight such as this and I have always wanted to put my 'gat' on automatic and let rip. It's fair to say sir, I simply got carried away."

There was a pause and then his words were echoed by others "Me too Sir" and "Sir, probably the same here" and so it went on, over 1,100 rounds were returned in the space of three minutes and most certainly our point was made as to a willingness to take a robust stance when under fire! Although seriously, the willingness to engage and demonstrate our intent was the required and expected reaction.

Left: B Company battalion five aside Football Champions, Cotswold Camp 1994

Below: including Sergeant Steve Musto, Lance Jory Corporal Deacon, Corporal Wyatt, and Lieutenant Gary McDade

Major Simon Gray (retired Lieutenant Colonel MBE Rifles), Goražde Force, B Company Commander, 1 RGBW (December 1994–March 1995)

Simon Gray with the three B Company translators

Today, as I reflect on my operational tour to Goražde so many years ago, after which more followed in Bosnia, Iraq and Afghanistan, alongside countless experiences in Somalia, it is fitting that someone wishes to tell the 1 RGBW Goražde Force story. Others have published the 1 DWR and 1 RWF perspectives; however the middle of the three battalion tours, conducted during a harsh Balkan winter, has until now remained untold. I am delighted that Maurice has committed to print his memories and reflections of those that served in the enclave. During the tour, his humorous and well-written B Company notes kept the vital rear link with our families informed and entertained, always with a focus on the individual.

Background

In December 1994, I was serving in Headquarters 1 (UK) Armoured Division as a junior staff officer based in Hereford, Germany. Married with two young children aged four and two; we had thoroughly enjoyed our time living on the continent. Professionally the division was an exciting place to work. The focus after the fall of the Berlin Wall remained on Cold War fighting, however our armoured units had, and were, conducting operational tours in the Balkans. The situation in Bosnia was therefore familiar and after notification of my appointment and deployment, the Divisional Commander and Chief of Staff ensured that I was well supported in my individual pre-deployment training. I shadowed 1 RHF on the ranges at Sennelager and in their exercises. The contrast between my former regiment, 1 DERR, and the jocks from Glasgow was acute. Previously I had served on operational tours in South Armagh and on a residential tour in Northern Ireland. I had also shaped my blue beret in the Cyprus sun on a six-month UN tour (UNFICYP).

First Impressions

The prolonged entry to theatre and into Goražde via Kiseljak, Sarajevo and eventually a convoy through numerous checkpoints, including the obligatory stop at each, provided a stark introduction to the realities of wearing a blue helmet amid a civil war. I wasn't the only new boy, however, joining the battalion at the mid-tour point, being accompanied for the journey by Major Ed Brown, the new OC A Company.

B Company, as has been described, occupied a series of observation posts (OPs) and check-points (CPs) on the right/eastern bank of the River Drina and a headquarters in the sports stadium on the west bank. The terrain was impressive and distances between the warring factions shockingly small, and more so was the impression left by the oversized population that had been forced to seek shelter and squeezed into Goražde.

It was sobering to note that the views and vistas were made possible because every tree that could be chopped for firewood had been done so, stripping the hillsides and being stockedpiled in town for cooking and heating. The brutal reality of war was clear to see with every building marked by shellfire, but most shocking were the areas of houses without roofs, where homes had been subject to systematic ethnic cleansing, leaving them destroyed and hollowed out.

Threading its way in the valley bottom, the not insignificant River Drina flowed northwards crossed by three bridges linking the two banks of the town. Superimposed amid chaos and war and located by necessity in exposed positions, were a series of OPs and CPs. Each had undergone winterisation work and on first sight the finished dug in positions were hugely impressive. The CPs and company lines had not been inherited and the innovation and self-improvement to improve the overall living conditions was startling to see.

Meeting the senior commanders from each side for the first time, accompanied

Far left: OP1 B Company

Left: OP2, B Company

267

by Patrick Tomlinson, was an interesting experience. Their blank expressions hid what they really thought, as they contemplated their third UN company commander in four months.

It was at one of these meetings that my dislike for the local slivovitz fruit brandy (made from plums), was quickly established. This putrid drink would materialise at the start of every meeting with a clear expectation that three shot glasses were required to be drunk before any meaningful discussions could occur. It was clear that during the war, supplies had to be maintained and it was obvious that the premium quality bottles would not be wasted on UNPROFOR. Not for the last time did the excellent Company Sergeant Major Brian Philips step up and drink my share, allowing me to remain focused and without the confusion of a 45% proofed alcoholic haze. More so, CSM Philips provided continuity at these early meetings, as I sought to form some form of relationship with the two local commanders, Captain Kepich, from the Bosnian Serb Army, and Commander Salko, the BIH Brigade Commander. We met a couple of times weekly, and/or on request usually following a local incident. Looking back, I am surprised that they gave me as much time as they did, when in the circumstances it would have been easier to have prevaricated and delayed any meetings or simply ignore us all together.

Most important were the B Company soldiers. Despite the environment and

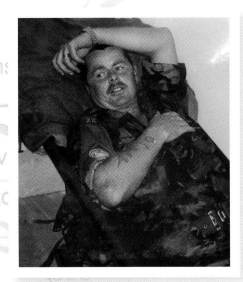

Above: CSM Brian Phillips, B Company at rest

Right: B Company Headquarters, Cotswold Camp

climatic conditions, which gradually worsened as winter deepened, constant throughout this austerity was the cheerfulness and adaptability of each of them. It cannot have been easy for the company to switch company commanders mid tour; however, the resilience of all remained constant. Three months into the tour, they were very experienced in the local pattern of life and adept on the ground. The rest and recuperation (R&R) plot was in full swing and the reality was that everyone needed to work a bit harder to cover the manning shortfall created by R & R, however, this was one issue that was never going to cause any complaints. In short, I was impressed.

Routine

Each day after the commanding officer's morning update, Company HQ aimed to patrol the company area and visit the OPs and CPs and walk the confrontation line. OP 1 the furthest and highest location from the centre of Goražde, was usually reached by Land Rover, up a particularly muddy track. However for the remaining locations it was often best to patrol on foot, particularly as the winter conditions worsened. During these daily excursions, you could see the living conditions for the local population and internally displaced, all under siege from the Serbs, was dire. In places mountains of rubbish littered the streets due to there means or location where it could be safely disposed. There was a real desperation about the place, and each day we crossed the river via one of the three bridges known as A, B, or C, all of which had been regularly raked by heavy machine run and direct tank fire.

The absence of electricity due to the main power lines having been blown up, forced the Goražde residents to improvise. Their efforts clearly top any other form of ingenuity that I have seen since in any conflict worldwide. Car axles, a washing machine, oil drums for flotation, wood to form a raft and water wheel paddles, telephone cables to relay power and a battery left during daylight hours to charge on the bridge, together formed a floating water wheel, which was secured to the bridge superstructure by the former power steel cables. One bridge alone had twenty waterwheels secured to it.

Unfortunately for the population, the local hospital was located on one bank and with the town split any casualties from the other side needed carrying to seek medical attention. Under direct fire, this was all but impossible. Company HQ was delighted to test the newly opened bridge under a bridge. The townsfolk, at considerable risk to themselves, had drilled through the surface tarmac and concrete and suspended steel wires vertically underneath the bridge. These were linked horizontally with a walkway wide enough for a stretcher bearer to carry casualties across the river protected by the major bridge above them.

The steady erosion by the Serbs of the battalion fuel reserves led to further company improvisation by the CQMS, Colour Sergeant Hansen. For a fee, the company resupply could be conducted by two donkeys pulling a cart. This, however, required an escort with a UN flag prominently being displayed to reassure respective warring factions that the resupply was legitimate. Ultimately access could only be guaranteed to the rough proximity of a CP or OP, after which all stores including water and rations required manhandling by the company. With access tracks only allowing single file, the riflemen slung their weapons and using a stick carried two jerry cans slung between them. The Saxon vehicles at this point remained in a static position at each location with only enough fuel in each vehicle to conduct daily engine running and an emergency drive out of Goražde if required.

On Sunday, 18 December 1994 the company communications were significantly enhanced by the laying of communications wire linking the CPs and OPs by the company signals detachment, led by Corporal Wyatt. Unlike today, company radios at the time were insecure and relied on codes to pass sensitive information. It is all very well laying line whilst on exercise on Salisbury Plain, but to do so in Goražde in difficult terrain, during mid-winter and under threat, was a considerable feat and not least required the agreement of the Serbs to do so. Once laid, the wires significantly aided the passage of information, but they did require checking regularly to ensure that they remained secure.

Mules and donkeys were ever-present on the streets of Goražde and a key part of 1RGBW's internal distribution system

270

Winter

By late December 1994 and mid-January 1995, the days were particularly cold and frosty. The cold weather brought a respite from the impact of mud and heavy snowfall brought new challenges, particularly to movement, even if it did most effectively quell the impetus of the war. Snow drifts up to a metre-deep covered tracks and paths. When combined with extreme temperatures of -15 to -20C, conditions for operating safely and professionally became more challenging. In such conditions it was not easy to maintain sentry duty near the Serbs and BIH front-lines, while stood in a steel vehicle or sandbagged position in freezing

The hard winter and snow made convoy movement particularly challenging

271

conditions, and it is a tribute to the riflemen and junior commanders who took it in their stride. It is no surprise that the B Company post operational report commented adversely on the lack and inadequacy of the issued clothing. It seems bizarre today, particularly when viewed in comparison the outstanding clothing issued in the later stages of the Afghan campaign, that in 1994 the equipment and clothing required to cope with the expected and known winter weather conditions was slow to arrive despite existing for Arctic use. Equally bizarre is that the issue did not take place before the deployment. It was no problem to wear civilian clothing under uniforms; however, the headdress question did require reiteration not to wear black beany hats for fear of being mistaken for the warring factions who all wore them.

Ever resourceful, the B Company solution was to honour the long-held tradition of buying commercial kit and clothing through the Gloucestershire-based and suitably named company, Cotswold Camping. The Company's second in command, Maurice, negotiated a 20% discount, which became 37.5% with no VAT being paid on orders, and then coordinated a weekly order. Not surprisingly, the company orders went into overdrive and achieved preferential customer status almost immediately due to the sheer quantity of its orders. The only negative side was the interruption of BFPO postal deliveries due to the Serb disruption of resupply convoys, and of all things, a pilot strike by Croatian Airline over the Christmas period, which affected eagerly anticipated deliveries*.

*Whilst on operations I coordinated and arranged an agreement with Cotswold Camping for the soldiers to have a 20% discount, enhanced by a further 17.5% because of no VAT on any goods purchased, being abroad, ordered from the manuals sent to us hard copy. Each item was individually wrapped, which ensured the Serbs would not steal them at checkpoints (agreeing not to seize personal Royal Mail stamped letters or parcels). The orders were taken at night over the radio, post daily activity checks. It was an unusual practice, with the regimental number being read out e.g. "Pax 73542789 1 x Item 603 Green XL (which I recall was a much sought-after Buffalo Jacket). The Serbs listening in must have thought this a strange code and a hidden agenda, when in fact it was simply an advanced version of online shopping!). In total, the soldiers of 1RGBW spent more than £27,500 throughout the deployment, delivering a lot of parcels and a lot of happy openings upon arrival).

The townsfolk dealt with the freezing conditions as best they could. Collecting drinking water was an onerous but critical task in the sub-zero conditions.

Snow melt caused further problems, mud, mud and more mud. Former tracks were no longer navigable and required Royal Engineer specialist plant to regrade the surface.

272

Change

After a ceasefire agreement was reached in early December 1994, brokered by the former US President, Jimmy Carter a Cessation of Hostilities Agreement came in to effect on 1 January 1995. It was due to last four months during which negotiations were to be conducted to secure a Comprehensive Peace Agreement. Goražde Force was to implement the agreement whilst maintaining the existing mission.

B Company received new orders to establish a liaison HQ near Osanica Bridge, where earlier in the tour the company had experienced an exchange of fire, and were now tasked to develop and extend its liaison within the Goražde Force Area of Responsibility. This would involve a redeployment and foot patrols of front lines previously not visited in the enclave and to record and report minefields, locations of heavy weapons and troop concentrations, whilst at the same time handing over some of our OPs to the Ukrainian battalion.

Of immediate concern were the Christmas festivities. The Battalion HQ had organised a 1 RGBW Christmas show for the local children, where the prime requirement was the distribution of vast quantities of sweets. It was no surprise therefore to find waiting outside the Cotswold Camp gates early on Christmas morning a large cohort of young children, who after their first sugar rush for two years hoped for more! Notedly, the support from the home front and regimental counties was superb, postal disruption permitting. It was touching and hugely reassuring to receive an iced regimental Christmas cake, and even although it could not be delivered to Goražde due to convoy priorities, the dispatch of Lucozade from the Forest of Dean was much appreciated.

Within the company, the second in command and Private Russell regrouped with four other members of the battalion's marathon team to run the twenty-six miles from Visegrád to the Goražde Hospital to raise money for the charity Sight Savers. The second in command has his own story to tell of that marathon and I will leave it to him to do so. However, after a magnificent effort, £500 was raised. On a slightly shorter journey, but sensibly undertaken by Land Rover, the Padre, CSM and I departed with supplies of beer, freshly cooked turkey and all the trimmings, rum and hymn sheets to visit in each B Company location.

Decorations, hats, antlers, Rudolph noses, Christmas cards and even Christmas trees with tinsel featured in each location. Despite a blanket of snow and the climatic conditions, a carol singing contest to be judged by the Padre was held. I have no recollection of who in 1994 was judged to have the X factor, however for many it was the first Christmas away from home and despite being spent in the most demanding and trying of circumstances, it proved to be a good day. Within Cotswold Camp, tradition held true as the officers and senior NCOs served a

273

traditional Christmas meal to the soldiers, a not too insignificant achievement by the outstanding chefs, who due to the shortage of fuel on the day were cooking on open fires.

Visitors

The Serbs, deliberate policy to disrupt travel to Goražde had one positive impact, we were not inundated by visitors. What it did mean however, is that when notified of a visit of importance it was highly likely to be a VVIP. The New Year started with a visit on 7 January 1995 from Lieutenant General Sir Michael Rose, Commander UNPROFOR. He was to be accompanied by the BBC veteran war correspondent, John Simpson and a camera crew from the BBC Panorama programme, aiming to produce a documentary. This was to be the first media visit into Goražde.

Originally commissioned into the Gloucestershire Regiment while a TA officer, General Rose's visit was very much viewed as an opportunity to highlight to the Force Commander the newly formed battalion's work and professionalism. The commanding officer, for ease of access and to achieve maximum effect, opted to visit B Company's OP2 located in a spectacular position on top of the Pargani ridge overlooking Goražde, and visited CP3 en route.

The visit was deemed a success. John Simpson was clearly struck by the adaptability of B Company's living and working conditions and the task to hand. 'Rose's War', the resulting documentary, was positive about Goražde Force's contribution. Although they were not listed by name as the credits rolled at the end of the programme, Sergeant Musto, Corporal Redgewell and Private Lawson-Innes featured prominently at CP 3 and Cpls Lewis and Drew at Blackadder's Lair, OP2.

In February the visit programme repeated itself, this time with the Chief of the General Staff, General Sir Charles Guthrie, enjoying the view from OP2. The battalion in the circumstances was perhaps lucky not to have had the succession of visitors compared to other deployed units; conversely it did mean that the story of Goražde Force and specifically 1RGBW's became known only to a few.

The 1 RWF Reconnaissance Party also visited during what was a particularly cold and snowy early start to the New Year. It was clear from their expressions that they were initially taken aback, with the visit certainly re-energising the urgency in their unit training. For me, it showed that B Company had adapted and taken in their stride the circumstances in which they found themselves. Conditions, even for me a relative newcomer, had become normalised rather than exceptional and tasks were continued without fanfare. The danger of becoming complacent or bored remained, with changes made to avoid issues evolving.

New Tasks

In accordance with Goražde Force's attempts to implement the Cessation of Hostilities Agreement, B Company was ordered to conduct liaison operations. This presented a dilemma of the balance to be devoted to my main effort verses wider tasks. Thankfully with a now very experienced team in place (2IC Captain Maurice Evlyn-Bufton; WO2 Johnny Yemm as the operations warrant officer: 4 Platoon 2nd Lieutenant Cook, although newly arrived was ably supported by Sergeants Desborough and Hammett; 5 Platoon Lieutenant Charlie Maconichie and Sergeant Musto, 6 Platoon; 2nd Lieutenant Gary McDade and Sergeant Sayers), which meant that, along with CSM Brian Philips and my Rover Group, we could venture further afield and into the enclave.

In my absence the routine events continued with huge potential for a sudden rise in violence. One such incident on 12 January 1995 saw two-foot patrols stopped by BIH forces from patrolling on the Pagani feature. Eight Muslim soldiers surrounded a four-man B Company patrol and despite weapons being cocked the patrol remained calm and defused the situation. This enabled me to protest vigorously to the BIH and to Commander Salko, who had no option but to apologise and, in my presence, call his leaders on the line to inform them not repeat this performance.

Captain Matt Shaw (IO) reviews a Serb 40mm Bofors gun above Goražde

The value of repeatedly visiting both faction's commanders began to be realised. The respective Serb and BIH passage of information was at times circumspect and they welcomed in our discussions about the wider international perspective. The meetings allowed me to seed well in advance my intentions to venture further afield, hoping to reduce risk to the company as we explored and exploited new areas, which were not used to a UN armed presence.

At first the daily activity reports of firing incidents dropped significantly, except for Serb celebrations of their Orthodox New Year. Specifically, and memorably, my initial visits to the Osanica Bridge proved interesting. Accompanied by Engineer and EOD specialists, our journey was trouble-free. Commander 801 Brigade agreed to show me his positions defending the bridge. Trenches and strong points inside the adjacent building provided commanding oversight, and mines and obstacles on the bridge denied access. Our presence attracted the Serbs' interest on the adjacent river bank and we attempted to communicate across the divide. The problem was that the female interpreters' voices did not carry across the distance and the Muslim positions recognising this began to convey the messages in a more forceful and louder manner. It became apparent from the translations that our initial greetings had unlocked a meaningful exchange of words between enemies, who proceeded to talk about the conflict from a very local perspective to the extent that they agreed a temporary and very localised ceasefire.

Visits to 802 Brigade in Zorovici and Haniste followed, and having had no interaction at all with the UN, the commander and staff were very happy to talk and mark on our maps the confrontation lines and locations of respective heavy weapons as well as socialise.

Frustratingly, early success was not long-lasting. Our local interactions were reported up through respective chains of command, who appeared uneasy at to what was happening in remote areas and sought to curb our initial contacts. Regardless, we established a permanent presence at the Osanica Bridge on a daily basis between 1000–1445 hours, which despite local BIH support was not reciprocated within Goražde. On the Serb side, our greetings were ended by a curt message that if we continued to shout across the river, we would be shot! Connections counted and after talking in Goražde with Salko, it transpired that his brother was a local commander near the bridge and cooperation increased further.

In late January 1995 B Company was tasked to provide a Saxon vehicle and team to watch a school in Vitkovici, which had been forced to close due to harassing fire across the Drina from Serb positions. Our presence reduced the firing, allowing normal schooling to resume with the odd exception of a sharpshooter, who clearly enjoyed firing infrequent single shots over our heads. The school buildings had suffered considerable damage and to help, Lance Corporal Edwards 33 and Private Taylor provided 'chippie' support and sought to replace the missing glass windows with the ubiquitous UNHCR plastic sheeting material. The children and staff were most grateful and the two were guests of honour at a school party held in late February.

B Company supported a UNHCR medical and social repatriation of Muslims to Sarajevo and Serbs to Kopaci; facilitating the security of the movement from the pitiful Goražde Hospital to Cotswold Camp and then onto Kopaci. To enable the task, manning in established positions was reduced to a minimum. Many local Muslims and Serbs were leaving Goražde for the duration of the war and 10kg of personal kit was permitted to be carried. Some proved to be extremely nervous, unsure of their fate when crossing front lines and how they would be treated by

Left: Captain Susie Griffin (SO3 Comd Info) centre with Privates Hacker and Lawson-Innes assist a Muslim child during the medical evacuation

Above: Private Lawson-Innes carrying an injured Muslim man prior to the evacuation

Above: Captain Susie Griffin (SO3 Comd Info) and Privates Cox assisting a Muslim elderly lady during the evacuation

Left: Four soldiers assisting an elderly Muslim into a Norwegian ambulance during the evacuation

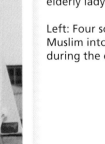

police checks even whilst being transported by the UN. On the day before the operation 150 armed BIH soldiers were reported to be moving from Factory Valley to Bridge A, which was one of B Company's responsibilities to secure. Local feelings were high, some connected to the repatriation of Serbs trapped in the enclave and the loss of possible bargaining tools and rumours of bribes being paid to secure names on the agreed list. The following day, 31 January 1995, 117 Muslims out of the 128 listed were moved (eleven voluntarily refused to leave), and fifty-four Serbs and one parrot! were moved to Kapaci once the Muslims had safely reached Sarajevo. The stark realities of conflict were laid bare for all involved as the sick and vulnerable were removed from immediate harm's way.

In early February, it was clear that the rumoured BIH patrol routes linking the Goražde enclave to Sarajevo were succeeding. Local BIH troops on 2 February suddenly began wearing uniforms. In contrast, our UN local shortages were further compounded by the UN failing to pay its gas bill, leaving Goražde Force with only fifteen gas bottles left at a time when, although the weather was fine, a 10-knot wind reduced temperatures to -10C to -15C.

Commander 802 Brigade announced his Valentine gift to me by giving unexpected permission to visit the remote hamlet of Haniste for a joint 802 Bde/B Company reconnaissance, to be followed by the establishment of a patrol base between 22–25 February. Meanwhile, this good news was tempered closer to home by extensive new digging close to CP 1, which had Captain Kepic asking demanding questions. I explained that the Muslims were increasingly concerned about the forthcoming spring offensive and were naturally adding further protection. The recce to Haniste was conducted in deep snow and with the lack of any vehicle activity in that part of the enclave movement was slow and challenging. A suitable vacant house was sourced as a base and local arrangements agreed. Sergeant Musto led a ten-man three-day Haniste patrol and for the first time placed a UNPROFOR presence in a very remote area of the enclave on the confrontation line, thankfully without incident.

Towards the end of February, coinciding with a noticeable thaw, the number of firearms violations rose quickly and with such reports our interpreters were being verbally abused daily. Samira, and her sister Selma were young women and with Haris completed a remarkable job of interpreting for us daily. B Company were protective of them and many returned from R&R with items to contribute to their welfare, including sweets, books and sanitary products. Despite my robust comments to Serb commanders reminding them of their legal obligations, their soldiers continued a constant stream of sexual verbal abuse, making clear their intentions should they overrun Goražde. At first the girls kept quiet about the abuse, but it was clear from their pained faces what was being said. The ethical situation was incredibly distorted, as at other times the same men talked about their wives and families. Meanwhile fresh digging continued, sometimes with a hundred Muslim men and women at work, busily extending the BiH trenches. Meetings with Kepic and Salko had become noticeably tenser, delivering a challenging atmosphere, and alongside these rising tensions, we continued to confiscate weapons from the supposed civilian Serbs within the 3km circle.

My handover to Major Richard Westerly RWF, with the obligatory handover photograph on 'posers rock' and the company extraction, passed smoothly and on 3 March 1995, B Company finally departed Goražde.

Subsequently whilst serving as a US exchange officer, (Deputy G3, 1st (US) Cavalry Division) in 1999, I was deployed from Fort Hood, Texas, to Tuzla, and whilst there was asked to take a team to Goražde to walk and talk through our UNPROFOR experiences. We flew southwards in two Black Hawk helicopters and met up with a ground convoy. Starting at the remnants of the former Cotswold Camp, we retraced a typical patrol over Bridge A, CP 3 and up to OP 2. Most found it remarkably hard going and I stopped frequently, pointing out key features. Our route to OP 3 was blocked by an almost impenetrable mass of fresh regrowth from the old tree stumps and we returned to the town centre.

Before leaving and visiting the RGBW memorials, I stopped at a house beside Bridge Bravo that I remembered and knocked on the main entrance. Samira opened the door and looked at me totally shocked, her cries and tears brought Selma running from a back room, as well as one of the former A Company female interpreters. By pure coincidence they were in town for the first time in six months visiting family. Samira, who had been pregnant at the end of our tour, introduced her son and in the brief time available caught up with our news.

In 2017 I returned to Sarajevo to deliver a course to senior leaders from Bosnia and Herzegovina, many of whom were senior former commanders. During the break, one of the female interpreters approached me and said that she had been living in Goražde during the UN presence and was at the time 15 years old. During the week we talked extensively, and she passed on my greetings to the B Company interpreters, whom she knew well. Each now has families of their own. Amid our discussions she highlighted many times that many owed their survival to our presence.

B Company had an extremely successful tour in the most demanding of circumstances. Their resilience, courage, restraint and deep-rooted sense of humour were found in abundance and more so remarkable, found in the face of adversity. To a soldier and to a man, and to the women that were our interpreters, all demonstrated a maturity, empathy and compassion beyond their age.

These are my abiding memories of the team with whom I was proud to serve.

279

14th November 1994

A convoy is leaving tomorrow morning, so I thought I would take the opportunity to scribble a few lines to keep you up to date with not so warm and increasingly cold Goražde (more of this eternally resident subject later).

Regarding the escalation of the local and regional situation, you will most likely be more up to date with the situation than we are, as we are in a media lock-out zone. The level of readiness and activity continues between the warring factions and our own readiness and activity, patrolling and other, increases and matches the BSA and BiH activity accordingly. There is a calm in our resolve amidst the surrounding noise and unfolding chaos.

Patrick, my Company Commander, remains Patrick and his trustworthy team around him remain in good order. We trust him, and he obviously trusts us. It is a good position to be in, a united leadership team in a corner. I know if it came down to it, our localised team of B Company would be united and capable. This is most important for us, our primary responsibility being the soldiers of B Company themselves. He came to Goražde and to lead B Company with his recent responsibility in Northern Ireland still carrying painful memories, as a soldier was lost under his command on this tour. I believe this experience has helped us, is he is acutely aware of assessing the risk to his soldiers, but also believe he is helped by the fact that he has found the best of 1 Glosters and 1 DERR under his command.

Now for something different.

Sunday 13th was Remembrance Sunday. Like so many in the UK and abroad, serving soldiers, retired soldiers and future soldiers gathered to recognise the sacrifice of those that have served with and before them. There was, of course, a poignancy to our service for the four we had lost recently on this tour. This thought was most certainly present at our thanksgiving and remembrance service.

On a lighter note, on the muddy square in the centre of Cotswold Camp our man of God, Patrick Irwin, a neoclassical eccentric battalion Padre of Oxford University heritage, who is given to periods of uncontrollable enthusiasm, leapt forward with vigour and admirable gusto to give a sermon reminiscent of a Monty Python character (visualise John Cleese in his pomp and there you have it!).

Having led the singing of four inappropriate, timeless and, thanks to Patrick, tuneless hymns, he set forth on a remarkable speech that rebounded from one inconsequential point to another and concluded with the rather austere, but appropriate words 'we will remember'. Unknowingly, the Padre was right, because after that nuclear-powered screwball performance there's no bloody way any of us will forget!

As if to remind us of the poppy fields of Flanders, God, in his infinite wisdom, had delivered sufficient rain the night before to turn the camp into a scene reminiscent of the Somme, Ypres, Passchendaele or Mons.

You could see the soldiers all carefree, casually flicking the sodden mud on to the rear of the soldier to their front, unaware of a soldier doing the same to their rear. We then had lunch and I had the pleasure to sit opposite the star performer of the day, Padre Patrick Irwin, the very Reverend Lunatic, whose spiritual boss is holding the most senior position in the ultimate higher formation!

Is it me or do men on taking the cloth get issued a bonus pack of nasal hair? Throughout lunch the only thing that grabbed my attention was the rarefied and copse-like collection of hairs that appeared to be growing from the Padre's proboscis with gay abandon. I did manage to finish my ornately coloured and overcooked pasta surprise (the surprise being that it was cooked or edible), despite my attention being taken by the new forest, a regimental Forest of Nasal-Dean, that sprouted and grew before me!

It's five to one on the morning of 15th November. I feel remarkably awake and strangely jolly, despite the intensity of the situation that surrounds us. It's day 76 of 194.

Give Tess a pat on her proboscis, a nose which correctly carries hair and is of added attraction!

Storm clouds gather above Cotswold Camp, November 1994

281

15th November 1994

Our main problem remains the convoys coming in and out of the enclave or, to be honest, not coming in or out, with the Serbs tightening their grip on movements around the enclaves. Running in parallel, the Bosniaks are stonewalling UN commanders at all levels. Effectively we are being frozen out of relevant dialogue between the two that helps us at any level maintain meaningful communication between the warring factions.

One must ask what, if anything, the UN can achieve in Bosnia when both sides appear resolved and determined on war. War appears the singular and only path to resolution to the present impasse and not a peaceful resolution to be discovered through constructive discourse. The UN must [post haste] assess what is its [and therefore our] aim. Can we achieve it? At what cost to the UN and what cost will participating countries accept to achieve this aim?

Presently we are caught between the devil and the deep blue sea, with little or nothing being achieved except the delivery of humanitarian aid and protection of the innocent, the women, children, elderly. We hold the status quo, and a fragile position it is to hold. This may be enough most will say, as indeed it is an achievement, but the onus of responsibility for their mid to long-term welfare cannot be our concern. Their leaders, political or military, should be considerate to this need and this grand ambition, brave and forward-thinking in its pursuit, rather than focusing their efforts on ill thought out and largely unachievable short-term military objectives, whilst their people suffer. Sadly, this pursuit is many leagues above my pay grade, as I am but a lowly infantry captain!

Of far greater importance at a local level is that unfortunately I sprained my ankle yesterday on my daily pursuit of fitness and healthy fortitude, oh foolhardy me! I was running around the athletics track when my right ankle rolled to the right. "Matters not," I thought, "It is but a sharp pain soon to pass and disappear." I ran on for another ten laps. Awoke this morning with a dwarf hammering nails into my right foot, or so it felt!

If I was a dwarf, I would not be Happy, but Grumpy and deserve to be punished for such a self-inflicted injury! I should be back on my feet in three to four days. However, the gymnasium is still accessible for trimming my waistline. Exercise each day acts as a release to frustrations and boredom; these are plenty I assure you!

The soldiers' morale remains high, adapting well and accepting each change imposed on them with remarkable fortitude. It is however grossly unfair that, unlike the French, Canadians, Ukrainians and Pakistanis, all around us on UN duty in Yugoslavia, that we do not get UN pay. We consider ourselves the most professional force here [if not in the world, a delightful British self-confidence founded on the self-belief bred at Sandhurst and carried forward into regimental life] but here we are less paid and rewarded for doing more than those around us. I am not on duty for extra pay, but fairness would be a good position to find ourselves!

We get paid 80p extra per day to live in poverty and austerity in the recognised hardest area in Bosnia, because of our volunteered professionalism. Six months without fresh food, living in mud holes, no luxuries and away from our families. What do we get? A pat on the back for our hard and loyal work. This loyalty can be stretched too far; we deserve at least what other UN duty-bound soldiers and servants are paid and, indeed, as a professional force this payment would be justified. It is an understandable gripe of the boys and one I listen to daily and support, whilst not openly airing my thoughts, as one must remain aligned to the corporate message!

Should a Ukrainian or Pakistani Corporal or other nationality be paid as much as a British Colonel? Remarkably here on operational duty in Bosnia and within the UN forces they are, as our government retains the UN payment and does not pass it on to the soldiers, as other nations do. As the echo of the soldiers proclaims regularly on this point, in a distinctive West Country accent "Sir, this is bollocks, just bollocks!"

I've said my piece, peace be with you Mum and Dad!

The Ukrainian BTR-four wheeled armoured personnel carrier could be found stationary at the limited OPs allocated to their command.

23rd November 1994

Just when you believe this forsaken place is returning to comparative normality the Holy Father delivers another dose of the unexpected. This is an issuance that he appears to have held on reserve for Bosnia-Herzegovina. Thank you, Lord!

No doubt you are aware of the Bosniaks' and BiH's latest attempts to go on the offensive throughout Bosnia: Bihac, Sarajevo, Mount Igman and Gornji Vakuf. Encouraged by limited success, the rest of the BiH forces think: "Now hang on a second, if our boys in Bihac can flex their muscles a bit, then I'm pretty sure we should."

These individual actions, whilst we are assured by the Bosniaks are a co-ordinated effort, appear disparate and badly co-ordinated and with no specific point of effort. However, supposedly importantly, they are doing so in contradiction of the UN mandate, but to date no sign of UN discontent has been expressed as to these Bosniak misdemeanours.

Naturally "Ivan the Terrible", or so he is portrayed (the Serbian), sits back and makes his own assessment. "Now hang on," he says similarly, whilst scratching his Balkan beard. "These meandering Muslims are attacking us from within and out of UN safe havens, not in keeping with the rules at play, so what can I do to retaliate?" Naturally any act Ivan undertakes will be an act of aggression and as such the UN will voice its discontent quickly. Enter NATO and the U.S.-led "let's bomb Johnny the Serb" campaign! He is the bad boy after all, isn't he? Who suffers when the U.S. bombs the Serbs? They do of course, but also all UN troops on the ground, the recipients of revenge.

Now, I am not saying that I am pro-Serb, as I am not and they are responsible for some terrible, unforgiveable, heinous actions and crimes, but the BiH are also to be found guilty for the role they have played. We need a fair distribution of blame and recourse and must try and retain some objectivity. After all, it is the leadership of the Serbs that must carry the blame, as not all Serbs are dispossessed of any sense of humanity. To recall and refer to a marvellous assessment by one of the soldiers: "Sir I'm not a politician and I'm not paid to make decisions, but surely the only people who deserve a good kicking now are the Bosniaks." His view is that the protagonists are presently the Bosniaks, the Muslims, and they are threatening the fragility of peace through their actions and this fractures our own security. Their actions are seen as being a necessity, being caught in a cycle of despair, but it appears we are caught amidst this madness and despite our best efforts, our purpose is sorrowful in its pursuit of success, long-lasting peace.

Comparative to other areas of Bosnia, Goražde remains comparatively quiet,

284

not that these warring factions are nearing any sort of agreement in our area, but it is merely because the Serbs are busy elsewhere and the Bosniaks are not quite ready to mount effective offensive operations themselves. If everything holds at this state for two to three more more weeks, then the winter snows will curtail any military activity and guarantee 1RGBW a quiet Christmas.

I have continued with my fitness campaign and today, partnered by Matthew Shaw, set a new Goražde force record of 20 minutes 57 seconds for the four mile Drina River circuit. Can I maintain this level of enthusiasm for burning the rubber soles of my trainers until March 1995? Probably, as there is little else to do! However, although training hard in the gymnasium, I have sadly had to resign myself to no modelling contracts with jockey Y-fronts due to inheriting Dad's legs. A fine set of pins if you ask me, a sparrow's legs poking from the bottom of a nest others say!

Back to my day job and the question of leadership. It is a subject I have dedicated much time to understanding in my readings, from Alexander the Great to Wellington to Montgomery and most significantly, Colonel Carne of Imjin and 1Glosters fame! When considering the requirements of leadership here in Goražde, you do not just need fire and brimstone leadership, as it is not healthy to have all the officers in battalion with a downward focus and strength. You need leadership that is upward and outward looking and to this end Battalion Headquarters has a good mix on this front, from the CO to his very capable OPs officer and 2IC, who is considered and calm in demeanour and action. It is a good balance to have this at the heart and centre and company commanders that bridge this effectively into their duties on the ground. Both Ian Harris (A Company) and Patrick Tomlinson (B Company), are well respected by their men, and literally in the trenches, whilst being able to manage upwards into battalion headquarters effectively. You cannot be splendid and excellent in all areas (apart from my fine self of course!), but understanding your strengths and, more so, your weaknesses and how best to fill these with the strengths of those about you is a talent and one that can make a good leader, great. This is the art of leadership you could argue. Between us across the battalion all and any gaps are filled with appropriate capabilities.

I am fortunate, however, for being directly under Patrick T. He is stern and has a robustness about his leadership style, is brutally efficient and professional, which secures respect by all ranks. Unfortunately, he leaves on December 14th and I understand is being replaced by a younger and less proven company commander, Major Simon Gray. Simon has a task on his hands in picking up from Patrick, but I will do my best to help in this transition.

Considering the above, it is appropriate to point out B Company has a very strong and noticeable 'Gloster' influence. This, beyond all, will be my abiding memory of serving in the British Army, to have been given the privilege to command the men of Gloucestershire and Bristol, and I hope to have held their respect. These memories are priceless, which has been enriched at the end of my service by serving with the men of Berkshire and Wiltshire, where there are some very fine men to be found also.

Unfortunately, the RGBW is not the regiment I joined, where the Ministry of Defence appears determined to erode all that was unique and irreplaceable about the regimental system of the British Army. The 'Glorious Glosters' will remain my regiment, but RGBW has also found a place in my heart through this tour. I am a little bias of course, but such blind regimental loyalty, even if misplaced, is a unique and adds strength to the British Army. I fear the regimental system is to be lost in ongoing cuts and with it much of the distinct identity found within the army.

A DESIRE FOR HOME

Captain Matt Shaw
(Intelligence Officer) and
Captain David Brown
(Operations Officer)

The rolling Cotswold hills scramble from the edge of a market town
Patchwork speckled fields rich in colour, yellow, green, golden brown
Dry stone walls carefully laid by hand meet fresh waters passing by
Deep hidden waters of Severn, Thames, green valley River Wye
Hold images of olden days and men sitting beside their flocks
Listen and we hear them whisper of legends and long-lost tales
They speak of simple days of hardened men of an earthy stock
They mourn a changing England, their blessed home and history
Silent pockets of a countryside enriched by ancient mysteries
A country that lives and thrives and shines a most glorious past
Modest men with simple tasks have created a story unsurpassed

THE RIFLE COMPANIES AND THEIR COMMANDERS

"We were not inundated with visitors [due to the Serb blockade]. What it did mean, however, is that when notified of a visit of importance it was highly likely to be a VVIP."

Lieutenant Colonel Patrick Davidson-Houston with UNPROFOR Commander, General Sir Michael Rose, late summer visit

Lieutenant Colonel Patrick Davidson-Houston with UNPROFOR Commander, General Sir Michael Rose, mid-winter visit

Lieutenant Colonel Patrick Davidson-Houston with Martin Bell

MEB with BBC reporter, Gorazde

"At the very moment
I concluded the service,
the sniper fired into the
cemetery. It was not a time
to give in to threats.
I recall announcing clearly
and loudly, the priest will
carry on."

CHAPTER 11

THE PADRE

THE PADRE

Patrick Irwin is a remarkable man, he's tall and greying and
quaintly peppered trim

Adept at things godly and fatherly counselling, he listens
with patience to every Tommy's whim

Divinity and theology learnt while studying, applied to
soldier's gaiety with a tipple of Gordon's gin

Righteous and religious with a forgiving heart on sin,
enjoying entertaining and caring not to win

Eccentric and effusive memories recall, the Lord's word
delivered with cheerful bobbing grin

29th January 1995

Note: Captain Patrick Irwin was the 1RGBW padre for the Bosnian tour 1994-95.
Written on 29th January 1995 after an impromptu service at Rogatica checkpoint.

Memories of the Battalion's Padre
Patrick Irwin

I had envisaged incorporating Patrick Irwin's memories within the chapter covering religion, but as my investigations and interviews unfolded, it became obvious he was held in such high regard by so many that had served with him that his contribution needed to be noted differently. In his short time in Goražde as the battalion's padre, he created colourful memories and offered words of counsel that had remained embedded in the consciousness of many. These were held to such an extent I felt it appropriate to include his memories, but to give them their own stage.

As I outline in the chapter on religion: "His eccentricity made religion approachable, enjoyable and believable. He was a figure in the shadows but offered a point of contact with no allegiance and outside the framework of rank and order of army life, and one the soldiers needed."

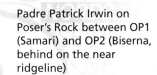

Padre Patrick Irwin on Poser's Rock between OP1 (Samari) and OP2 (Biserna, behind on the near ridgeline)

Here are some memories offered by Patrick:

Taking Communion

On Sunday evenings, I used to conduct worship in the cookhouse tent. This was next to where the cooks prepared the evening meal and therefore had the simple advantage of being warm. I used to conduct Prayer Book Evensong (with hymns) followed by Prayer Book Communion for those who wished to remain. I had taken with me to Goražde the old Army Field Service Book in preference to its successor for two reasons:

1. It was more compact than the newer version, which was far too large. (This fault has now been rectified, with the Field Service Book again small enough to fit in a pocket.)

2. The old book also contained a good variety of hymns. Its successor had far too few.

I may well have been the only chaplain in the 1990s to deploy with the old Field Service Books, but I remain convinced that I made the right choice. Those who worshipped on Sunday evenings in the cookhouse tent in Goražde enjoyed the familiarity of traditional language and the opportunity to sing well-known hymns.

Remembrance Sunday – 22 Services remembered

"On Remembrance Sunday 1994 Commander Goražde Force (the CO) decided that all four of the national contingents would sing their National Anthems.

The hundreds of Britons had no difficulty with God Save the Queen and the Ukrainians formed a choir of fifty to sing their National Anthem (after they had learned it!). Nineteen Norwegian medics sang the Norwegian National Anthem quietly and elegantly. The French, however, were not very happy with the arrangement.

Four French sergeants were serving with us, and of these one was always on duty on the radio. One of the sergeants approached me to explain their concern, "Mon Pére," he said, "We are professional soldiers, not professional singers. It is not possible for three of us to sing La Marseillaise in the ceremony."

I assured him that he and his colleagues need not worry; I would sing the French National Anthem myself as a solo. This I did at full volume. Afterwards I was told that my singing was reminiscent of the French rugby stadium in Paris, which may have suggested that the volume was more notable than the delicacy of intonation.

The Central Remembrance Sunday service was a memorable occasion, with live shellfire in the background punctuating the Two Minutes' Silence, naturally made the more poignant due to the loss of our four comrades in September.

I took the opportunity provided by Remembrance Sunday to dedicate a memorial on the Bosnian Serb side of the ceasefire line to a British soldier killed earlier in the conflict. He had been killed by the Bosnian Serbs and it was rather poignant to hold the ceremony with the soldier's colleagues in front of the men who had killed him. Thirty minutes later these British soldiers joined other Bosnian Serbs for a joint Remembrance Day service, remembering the allegiance between the United Kingdom and Serbia.

In the evening of Remembrance Sunday, I conducted a service in French for the French sergeants and their invited guests. Afterwards we had a very jovial reception. Many of our soldiers were out in the OPs and so I travelled round them conducting short ceremonies over the Remembrance weekend. In all I conducted twenty-two services!

Christmas 1994

The Norwegian medical unit was based opposite our medics and I came to know them well. Shared accommodation for both sexes was normal in the Norwegian Army and the Norwegians were fascinated by our concern to provide female accommodation for visiting RLC drivers.

I was similarly fascinated to read the briefing material provided for Bosnia, which was much better than anything provided to the British soldiers. I still remember being asked in all seriousness by a British subaltern if the Bosnian Muslims were Christian. Such a question would be inconceivable now.

I conducted various services in Norwegian for the Norwegian contingent, including a memorial service for a Norwegian soldier killed elsewhere in Bosnia, traditional candle-lighting ceremonies on Sundays in Advent, and a Christmas service.

I had sent a copy of my draft Christmas service to the Norwegian chaplain in Tuzla, the Dean of Stavanger Cathedral, who would become a good friend of mine, asking him if it would be appropriate. He replied graciously that it was excellent, and he would use it himself in Tuzla!

Norwegians celebrate Christmas on 24th December and so we could have the Norwegian service and dinner before moving on to the British celebrations. The Norwegians were surprised in the British service to hear mention made in the reading about the Wise Men of King Harald, rather than King Herod. I spotted this error and told the reader to apologise to the Norwegians afterwards, which he

292

promptly did. No insult had been intended to King Harald of Norway!

On Christmas Eve, we had a splendid Midnight Mass and I also took Christmas services around the OPs; it was very picturesque singing Christmas carols in small groups in the snow. However, my most memorable service that Christmas occurred by chance. After Midnight Mass I walked around the camp to visit the sentries. At the back gate, I found a young soldier from Somerset on duty. He told me that at home he used to go to church at Christmas with his girlfriend and he was sorry that he had not been to church this Christmas. Had he told his N.C.O. that he wished to attend the Midnight Mass, he would probably have been allowed to do so, but at least he was now talking to the right man! I had all the kit for Midnight Mass and nothing else to do, so I celebrated another full Midnight Mass in the ruins of the bus station for a congregation of one by the light of the security light. I used part of a wrecked bus as an altar.

I was also keen to contact the Ukrainian soldiers, who formed part of the U.N. Goražde Force. I asked the major in command if I might visit his troops, but he told me that all his soldiers were atheists. I doubted this but explained that it would be useful for his soldiers to know who I was as I was often meeting them at checkpoints.

One of the hundreds of Christmas cards sent from the children of Gloucestershire to the serving soldiers in Goražde, Christmas 1994

I was duly invited to visit the Ukrainian company. When I arrived, the soldiers were all drawn up as if for the visit of a V.I.P., so my first task was to persuade them to relax. Through an interpreter, I told them about the work of army chaplains in general and my own responsibilities. After my address the soldiers spontaneously lined up to meet me. One after another they told me that they were Christian believers, often indicating the crosses that they were wearing round their necks.

Most Orthodox Churches still follow the Julian calendar, so Christmas is celebrated on our 6th January. On this date I was on leave, but I chose the Orthodox Feast of St Nicholas (our 19th December) to visit all the Ukrainian OPs in turn. At all of them I handed out Orthodox Christmas cards I had obtained from England and seasonal food and said prayers. At the final OP, manned by the Ukrainian recce platoon, I was asked by one of the soldiers if I would celebrate the Liturgy for them. I pointed out that I was Anglican rather than Orthodox, but the soldier replied that they did not have an Orthodox chaplain and the Bosnian Serb Orthodox priests never visited them, so there was no chance of their having an Orthodox Liturgy that Christmas. I duly celebrated the Eucharist in English, using my interpreter to translate what I was saying. The soldiers were most appreciative.

The one who had asked me to celebrate the Liturgy for them now presented me with his Ukrainian Bible. It was a Gideon Bible and I thought how interested the American businessmen who had paid for its production would have been to hear how it had travelled with the soldier from Kiev to an OP in Bosnia to be given to a British Army chaplain.

The Serbian Orthodox Church of St George (*built 1454*)

"I used to meet the local Bosnian Serb Orthodox priest and took an interest in the medieval Orthodox Church, just beyond the ceasefire line, which our Engineers re-roofed. It was the second oldest Orthodox church in Bosnia–Herzegovina and as such of considerable interest to the Bosnian Serb leadership.

On inspecting the building, I realised that a side-chapel in it had been used for Roman Catholic worship. This the Orthodox priest and local authorities strongly denied, but I suspected they were lying. I arranged to speak to a Bosnian Serb soldier and to a local architect, both confirming that Roman Catholics had used the chapel in the church for worship in the past.

Now the church has had a further restoration and a little exhibition at the church tells the story of this restoration but makes no mention of either the Royal Engineers or of the fact that Roman Catholics had worshipped in the chapel.

On one occasion the CO and I were invited by the Bosnian Serbs to attend

St. Georges, Goražde, 2012

the dedication of a church. This was a propaganda ploy as we were kept waiting until the church service was over and then invited to join the celebratory lunch, at which time some released prisoners were welcomed. This was duly filmed by the Bosnian Serbs, who had cannily ensured that the UN would feature in their shots.

Afterwards I insisted that we wanted to visit the church and the Bosnian Serbs reluctantly took us to see it. Once inside I delivered an extempore lecture on Orthodox Church furnishings to make the point that we were interested in such things.

Meetings with the Mufti

I had regular meetings with the Mufti, the religious head of the Muslim community in Goražde. I always knew in advance the atmosphere in which the meeting would be held. If the relations were good that day between the government in Sarajevo and the United Nations, then our meeting would be a friendly affair. If there were difficulties at national level our own meeting would acquire a certain tension.

We often had very enjoyable conversations. The Mufti would tell me that I should become a Muslim, because so many of the Bible stories could be found in the Koran. I would reply that this was because the Muslims had taken them from the Bible, so he might as well become a Christian.

Sometimes I had a difficult wicket on which to bat. Two occasions spring to mind:

1. Once I had to explain to the Mufti that the pantomime put on by our soldiers for the local children in the theatre was not intended to convert the children to Christianity. I pointed out that we had not been telling the story of the baby Jesus or singing religious carols with the children, and in any case in England pantomimes tended to be regarded as seasonal fun rather than Evangelistic opportunities. A memorable feature of the pantomime included by the Engineers based on the Pied Piper town of Hamelin was an evil rat. Rat means war in Serbo–Croat and so the story contained the subliminal message that "war is bad". The Mufti was particularly annoyed about the pantomime because the UN had refused to bring him a supply of Korans. (The UN realised that the books would never be allowed through Bosnian Serb lines.).

2. On another occasion, a young captain running the camp's Christmas show thought it would be amusing to impersonate the town's community leader. Whilst well meaning, this turned out to be not the best of ideas, as his warblings were carried by loudspeaker across the town to the Bosnian Serbs in the hills. The captain's colleagues had to pacify the Bosnian Serbs, who feared that the calls being heard from the camp were a prelude to an attack from Goražde, and I had to similarly explain to the Mufti the following morning that the behaviour of this young officer was not intended to insult Muslims, which indeed he had not intended to do so. I took some time, however, to explain that the English fondness for portraying comical clergy was not perceived as anti-Christian."

Founding the Croatian Association of St Dominic

Within Goražde there was a small Roman Catholic community, whose priest had fled. I used to take services for this community in Latin and English (with an interpreter). I helped to establish the Croatian Association of St Dominic for them, with myself as its chaplain. We used the term 'association' rather than 'church' or 'parish' to make it easier for Muslim spouses to belong to it.

On Christmas morning, I set out from the camp to take a Christmas service for the local Roman Catholics in the UNHCR centre. Into my Bergen (rucksack) I had placed the liturgical items that I needed for the service and a couple of

Christmas cakes and a 100 mince pies. En route, we were surrounded by hundreds of local Muslim children chanting 'bon bon'. They were firmly of the opinion that Christmas was a time when they should be given sweets, with some demanding to know what I had in my Bergen.

I told the British interpreter with me to say that the Bergen contained books and other items needed for the service, which indeed it did. On arrival at the UNHCR centre I unpacked the Bergen and the interpreter was horrified to see the cakes and mince pies emerge. He accused me of lying, but I pointed out that my reply had been strictly true. I added that if we had revealed the quantity of food with us we would never have succeeded in bringing it through the crowds of children. After all it seemed reasonable for us to share our Christmas food with our fellow Christians.

I also took with me a choir formed from the Norwegian contingent, which sang some beautiful Norwegian and international carols. The local Roman Catholics were thrilled.

The priest will carry on!

At All Saint's Tide it was traditional for the local Roman Catholics to visit the graves of their relatives. The local Roman Catholic cemetery had originally been an Austro–Hungarian military cemetery, linked with the military hospital in Goražde.

I arranged for the Muslim Civil Defence team to tidy up the cemetery and for the Austrian equivalent of the Commonwealth War Graves Commission to send us ribbons, which we attached to home-made wreaths and these were ceremoniously laid at the Austro–Hungarian memorial. The Austrians were thrilled by this and both the foreign minister and the defence minister of Austria wrote me letters of appreciation.

On All Saints Day, I celebrated a Eucharist in the cemetery, which was to be followed by a procession. The Roman Catholics gathered outside the UN camp and walked in procession under our protection to the cemetery. We had informed the Bosnian Serbs that a service was to be held in the cemetery under UN auspices.

We knew that a Bosnian Serb sniper was positioned overlooking the cemetery (on a previous occasion a bullet fired from his position had passed between me and the NCO to whom I was talking.) At the very moment that I concluded the service in the cemetery the sniper fired into the cemetery. Our soldiers took up firing positions and the congregation waited to see if I would lead the planned procession or call it off. It was not a time to give in to threats, announcing clearly and quote loudly I recall 'The priest will carry on' and set off at the head of the procession through the cemetery, singing an appropriate Austrian Easter hymn, a resplendent sight in the abandoned Roman Catholic vestments that I had borrowed for the occasion.

Fortunately, the sniper did not fire again and that night the incident was mentioned on the BBC World Service News, though I was irritated to hear the service described as an inter-faith ceremony, as it was a normal Christian service. It was attended by the Mufti in the way that local religious leaders used to attend festivals of different traditions in the harmonious days before the war. Ironically, the service in the Austro–Hungarian military ceremony took place on the anniversary of the Battle of Vittorio Veneto in 1918 in which the Glorious Glosters participated in the decisive Allied victory over the Austro–Hungarian army."

Donkey Mail and Postman Padre-Pat

When the Bosnian Serbs refused to allow us fuel supplies and our vehicles could no longer be used, there was a danger that mail deliveries to the OPs would be suspended.

Soldiers on operations look forward to receiving their mail, and I immediately volunteered to act as postman. I would fill my Bergen with letters and parcels and accompany patrols to the various OPs, collecting any outgoing mail at the same time. I enjoyed my role as Postman Pat, and my new role guaranteed me a warm welcome wherever I went!

Eventually transport with mule carts were organised, and I rode on the first one, driven by the indomitable Corporal Hack.

Sergeant Desborough and the author prepare the Royal Mail Mule Train for its next venture into the mountains

WE SANG JERUSALEM

At Rogatica we sang Jerusalem
As if standing in Cheltenham Spa
With silent thoughts of loved ones
High lifted voices to praise the Lord
Frosted fingers touch hand in glove
All men and women in true accord
Their distant parents dream of Bosnia
And their Lord, they sing, Jerusalem.

In the shadows the soldiers cluster
Half-filled circle of a blue beret crowd
Green shoulders touching in the cold
Throughout Rogatica the song is heard
English voices sing both clear and loud
Everyman's heart most safely stirred
Duty and loyalty were well endowed
Calmness born amid local disconcert

Then we stood and sang for Jesus
We were soldiers of the cross
Lifting high his royal banner
To his trumpet call we would obey
No flinch or stutter or nervous stammer
To break us from that glorious day
We could not suffer a holy loss
As we stood and sang for Jesus

O Lord of love and mighty power
Protect us from tempest, fire and foe
For we shall rise and sing to thee
For those that walk-in foaming deep
Or those in peril on the sea
Your hand in mine I will sleep
Then guide and show me where to go
A rifle my shield in this violent hour

Did your holy feet touch this land
Did you walk these hills of green
Or did your fingers of desire
Miss this time that now unfolds
Turning meadows to fields of fire
And warmest hearts to hearts of cold
More pain and hunger than I have seen
Souls that have missed your loving hand

We sang at Rogatica to my Lord
Alleluia! Praising him we could hear
As his soldiers held the cross on high
And swept across this Serbian sea
We could not let these children die
God hear us sing and set them free
In that rising morn we showed no fear
We honour you with hallowed sword

3 February 1995.

Note: Written at Rogatica checkpoint, central Bosnia.

The Padre, Sergeant Major Yemm and the author sing Jerusalem

25th November 1994

The days slip by and with the infrequency of the convoys going out of Goražde, this letter will probably arrive hot on the heels of my last letter about Topalovic (or even before it!).

Last night I had a bizarre and quite surreal evening. After obtaining permission from our great leader, the Commanding Officer, he allowed us to hold a birthday party for one of the Sergeants, a member of 2:2 SAS, attached to IRGBW in Goražde.

A dozen or so RGBW officers attended, including the eccentric Padre. The latter gave a novel foot-stomping demonstration (and us much amusement), whilst dancing to the rhythmical tunes of various '60s and '70s tunes and songs. In attendance were the translators, local representatives of the UNHCR and half a dozen BiH soldiers. The cooks, or slop-jockeys as they are affectionately known, whipped up a light, colourless and remarkably tasteless buffet. We were issued our single can of Boddingtons, my first alcoholic drink in ten weeks, and were kindly offered by the BiH to partake in the now expected ritual of slivovitz drinking. I kindly refused, as the tastes and smell of this liquid from the devil's arse and hell's lavatory will be the lingering taste and memory of my six months in Goražde!

There we were, dressed in combats with pistols at our sides, dancing with our Yugoslavian translators, helmets and body armour lounging leisurely on the chairs surrounding us. The whole gathering was listening to English pop songs or American bands on the smallest of JVC stereo systems you could imagine (better used for a music festival for mice), in the presence of BiH soldiers looking inquisitively on at the UN soldiers conducting poor impressions of John Travolta or even poorer ones of Elvis Presley!

Whilst our tomfoolery was going on, outside the town of Goražde remained blackened and silent, shadows disguising the presence of Bosniak and Serbian soldiers occupying positions around the town and on the surrounding hills. The evening ended sharply at 2330. Unlike any evening of joviality in England, there were no clubs, pizza stops or wine bars to move on to, no "back to my house for coffee" (or other), no refreshing walk in the crisp hours of darkness. As we stepped outside, we were met by the beams of the white UN Land Rover with Lance Corporal Mason tucked inside ready to carry us back to reality, back to the shadows of the Saxon, the characterless Italian Portacabins and the warm, but welcoming, army issue sleeping bag. I climbed into bed and read a few pages of my latest literary challenge, Catch 22 by Joseph Heller. I am unsure if I managed 4 to 5 pages, as the next thing I knew it was early morning and Robinson was delivering his morning call, accompanied by a cup of "kick-starting sweet and luxurious tea", and so another day begins. Day 87 of 194.

Šljivovica: "the taste and smell of this liquid from the devil's arse and hell's lavatory will be the lingering taste and memory of my six months in Goražde!"

ENGLAND IS CALLING

England is calling, my home, my heartfelt fallow pastures sing to me
Her green meadows will be peppered with spring flowers now
I see framed falling light of a reddened sunset Cotswold matinee
Light caps river banked tearful willow trees that take a final bow

Golden light streams through the soft leaves of new spring growth
Flickering light that bears and holds shadows like mother with child
Words leap from shadows as if fingers of light offering a godly oath
No harshness in their brightness of pastel colours and gently mild

Like fluorescent light found at alter end in Gloucester Cathedral
The sunset bids farewell to the day and welcomes in the night
A badger and fox call and owls and bats gather for the midnight ball
In the light of the moon that coverts the fields cobalt blue and bright

This is my calling and the beckoning of my beloved country England
Captured in the moment when the light of sunset bids the day farewell
Like the spiralling arms of the ancient wizard and his swirling hand
Oaken wand breaks the day and summons night with hallowed bell

6th December 1994

This is going to be a note scribbled in haste as a convoy, we are led to believe, is on its way to Kiseljak tomorrow. Apart from the engineer convoy that arrived on Sunday having been 'held hostage' for seven days, we have not had a convoy into this Goražde since November 20th. I wonder how many letters are stacked in Kiseljak waiting to be transported and delivered to the boys in Goražde. Imagine 500(+) soldiers all pending Xmas parcels, goodies, cakes, chocolate, letters, presents galore. How many trucks will be needed? How many trucks will the Serbs allow in?

The convoy delays and infrequent arrivals have become part of life in Goražde. Whilst they create temporary hardship and take away any sense of luxury we could enjoy through the delivery of heartfelt letters, fresh food or diesel that keeps us fully operational, you can and do cope with such shortcomings. The frustrations and humiliation at having to be subservient to the Serbs at checkpoints, whilst galling, can also be accommodated, although this imposition does dig deep into the psyche of the soldiers, proud as they are to be professional and British.

More than anything else, I think the delay and infrequency of mail delivery does have an eroding impact on morale, especially in the run-up to Christmas when your thoughts are more so at home with the family, especially those with children.

Fresh food can be replaced by ration packs, no diesel and you can walk or even buy a donkey, no letters leaves a void. There is something timeless and perfect about handing out the mail, parcels and letters. The rustling sound of an envelope being ripped open, the silence that follows as the words are read and reread. Knowing your loved ones, family or friends have taken time to sit and write to you, and knowing it is their touch which was the last on the paper in your hands is precious.

I have been reasonably well received on the letter front. Having put pen to paper religiously in my first few weeks, writing to many friends with enthusiasm, it now appears to be paying dividend. I respond to those that have written, although I will not chase friendship with others I have reached out to in the hope they can find time, 30 minutes or so, to write a few scribbled words. There's probably no intent in not writing, but I know I would find this time to write if I had a friend away and found a letter on my doormat one morning. If nothing else, it's courteous and simply the right thing to do.

I have heard from Nick Argles and Lucy Watts on several occasions, Sarah Davies, Caroline Watkins, Georgie Smith, Richard Tams, Juliette Thwaites, Binks (Alistair Cordon-Lloyd), Matthew Stone, Jeremy Welch, Charlie Barton, Aunty June, Claude Rebbeck (Regimental Secretary) and many others. It is warming to hear from so many friends at home and I feel privileged to have such a rich tapestry of friendship. I am, however, disappointed, to not have heard from some friends I had thought close.

I feel jealous about their freedom, their lives as a happy go lucky civilian, and this is key to understanding why I wish to leave the army. Time spent in service has been rewarding, not least now, as they will not have had this experience or the privilege of commanding the men of Gloucestershire and more laterally, Berkshire and Wiltshire. I am looking forward to this freedom but will similarly miss what I have now and have had in service.

Back to my daily business. No convoys and therefore no fuel. No fuel and therefore more foot patrols. Bloody hot when we first arrived, too hot with the summer temperatures reaching 80F+, now the other extreme, crisp cold mornings with heavy mists that remind me of the Brecon Beacons. It grasps and holds tight to the extremities, and the fingers, ears and nose feel the early brutality of a Yugoslavian winter. Early brutality, as we understand mid and late winter will be more brutal still. I pity the poor private soldier on sentry throughout the night, where the wind chill factor, the temperature can drop to -15/-20 on the higher reaches of the Senokos and Samari.

Samari, what a 'to do' about my poetry! Would Mr. Banks (my English master at Adams) believe it? It's amazing what levels of advancement can be found with a little dedication, a little imagination, a retreat of 6 months to the English Literary School, Goražde, Bosnia and the input of one eccentric priest! I am delighted, of course, that Sentry on Samari has found a fan or two! You said it will be published in a book of modern English poets? There can not be many therefore!

One month, four days until leave. I can smell Boddingtons on the wind, Mother's Sunday honey-roasted gammon and the loving loyalty and attention of Tess 28/LXi, the Regimental Dog.

Lieutenant Gary McDade and the author on a winter patrol en route to OP3

14th December 1994

Once again in haste, I scribble furiously to finish a letter and for it to catch the convoy leaving early tomorrow. Convoys are so infrequent that the sense of urgency to put pen to paper has diminished, as all letters will be so out of date upon arrival, but I hope late news is better than none!

Tonight, is the last night that Patrick commands B Company. He leaves tomorrow morning at 0600 for England and, I am led to believe, to be Chief Instructor at Sandhurst. He has been a pleasure to work with: knowledgeable, stern, fair, commanding respect and leading by example. As a leader, his main asset is his ability to demonstrate trust and yet guide his men, and he draws out the best qualities in his senior and junior commanders by giving them responsibility; he trusts them. He did, in his closing speech to the Company, pay me a fine compliment, warranted or not, when saying: "Maurice has made my job of command a pleasure, in that he has worked with high degree of professionalism and in good humour throughout. The decisions I have made have always been with the counsel and views of my 2IC." As I said, he is a damn fine fellow and obviously astute!

I feel sure that Patrick will go on to command the battalion and do a very good job of it. However, he like so many others, has questions about his future in the Services, due to the uncertainty of the armed forces during a period of change. Significantly, his wife Charlie, appears set on him leaving the forces. Ultimately, I have no doubt this will be the card that forces his hand, as it is for many when love of family comes head-to-head with your love of service.

The policy being followed and pursued steadfastly by the government, in driving down head count and capability whilst increasing operational duties, is and will lead to a brain and quality drain from the forces. This appears short-sighted in my opinion, especially as we are entering a period when the Armed forces will need to change their focus post-Cold War to deal with new international demands and who knows what threat, for example Bosnia. This issue, this challenge, will be on the governmental and international agenda in future years, as we are entering a period of global change. I am not sure what is coming, but the status quo provided by the Cold War will be replaced I feel with something more sinister, more open and divisive, a social, racial or religious divide perhaps, as we have found in a microcosm in Bosnia.

Enough of this, Patrick and I had a good, no better than that, great working relationship. The new OC, Simon Gray, is younger, has much less experience than Patrick, but seems a nice enough chap. As Robinson, my energetic and 6'2" radio operator from the West Country said: "Sir, Major Gray thinks he's the Daddy

Right: The irrepressible Private Robinson and the author high up in B Company's sector

now, but we know who's the Daddy. He's about 5'8" and runs like a greyhound with a bouffant hairstyle and has a ridiculous name! We'll sort 'im out no problem boss!"

Not long until Christmas now, two missed out of the last three isn't that bad, it could have been a hat-trick. What will be happening to me this time next year? Who knows? Twenty-seven days until leave - only twenty-seven. Considering that we've been here for 109, I don't think I have long to go for a brief taste of freedom, of normality and I hope, boiled ham, roasties, parsley sauce and peas, such a simple delight and one that I am putting in an advance order, Mum!

Right: GPMG (SF) machine gun, OP1, looking down into the valley below and trained onto the principal Serb positions below.

FIRE REPORT AS AT 0100 HOURS

Guzump - ripple, ripple, ripple
Echoes from mountains high
Of heavy weapons exploding
Fly through spring time sky

Sssump - waffle, waffle, waffle
The rocket tube ignited
Of anti-tank exploding
From battle trench is sighted

Crackle - fizzle, fizzle, fizzle
Of tracer burning bright
Of rifle breach discharged
The red illuminated night

Guzump - Sssump - Crackle
Heard throughout the day
Of rifle, gun and rocket
Shows war is here to stay

Note: Written December 1994 after a long, cold and snow white patrol.

"This time I hoped I could complete the marathon without stopping, or rather being stopped. It was unfinished business, you could say."

CHAPTER 12

A STORY OF TWO MARATHONS

Two memorable days in my life are intrinsically linked by the commonality of the event, its location and cause. They are the running of a marathon in Goražde, and both for a charity. There are twenty years between the two; the first was undertaken on Christmas Day 1994 and the second in early April 2015. In 1994 I was twenty-five years old, a captain in the infantry, had not been drinking for four months, was running and patrolling every day across the Yugoslavian mountains and was by any standards as fit as a butcher's dog. Roll forward twenty years and I am a desk-bound company director, overweight, despite my best efforts to lose it in preparation for the marathon but hoping my body memory would carry me through the day.

What gave me the purpose to run the second was the charity I had set up after my visit to Goražde in 2012; The Goražde Children's Foundation, Bosnia. Its foundation and this part of my Bosnian journey is outlined in more detail in another chapter but having established it with an aim to raise funds to help the primary school in the town, I needed something, an additional purpose or event on which to focus my fundraising efforts. I determined I would run a marathon, ending up at the school but starting in the hills above the town. It was an echo of when I had run a marathon from Višegrad, downriver from the same town on Christmas Day 1994, ending that day at the hospital in Goražde. I had originally thought and hoped of replicating this same run but had been advised against it due to the uncertainty of being able to start and run the majority through the Republika Srpska. As it happened, the revised route allowed me to pass en route the memorials to my four fallen comrades, so it proved a positive turn of events.

This time I hoped I could complete the marathon without stopping, or rather being stopped. It was unfinished business, you could say.

I had, in my day, been a good runner, a gift from my father, also a very good cross-country runner, and I invariably found myself at the front or in sight of it at battalion level. It was with this background that in 1994 I had convinced my commanding officer, the then Lieutenant Colonel Martin Vine, to allow me to run a series of marathons to raise money for the charity Sightsavers, raising sufficient to give sight back to 300 children in Bangladesh. This was aligned to 1994 being the tercentenary of The Gloucestershire Regiment, founded on 5 March 1694 by John Gibson.

By the spring of 1994 I had completed the London, New York, Ottawa and Cairo marathons, the last being run between the great pyramids and along the cluttered back streets and festering canals and waterways that surround the city en route to the pyramids of Saqqara. The races had been completed in back-to-back fashion all within the previous ten months, with the aim being to undertake a final and fifth marathon in Kenya. I was running comfortably under three hours, as I did in Egypt, and hoped to break two hours 45 minutes, which I had set as my target for the final marathon in Kenya. There were links and reasons for each; London being a home marathon; New York as my regiment held the US Unit Citation of Honour, which had been awarded to it after the Battle of Imjin River in 1951; The Royal Canadian Rifles was a sister regiment, just as the Kenyan

The Glosters 300 Marathon Team, the Pyramids Marathon January 1994

310

The Glosters' marathon team run through the rugged and desolate terrain that would take them back to the Great Pyramids

Forces were. A trip to Kenya would also be nodding my head to my father, as he had served in the country as an officer in the King's African Rifles, fighting in the Mau Mau uprising in the early 1950s.

However, with the deployment to Bosnia, the final leg was cancelled, my patron, Martin, being replaced by the new commanding officer, Lieutenant Colonel Patrick Davidson-Houston, who gave his blessing for a proposed running of a six-man marathon on Christmas Day that year in Bosnia. This only came about that October, after we had been in Goražde for some weeks, when I put forward the suggestion. Christmas Day was a few months away, with training getting under way with daily runs through the town and helped by my day-to-day patrolling duties into the mountains.

Twenty years passed and on Christmas Day 2014 I was out running too, this time across the rolling hills of the Cotswolds near my home. It was in preparation for a marathon in Bosnia, I had recovered my fitness well and felt confident, running the six miles into work daily and stretching out ten-milers at the weekends. I pushed too hard too early, failing to appreciate I was not that young man in the Army that I used to be and in January had to take six weeks out due to injury. However, mentally I felt strong and knew, despite it being a painful experience-in-waiting, that I could get through the day. I had also convinced five of my team from work to join me, all some twenty years younger than me, and more so a good friend of mine, Chris Severson.

311

Chris is American, a former Top Gun-trained F/A-18 instructor pilot ("I'm known as Whizz to my flying buddies"), and he had been convinced foolishly over a couple of bottles of red wine that this would be a good thing to do. An interesting statistic we had calculated, as we stared into the empty wine glass, was that in his previous job as a jet fighter pilot, when he was in the cockpit of his F/A-18 jet he would have taken approximately 80 seconds to cover the 26 miles 385 yards of the marathon at the jet's top speed of around 1,900km/h. We agreed, however, that without the help of two General Electric jet engines and relying only on a pair of aging Nike trainers for propulsion, a sub-four-hour marathon would be a result of significant proportions.

We arrived in Goražde in car and in convoy, having driven from Dubrovnik. Chris had brought his family, his wife, Missy, and his three daughters. I had with me my wife, Joanna, my two sons, Simon and Monty, and my mother, Diana. For my mother this was a trip to connect the dots, to see the places written about in my letters and to see where her son had soldiered. In the third car were five team members from work. We were met by Nihad, who had been born and raised in Goražde and was now working for the British embassy in Sarajevo. He had been a young boy in 1994 and had witnessed the worst days of the war. Having been introduced to him in 2012, he had enthusiastically taken up the baton to support me in my endeavours to help the townsfolk of his childhood. Nihad subsequently wrote a chapter to be found at the beginning of this book that outlines his childhood memories during the war.

I had managed the expectations of all in the convoy on the standard of accommodation, knowing they would be pleasantly surprised when they arrived in the mountain lodge high above Goražde. The lodge was owned by the previous commanders of the BiH Army in the area, and was extensive, new and comparatively luxurious. It was far from the deep green, standard issue British Army sleeping bag (the affectionately known gonk bag), that had been my resting place when in Goražde in 1994 and the Observation Posts or Portakabins that been home.

We woke early on the day of the marathon, ate well and then Chris, Huw, Jack and I boarded a bus to take us to the start line. The hills were still covered in snow, the trees still bare and leafless, yet there was a beauty in the barren land and the greyness of the morning. The view down the valleys below us were breath-taking; this was Yugoslavia and Bosnia at its most beautiful. There was no crowd, no start line, no signing in. We were met by a police car and, rather worryingly, a support ambulance. Two marathon runners from the Bosnian Army had also joined us. They were tall – very tall – and very thin.

Without ceremony we stood on what we thought would make a good point

Left: The start line was found high in the mountains above Goražde (from left: Chris 'Whizz' Stevenson, Huw Fullerton, Jack Gooding and the author)

to start; six of us, the two Bosnians like book ends either side of different-sized, aged and disconnected volumes. The two giraffes, as I called them to my and no one else's amusement, skipped from one of us to another, as we found our own pace and drifted apart. I was full of energy as we started and was running well, but in the coldness, I was also taking in my surroundings, passing the occasional farm house, some rebuilt, some still rack and ruin. As we went past the junction that would take us back to the lodges and our accommodation, the road climbed once again, and I passed a fading sign that pointed to Sarajevo, 61km. This corridor had been the lifeline that had linked the enclave to the great city to its north and as I thought of this passageway of hope and equally of terror, the hill flattened and down below me in the distance you could make out the industrial parts of Goražde. The uphill now largely behind me, gravity helped my acceleration and it felt all to the good coming off-track momentarily to touch the memorial stone to Ben Hinton. Here was a moment and a single reason that had bought me to this place.

Below: The author, 61 km to Sarajevo, and 26 km to the finish line in Goražde

We were all in good order as we dropped down into the town, at the 21-mile point, painfully and emotionally having to

313

turn away from it to run back up the next valley. In doing so we reached, touched and passed the memorial stone dedicated to Philip Armstrong, Martin Dowdell and Chris Turner. At the final turning point, we gathered as a group and started our decent back into Goražde and along the same road we had just ran, which was becoming increasingly painful under foot. The cloud of not having trained as hard as I should had caught up with me, but I was lifted by the sight of my eleven year-old son, Simon, waiting on the side of the road, dressed neatly in his Cheltenham Prep running gear. "Come on Dad, five miles to go," he joined me and bounced along like Tigger as I flowed down the hill like an oil tanker.

As we entered the streets of the town, unknown to us the school had gathered, lining the roadside. As we crossed over the bridge, Bridge Bravo to me, they fell in behind us and, to the echoes of screaming and happy children, we turned the final corner and came into the school playground. With one last effort, trying desperately to look as if this was all in a good day's work, the marathon was done. There at the end was my wife, smiling and holding Monty, and my mother smiling and offering immediate comment, "Silly boy, you shouldn't be doing this

The team stopped momentarily at each memorial en route to Goražde. The author was joined here by his 12 year old son Simon to run him to the finish line

IN MEMORY OF
THREE MUCH LOVED SOLDIERS AND FRIENDS
PTE PHILLIP ARMSTRONG
PTE MARTIN DOWDELL
PTE CHRIS TURNER
A COMPANY – 1ST BATTALION
THE ROYAL GLOUCESTERSHIRE BERKSHIRE
AND WILTSHIRE REGIMENT
KILLED AT THIS SPOT
ON 12 SEP 94
IN A VEHICLE ACCIDENT
WHILST ON AN UNPROFOR PATROL

at your age." And so, it was to the echo of Captain Mainwaring and "Stupid boy Pike" that I made my way for an unwelcoming cold shower. Soon I was greeted by the headmistress, her teachers and the school, and their celebrations and heartfelt thanks demonstrated by unexpected plays and music. This was a run worth doing and, at 3 hours 58, a result of significant proportions!

Ironically, twenty years earlier, when living in austerity, I had finished the day with a warm shower, but had started it similarly in the snow and cold.

I had been training for many months and had completed a number of marathons already that year. Upon deployment I had carved out with Patrick Tomlinson, my company commander, a right to lead a daily three to four-hour patrol into the hills

Crossing over Bridge Bravo en route to the school, 41 kms into the marathon

and had managed my own time to also do a daily four mile run. This took me around the town and, memorably, over Bridge Alpha. The route was mined, with a marked path taking me through the mines lying cold and expectant.

Members of my marathon team had not been as lucky as me, as they had found themselves largely static in the OPs. Although they kept fit, my aerobic fitness levels were helped enormously by my daily routine. Undeterred, they all agreed heartily to join me on Christmas Day to run a marathon from Višegrad, some twenty miles down from Goražde, to complete our five marathons and hopefully raise further funds in doing so. Having wished each other happy Christmas, we climbed into the back of the Saxon and headed for Višegrad. The Serbs and the BiH had agreed a temporary ceasefire for Christmas Day and had also agreed to allow us to run the marathon. They provided us with a Serbian officer, Captain Kornovic, to accompany us, as we slowly navigated our way back to Goražde and through the various checkpoints, ultimately to cross over and through the front line that divided the two forces.

We had agreed the start point to be the middle point of the ancient and historic bridge over the River Drina in Višegrad. The bridge had been made famous by the success of a book published in 1945 called The Bridge on the Drina by Yugoslav writer Ivo Andrić.

Andrić's book tells the unhappy story of a young Serb boy from the Višegrad

315

area. As part of the Ottoman's devşirme levy during their 500-year-long occupation of the Balkans, he was forcibly taken from his mother, as many Christian boys were at the time. The boy's mother runs after her son, crying, until she reaches the Drina River and can go no further. She watches her son be taken across on a ferry, never to see him again. The boy is given a new, Turkish, name – Mehmed-paša Sokolović – and he converts to Islam. The boy does well for himself in his life and receives promotion after promotion until he eventually becomes the Grand Vizier and remains so for the next fifteen years, even managing the Ottoman Empire's expansion into Central Europe.

However, despite the success he has achieved in his life, he is scarred by the troubling memories he has of being taken away from his mother at a young age. At the spot by the river where he left his mother behind, he arranged the construction of a bridge in memory of her and the day they separated.

From Joe Sacco's
"Goražde: A Safe Area"

Prior to the Balkan War the bridge carried the romantic echoes of this story, and in some way, you could argue it metaphorically carried a message through time of the bridge that existed between the two faith communities of Islam and Christianity that resided either side of the Drina.

However, it had become infamous during the Bosnian War as it was from the mid-point of the bridge that many Bosnian men, women and children had been thrown to their deaths.

It is estimated that in the buildings on the slopes above the town, the fields and mountains overlooking the bridge, that some 3,000 Bosniaks, Muslims had been murdered during the spring and summer of 1992. The town had been used as a centre for brutality, torture and rape. The viciousness of the crimes of violence committed by the Bosnian Serbs in the Višegrad massacres and the effectiveness with which the town's entire Bosniak population was either killed or deported by Serb forces in 1992, long before Srebrenica, have been described as epitomising the genocide of the Bosniak and Muslim population of eastern Bosnia carried out on orders from the Bosnian Serb leader Radovan Karadžić and his military counterpart, General Ratko Mladić.

When we stood on the bridge on Christmas Day 1994 the two sides were still very much at war and these terrible, unimaginable actions had been recent. It was with these echoes and not the romantic ones from Ivo Andrić's book, that we set ourselves ready for the marathon ahead, standing in our shorts and running vests on a cold, snow-clad Christmas Day. The juxtaposition of our situation and purpose to that of the Serb soldiers who looked on with bemusement could not be lost. The uniqueness of what we were about to do was not lost also; this would be a tale to tell.

In front of us would be a white-painted UN Land Rover. In it would be two British soldiers, a translator and a Serbian Army officer, Captain Kornovic. To our rear would be a white-painted armoured Saxon, with driver below and gunner above and the letters UN painted clearly in black on its flanks. This was our convoy; two vehicles like mobile book ends to six soldiers all running for charity, through a war zone on Christmas Day.

An elderly Serb woman looks over the arched bridge at Višegrad

If you ever get the chance to drive between Višegrad and Goražde and your mind is unfettered from the evidence of the past, then you will find this experience uplifting. The Drina Valley is breath-taking. High cragged peaks climb from the valley below, as the turquoise blue waters of the river rush past you. The riverside road holds tight to its edge, following the contours of the Drina as it turns, twists and carves its way through the mountains. Occasionally you will pass under a covered bridge, the type you find in the European Alps that hold up the snow in winter, when suddenly you are thrown into half-light as you enter a tunnel burrowed through the rock, until sunlight spills into the tunnel to welcome you as you exit its shadows. This was our route and path on that Christmas Day and one that filled your heart with joy as your lungs were filled by the crispness of the mid-winter air.

My good fortune in being able to train and therefore keep myself at a high level of fitness slowly became apparent, leaving me ahead of the other team members and running strongly towards Goražde. The run had become increasingly a silent and lonely one, all be it I felt good and was looking forward to the closing miles. I had been accompanied throughout by the soft echoes of my trainers repeatedly, repetitively hitting the road below and the occasional sound of the Land Rover ahead, with the distinct whirring of its wheels that it makes on Tarmacadam as it accelerates away. At Kopači on the outskirts of Goražde, and the forward urban stronghold of the Serbs, the Land Rover was parked on the side of the road. By its side stood its four occupants.

317

Through the translator Captain Kornovic explained he was going to wait here for the other runners, as Goražde was only three miles away and I could make my own way to the end. I waved enthusiastically and passed them, hearing the Land Rover start up and then hasten away back down the road towards Višegrad and the other runners, leaving Kornovic on the roadside and in anticipation of their arrival.

The road curved around to the right and then back again, and as it did, you could see the confrontation line and Serb trenches and positions running up the slope to my right and down to the river on my left. In the near distance I could see the houses of the town coming into sight and closer still the Orthodox Church, rather appropriately, for an Englishman abroad, called St. Georges. The demarcation line between the two forces was 200 metres, reminiscent of the images you may have of the First World War. On the road, I knew there were three checkpoints, the nearest being the Serbs', the middle one being the UN post manned by Ukrainians and the third that of the Bosniaks and their forces, the BiH.

As I came to the Serb post, a ramshackle building of brick, corrugated iron sheets and other, I had expected to be stopped or waved on, but neither happened, it was silent. I ran past not giving it a second thought, but as I passed, perhaps 30 metres or so, I heard the shouting of "zaustaviti, zaustaviti" behind me. My very limited Serbo–Croat had picked up the "stop". Stop, stop, it came again, but louder, "Stop ili pucam." Perhaps mercifully I did not know at the time that "ili pucam" meant "or I fire". Regardless of my lack of understanding, I stopped within three to four strides and turned to see a Serb soldier waving his AK-47 at me frantically, cocking his weapon as he moved forward and beckoning me to put up my hands whilst continuing to shout, this time "Musliman, Musliman". As I stood there, in my running shorts and regimental running vest, with my pearly white legs poking out from the shorts like sparrow legs from a nest, my hands raised above my head, being called a Muslim by a Serbian soldier brandishing an AK-47, the rather ridiculous, precarious nature of my position dawned on me.

My first thought, however, was not one of explanation, but that rather annoyingly I had been stopped when most decidedly I was on for a very good time and 2 hours 45 minutes was not just achievable but was mine to lose. Foolishly I dropped my hands to stop my stopwatch, my logic being that once this had been resolved I could start it again and this would be a worthy explanation as to why I had stopped. My adversary, an unusual marathon roadside official, did not see my logic and this sudden and unexpected movement threw him into a torrent of high-pitched abuse, which I presumed to be offensive. I continued to profess my innocence to be a Muslim and therefore could not possibly part of the BiH, as he came towards me. My response was limited to "Nista, nista, UNPROFOR" ["No, no, United Nations Protection Force"].

318

I can remember him being a young man, unshaven, and as he got close his breath smelt of slivovitz. He had calmed down a little by the time he got to within a foot or so of me but was still insistent on half-shouting and repeating the accusation that I was a Muslim. As he did so, a second Serb soldier appeared from the checkpoint. This I felt sure would be my salvation and the voice of reason. The man in front of me turned, talking quickly and occasionally punctuating his sentences with "Musliman", to which end I gathered he was making clear his thoughts on who or what I was.

I leant a few inches to the right, hoping to catch the eye of the second Serb, and in doing raised my right hand, moving it in a rotational manner, as if calling someone on a telephone (I had hoped this would be the interpretation). "UNPROFOR, UNPROFOR, Captain Kornovic, Captain Kornovic," I repeated, hoping he would disappear into the checkpoint and I would hear the radio being wound up, frantic voices and an apologetic soldier exiting the metalled shed. The soldier before me did not take well to my efforts, pushing the barrel and end of his AK-47 into my forehead and continuing with new purpose to shout his accusation. I knew there was a bullet in the chamber as he had loaded his weapon earlier. What I couldn't determine as I stared down the barrel into his face, was whether the safety catch was on, although I felt it unlikely to be so. Having handled many AK-47s, and confiscated a few in recent weeks, I knew the safety catch to be on the right side of the weapon, my left as I looked down the barrel, and I knew also it was easily slipped on and off. His hand was holding the weapon in a way that covered the safety catch and obscured my view.

His comrade moved forward as this was happening, went behind me and then the barrel on my forehead was replaced by what I presumed was one on my back. This was, in some strange way, progress. Many of my friends have asked me what this felt like, and to be honest it is difficult to explain. It was certainly not fear, nor was it a cold, rational response. It was more a void of emotion, although I can say there was a type of out of body experience to the whole episode, as if I was watching the event unfold and was looking at myself at its centre. Later that evening, when back and having showered, eaten and resting in my gonk bag, I can recall a cold shudder as I reflected unconsciously on the day's events.

I was taken, half lifted, to the checkpoint and spread-eagled, with my hands now resting on its side and my legs stretched out below me. I suppose I must have been cold at this moment but cannot recall this coldness. I am not sure how long I had been in this position, continuing to listen to their rantings, when I heard a Land Rover pulling up behind me and looking sideways I could see Sergeant Steve Mustoe jumping out with his SA80 in his hand. I could tell his natural inclination was to resolve the situation on his own and with the support of whosoever was in the Land Rover with him, but after a staccato conversation, punctuated by unhelpful contributions from my Serb friends, Sergeant Mustoe climbed back in and sped off in the direction of Goražde, I could hear him talking on the radio as he departed.

Christmas Day 1994 was becoming a memorable one, as I remained in position, starting to feel the cold leaning against the checkpoint as my commanding officer turned up in the Land Rover, accompanied and driven by Sergeant Mustoe. After a passage of words between him, his translator and the Serbs, it was clear little progress was being made and the Land Rover disappeared once again, returning within minutes, this time with Captain Kornovic on board. He leapt from the Land Rover, shouted a few words at my two hosts and immediately they dropped their weapons, smiled and rather bizarrely started to pat me on the back, as if old friends standing at the bar.

An explanation was forthcoming, a simple mistake, a matter of poor, or rather no communication. I had run through the checkpoint at about 11.10 that morning. At 11 there had been a change of guard, except the offgoing guard had forgotten to brief the oncoming guard as to the events that would unfold that day and that half a dozen UN British soldiers would be running through the checkpoint later that morning, accompanied or not by Captain Kornovic.

With the commanding officer's permission, I nodded, thanked Kornovic, pressed my stopwatch and headed into town, finishing at the hospital some minutes later. The time by my watch when I finally stopped showed 2 hours 48 minutes, my time on my Army watch from the start in Višegrad, showed 3 hours 30 minutes had passed. My stopover at the Serb

Gloucester Citizen, 25th January 1995

■ The party of soldiers from the Royal Gloucestershire, Berkshire and Wiltshire Regiment who went on a sponsored run – through a Bosnian battlefield. ★

Battlefield run for their money

by Christian Otton

THE two sides in the Bosnian civil war laid down their arms on Christmas morning to allow Gloucestershire soldiers to run a marathon for charity, it has been revealed.

Eighty years after German and British troops facing each other in the trenches of France held a First World War ceasefire in a seasonal gesture of goodwill, the Bosnian Serbs and Muslims held their fire for six runners from the new Royal Gloucestershire, Berkshire and Wiltshire regiment.

Orphaned

The soldiers ran between Serb and Muslim held areas, raising money from sponsors for children orphaned by the conflict, and more than £500 for the African blind charity Sight Savers. Locals lined the streets to cheer them on.

The temporary cease-fire allowing the six to run the marathon distance of 25 miles from the Serbian town of Visegrad to the besieged Muslim city of Gorazde was arranged by the group's commanding officer Lieutenant Colonel Patrick Davidson-Houston.

Details have just been released of the special fund-raising mission.

The team left Visegrad in the early hours of Christmas morning.

They then headed 20 miles west along the River Drina to pass through the Bosnian Serb check-point up to No Man's Land.

They passed a United Nations checkpoint manned by Ukrainian soldiers while 500 metres further on, the Moslem police waved the team into Gorazde.

The last three miles took the soldiers into the centre of town and onto the front-line line at the hospital.

First over the line was Captain Maurice

Evlyn-Bufton, followed by the group's other officer, Captain Matthew Shaw.

After a short break the team returned to their observation posts.

Shortly after, from the hills above, came the familiar sound of gunfire.

It was not the Glosters' first fund-raising venture for Sight Savers.

Remarkable

Runners from the regiment have already completed marathons in New York, Ottawa, London and even in the sweltering heat of Cairo.

The long-term aim is to raise enough money to restore sight to 300 children in Kenya.

Geraldine Stevens, director of fundraising at Sight Savers International, said "We are delighted with what has been achieved by these events in what were very difficult circumstances.

"It is remarkable."

checkpoint had therefore been forty-two minutes. A lot can happen in forty-two minutes; it is, after all, the answer to life, the number forty-two, as determined by Douglas Adams in his The Hitchhiker's Guide to the Galaxy, where the "Answer to the Ultimate Question of Life, the Universe, and Everything", as calculated by an enormous supercomputer named Deep Thought over a period of 7.5 million years, is forty-two. It's a number I retain some affection to this day!

Above: The winding road into Goražde that was the closing miles of the Christmas Day marathon, taken October 1994.

One question remains unanswered: Where amidst this were the Ukrainians? I asked myself this question later that day, although perhaps if a lesson was to be taken from this adventure, it is if I had trained a little harder I could have got through the checkpoint some ten minutes earlier and therefore before the handover! If I had, then I doubt, without a story to be told, my marathon in Goražde in 2015 would have happened. Neither would I have crouched on the roadside by the nearby Orthodox Church in 2012 reflecting on the moment on Christmas Day 1994 when I found myself looking down a barrel of an AK-47, neither would I have subsequently raised the funds I have for my charity since 2015. Sometimes lack of training, not being as fast as you hope, poor communication and unfortunate timing can pay dividend; albeit some distance down life's road!

Left: Old comrades return journey, on the centre of Višegrad bridge 2012

26th December 1994

Yuletide has arrived. Usually, at this time of the year, I am en route to Shrewsbury to pick Dad up, more often than not from the pavement, after his festive drinks with the rest of the Barclays crew! OK Dad, not quite the pavement, but shall we say you are at least merry, tipsy or "rather damn happy!"

Our first stop is always Tanners the Wine Sellers and, encouraged by a lunchtime beverage, we know the chief (Dad) always buys excessively, to be reprimanded by Mother on our victorious return. "But Di, it's only once a year." And every year the family and our friends have little difficulty in finishing the alcohol that was bought in excess and in haste! It is indeed but once a year, as it takes all 364 following days to recover! A fine and festive tradition Dad and one I hope will remain intact for years to come, even into your retirement.

I believe the annual Boxing Day golf match with Uncle John will be off this year. What a shame that the whisky flask will be shared by only three! Does this mean the curtailment of the match even earlier than before? Will Uncle John manage to keep focus on one, two or three balls as he staggers to the 3rd or 4th tee? His ability to handle Scottish water is not as tested as Dad's and it remains our year in, year out strategy to feed UJ the Scottish water with a steady flow to our benefit! He is the only man that can claim to see two balls before him on every tee after the second and still make the best effort to see himself through to the 9th and into the bar to top and tail this annual festivity and participation of Scottish folklore and revelry! I will miss this annual walk and talk and hope it has gone well without me.

In Goražde, the festive season has arrived and been announced with a fresh snowfall. It covers the ground and softens the pot and shell holes that are littered throughout the town and surrounding villages. The hills around us are resplendent in their covering and for a moment you can feel festive and childlike, and all is normal, beautiful even.

Our first celebration is a children's panto. As the in-house script writer for B Company, I scribbled a play and pulled it together as a panto-story, to be acted out by the accommodating Company headquarters crew. It is a traditional theme of good versus evil, where good naturally triumphs in the end. King Rat of the Drina has ruled Goražde land for many years and its children pray for a saviour. Mr Bon Bon (equals sweets in their language) arrives, but only keeps his power by the children shouting his name. The shouts replace the endearing and usual "he's behind you!" of English fame! King Rat eats Mr Bon Bon's sweets, but as he is evil they are not sweet but bitter and poison him. He is driven from the land and

322

Mr Bon Bon awards the children by showering them with sweets (which we did literally!). Not a bad little effort, the children's delight became our own!

What else? A carol service, gun fire for the troops at 0630 on Christmas Day. While this is going on I have been transported to Visegrad for my marathon. No more to say on this, I will tell you more on leave. It was cold and eventful is all I can tell you!

Having finished the marathon, I was back in Goražde in time for Christmas lunch. As tradition, has it, the troops were served by their officers and senior non-commissioned officers and they take every advantage of this change in role, with hands up and hefty and loud demands, "More wine over here" and "take my plate away" and so on!

The day crept by with happy smiles, meetings and festive greetings for everyone you pass, and then the SNCOs and Officers had an evening dinner. There is something uniquely and wonderfully British about its Army abroad at Christmas. The limited spots for calling on Christmas Day were more meaningful, as you imagined the young children unwrapping presents without Daddy at home, being passed the phone to wish him happy Christmas and to thank him for all the wonderful things before them, inevitably finishing with: "Daddy will be home soon, love you, pass the phone back to Mummy".

New Year, a week away. What celebrations shall we have to welcome in 1995, who knows? I'll be on countdown to R & R by then. Fourteen days until I leave Goražde, nineteen days until the welcoming lights of Birmingham, that will be the first and last time Birmingham will seem so welcoming!

Happy Christmas and New Year to all my family, I will see you all soon!

Far left: The children of the three shires sent hundreds of toys for the children of Goražde, and once they finally got through the Serb checkpoints and embargo, were distributed by the soldiers to the joy of the recipients.

Left: Christmas card sent by a young child from Gloucestershire

VIEWED FROM A COTSWOLD MEWS

This war beaten country has been wrenched from the free
Which back in England had meant nothing to you or me
I'd read the daily papers and seen the colourful news
When sat content and warm in stony Cotswold mews
I'd scribbled notes on Goražde a town with giddy name
Heard of Muslim enclaves and Serbs that gather blame

Sinister men with iron fist and a regiment of armour
Turned a deathly soldier from simple hill top farmer
Surrounded by the old and dying and those sadly done
I knew of the Bosnians' fate and desire to live as one
I'd listen to the crying babies and of charities in need
See outstretched aging hands and hungry mouths to feed

I thought I knew the truth of Bosnia's vibrant history
A gallant and colourful story and one full of mystery
Above this town I'd climb rolling snow swept peaks
I'd live with its people throughout the winter's weeks
I would see a broken heart of a mother and her child
Elders praying for peace amidst the meek and mild

It is not the lowly husband or wife and lonely child
Or the failure of mankind and a society left defiled
That leads this country onwards and forward to despair
Detached from their people that no longer seem to care
It is hope that is the casualty and one that sings its song
Of the vile and chaotic carnage and all that is wrong

I'm returning to England and stony Cotswold mews
To read daily papers and watch the colourful news
I will see the hill top houses and paths underfoot
All laid bare from where the fallen trees were cut
My thoughts remain with the people of this town
Robbed of hope and of humanity's golden crown

Note: Written March
4th 1995

324

7th February 1995

Apologies for the late arrival of this letter, it will be almost the end of my tour by the time you receive this letter. Well spent and welcoming, lovely time at home, were followed by my flight from Birmingham on the 24th back to Yugoslavia, and it was not until 31st that we finally arrived back in the distant Bosnian holiday camp of Goražde.

Arriving at Gornji Vakuf, we ventured forth to Kiseljak. Unfortunately, the road was treacherous, snow bound and we encountered a series of road traffic accidents. We returned to Gornji Vakuf eight hours later, having failed to get through. On finally arrived in Kiseljak (our rear administration centre), we found we had failed to make the deadline for this convoy and spent three days living it up in the Kiseljak hotel (or rather the Battalion's rear support headquarters). Finally, when on route to Goražde, we spent another night at the Rogatica checkpoint, almost obligatory, before returning to Goražde. Seven days to get from home in the U.K. back into Goražde!

At Rogatica we had an early morning service conducted by our ever-present eccentric Padre, Captain Patrick Irwin. The poems attached include 'The Padre' and "We Sang Jerusalem", inspired by a surreal if not entertaining experience whilst at Rogatica. Namely the Padre offered and we all accepted to take communion and this was followed by the most resounding rendition and singing of Jerusalem, which warmed our hearts and left the observing and listening Serbs a little puzzled.

What of Goražde? The thaw has arrived and with it the battlefields of the Somme, Ypres and Passchendaele. We had rather hoped that the snow was with us for the duration and would keep the OPs and CPs intact and cover the carnage of the camp. Not to be. This is, apparently, an extraordinarily early thaw and beings in the first hint of spring.

We hope that this does not encourage early activity by either warring faction. The Serbs expect and are planning on a renewed offensive, the Muslims fear one - a dangerous combination. As for me, I am not sure what to think but there's a niggling, no far more than this, a troubling sense of pessimism about the evolving situation. Neither side is ready or content to conduct constructive peace talks beyond the fragile peace accord that tinkers daily on the verge of disintegrating. The UN remains ostracised and the situation on the ground remains largely misunderstood by the world's politicians, and just as importantly the media. An example being today when an ABC television crew arrived to film an hour-long documentary, with us insight, about where the UN and UNPROFOR got it wrong last April, they stood and photographed and made assertions, and left no doubt full of self-confirmation as to their assumptions. Ironically they did this escorted into the pocket and protected whilst in it, by soldiers of the UN - can we ever do anything right?

I've been rather taken by this poetry bug and have scribbled happily since my return. What I, or rather the Padre, noticed was the underlying religious tone and sentiment throughout my writings. Am I that godly or religious? My interest in divinity and theology has always been muted, but I know it has been there and never questioned it, who knows what this sub-conscious discovery may mean. As I reread my poems, I realise some are OK, some less so and some not worthy of a second glance. However, their writing has served a purpose, regardless of their quality or lack of it, as they have helped shape my thoughts and emotions whilst being here. I've taken time to revamp some of my older ones, hopefully to improve them a little, as even Wilfred Owen altered some of his many years later I understand, so this I consider not to be cheating the reader!

Cotswold Camping is a saviour, for many of us in IRGBW! I've booked Roger's jacket along with one for myself and that should be sent directly to home (Brooklyn) late February/early March. He can pay me on my return - as they say out here "Nema problema". I have a feeling the Cotswold Camping adventure and post deployment accounts and reconciliation are going to take a little time to sort out on my return to the UK, but at the end of the day the soldiers have enjoyed some great bargains, many have kept warm over the winter months because of it and it created opportunities to undertake magazine browsing and shopping whilst resting in their OPs or CPs. A little work when I am back to make good will be nothing when weighed against its success.

Running short of time - and of space - hope all is well on the sunny and rolling hills of Shropshire. Also enclosed is the end of tour article for B Company and a copy of our musical we put on in November.

With all my love, Mart Xxx

14th February 1995

Today, as you can see, is Valentine's day.

Having detached myself from the rigorous infighting of man-woman and woman-man; the resident questions of 'does she like me?' usually followed by 'is this effort all really worth it?', and having resigned myself to zero incoming interest this year, I find a card arriving today from London from an mysterious Miss 'X'. The card read 'I'd walk a million miles for one of your smiles – even to Bosnia!' It begs the question, 'which lost soul and sad girl has fallen so lowly in hope in finding love that she should send a card to me, my name no doubt resting firmly at the bottom of the list and barrel and secondly, how prepared would this hopeful young lady be to meet my invariably inconsistent emotional demands after walking a million miles?' She may be metaphorical in her writings, but it is a hell of a long way to go to meet disappointment, namely me!

The tour is very nearly over. We have, I strongly believe, achieved much since our arrival in August 1994. General Guthrey visited last week. As Chief of the General Staff he is the highest-ranking officer in the Army. He returned to England to report "In my 2 years as CGS, IRGBW is the best battalion I have visited", high praise indeed or rather this is what we have been told he said, I am still seeking documented evidence!

Sadly as we look to leave, the political indifference of the Muslim and the Serb leaders makes me believe war will come again in April/May and this time the UN will be incapable of doing anything about it and will be forced to leave Bosnia. I would not say incapable at the ground level, most soldiers at the coal face are more than capable, but incapable at the political level. A rather pessimistic, but sadly realistic view.

With the end in sight, I am now finding time for reflection, as I know I will be leaving this valley soon. You look at the daily things that have left an impression. I think of the colours of this valley, where there is much more than the grey and war torn buildings to inspire you. The summer, autumn and early spring seasons have allowed us to see this valley in many colours and I think, when peace comes to it again, it would be a beautiful place to live. Sadly there will always be the echoes and shadows of the past, but it will recover someday I am sure.

The weather was glorious this last week. An early spring in the Yugoslavian mountains melted the legacy of winter and dried the tracks and fields. I took a long patrol up through Porgani, Kolijevka, Bran Potok, Gaj village and up to the high placed hamlet of Brdo, perched on a ridgeline. From here the view is breath-taking. On route we called in at several Serb positions, all now friendly to Kapetane Maurice and his motley crew. In a strange, perhaps unforgiving way, I have a number of friends or at least friendly acquaintances amidst this gathering of foreign soldiers (or am I the foreign soldier?) In a stranger way, I will miss Goražde and both its happy Muslim community and the Serbs. They are both as good and as bad as each other, but at its core this situation for both sides is intensively sad, tragic even.

It is now two weeks to go, this will be my last letter home and I may well be home to greet and open it. Two more weekly calls home to you should see me through and to my return (glorious I hope) on March 8th. I am energetically photographing all and everything to record my visit to this battle-torn country and one day hope I may make a record of this adventure. It has been live changing, memorable, a privilege and a fitting end to my short military career.

Enclosed are a couple more and final poetic scribbles. I rather like 'The Forest', more so, the man I wrote it for and largely about, WO2 Yemm, a true Forester and an inspiration. You must read it is a west country accent for it to serve its true purpose, to be a poem in admiration of the Foresters!

THE FOREST

Ow bist gwain on?
Young rustic man from Bream
Did ask his Forest friend
Who stood by Severn stream.

He didn't care a tinker's cuss
For mines closed at Berryhill
Or miners' rights of ninety days
And rusty shovels standing still.

Up an' out a black cloud bust
From depths of Lightmoor colliery
Lifts high the blackened coal
The golden dust of Lydney.

T'were a gert big oak tree
That grew from sodden soil
Hiding coal and iron ore
Dug with young men's toil.

Never tha' wuz till Autumn
When summer turns to breeze
Clock tower rings in Coleford
Not heard at Mayhill trees.

Couch-grass, docks an' nettles
At St. Briavel's monastery
Badger, deer and rabbit
To Forest glade at Yorkley.

The Varest velt quite peaceful
Jacob's Ladder, on Giant's Chair
Above Whitecroffs marbled streets
To carnival and summer fair.

A bunch of so'jers blocked tha way
At Cinderford's cenotaph
A group of spritely Glosters
That love to sing and laugh.

A qwart o'two o'zider
Old Forester takes in hand
Ridler, Yemm and Damsel
Names born in Forest's land.

Zundy clobber wiv polished bwoots
To ancient Forest church
On Forest paths to Drybrook creep
For wooden cross they search.

Sparklin' white an' billowin'
Rushing streams do rally
Race to Symond's Yat
To green Wye and Severn Valley.

Fer the Varest's 'eaven on Earth
Such beauty never seen
Royal oak, beech and ash
Enchanted Forest of Dean.

14 February 1995

Note: Written for Sergeant Major 'Jonny' Yemm. A true Forester from Cinderford and the oldest of his kin within the 1st Battalion. Inspiration was further given by Keith Morgan's poems, especially his second collection called 'Albert's dree Wi'ker'.

A letter to the author from Major Nicholas Barne on behalf of The Duke of Gloucester to congratulate him on his success

From
Major Nicholas Barne

KENSINGTON PALACE
LONDON W8 4PU
TELEPHONE 071-937 6374

2nd March 1994

Dear Maurice,

The Duke of Gloucester has asked me to thank you very much for your excellent report concerning Gloster Marathon Man.

His Royal Highness was delighted, though not surprised, to read of your great successes and sends his congratulations to you and to the team and The Duke is very much looking forward to being able to meet everyone personally on Saturday 19th March at Royal Air Force Quedgeley.

Yours sincerely

Nicholas Barne

Captain M C Evlyn-Bufton

"1992 to 1995 left Bosnia-Herzegovina in turmoil; it was a war which consumed the entire country and its people. At the heart of the trauma was Goražde."

CHAPTER 13

A VIEW FROM THE INSIDE

BY MUHIDIN (MUKI) TUTIC, UN INTERPRETER ATTACHED TO BRITISH ARMY

The events that occurred from 1992 to 1995 left Bosnia–Herzegovina in turmoil; it was a war which consumed the entire country and its people. At the heart of the trauma was Goražde, which was a high priority of the Serbian political and military intentions, occupying a strategic location as it did between Foca and Višegrad, two principal Serb locations; thus, it was an area the international community sought to provide help in Bosnia. The UK initially sent troops into Bosnia as UNPROFOR, entering Goražde in the spring of 1994.

At the time, I recall distinctly, that the official UK political stance was not favoured by the Bosniaks; partly due to the UN's behaviour and work in the past, and partly because of the UK distancing itself from taking a firm position in the debate raging over Bosnia–Herzegovina (or this was our perception). Hence, when the first arrival of the UK soldiers to Goražde came at the beginning of April 1994, the people of Goražde were wary of their presence. At the same time on both sides of the divide, those who liked (arguably the Serbs' historic position) or originally disliked the UK (the Bosniaks' position) gave full credit to the UK's troops as they quickly proved themselves to be fully capable and commendable soldiers, something everyone, both sides, civilians and soldiers, agreed upon. The people of Goražde were aware of the UN and their high-brow position, but also of the importance of having reliable UN troops in place in Goražde.

The people of Goražde had abbreviations for everything, including names for the troops. The Russian Battalion were "RUS BAT", the French Battalion were "FRA BAT", and "UK BAT" was renamed "SHOOT BAT", aptly reflecting their ability and willingness to engage in combat to protect themselves or others around them without hesitation.

My perception was that the UK troops were often willing to risk breaking the rules for the general good or to make the right moral decision, regardless of its implications. They believed it was more important to do the right thing, rather than just follow official orders. This was important for the town's people to see, as there were constant disagreements that arose from what appeared to be nonsensical issues and matters, mainly caused by the uncertain political situation and the reality of this when played out on the ground. Adopting a no-nonsense approach was important and gave the British credibility on both sides.

Undoubtedly the UK troops in Goražde were highly exposed, occupying the ground between two enemy sides, and when they were expected to do what their UN mandate told them despite the difficulties of its relevance on the ground they simply did it, all three British battalions deployed to Goražde equally so. They did so with professionalism, compassion and on occasion humour; they can and should be proud what they did for my people and the legacy they help leave behind.

Goražde, 1994: Rumours of Serb atrocities against the Muslim population in and around the town prompted General Rose to send the SAS to qualify these rumours. Once inside, the SAS took up position in a bank and called in regular sit reps.

An SAS trooper, Fergus Rennie, was killed when his Land Rover was ambushed when attempting to find a route back into town. Muki was his driver on that day and on 11 November each year he attends to the fallen SAS soldier's memorial, resting above the town of Goražde

SPRING ARRIVALS – WE BID FAREWELL

The long-awaited spring has come early with sun shining forth
The eternal winter has left these mountains and has bid farewell
Freshly blowing from the north winds caress each lonely valley
Deep pools of melted snow are left where rushing steams do rally
These spring time breezes on freshened cheeks are felt anew

On surrounding hills soldiers cry and sad songs can be heard
Packed of memories of men and boys that alas have died
We are bid farewell by a lonely songbird's soulful melody
On a last patrol as we clambered the paths to our destiny
To high windy peaks and to clouds we have broken through

Many seasons this town has been wedded to this war
More years will pass with stories told from tightened lips
Through scarred and bitter town we had walked alone
Among fathers', mothers' and children's memories blown
Hollowed and blackened eyes tearful with morning dew

I will not forget and leave this day with my six months spent
What achievement can we recognise for us to take away
We left with no ceremony and no rattling or rolling drum
No music to create harmony or a silence that made you numb
We leave you and behind us is the valley's heavenly view

3 March 1995, on leaving Goražde.

Members of 1RGBW ready themselves for the final
journey home and back to England.

335

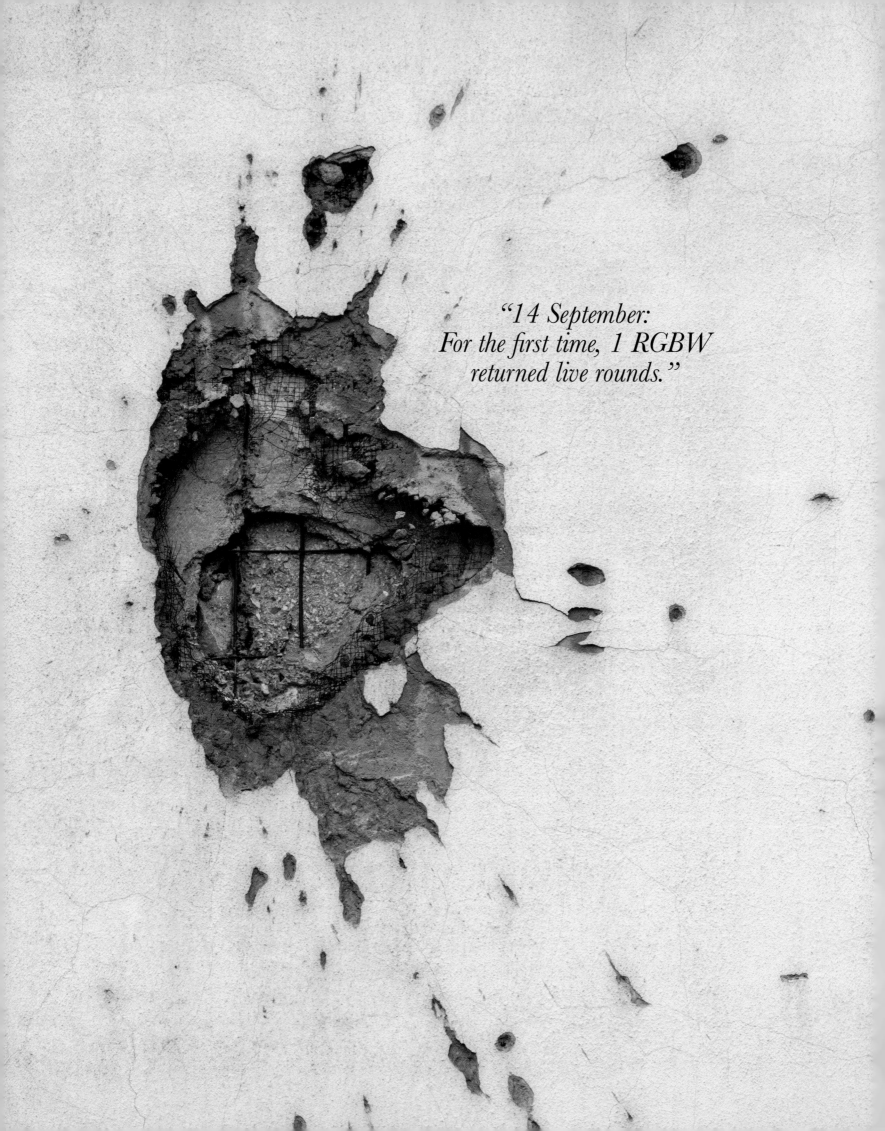

*"14 September:
For the first time, 1 RGBW
returned live rounds."*

CHAPTER 14

LIST OF SIGNIFICANT EVENTS AND DIRECT TARGETING OF 1 RGBW BRITBAT

2 SEPTEMBER 1994 – MARCH 1995

A s written and extracted from the end of tour battalion magazine.

1994

5th September	During a recce of an alternative site for OP 11 Colour Sergeant Griffith and Sergeant McTaggart were engaged from a BSA position by one 40mm exploding round.
8th September	Bugojno go to state red for the first time when sixteen artillery rounds impact on the town.
14th September	For the first time 1 RGBW returned live rounds. While awaiting REME assistance a B Coy patrol was engaged by a series of BSA positions around the Osanica Bridge. 1,100 rounds were returned into four separate BSA positions (five BSA casualties were subsequently reported). Private Jones 04 received a minor wound to his buttock.
15th September	The CO and UNCIVPOL went to inspect the contact of 14th September. Once again UNPROFOR personnel were targeted and 381 rounds were returned.
16th September	Two hand grenades were thrown into Bugojno Camp.
17th September	A drunken BSA soldier fired a burst of MG fire over the top of OP 7 (A Coy).
19th September	The BSA fired nine 40mm rounds at OP 11 (Recce).
20th September	A BSA grenade thrown at the BiH detonated 30m from OP 8 (A Coy).
21st September	A BSA position engaged OP 5 with bursts of MG fire. The

	OP returned both GPMG and SA fire (A Coy 1 Recce 0).
22nd September	OP 11, abandoned for better observation at OP 14 only forty-five minutes earlier, was engaged by four BSA artillery rounds, two of which were direct hits (A Coy 1 Recce 1). OP 5 was once again targeted by BSA SA fire (Coy 2 Recce 1). Recce Platoon, not wanting to be outdone by A Coy, were then engaged by 40mm rounds into the front bank of OP 14 (A Coy 2 Recce 2).
24th September	OP 1 (B Coy) was engaged by ten rounds of BSA fire. OP 1 returned fire with the GPMG. A BSA doctor was reported visiting the firing point the following day.
26th September	OP 14 (Recce Platoon) was engaged by a 40mm Bofors gun.
28th September	An A Coy foot patrol near OP 9 was engaged from a BiH position on the Vranovina feature. The patrol returned sixty-nine rounds and then sat out a crossfire between the BiH and BSA.
29th September	Another A Coy patrol from OP 9 was engaged by the BiH.
8th October	While A Coy QRF Saxon awaited a UNHCR convey it was engaged by BSA SA from the East Bank.
10th October	Four 20mm rounds landed near Op 14 (Recce Platoon).

338

Left: Private Leach (A Company) looking down from the Senokas feature into Goražde

17th October	11 BSA artillery rounds landed 300m from OP 14 (Recce Platoon).
18th October	While B Coy was escorting a UNHCR convoy, the convoy was engaged from a BSA position, killing one of the UNHCR drivers. TACP deployed and provided two F-18, two Mirage and two Mirage 2000 for air cover.
19th October	Op Thin Out (movement of Coy (-) to Gornji Vakuf) was implemented by C Coy Group when a hundred rounds of artillery landed in Bugojno.
23rd October	A30C patrol was engaged by approximately eighty rounds of SA fire whilst at OP BM 8. The patrol returned 583 rounds.
24th October	An A Coy patrol was engaged by the BSA from the Paligovina feature. Goražde Engineers were engaged by 12.7 and 82mm mortars while wood cutting!
25th October	An A Coy foot patrol was engaged by BSA MG fire in the outskirts of Obarak.
28th October	An A Coy foot patrol was engaged by a combination of MG and SA fire while in Factory Valley.
29th October	An A Coy foot patrol was engaged by BSA SA fire in the outskirts of Obarak.

1st November	During an All saints service in the Catholic cemetery in Obarak, Goražde, two SA rounds 'whistled' overhead. The Padre, unflustered, raised his hands and said 'the Padre shall continue the service'. Meanwhile, in Bugojno four SA-2 rockets were fired into the town, causing much damage to the camp. Op Thin Out was instigated for the second time.
8th November	An A Coy patrol on the Senokos feature was engaged by three rounds from a BSA sniper. One round hit Sergeant Lewis in the leg and another hit Private Temme in the leg. Neither casualty was serious. A Recce Platoon patrol (14A) was engaged by one SA round from the BSA near to the Osanica Bridge. A water patrol from OP 9 was engaged by BSA SA fire.
9th November	A BSA soldier on the Right Bank of the Drina put on a firepower demo for all in Goražde. The B Coy soldiers at OP 2, some twenty metres away, were more than a little surprised by this! In a follow-up, the next day, several weapons were confiscated.
12th November	Private Evans, a member of an A Coy patrol using a cleared path, trod on an AP mine. This locally made mine pierced his boot and broke his foot.
17th November	OP 5 went to state red when an RLG impacted close to the OP.
20th November	A BSA grenade detonated close to the rear of OP 6. An A Coy patrol was pinned down by sustained BSA HMG fire. The patrol commander deployed his GPMG as best he could and returned fire. At this, all BSA positions on the Paligovina feature opened fire. The patrol now used SA and GPMG to return fire. Some minutes later an A Coy Saxon arrived on the road below and engaged the BSA with the L37. The patrol extracted, under fire, using smoke to the safety of the Saxon (which took hits in the tyres).
24th November	A Recce Platoon patrol was engaged by two BSA SA rounds in the area of the Osanica Bridge.
27th November	The outgoing convoy held at Ustiprača had a burst of MG fire and an M80 rocket fired over the top of it.
29th November	Recce Platoon in OP 12 was engaged twice by the BSA from Kolovarice. OP 12 returned fire with their L37, GPMG and personal weapons.

2nd December	An A Coy foot patrol in Obarak was engaged by the BSA from the Senokos feature. Corporal Willes was struck on the arm, causing minor bruising.
4th December	Ten rounds of SA fire were fired at Corporal McKee inside Bugojno Camp. No casualties were sustained.
5th December	A joint TACP and UNMO patrol was pinned down in the north of the Goražde pocket by BSA 14.7mm, 20mm, 37mm and 82mm mortar fire. After three hours, darkness came and a twenty-five man BiH patrol extracted them. On withdrawal the patrol was engaged by mortar DF.
6th December	A foot patrol from OP 14 was engaged by SA and HMG fire in the Osanica Valley. The patrol returned GPMG fire but was pinned down for forty minutes. TACP and the B Coy QRF were tasked, but the patrol eventually threw smoke and extracted.
7th December	A JCO patrol to the NE of Cotswold Camp was engaged by two bursts of MG fire from a BSA position. One of the JCOs lost a finger and fractured another. OP 5 was engaged by one SA round from the BSA on the Senokos.
16th December	Fifteen SA rounds were fired into Bugojno Camp, smashing several windows in the accommodation.
17th December	An A Coy foot patrol leaving OP 5 was engaged by seven SA rounds from the Senokos feature.
19th December	A vehicle patrol from OP 9 was collecting water at a nearby spring when it was engaged by three MG bursts from the Vranovina feature.
21st December	Salamanca, with both the GF Chief LO and GF BSA LO inside, was hit on the offside window by one SA round when leaving the BSA HQ in Kopači.
23rd December	A Bosnia-wide ceasefire was signed today.
25th December	Capt Evlyn-Bufton at the twenty-five-mile point of the Visegrad Marathon when passing through the BSA checkpoint into Goražde was confronted by a pistol, held to his head, and replied, 'I say old chap, don't you know who I am?' He reached into his pocket and realised he had forgotten his ID card. In a separate incident, Father Christmas reported Bugojno 'cold but all in good spirits' and Kiseljak 'full of spirits'. Unfortunately the guards at Rogatica said that as Rudolph and Prancer were not

manifested, he was to return to Sarajevo, and so was unable to reach Goražde. The Split Liaison Detachment were on minimum manning throughout this incident.

31st December
A Bosnia-wide Cessation of Hostilities Agreement was signed today. To greet this tremendous news SA rounds were fired into the accommodation at Bugojno Camp – sixty rounds were returned.

Patrolling the Vranovina ridgeline 1995

20th January
The BSA fired three rounds over the top of a B Coy patrol at Vitkovici School.

30th January
A single low-velocity round was fired over the main gate sangar sentry at Cotswold Camp.

1st February
A drunken BSA soldier fired one SA round over CP 1 (B Coy).

20th February
Five SA rounds were fired over a B Coy Saxon overlooking the Osanica Bridge.

22nd February
One SA round was fired into an A Coy OP, narrowly missing the sentry.

VIP Visitors Received by 1 RGBW (Goražde)

Date	Visitor
19th October 1994	Lt Gen Sir Michael Rose KCB CBE QGM MA (Comd BHC)
18th January 1995	Lt Gen Sir Michael Rose KCB CBE QGM MA (Comd BHC)
25th January 1995	Brig A. Behagg MBE MA (Comd TSC (G))
25th January 1995	Brig I. Johnstone (Comd CATC)
2nd February 1995	Maj Gen MD Jackson CBE (GOC 3 (UK) DIV)
2nd February 1995	Lt Gen De la Presle (Force Comd UNPROFOR)
5th February 1995	Gen Sir Charles Guthrie GCB LVO OBE ADC Gen (GCS)
21st February 1995	Col H. Smith OBE MC (DComd BRITFOR)

The journey home, their duty done

343

A LITTLE TIME WELL SPENT

Four seasons we have seen renewed
A summer and seven months remained
To reddened leaves of autumn viewed
Fresh spring morning breezes reigned

Climbed fair mountains and every rise
We listened to the Drina's roar
Blue waters we saw with our eyes
Rapid whispering of love and more

And on those tracks where bloodied fell
Young men had died to leave distress
Marked with a soldier's death did quell
Lost on lonely hills of loveliness

Where deep valleys run east to west
Above broken town as if a slave
To orphaned daughter sorely blest
Her shadow rests by parents' grave

We will depart with time well spent
And bid farewell to foolish men
Of playful children, the innocent
We will return, we know not when

27 February 1995, arrival of IRWF.

"Here the blue beret of peacekeepers did briskly walk where a fatherless child reached out a hand of hope."

CHAPTER 15

BOSNIA IN THE INTERVENING YEARS

Upon leaving Goražde in March 1995, to the old comrades' return in June 2012.

The Legacy of the Dayton Agreement

Bosnia and Herzegovina becomes a confederation of two entities – the Federation of Bosnia and Herzegovina and the Republika Srpska, as well as the district of Brčko. Each of the entities has its own constitution and extensive legislative powers.

Since its 1992 independence and the 1995 constitutional framework of the Dayton Agreement, Bosnia and Herzegovina followed a path of state-building, while remaining under final international supervision through the figure of the High Representative for Bosnia and Herzegovina.

1996
The International Criminal Tribunal for the former Yugoslavia begins in The Hague. Dražn Erdemović, a Croat who fought for the Serbs and took part in the Srebrenica massacres, is the first person to be convicted. He is sentenced to five years in prison.
1997
International conference in Bonn extends powers of High Representative.
1998
Elections see nationalist politicians do well. The first Bosnian Muslims and Croats are convicted of war crimes in The Hague.

2000

Moderate parties do well in elections in the Muslim–Croat entity, but nationalists gain the upper hand in the Serb entity. Results force main Serb nationalist party to form a coalition headed by moderate Prime Minister Mladen Ivanić.

March 2001

The Croat representative in the collective presidency, Ante Jelavić, is dismissed as his party threatens to an independent Croat Republic.

May 2001

Bosnian Serbs in Banja Luka and Trebinje use force to break up ceremonies marking the reconstruction of mosques destroyed during the Bosnian war. Several Muslim refugees are injured, cars are set on fire and international delegates are forced to shelter in local buildings.

THE HAGUE FINDS BOSNIAN SERB GENERAL RADISLAV KRSTIĆ GUILTY OF GENOCIDE

August 2001

Hague war crimes tribunal finds Bosnian Serb General Radislav Krstić guilty of genocide for his role in the massacre of thousands of men and boys in Srebrenica. Krstić sentenced to forty-six years.

Three senior Muslim generals indicted to face war crimes charges.

December 2001

Amid growing international pressure, the main Bosnian Serb nationalist party, the SDS, votes to expel all war crimes suspects, including wartime leader Radovan Karadžić.

May 2002

UK politician Paddy Ashdown becomes UN High Representative.

October 2002

Nationalists win back power in federal, presidential, parliamentary and local elections.

Former Bosnian Serb President Biljana Plavšić changes her plea at the UN tribunal in The Hague to one of guilty of crimes against humanity. The remaining seven charges are dropped. She is subsequently sentenced to eleven years in prison.

January 2003

Three months after elections, parliament approves a new government led by Adnan Terzic.

EU officially embarks on its first foreign security operation by taking over policing duties from UN.

March 2003

A mass grave is discovered near Zvornik in eastern Bosnia, close to the Serbian border. More than 600 bodies thought to be those of victims of the 1995 Srebrenica massacre are eventually removed.

April 2003

Mirko Šarović, Serb member of presidency, resigns following a report by Western intelligence services on an affair involving illegal military exports to Iraq and allegations of spying on international officials.

High Representative Paddy Ashdown abolishes the Supreme Defence Council of the Bosnian Serb Republic. He also alters the constitutions of the Bosnian Muslim/Croat Federation and Bosnian Serb Republic, removing all reference to statehood from both.

Borislav Paravac of the Serb Democratic Party replaces Sarovic as a Serb member of the presidency.

July 2004

Celebrations mark the reopening of the rebuilt 16th century bridge at Mostar.

EU PEACEKEEPERS TAKE OVER

December 2004

NATO hands over peacekeeping duties to a European Union-led force, EUFOR.

March 2005

High Representative Paddy Ashdown sacks Croat member of presidency Dragan Covic, who faces corruption charges.

May 2005

Ivo Miro Jovic appointed Croat member of presidency.

June 2005

Bosnian unit with members from all three main ethnic groups heads for Iraq to support forces of US-led coalition.

October 2005

Entity and central parliaments back establishment of unified police force.

November 2005

EU foreign ministers give go-ahead for the Stabilisation and Association Agreement (SAA) talks.

January 2006

Christian Schwarz-Schilling takes over from Paddy Ashdown as UN High Representative.

February 2006

International Court of Justice in The Hague begins hearings in genocide case brought by Bosnia–Herzegovina against Serbia and Montenegro.

SREBRENICA TRIAL

July 2006

Largest war crimes trial to date over the 1995 Srebrenica massacre opens at the UN tribunal in The Hague.

October 2006

General elections reflect ethnic divisions, with Serb entity voting to maintain split from Muslim–Croat entity. In the run-up to vote, Bosnian Serb leadership threatens to seek complete succession if moves are made to end the autonomy of the Serb entity.

December 2006

Bosnia joins Nato's Partnership for Peace pre-membership programme after the organisation overturns a decision to exclude it because of its failure to catch Radovan Karadžić.

January 2007

Nikola Spiric, a Bosnian Serb, is asked to form a government after party leaders agree on a coalition.

February 2007

The International Court of Justice rules that the 1995 Srebrenica massacre constituted genocide but clears Serbia of direct responsibility.

May 2007

Zdravko Tolimir, one of the top fugitives sought by the UN war crimes tribunal in The Hague for his alleged role in the Srebrenica massacre, is arrested.

July 2007

Miroslav Lajcak, a Slovak diplomat, takes over as High Representative.

November 2007

Nikola Spiric resigns as prime minister in protest at EU-backed reforms the High Representative wanted to introduce.

June 2008

Former Bosnian Serb police chief Stojan Zupljanin is arrested near Belgrade and transferred to The Hague to stand trial for war crimes.

Bosnia signs Stabilisation and Association Agreement (SAA) with EU.

KARADŽIĆ CAPTURED

July 2008

Celebrations on the streets of Sarajevo at news that former Bosnian Serb leader Radovan Karadžić, wanted on war crimes charges, has been arrested in Belgrade after nearly thirteen years on the run.

October 2008

Nationalist parties do well among all three ethnic groups in local elections, leaving Bosnian politics divided firmly along ethnic lines.

March 2009

Austrian diplomat Valentin Inzko takes over as High Representative.

May 2009

US Vice-President Joe Biden visits Bosnia and tells local leaders to work together ahead of the expected closure of the Office of the High Representative.

July 2009

Report by High Representative Inzko on progress towards full sovereignty says Bosnian leaders are undermining state institutions despite international condemnation.

CONSTITUTIONAL STALEMATE

October 2009

EU and US-brokered talks aimed at breaking the deadlock on constitutional reform end in failure.

Trial of former Bosnia Serb leader Radovan Karadžić begins at UN tribunal in The Hague. He faces eleven counts of genocide, war crimes, crimes against humanity and other atrocities.

February 2010

Bosnian Serb Republic passes law making it easier to hold referendums on national issues, in a move seen as a challenge to the international High Representative's authority and potentially paving the way for a referendum on independence.

March 2010

Bosnian wartime leader Ejup Ganić is arrested in London at the request of Serbia, accusing him of war crimes. A court later blocks a bid to extradite him.

October 2010

The Serb Nationalist party led by Bosnian Serb Republic premier Milorad Dodik and multi-ethnic party led by Zlatko Lagumdžija emerge as main winners in general election.

RATKO MLADIĆ ARREST

May 2011

Serbian authorities arrest former Bosnian Serb military chief Ratko Mladić, one of the world's most wanted war crimes suspects.

December 2011

Bosnia's Muslim, Croat and Serb political leaders reach agreement on formation of new central government, bringing to an end a fourteen month deadlock, since the 2010 general election.

January 2012

Parliament elects Croat Vjekoslav Bevanda as prime minister under the December Agreement.

May 2012

War crimes trial of Ratko Mladić opens at The Hague. He faces charges including genocide and the massacre of more than 7,000 Muslim men and boys at Srebrenica in 1995.

July 2012

Large crowds attend the mass funeral of some 500 newly identified victims of the Srebrenica massacre.

December 2012

Bosnian Serb ex-general Zdravko Tolimir is sentenced to life in prison by The Hague UN war crimes tribunal for genocide over the Srebrenica massacre. A close aide to the then Bosnian Serb military chief Ratko Mladić; he was arrested in Serbia in 2007 after two years on the run.

SEVENTEEN SUMMERS

Distant the terracotta slates are shimmering red
Where once shadows of fallen homes restless stood
Echoes of a fractured family's dying brethren bled
Who sought answers amidst pain for common good

The hillsides are now covered in green life anew
Deep rich the innocence of a young sapling's life
Reaching from dusted ground and breaking through
Each seed born from hallowed earth speaks of strife

There are no empty graves to be filled with the fallen
No shovels standing still in desperate expectation
Nowadays white marbled tombs line fields sadly swollen
Silently laid still the sleepless souls of a generation

Rusting iron walk under river bridge swings silently
Safe shadows run above the Drina from Serbian threat
The shameless face of a religion worn devoutly
Once guarded by Muslim men with gun and cigarette

Seventeen summers and white winters have long past
Where peppered rifled walls chit chatter with fear
And crowds of happy wandering people do contrast
To the patrolling soldier and cheery British bombardier

Here the blue beret of peace keepers did briskly walk
Where fatherless child reached out a hand of hope
A young Gloucester lad of foreign land paused to talk
Sweet innocent teenage years finding depth to cope

Listen to the town's joyful sounds of a happy freedom
Of the lights at night that speak of a homely station
A heartfelt hope that a recent past will give wisdom
To the birth of a nation as a civil war's citation

Written 2012, Goražde.

353

"Although the passage of time would heal wounds, for many the loss of loved ones during its bloodied days would never be forgotten."

CHAPTER 16

LEST WE FORGET

OLD COMRADES' RETURN JOURNEY

In 2011 Ian Harris contacted me, asking if I would be interested in joining him and other old comrades on a return journey to Goražde. Tied to this commitment were fundraising responsibilities, such as funds to pay for the refurbishment of the two memorial stones for the four soldiers the battalion had lost in 1994.

There was no hesitation in my answer, returning to Goražde had been something I had thought about for many years and had set as one of my ambitions and must-do tasks. Since leaving the Army in 1995 I had fostered and fed an increasingly colourful reminiscence of my time in Bosnia, attaching possibly a disproportionate level of importance to it. My short military career had a memorable beginning when passing out of Sandhurst and then ending with the pomp and circumstance of the tercentenary of The Gloucestershire Regiment and the polar experience of an operational tour to Bosnia. However, it was my time astride the banks of the River Drina and patrolling the hills above Goražde that was the high point of my Army service.

With Ian's organisational skills and his passion for getting this done, I knew this was an opportunity not to miss. Through this reconnection, memories came flooding back as old characters reappeared in my life: Colour Sergeant Johnny, the Forester Yemm, Corporal Slug Southern and Andy 'king of comedy' Paddon, all came from my past and crashed into my present. It gave impetus to my nagging desire to write a book about mine and the soldiers of 1RGBW's experiences in Goražde, an idea I had played around with for several years. Due to this unexpected prompt, I found myself travelling throughout the country to meet old faces, interviewing regimental contacts to listen to their memories, opinions and thoughts of their time in Goražde.

Right: Corporal Morley following a weapon confiscation

Nearby in Gloucestershire I met the former Sergeant Mad-Dog McTaggett, travelled north to Darlington to meet Corporal Morley and into London to have a beer with Lieutenant Gary McDade, and my first company commander in Bosnia, Major Patrick Tomlinson. I concluded this initial flurry of meetings by looking upon Buckingham Palace and having a coffee with the now Brigadier Patrick Davidson-Houston, in 1994 a lieutenant colonel and the commanding officer of 1RGBW. All were happy to offer time to discuss their reflections and share their views on their deployment and experiences in Bosnia.

What gave deep colour to this journey and unfolding reunion was reconnecting with the Rev, Andrew Grant, who had now become the very Reverend by name and by profession. Hand-in-hand was the news that his spiritual colleague, Patrick Irwin, would be part of this returning group. Patrick had been the battalion's padre in Goražde and had made an impression upon me, not least in encouraging my writing, which I often found to have a religious undertone.

My poems and letters written in Goražde had given a voice to my privately held Christian beliefs and enabled me to reconnect with my upbringing in the

Below, from left: Sergeant McTaggart, Private Froom, Corporal Whiteway, Private White and Corporal Riddel, Recce Platoon, OP12 overlooking Kolovarice, Goražde 1994

356

1970s, which was framed by Christian teachings. I came from a godly family, Sunday School and church once a week. Godly in a quiet, unassuming way, as my parents were involved in the Christian communities of the various villages in which we had lived and raised us with the principles you find in Christian schooling. However, we were far from being high church or openly preoccupied in our commitment to the church. This spiritual journey of enlightenment had started in Goražde and came full circle in 2013 when I married Joanna. The priest who married us was Andrew Grant and he subsequently christened two of our sons, Monty and Alfie. Meeting Patrick and Andy in 2012 was ample reason therefore, for me to be involved in the proposed old comrade gathering and it became one that would pay unforeseen emotional dividend.

The initial momentum and activity in relation to my planned book was lost after the visit to Goražde. In the three years that followed, I set up a new business with work in London, New York and Singapore, got engaged and married to Joanna. We had two boys with Monty and Alfie and I adopted Simon, Joanna's son, to become mine also. We moved to a new house three times in this period, searching for the

right spot, and I set up my charity The Goražde Children's Foundation, Bosnia. I returned to Goražde in 2015 to run a marathon and to see the works in progress at the primary school in the town, the beneficiary of my charitable efforts. Amidst these wonderful and whirlwind series of events any time to write was lost, to be found again in 2016 as I entered calmer waters.

As I reflect on the last five years, it is clear-cut that the return visit to Goražde in 2012 had been decisive in feeding and facilitating some of the events that followed and have in no small part shaped or rather, reshaped my life. Whether it was gaining a sense of perspective or reconnecting me with a time I felt I had a deep-rooted purpose and could be

Above: The Reverend Andrew Grant marries Maurice and Joanna, 21st March 2013.

Left: Andrew has christened both of Maurice and Joanna's sons, Monty and Alfie in Gloucestershire

proud in my endeavours, I do not know exactly; but from the 2012 visit my life took a positive turn, taking me forward with an increasing level of happiness and contentment.

In June 2012, we had met at the Marriott Hotel at Heathrow, a hearty bunch and many good men listed. I arrived a little late and as I came into the room Ian had booked for a collective briefing, the distinctive West Country tones met my entrance, "Bugger me sir, you've had seventeen years to get here on time and you're still late." Joey Deacon, a true Forester, smiled and triggered general laughter at my expense. "Hello Joey, good to see you, but I think we can drop the sir, I left the army over fifteen years ago." Joey shifted in his seat, "That's fine sir, in 1995 I didn't mean it and now I just find it funny." Joey had been, and was clearly still, quick-witted and brutal in his wit, just as was Andy Paddon who added upon seeing me, "Have you not stopped eating since you left Bosnia sir?" Admittedly I had grown somewhat, and it was nice to be reminded so openly and so eloquently.

We were up early next morning and boarded the plane to Sarajevo and just under four hours later we landed. As it had been the day I had arrived in Sarajevo some seventeen years earlier, the sky was perfect blue, and the sun was shining. The airport was a very different place to the one we had driven into in September 1994. Then we were welcomed by the French army, wearing the distinctive UN blue covers on their helmets, and the airport was full of military activity today we were ushered through passport control, picked up our baggage and walked through the newly laid marble halls of the airport and into the sunshine of a summer morning in the Bosnian capital, this day as expectant and excited tourists.

Lance Corporal Joey
Deacon, 1994 Goražde

Boarding the minibus we travelled into the city, the high hills surrounding it climbing from the basin that cradled the historic capital. Cars queued, people queued, shops were full, and the occasional cyclist drifted by. Life appeared normal in this once battle-torn town. There was plenty of evidence of reconstruction, but amidst this you could find and see the physical scars of war. High buildings and blocks of flats carried pockmarks, the distinctive star-like marks of artillery and mortar exploding shells, or the smaller marks of rifle and machine gun fire. The physical scars of war were still present if you looked for them, just as my readings in the weeks before outlined how the psychological scars of the terror of war were very much resident in the city's aging population.

Having debussed and unpacked, we had a day's sightseeing ahead of us. Our first stop was the panoramic view of the city from the site of the crumbling edifice of the 1984 Winter Olympics. As the bus climbed the winding roads to the hills above us, the memories of the day we drove out from Sarajevo in our white-painted Saxons were clear and at the forefront my mind. The view from the hills above Sarajevo are striking, but it also shows how helpless the people of the city were once these hills were in Serb hands at the height of the war. From here they had rained down shells and machine gun fire indiscriminately into the city, the slaughter had been horrific and the situation heartrendingly precarious.

The image of General Mladić in uniform pointing down into the city during its siege (5 April 1992 to 29 February 1996) is one of the iconic images of the Bosnian War, which captures both the situation facing the innocent civilians of the city and the man who was directly and collectively responsible for their suffering.

From this panoramic point, we walked to the derelict ruins of the Olympics. The curving tunnel of the bobsleigh run was overgrown and peppered with colourful graffiti. It is a strange place with strangely conflicting echoes. It is as if you can hear the cheers of the watching crowds of the Olympics, as the four-man bobsleigh teams would thunder down and through the iced tunnel of the luge, but then amidst these cheers you can hear the thunder of artillery fire and the screams of people suffering at the sound of this thunder. That afternoon we gathered in a bar, drank local beer and talked merrily. It was a good day and time for recollection. And, as there had always been, however dark the hour, time and occasion for laughter.

The next day, Goražde was our destination. In 1994 and 1995 this journey would take from two to ten days, depending on the weather and more so the bureaucracy and intransience of the Serbs. This journey had previously been a tortuous and elaborate one, winding through Serbian territory, the drive broken by various checkpoints, often having the hospitality of the Serbs forced upon us, often momentary stops rolling into multiple nights. Not so this day, as the seventy or so miles from Sarajevo to Goražde on open and refurbished roads took us two hours, even with traffic. Our single stop en route was at Rogatica, an infamous checkpoint. Infamous as the small town had been for the location of suspected ethnic cleansing and slaughter, and notorious as the final checkpoint for UN forces throughout 1994 to 1995, it provided many moments of brinkmanship and tension as the Serbian guards would find pleasure and amusement in the authority they held over us.

The first sight of Goražde was from the peaks above it. It was striking in its difference, the landscape below us was one filled with colour. The hillsides, barren and stripped of woodland in 1995, were now full of new growth and young trees; the verdurous augmentation of the leaves of summer adorning the valley sides with a hundred shades of green. The hillsides were framed above by a perfect blue sky and below in the town the rusty orange of the newly-laid terracotta tiled roofs and principally whitewashed houses was a spectacle. The town we had left had been shades of grey, where roofs and windows were broken and offered

"The hillsides were framed above by a perfect blue sky. Below in the town, the rusty orange of the newly-laid terracotta tiled roofs and principally whitewashed houses was a spectacle."

dark shadows, and where the white walls of houses had been brutalised by war, artillery and gun fire. Running through the town were the turquoise blue waters of the River Drina and crossing it from one side of the town to the other were the three bridges, previously known as Alpha, Bravo and Charlie. With this colour-filled countryside, here was the first sense of a town reborn.

We stopped at the large concrete edifice that held the welcoming sign for the town, which you would have expected to have been one thing they would have refurbished, but perhaps appropriately for us it had not been. The town unfolded before us, distinctly familiar, as fingers pointed and voices were raised as memories flooded back. There were things to do and places to see, but we were ever-conscious of the main business and reason for our visit, the rededication of the memorial stones.

To start our tour Ian led us to the stones and we walked the paths and routes we would have driven and patrolled some seventeen years earlier. More pointedly, we were delayed witnesses to the exactness of momentous events that unfolded in 1994, as Ian described what led to each tragic accident. For many, especially those aging soldiers by my side who had been close friends of the fallen – or in such

Upper Left: Old comrades
gather at the former site
of OP5

cases as Andrew Grant and Mick Stacey, who had survived one of the incidents
– it was clearly an emotional reunion with the past. I had been on the opposite
bank at OP1 when I heard of the first incident. I could remember the radio
message clearly, but for some amongst us, they had been at the point of tragedy,
been within it, first to respond, or in Ian's case, the leader who had to deal with
each happening.

This was a sobering and yet cathartic experience, and under the mid-summer
sunshine and surrounded by new growth and softened boundaries, the dusty

Left: At the middle of
the bridge of the Drina,
Višegrad 2012

361

paths we trod felt soft under foot and gave time for thought. Tomorrow we would return, more appropriately dressed, and would pay our dutiful respects.

Later we visited the athletics track and sat on the steps that rested by the Portakabins of Cotswold Camp. We ran a short race, a dash of 40 yards or so, and were led by Patrick Irwin to lay a wreath at the Catholic cemetery before travelling south along the riverside road to Višegrad. We walked over the famous bridge, its eleven arches rising and falling perfectly, and took a cold beer looking over the rushing waters below it. The bar's residents, largely men smoking rolled cigarettes, coffee in hand, looked on at us with disdain. There was a noticeable difference in the people of Goražde to those of Višegrad. Here they were cold, distant and unwelcoming, although neither group knew who this crowd of western men

The 40-yard dash for the aging comrades

were, despite assurances by some welcoming dignitaries in Goražde who claimed "the whole town knew who we were". It was surprising, we thought, how well they kept this thought to themselves without a second look as we walked by! It mattered not.

Returning, we stopped at what would have been the confrontation line. No signs were left, no evidence of this defining boundary, although on the roadside a large, metal bin with the faded letters 'UN' could be seen. I took a moment to crouch on the roadside by the Orthodox church and reflected on the moment on Christmas Day 1994 when I had been stopped approximately at this same point, 24 miles into a marathon and had forty-two minutes of unique entertainment, where unfortunately I was the forced actor upon the stage. Today was hot, very hot, and that day had been cold, snow-covered and grey. My moment was short spent, as soon we were setting tracks to the south bank.

Our destination was two-fold, being the opportunity to navigate our way to Poser's Rock and hopefully to find evidence of OP1 amidst the undergrowth. We were accompanied by Mirsad Crljenkovic, previously BiH second in command of this area during the war. He took us up an overgrown path and through the translator made it clear that here or hereabouts was OP1. It was hard to envisage, as we were surrounded by trees, growth and bushes. Some seventeen years earlier the route to OP1 had been clear, with a dusty path taking you to the isolated summit of Samari. Then from this cleared hilltop you had an unrestricted view further south into the valley beyond, and from the near side, down into Goražde. In between, the Serb position of the red house had been prominent and clear to see, but not today. There was no view, no line of sight, no evidence of our previous

362

residence. Shortly afterwards there was a cry and a hand held high. Loose in hand was a white fragment of a sandbag, and then another and more. Here amidst and hidden in the undergrowth was the decaying evidence of the former station of the British soldier on UN operations above the town and enclave of Goražde.

Above: Mirsad standing where OP1 once rested: uncovered UN white sandbags

With this success, we showed our intent to move to Poser's Rock. This was a walk those of B Company and I would have taken tens of times. Today either side of the path was lined with red tape and the occasional yellow sign, signifying areas of danger, largely non-cleared anti-personnel landmines. This task had been ongoing for many years, a painstaking one that would take many more years to complete before the children of the town could run freely through these woods. The walk and our collective will to get to the viewpoint was well worth it and as we posed, laughed and took in the view, I noticed Mirsad was withdrawn, head bowed. The translator explained that the last time he had been there was on a day in February 1994 when his brother had been killed some metres from that spot as the BiH fought to hold the high ground from the advancing Serbs. Unprompted and modestly handled, Andrew took us

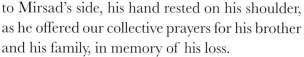

to Mirsad's side, his hand rested on his shoulder, as he offered our collective prayers for his brother and his family, in memory of his loss.

Andrew bridged the two great religions of Christianity and Islam in that single moment, perfectly offering the hand of friendship and solace in his words. Later that day, as we dined alongside the river, the sister-in-law and the wife of this fallen brother came across to Andrew and hugged and thanked him for bringing the memory of her husband

Left: The author returns to Poser's Rock seventeen years after he last stood upon it

Below: The author revisits Cemetery Valley, now marble stones rest in rows where once earthen mounds and rows of pre-dug graves could be found.

into the present. Two moments that bound the past with the present and bought focus to the reality of the legacy of war. Although the passage of time would heal wounds, for many the loss of loved ones during its bloodied days would never be forgotten.

Having travelled and toured throughout the day, we barracked in the mountains, a luxurious log cabin complex owned and run by previous leaders of the town. We ate and drank well, talked into the early hours and the next morning rose early. Having journeyed in dress-down, mostly with T-shirts and jeans, now blazers, regimental ties and polished

shoes were the common uniform for the day. Not far from the accommodation, down the main roadway heading into town, we gathered at the memorial to Ben Hinton. On his stone, it read "In memory of a much-loved soldier and friend, Private Ben Hinton, A Company – 1st Battalion, The Royal Gloucestershire, Berkshire and Wiltshire Regiment, killed in a vehicle accident on 9 Sep 94, while serving from this UNPROFOR base". Either side of his stone stood the robed figures of Andrew Grant and Patrick Irwin. Surrounding his plinth, we stood silently and looked down the valley into the distance and Goražde. This view had been a wonder to so many young soldiers, looking down on the Yugoslavia mountains, but today it was only identified with Ben Hinton and the view he would have for eternity.

We each took turns to bow our heads, touch Ben's stone and then left, heading down the valley to our second stop and moment of remembrance, at the bottom of the hillside in what was known as Factory Valley. The stone memorial was the same in shape, simplicity and size, only the names of privates Phillip Armstrong, Martin Dowdell and Chris Turner and the date 12 Sep '94 differed. The townsfolk and its dignitaries had turned up in good numbers and were most certainly sincere in their own thanks and remembrance. Our duty done, and our comrades remembered, we had but a few hours left and time to reflect. One last invitation was yet to be fulfilled and attended.

RGBW RETURN TO GORAZDE

SERVICE OF RE-DEDICATION OF MEMORIAL STONES

To

PRIVATES BEN HINTON, PHILLIP ARMSTRONG, MARTIN DOWDELL, AND CHRIS TURNER

OF

THE ROYAL GLOUCESTERSHIRE, BERKSHIRE & WILTSHIRE REGIMENT (RGBW)

GORAZDE, BOSNIA & HERZEGOVINA   JUNE 2012

Above: Programme of the 2012 memorial services held at the two memorial stones to the fallen

Right: Old comrades pay respect at the memorial to Private Ben Hinton

The school had invited us to come and see today's rising generation, the children of those we had come to protect, and gifts were distributed by us to one of the classes. As we parted we were taken into the main hall and sat in two smart rows of battered and well-used plastic chairs. A school master entered with children aged five to perhaps eight or nine and then they broke into song. The music was harmonious, that pleasant sound of a collective group of children, seemingly untrained when singing alone out of tune, but when together, a heavenly voice.

Above: Goražde Primary School, winter 1994 amid the war

In translation and summarised, they were thanking us and the British soldiers for saving their parents' and grandparents' lives. It was unexpected, possibly the most perfect end to our visit, and as we talked to the headmistress as we bid our farewells, I made a spontaneous offer that would take me on an adventure for the coming years. "We came here to salute the past, to remember our fallen comrades. What can we do to help the children and the future generations of Goražde?" I was uncertain of what we could do but felt compelled to offer. "English is a language that would offer a route to opportunity for many of our children, if any gift could be given, your language would be it," came the headmistress's reply. She detailed this clearly and without expectation, just a simple statement as if it had been said many times in the teachers' restroom when they discussed what they would do if money was no object. At that point I made a resolution to deliver on my unstructured promise and weeks later GCF Bosnia, The Goražde Children's Foundation, Bosnia (www. gcfbosnia.org) was born. In giving to today's children of Goražde the gift of my mother

Above: Year 7, Goražde Primary School and, inset, school art

tongue, we would ensure in a small way the service of all British soldiers that came to Goražde, and especially those that gave their lives in the valleys above the school, would leave a positive legacy through their sacrifice.

In Rudyard Kipling's poem 'Recessional', the phrase 'Lest we forget' is used eight times to emphasis the dangers of failing to remember. Alongside a school playground in a small market town in central Bosnia, the children of Goražde are learning English in a new classroom named after four young men from the West Country who came to do their duty in 1994 and never returned to England:

Below: Evidence of the war remains all around, with modern day and obvious signs and more rusting evidence found in corners and on road sides

Below: Andy Paddon on the return journey, 2012

'Lest we forget, Privates Ben Hinton, Chris Turner, Martin Dowdell and Phillip Armstrong of the 1st Battalion, The Royal Gloucestershire, Berkshire and Wiltshire Regiment, died on operational tour with the United Nations, September 1994.'

Sanella and the Veg Family, memories of Corporal Andy Paddon (B Company)

June 2012, The Old Comrades Trip

When patrolling the B Company side of the River Drina we were constantly mobbed by children shouting "bon bon mister, bon bon". As in many other countries we had visited through our army careers, children had quickly grown to know that soldiers had sweets in their ration packs. Some were very lucky and were given them in passing and some were even luckier and got non-ration packed sweets, sent to the boys by their friends and families back at home. We were generous in our giving, as these children gave purpose to our tasks and as many of us had young children at home, seeing these children in such a desperate situation pulled on the heart strings.

On patrols, my section used to come across a young girl of maybe seven or eight years of age. She always stood in the background and never begged, she had the shyest, sweetest smile I had ever seen and we all noticed her and her gentle, reserved appearance. Unlike many of the other children, she stayed at the back, never begging or being cheeky, just waving occasionally and always radiant with her ever-present smile; a little gem found amidst this war-torn country and town.

Along with the other lads I took a real shine to this young girl, who we knew to be Sanella by name, and it wasn't long until she was being showered with all the sweets and chocolate that we could muster. As we got to know her, seeing her daily, I for one was amazed at her humility and maturity. Even though she had won our hearts, gaining much of our attention, she always took time and tried to share equally what we had given her amongst the other children.

After a few weeks patrolling, one day we saw Sanella standing with a lady whom we presumed to be her mother and as we passed she motioned us over

366

to her. In broken English her mother thanked me for the kindness we had shown towards her daughter, explaining her husband was either away fighting or had been killed, we couldn't determine which. What we did understand was the invitation she extended to visit her home, which we duly accepted, as this was part of our role, to forge relationships and build confidence in the community we had come to protect. When we came to her home she cooked us some food from the tins of army compo (ration packs) that we had given to Sanella.

What her mother managed to conjure up from our offerings amazed us all, it was cooked to perfection and almost unrecognisable. Whilst we chomped our way through our feast we met the neighbours, which was a family of three generations living in a house that had seen its fair share of shelling. There was a granddad whose English was limited to the two words "*Hitler loše*", which he said countless times, as we understood soon enough that he had fought against the German Army during the war. His daughter and her husband had three kids in their teens, the youngest girl had long flowing blonde hair, and from that point was affectionally known as Samantha Fox (a famous model at the time). It was hard not to notice that the whole family had been gifted with rather large noses and as we had one soldier in our team, a Private Green nicknamed 'Veg' for his perfect hooter, the family became known affectionately as the Veg Family.

As the months dragged by, I had many long conversations with the Veg Family and Sanella was never far from our side, always in our shadows. Her family showed overwhelming generosity to us throughout the remaining time of the tour and demonstrated more dignity and fortitude than any family I had encountered in the UK. It became common practice that as we gave whatever spare rations we had to her and her family, she would on occasion cook us up yet another comp-surprise; a welcomed addition to the mundane daily rationing and cooking we had in place in the OPs. They also seemed to have an unlimited supply of the devil's liquor, the dreaded slivovitz, which we partook on a very limited basis, putrid to drink and taste as it was.

The night before I left Bosnia, the family invited me and the boys for a surprise party. It was a very emotional event that saw poor little Sanella heartbroken, tears flowing as we bid farewell and as I said my goodbyes to this most gentle of souls, I made a promise to her and her family that after the war I would return.

On our return to Goražde some twenty years later, I wanted to keep that promise and upon arriving in the town I commandeered our interpreter and went in search of the home of the Veg Family. It was with some excitement that I knocked on the door of a home that was now well-repaired from the one I had last seen. Unfortunately, we quickly established from the people in the house that the Veg Family had moved and not left a forwarding address, just knowing they

had moved to the other side of the town. The interpreter could see the look of disappointment on my face and calmly offered. "Let's do what you do in the UK if you are looking for someone," I looked at him inquisitively, "And what is that?" He replied, "You'd go the pub and ask the locals, isn't that what you would do?"

We made our way to the other side of town and found a bar in the area we understood the family had moved into. I showed some photos to the barman and asked if he knew the children within it. He looked at me and smiled, "You must be Andy?" he said. Not surprisingly I was more than thrown by this and asked how he knew. He told me the children in the photo were his cousins and they had talked about a British soldier called Andy and of his kindness and that he had said one day he would return to Goražde, "I will call them," he added.

An hour later, members of the Veg Family arrived at the bar, the children I had left now with their own. Unfortunately, the grandad and Mr Veg had passed away (he had died only a few months beforehand) and we further understood Mrs Veg was living in a different area. They asked the small children to thank me for everything I did for them in the war, which they did, looking on rather bemused, although we had a wonderful and fantastic time together that afternoon, one of the most emotional times I have experienced.

Unfortunately, I never got to see Sanella as she was away at university, but I left with the assurance that she would be told that I came to see her and had kept my promise. It was disappointing to not see her, but equally heartening to find out that she had survived the war and was now living a full and happy life."

A letter to the editor, Tom Bailey

In 2011, when I was studying for the third year of my History degree at the University of Bristol, I came to learn about RGBW and its six months tour in Goražde. Mo ('only my mother calls me Maurice', he insisted when we first met) or EB, as his military friends and comrades call him, had got in touch with the university to ask if any history students would be interested in helping to research his book. I volunteered, met EB for a pub lunch and embarked on this unexpected journey, travelling with him to interview ex-RGBW veterans across the U.K. in Gloucester, Chepstow, London, Doncaster and York, and then joining the return trip to Bosnia in summer 2012.

When I started my research with EB, I knew little about the break-up of Yugoslavia: I had heard of Srebrenica, but not of the RGBW's peacekeeping mission to Goražde. I was five years old when their tour began, so it was not a war I read about in the paper or watched on TV at the time, like Iraq and Afghanistan. Instead, it fell into the category of history for me, though not a conflict which I had studied at school, like the World Wars or the Cold War.

Working with EB opened a new world to me, the armed forces, of which I had scarcely any knowledge. Much of it was an entirely new experience for me as I had not met anyone who had served in Iraq or Afghanistan before; for example, I met Danny Ashton in Gloucester. It was an insight and humbling to hear of his stories, if not slightly surreal. My grandfather had served in the Navy in World War II, but I do not have a military family. As a child I played with toy guns and was fascinated with the Second World War, but the CCF never appealed and a career in the army never beckoned. Instead, my 'adventures' were gap year travels in India and Central America, before going on to study history at university.

Having studied a module at university on combat motivation and why soldiers fight, it was satisfying to go beyond library books and journal articles to hear first-hand accounts of why the RGBW soldiers signed up to the army and their memories of the Bosnia deployment. It was interesting to hear the different views of those who had previously deployed in Northern Ireland, those who only had a tour of active service in Bosnia and then those who remained in the army after Bosnia, serving in Iraq and Afghanistan.

The 2012 trip to Bosnia and meeting the veterans strengthened my appreciation for the sacrifices made by the military. RGBW had an impossible mandate, sent in as peacekeepers into a bitter conflict with little inclination for peace on either side, a situation which they did their best to make a difference. It reminded me of the Tennyson lines: "Theirs not to reason why; theirs but to do & die". Depressingly, it confirmed that our government does too little for those who risk a huge amount on our behalf, such as the provision of substandard kit (the Saxons) or not providing sufficient support for soldiers after they leave the military and return to Civvy Street.

Tom Bailey with the author in what would have been Cotswold Camp 2012

Clichés were reinforced; the veterans confirmed the close, lasting bond between soldiers. There were undoubtedly differences between officers and the Tommy's, both in their backgrounds or their career paths after leaving the military. However, there was respect for rank and mutual affection that was balanced, during the return trip to Bosnia, by relentless mickey taking and good humour. I had not appreciated the strength of military pride in regimental tradition - in 2012, EB, a Gloster soldier to his fingertips, still seemed saddened, even aghast at the

369

reorganisation of the Glorious Glosters and their amalgamation with the Duke of Edinburgh's Royal Regiment into IRGBW some two decades earlier. However, it was clear he had a pride in the RGBW also and in no small part was writing this book to help the name of the RGBW, and those who served within it, to be remembered (as it was amalgamated again some years later, being brought into The Rifles and was therefore, as EB would say, 'merely a speed bump in the Army's history').

One common view was confirmed: the drinking stamina of soldiers was simply remarkable! I have no desire to ever taste slivovitz again!

Individual stories of the deployment were deeply moving and underlined just how life-changing the Bosnia deployment had been. Andrew Grant's account of the Saxon crash was completely captivating, a striking account of a terrifying experience. His description of how they were hurled around the inside of the vehicle as it rolled down the hill – it was like 'being in a washing machine with a load of bricks', was harrowing. His subsequent journey to priesthood was equally captivating. Each soldier had their own memory of where they were when the accidents happened, whether they were in the vehicle, nearby as a first responder or hearing it over the radio.

One poignant anecdote from Ian Harris brought out the absurdity of war: a Serb & a Bosnian soldier, in opposing trenches, started speaking before shouting broke out. A momentary local truce was clearly agreed, following which a middle-aged man emerged from each trench. The two men met in the middle, embracing, crying and sharing fish and cigarettes. It reminded me of the World War I story of the soldiers meeting in No Man's Land to play football.

EB's experience of being held at gunpoint by a drunken Serb soldier at the end of a marathon was another dreadful account. It was bemusing and shocking that he could have been killed while running a marathon for a good cause, on Christmas Day, because of a failure of communication (though he makes the story darkly amusing now, as with hindsight, he made the situation even worse by dropping his hands held aloft, to pause his watch, as he was conscious of running a good time!). Unsurprisingly, it deeply affected EB, and was a focal point when we spent an evening in Tetbury talking about his six months in Bosnia, sponsored I recall by a single malt whiskey or two!

I am very glad that I met EB and had the opportunity to learn about RGBW's deployment to Bosnia. It opened a new chapter of history for me and gave me an insight into the military, a world I knew little about.

I hope that everyone reading this book encourages their friends and family to read it too, so more know what the RGBW endured, the losses they suffered and the sacrifices they made.

"*Bosnia 2018: no eternal settlement and a fragile peace; corruption remains at the heart of politics alongside dormant and repressed nationalism.*"

CHAPTER 17

STEPPING STONES; WHERE NOW FOR BOSNIA? (2013–18)

April 2013

The president of the Muslim–Croat entity, Živko Budimir, is arrested on corruption charges. Budimir and four other officials are accused of taking bribes to arrange pardons for convicts. Budimir had refused to step down from office in the wake of a political crisis that blew up in 2012, splitting the ruling coalition.

May 2013

A UN tribunal finds six former Bosnian Croat leaders guilty of war crimes and crimes against humanity during the 1990s Balkan wars. The men are convicted of persecuting and murdering Bosnian Muslims and other non-Croats as part of a plan to create an ethnic Croat state in Bosnia.

September 2013

About 140 miners barricade themselves inside a pit near the northern town of Tuzla for two days in a dispute over pay.

October 2013

A huge mass grave – thought to be even larger than the one discovered near Zvornik in eastern Bosnia in 2003 – is located in the village of Tomasica in north-western Bosnia.

January 2014

Ratko Mladić refuses to testify at the war crimes trial of Radovan Karadžić at The Hague, denouncing the UN tribunal as a "satanic court" and saying that testifying could prejudice his own case.

February 2014

Hundreds of people are injured in protests in Sarajevo and Tuzla over high unemployment, which is perceived as a symptom of official corruption and inertia.

May 2014

The worst flooding in modern times leaves quarter of the population without clean drinking water as half-a-million people are evacuated from their homes. Defence in trial of former Bosnian Serb army chief Ratko Mladić on genocide and crimes against humanity charges opens in The Hague. He denies the charges.

October 2014

Party of Democratic Action emerges as largest party in general election. Proposes Denis Zvizdić as prime minister. He takes office in February.
Steps Towards EU Membership

March 2015

European Union foreign ministers and Bosnia sign Stabilisation and Association Agreement that has been on hold since 2008, raising possibility of Bosnia's joining Union if it carries out key political and economic reforms.

February 2016

Bosnia submits formal application to join EU.

March 2016

UN tribunal in The Hague finds former Bosnian Serb leader Radovan Karadžić guilty of genocide and war crimes – including genocide over the 1995 Srebrenica massacre – and sentences him to forty years in jail.

September 2016

Bosnian Serbs vote overwhelmingly to keep 9 January as a national holiday, despite the opposition of Bosnia's constitutional court. Bosnian Muslim leader Bakir Izetbegović denounces the vote as a breach of the Dayton peace accord that ended the country's war.

Bosnia 2018

No eternal settlement and a fragile peace, with corruption remaining at the heart of politics alongside dormant and repressed nationalism

"*What started as a passing remark to the headmistress of the primary school on the south bank of Goražde, which nestles amidst the streets I patrolled when wearing blue in 1994, was soon to become a central purpose in my life.*"

CHAPTER 18

GORAŽDE CHILDREN'S FOUNDATION, BOSNIA

GCFBOSNIA.ORG

What started as a passing remark to the headmistress of the primary school on the south bank of Goražde, which nestles amidst the streets I patrolled when wearing blue in 1994, soon become a central purpose in my life. Having made the promise to build an extension to the school to enable its children to be taught English, I felt instinctively that I should not, would not, renege on this promise. It was apparent that it would be a fitting and living memorial not just to those who we left behind, nor just our battalion, but to the British Army's contribution in Goražde. More so, the opportunity to make a real difference to these children appeared achievable.

Why I decided to do so, I am not exactly certain. Perhaps I inherited this sense of using one's position of privilege for good, as I come from charitable stock: my parents had committed much of their spare time to raising funds for various charities and playing roles as treasurer, president or chair to charitable causes. I can recall as a child, many times my father with a money box in hand, standing on the streets of Shrewsbury or Hereford (where I was raised), shaking it to raise funds on behalf of The Roundtable, or my mother doing the same for Ladies Circle, both social networking clubs that raised multiple thousands of pounds for worthy causes. Rattling charity boxes are an echo of my childhood, where an inner premise that giving is more enjoyable than receiving and giving back in some way is joyfully rewarding, was imbued into my make-up from toddling days.

My initial task was to understand what I had committed to financially, as this would drive my efforts going forward. Fortunately for my charitable efforts I have always been target-driven and have become more so since leaving the army and working in a sales-related industry. My target was established as GBP£25,000. This figure came about from a full and detailed quotation secured and presented by the school to undertake all works to build an extension to the school to home what they called an English-speaking laboratory and in the interim period I had added to my pledge the relaying of the school's war-scarred playground with Astro Turf. This was added as I wanted to give enjoyment to all children, those who excelled in the classroom and to those who acted out their dreams playing football daily. At school I was a dreamer and not an academic, perhaps then it was my own childhood wanderings on the rugby fields at school, playing football or touch rugby to the imaginary cheers of the Twickenham crowd, as I kicked the winning penalty of scored yet another inspirational try for England, that prompted this additional gift.

Regardless, I had now gone public to my friends, family and to many of my clients about this endeavour. In doing so I could not renege on my promise, which added to the 'should not' and 'would not' already urging me to fulfil this commitment. Friends and family would support me, but my clients were more important, as they worked in the banking sector, where salary and reward are comparatively plentiful, and, in their hands, I would seek to leverage and prise out the £25,000. Bankers, despite what many think, are generally a community of good, honest, decent folk (as my father was for forty years with Barclays), where their reputation has been tarnished by the greed of the few. It was their decency and the spirit of goodness I had seen in many that I would seek to access to make good on my promise for what I considered a deserving cause.

Initially I held a charity evening at The RAC on Pall Mall. I had been a member at the club for some years, enjoying its membership in no part as it was quickly becoming one of the few places on Earth where I was still referred to as 'young man' by most that frequented it!

I had invited some 200 bankers and whilst I had my own speech, my guest speakers were excellent and could not be more different.

The first was my oldest friend from school, Nick Jenkins of Moonpig and Dragon's Den fame. I invited him not because of his celebrity, which may have held interest for some, but more for his story of how he had made good and done so with a mixture of genius, hard work, charisma and an honesty throughout that enabled him to reflect and truly learn from his mistakes. His ability to speak and hold the audience was forged initially at school, when he was head of the debating society, before doing the same at Birmingham University where he studied Russian, going on to represent England in debating at the world championships. There are many men and women who have found success in business, who have been innovative and entrepreneurial, but few who have the additional gift to hold an audience with a natural flair as a true orator. Nick did so with self-effacing charm and wit, both in intellect and in humour.

The combination of Nick Jenkins (far left) and Dzenan Hadjy Hadzovic (left) made for a great evening.

Secondly, I had invited and flown from Bosnia, Dzenan Hadjy Hadzovic, a Goraždan I had been introduced to in Sarajevo in 2012. He was fascinating, charming, and a long-haired leader of a rock band in his spare time; a hard-working husband and father when not filling the music clubs of Sarajevo. His speech was delivered as a respite halfway through my own, aimed at offering a real insight to the terror of being under siege as a young child, to put my own endeavours in context, as being but a side-show to the real story of Bosnia during a horrific time. He told of his childhood days, of the blockade of Goražde, as a young boy facing terror, catastrophe, annihilation and surrounded by death, and then of the arrival of the United Nations and the British Army and of the unknown sound of the British machine gun that meant salvation. It was a wonderfully emotive speech, lacking graphic details, but eluding to the sights and sounds that left any person in the room with pictures forged by their own imagination that allowed the awfulness he had experienced as a child to be felt and understood.

We raised £7,500 on the night and the charity was in motion with over 25% of the initial target obtained.

My second fundraising effort was to run a marathon in Goražde, which is covered in detail elsewhere in the book (see chapter 12: A Story of Two Marathons) but added further funds alongside the regular plea I made to my banking community, mostly communicated at the quarterly forums I run for the Chief Operating Officer (COO) community in Toronto, New York, London, Singapore and Hong Kong. Many had been graceful in their giving and did so again when my third effort materialised.

I had long held a desire to write a book, but feared I lacked the ability, the articulation or imagination to do so. It came about somewhat by surprise, when encouraged to do so by two of my clients, Steve Krueger and John Weisel, partners at EY, the leading global professional services company. Steve, I had known for many

New York and London
charity book launch events
for No Place to Hide

years and upon joining EY, he introduced me to John, a bigger than life, fulsome and hearty American that, over a glass or two of red wine, thought it a good idea to take my various articles written about the COO and bring them together in a book. I accepted tentatively, knowing at best the audience to read the book would be narrow, the COO community and my mother, and not least I had concerns about being able to do so or the time to make good on this idea. Twelve months later I was giving a speech at Standard Chartered Bank's London headquarters, with Doris Honold, Group COO for the bank, hosting the book's launch (No Place to Hide, the role of the banking Chief Operating Officer) and three weeks later, at another event hosted by John at The Metropolitan Club in New York. The book's print and distribution were covered by the sponsorship of EY, with all proceeds of its sale going to the charity. Over £20,000 was raised, which led to the release of funds to meet the building costs of the planned English classroom and playground refurbishments, and change was left for more.

It was, however, a comment my mother made in London, when being quizzed by Doris and some others as to how proud she must be that her son had written and published such a book, that I remember best. My mother, a spritely and ever-young 83 year-old, replied pan-faced to the question, "To be honest, I didn't know he could read, let alone write!"

A year later, with the additional funds raised and the works completed, we ran a competition for the school and years six to eight (ten to twelve year olds). It was a writing competition and the title was set to compose an essay in not more than eight hundred words with the title 'I dreamt of a faraway place'. The prize for the best boy's and girl's entry would be a trip to the UK, two days in London, followed by a week at Cheltenham Preparatory School, the school my eldest son, Simon, attended. Its headmaster Jonathan Whybrow was delightfully supportive of this idea and he and his head of English read through the many manuscripts provided by ever-hopeful children to eventually pick two winning essays.

Two children in a faraway place, who had dreamt of England and learnt its language in a classroom built on the donations of many, would find themselves before the gates of Buckingham Palace and later before the headmaster of one of England's finest preparatory schools, in the county of Gloucestershire, the name given to its county regiment. Significantly, the school's Combined Cadet Force

(CCF) also wear the Back Badge on their berets, just as the soldiers who went to Goražde from 1RGBW some twenty years earlier.

Here are the winning essays, left word for word and comma for comma as they were written:

My name is Naida Efendić
I'm 12 years old and I go to 8th grade. I live in Goražde. I live with my parents and my brother. My favourite school subject is History. I play the violin and I love singing. My hobby is doing make-up. I love rock music and my favourite band is Sabbaton.

"Dreams are weird. They can lead you to the most far away places, the most beautiful lands and the largest fields. My dream took me to to the land of endless beauty. A land full of historical monuments, clear and blue rivers and everything else I read about in books. I got tired of walking so I sat down on a nearby bench. An old man with grey hair wearing a uniform was already sitting there. He had piercing, blue eyes and a proud smile on his face. „Good day", I said. He looked at me and answered: „To you as well girl. It really is a good day". I stared at one big green hill. „What are you thinking about?", he asked. "I'm thinking about this hill. It reminds me of my country. There is a hill like this there". „Tell me something about your country. I'm sure it is exceptionally beautiful", he told me while staring at the hill himself. „I'll tell you if you want to listen", I said laughing. „Of course I want to", he answered. „Well, ok". „The country from where I come from is far away. My country is known for its green expanses, rivers with magical names and beautiful cities", I said while the soldier was listening. „But what is the name of your country?", he asked. With pride, I answered: „Bosnia and Herzegovina". „I never heard of that country, what is its history?". „It is hard to talk about the history of Bosnia and Herzegovina. If I started talking about I would never finish. But my country is a hero", I said while watching a nearby river surrounded by colourfull. I think there were over 100 types of flowers there. Everything looked so magical and beautiful. I'm sure this soldier sat on this bench every day and viewed this beautiful landscape. „Please, continue. Your story seems very interesting. But how do you mean that it is a hero?", he asked me with a confused look. „Yes, that is correct. A lot of wars, conflicts and bad things happened in my country, but Bosnia survived all of it. And today is it proud because of that". The old soldier stared into the distance not saying anything. I did the same, I did not wish to ruin the beautiful moment. My surroundings were beautiful yet simple. „Is there any special place in your country that you love?", he asked while looking at a small lake near a

381

large monument. I thought to myself. Every city in Bosnia has something unique, but which city do I love the most? I know. That is Goražde, my birthplace. „I think that would be the place where I was born, Goražde", I answered. Nothing is more beautiful than Goražde. A small and serene place. Walks along the river Drina and the vast green fields. That, is my dream place. „The country from where you come from, Bosnia, sounds magical. You're lucky". I thought of the soldier's words. „You know, my country isn't the largest, it doesn't have the most money, but it is rich in order way. Its riches the people who live there. Defiant and proud Bosnia. That is Bosnia and Herzegovina", I carried on while the soldier carefully listened. „In my mind, I can imagine the things you told me", he said. „No, you can't imagine it. To understand it, you need to see it". I didn't even notice that it was getting dark while the stars above were watching these magical fields, rivers and streams. „I think it is time that I leave, it's already late", I said extending my hand to the old man. „Goodbye and good night. I hope we see each other", he shaked hands with me and then left. An interesting person in an interesting land."

My name is Adnan Ferhatović

I was born on March 31st 2003 in Goražde. I am going to Music school „Avdo Smailović" and Elementary school „Fahrudin Fahro Bascelija". I play accordion. I'm a traditional dancer, I also play handball. I love watching football, and my favourite football team is Manchester United.

"When I woke up, it was still dark and it was cold. I needed to get ready for school. I got up, brushed my teeth, had a sandwich and packed my stuff for school. When I got out of the house, it was a bit foggy outside. I started walking. It does not take me to much time to school, because I live near the school. As I was walking to school, suddenly I heard some strange noises. Far in the distance, I saw a silhouette walking towards me. I was trying to think about something else, because I did not want to show that I was afraid. Suddenly, I noticed that the silhouette walking towards me was a soldier. He looked really exhausted. He came near and asked me: „Boy, what is your name?'

I answered: My name is Adnan. „Listen, Adnan, I'm a soldier and I come from a faraway land. I go from country to country in search for places which are worth to visit. However, on my journey I got lost. Can you please help me and tell me where to go next?' I was confused and I did not know how to answer to his question. But then he continued. „What is this place called, where are we now ?' I answered: This is my hometown Goražde. „Oh, really", he sounded quite surprised. „ It seems to me that Goražde is a nice place. Can you tell me more about Goražde?'

Still, I was confused and I did not know what to do next. I thought for a second and then an idea came to my mind. „Are you hungry?", I asked the soldier. „Yes, I am." „Ok. Let's go to my home". We went back to my home. My mom was home and she was surprised to see me. „Adnan, is everything ok?" Yes, mom, everything is fine. I just met a soldier who is hungry and wants to find out more about Goražde. „Oh, well, then come on in, mr. Soldier. Soldier took off his boots and he entered the house. My father was sitting on the couch, smoking a cigarette. The soldier sat next to him. He looked at him with surprise and then he lit another cigarette. Mom brought the food to the soldier. He started to eat and soon he started to ask question about the food. „What is this?" That is pita, my mom said. It is very good, the soldier replied. After he was done with eating, we sat in the living room and started talking about why he should visit Goražde.

I told him to stand up and to come with me. We went out on the terrace. At the very moment, the sun started to rise. Slow, but warm wind started to blow. The birds chant could be heard in the distance. People were walking on the street going to work. The city started slowly to wake up.

You know why I love Goražde, Mr. Soldier? He said: „Please tell me." I love it not only because of the beautiful woods surronding the city. I love it because of the children laughs that you can hear on the streets. I love it, because we have the River Drina, the prettiest girl in the world. I love beacuse of the beach Žanj, and the rafts go down the river rapids. I love it, because of the people living in my town. No one will ever tell you a bad word, and everyone will welcome you into their houses. I love it, because this city has a soul. This city may be small, but it has a big heart."

Where is your hometown, Mr. Soldier? He did not answer. Then, I saw that he was lost in his thoughts. Few seconds later, he turned to me and said: „Adnan, I can not remember where my hometown is. I have been far away from my hometown for too many years and I forgot. I forgot my hometown. And, I do not want to travel anymore. I want to stay in one place. Adnan, can I stay with you?

Once again, I was confused with the question. We went back inside into the house. I asked my mom about whether the soldier can stay with us. She said: „Of course he can." The Soldier was happy with this decision and so were we. I was late for school, but I did not care that much about it. I wanted to ask the Soldier one more question. „Can you show me the pictures of your faraway land`? The Soldier answered: I would love to, but I think that there is no need. My home is now in Goražde, and I hope that you and I will create as many memories here."

383

What now for this charity, what future benefit can be designed and hatched? With the great success of the charity and how it has been able to resonate and find favour and support from so many, there are plans for a 2018 summer cycle ride from Sarajevo to Goražde, following the route taken so painfully and so slowly by so many when funnelled through Serb territory and from one checkpoint to another throughout the bitter winter of 1994 to 1995. There is hope of a twenty-five year reunion and an old comrades trip to Goražde in 2019, but in the interim a commitment has been made to build a new science classroom at the primary school.

How will his be funded? I decided some time ago to write a book about the soldiers of 1RGBW who also travelled to a faraway place many years ago. This book tells of their journey, adventures, memories, and of laughter and sorrow and of a spirit of camaraderie that is uniquely British. This book has been written in honour of their service and the four comrades they left behind. It is this book you have in your hands and in doing so, I presume you would have donated to my charity for it. You can finish your reading knowing every penny or dime or other that you gave went to the charity and that you have helped ensure, as Rupert Brooke so famously wrote, 'That there's a corner of a foreign field That is forever England'. That field can be found in a city in central Bosnia, amid its high-peaked and beautiful mountains, astride the turquoise and running waters of the River Drina, a city called Goražde and to this end I close by saying, thank you.

Right: After the laying of the Astro Turf

Below: The playground before its refurbishment

Left and below: The English classroom before and after its refurbishment.

left: The English speaking centre with books provided by Cheltenham Preparatory School

Below: The plaque outside the English speaking centre, Goražde Primary School

BIBLIOGRAPHY

The following publications and websites informed the writing of this book and are referenced as such. Where appropriate, every effort has been made to attain permission to reprint extracts.

All poems and letters in this book were written by Maurice Evlyn-Bufton during the period of 1994 – 95, unless otherwise attributed. All images have been either donated or reprinted with the correct permissions where appropriate.

Adams, D. (1977). The hitchhiker's guide to the galaxy. New York: Del Rey.

Andrić, I. (1977). The bridge on the Drina. Chicago: University of Chicago Press.

Antill, P. (2018). Military Involvement in Humanitarian Aid Operations. [online] Historyofwar.org. Available at: http://www.historyofwar.org/articles/concepts_humanitarian.html

Assets.publishing.service.gov.uk. (2016). UK Armed Forces Deaths: Operational deaths post World War II. [online] Available at: https://assets.publishing.service.gov.uk/government/uploads/system/uploads/attachment_data/file/512070/20160331_UK_Armed_Forces_Operational_deaths_post_World_War_II.O.pdf

BBC News. (2018). Bosnia-Herzegovina profile - Timeline. [online] Available at: https://www.bbc.co.uk/news/world-europe-17212376

Biblehub.com. (2017). Matthew 7:16 By their fruit you will recognize them. Are grapes gathered from thornbushes, or figs from thistles?. [online] Available at:

http://biblehub.com/matthew/7-16.htm

Bible Gateway. (2011). Bible Gateway passage: Galatians 5:22-23 - New International Version. [online] Available at: https://www.biblegateway.com/passage/?search=Galatians+5%3A22-23&version=NIV

Binyon, L. (2018). For the fallen, and other poems. Collingwood: Trieste Publishing.

Boswell, J. (1791). The Life of Samuel Johnson LL.D. [Oxford]: Henry Baldwin

Brooke, R. (2008). 1914 & other poems. [United States]: JM Classic Editions.

Building Stability Overseas Strategy. (2011). [ebook] Department for International Development, the Foreign and Commonwealth Office and the Ministry of Defence. Available at: https://assets.publishing.service.gov.uk/government/uploads/.../bsos-july-11.pdf

Coward, H. and Smith, G. (2004). Religion and peacebuilding. Albany: State Univ. of New York Press, p.215.

Dannatt, Richard, Ethics.iit.edu. (2012). Values and Standards of the British Army (2008) | Ethics Codes Collection. [online] Available at: http://ethics.iit.edu/ecodes/node/5512

En.wikipedia.org. (2018). History of Bosnia and Herzegovina. [online] Available at: https://en.wikipedia.org/wiki/History_of_Bosnia_and_Herzegovina#cite_note-Malcolm-0#cite_note-Malcolm-0

En.wikipedia.org. (2018). Siege of Goražde. [online] Available at: https://en.wikipedia.org/wiki/Siege_of_Gora%C5%BEde

Dictionnaire.sensagent.leparisien.fr. (n.d.). British army : définition de British army et synonymes de British army (anglais). [online] Available at: http://dictionnaire.sensagent.leparisien.fr/British%20army/en-en/#Gulf_War

European Commission (2015). Stabilisation and Association Agreement with Bosnia and Herzegovina enters into force today. [online] Available at: http://europa.eu/rapid/press-release_IP-15-5086_en.pdf

Johnston, D. and Eastvold, J. (2018). History Unrequited Religion as Provocateur and Peacemaker in the Bosnian Conflict. In: H. Coward and G. Smith, ed., Religion and Peacebuilding. [online] New York: State of New York University Press, pp.213- 242. Available at: https://zodml.org/sites/default/files/%5BHarold_G._Coward%2C_Gordon_S._Smith%5D_Religion_and_P.pdf

Jones, S. (2015). Wave of departures leaves British army under strength | Financial Times. [online] Ft.com. Available at: https://www.ft.com/content/d3624138-3610-11e5-b05b-b01debd57852

Harding, T. (2007). Troops leave Bosnia after a job well done. [online] Telegraph.co.uk. Available at: https://www.telegraph.co.uk/news/worldnews/1546552/Troops-leave-Bosnia-after-a-job-well-done.html

Hartmann, F. and Vulliamy, E. (2015). How Britain and the US decided to abandon Srebrenica to its fate. [online] The Guardian. Available at: https://www.theguardian.com/world/2015/jul/04/how-britain-and-us-abandoned-srebrenica-massacre-1995

Kayongo, J. (n.d.). The History of the Conflict in the former Yugoslavia: 1991-1995. [online] Web.stanford.edu. Available at: https://web.stanford.edu/class/e297c/war_peace/confrontation/hformeryugoslavia.html

Kipling, R. and Jones, R. (2001). The Collected Poems of Rudyard Kipling. Hertfordshire: Wordsworth Editions. p. 340

Luka, T. (2007). Troops leave Bosnia after a job well done. [online] Telegraph.co.uk. Available at: http://www.telegraph.co.uk/news/worldnews/1546552/Troops-leave-Bosnia-after-a-job-well-done.html © Telegraph Media Group Limited

Moe, C. (2006). Religion in the Yugoslav Conflicts, Post-war Perspectives. [ebook] Available at: http://file:///C:/Users/s.chappell/Downloads/67312-Article%20Text-81197-1-10-20171119%20(1).pdf

Popovski, I. (2017). A Short History of South East Europe. North Carolina: Lulu Press Inc.

Puddington, A., Piano, A., Dunham, J., Nelson, B. and Roylance, T. (2014). Freedom in the world 2014. New York: Freedom House, pp.100 - 104.

Rennie, D. (2001). The day 650 Glosters faced 10,000 Chinese. [online] Telegraph.co.uk. Available at: https://www.telegraph.co.uk/news/worldnews/1316777/The-day-650-Glosters-faced-10000-Chinese.html © Telegraph Media Group Limited

Sassoon, S. (2007). The war poems of Siegfried Sassoon. [Gloucester]: Dodo Press.
By kind permission of the Estate of George Sassoon

Service, C. (2016). Religious tolerance is good for society and the soul, says Pope during mosque visit | CatholicHerald.co.uk. [online] CatholicHerald.co.uk. Available at: http://www.catholicherald.co.uk/news/2016/10/03/if-you-are-human-mix-with-humans-pope-quotes-muslim-poet-in-speech-on-religion/

The Economist. (2011). Bosnia's long shadow over British foreign policy. [online] Available at: https://www.economist.com/bagehots-notebook/2011/03/15/bosnias-long-shadow-over-british-foreign-policy

The Economist. (2016). British military deaths. [online] Available at: https://www.economist.com/graphic-detail/2016/07/06/british-military-deaths

Velikonja, M. (1998). Liberation Mythology: The Role of Mythology in Fanning War in the Balkans. In: P. Mojzes, ed., Religion and the War in Bosnia. [online] Atlanta: Scholars Press. Available at: https://journal.fi/scripta/article/view/67312/27609